» Experimental Archeology «

Experimental Archeology

» edited by «

Daniel Ingersoll, John E. Yellen,
and
William Macdonald

new york   columbia university press

1977

Library of Congress Cataloging in Publication Data
Main entry under title:

Experimental archeology.

Includes bibliographies.
1. Archaeology—Methodology—Addresses, essays,
lectures.   I. Ingersoll, Daniel.   II. Yellen, John,
1942–   III. Macdonald, William, 1943–
CC75.E86   930'.1'028   77–4250
ISBN 0-231-03658-2

Columbia University Press
New York   Guildford, Surrey
Copyright © 1977 by Columbia University Press
All Rights Reserved
Printed in the United States of America

Scepticism is a powerful aid to scientific thought. Above all scepticism is justified in the case of creative scientists and is as indispensable as positive knowledge. One must be bold enough to cast doubt both upon the theories of others and upon one's own, and even upon the foundations of one's own science and its method, if one is to achieve a criticism that is not barren but alive. And scepticism is positive if it leads to a knowledge of the limitations of one's field of science, to the suppression of vanity and self-conceit, to an appreciation of realities.

A. M. Tallgren "The Method of Prehistoric Archaeology." *Antiquity* 11:154 (1937).

The unknowable cannot be taken as a standard of value.

W. W. Taylor "A Study of Archeology." *American Anthropologist.* Memoir 69:35 (1948).

The title of this book, *Experimental Archeology,* has been carefully chosen. Those whose definition of "experiment" is derived from the physical sciences may note with some dismay that not all of the studies presented here were laboratory oriented; in many, not all relevant variables were rigorously controlled. They may point out that no laws were derived, and no proofs demonstrated. But we would define "experiment" in the social sciences, which include anthropology and its subdiscipline archeology, simply as a systematic approach to the explication of data. Operationally this definition encompasses tests of hypotheses, replication of activities, duplication of conditions, construction of explanatory models, manipulation of methodological variables, and simulation of data-based observations.

Many archeologists would argue—and we would agree—that a proper focus of study for archeology lies in the relationship between material culture and human behavior. In working from "things" to "people" one shares the hope of all anthropologists that there are underlying cultural rules or laws which are susceptible to discovery. Any information bearing on this study may thus be considered "archeological data" regardless of the academic orientation of the investigator, and our choice of articles clearly reflects this belief.

It is our hope that this book will stimulate those interested in the past to recognize archeology as an expanded and expanding discipline, which continuously seeks to widen its data base and to broaden its perspectives.

This book is an argument for what we feel to be a useful procedure for archeological research. We wish to outline a series of *a priori* definitions under which the argument is presented in order to develop it with as much clarity and precision as possible. Admittedly, the definitions are open to debate and discussion, but it is to be hoped that the logical structure derived from these basic assumptions is not. Definitions are arbitrary and the ones we present are, in some cases, looser than those given by others. We do this primarily so that we shall not become embroiled in debates tangential to the central theme of this book. Archeologists have frequently expended too much effort in defending or attacking propositions outside of, although important to, the discipline—propositions in which they often have little expertise. We feel that, although we as archeologists should certainly be critically aware of the ongoing discussions in other disciplines, we should be primarily engaged in doing archeology.

There are almost as many definitions of concepts in anthropology as there are people interested in defining those concepts. The important thing to remember, however, is not what a definition is but rather how one uses it to facilitate understanding. We hope our definitions are precise enough to satisfy many, and loose enough to offend only a few.

THE DISCIPLINE

Archeology is a science. Specifically, archeology is concerned with the systematic study of the relationships between human behavior and its material correlates, including the environment in which that behavior occurs. It is important to stress that the goal of archeological research is the explanation of human behavior. Generally, although by no means always (as should become apparent from the studies included in this book), archeology tries to define these relationships in reference to past behavior. The explanation of human behavior is the goal of anthropology and this end is also the objective of the subdiscipline of archeology. Thus archeology is part of the science of anthropology; what differentiates it from the other subdisciplines within anthropology is the data archeologists use in pursuit of their goal.

Differences in the nature of data require alternative techniques of manipulation to provide access to understanding. The study of how one organizes problems of data collection, description, and interpretation is termed methodology. This study, an often neglected link between the much discussed Method and Theory of archeology, is the subject of this work.

Experimental archeology, then, is one method utilized in the study of human behavior; it stands as one among many but one which is, we believe, most useful given the nature of the data that confront archeologists and the problems considered most appropriate to the discipline.

EXPERIMENTAL ARCHEOLOGY

In the past, the term "experimental archeology" has generally referred to imitative or replicative studies in archeology (Ascher, 1961). We would expand its use to include not only replicative studies—several examples are presented in part I of this book—but also tests of method and technique and theoretical principles relating them (see part II). We would also include studies of the processes of site formation and deterioration (part III) and studies of the relationship between material and nonmaterial culture in societies functioning at present (part IV). Experimental archeology, then, explicitly attempts to apply experimental methods in the areas of data collection, description, interpretation, and explanation. Every possible attempt is made to define and control as many relevant variables as possible within the framework of archeological data and its inherent problems. Experimental archeology, in other words, seeks to test, evaluate, and explicate method, technique, assumptions, hypotheses, and theories at any and all levels of archeological research. The object of this approach is to define and control as many variables as possible in any given research situation.

Basically, an experiment is the test of a hypothesis in which at least one variable is controlled. The more rigorous and useful experiments are those in which a larger number of variables may be so treated. The most information can be derived from those experiments which control all but one variable: the one which is being tested.

In archeology there are four distinct categories of experiment: controlled replication of recovered artifacts or known activities; testing the validity of methodological assumptions by applying them to known data or known results; "contextual"; and those dealing with ethnographic data.

The first, and perhaps the best known, category is the controlled replication of recovered artifacts or known activities. Through imitative experiment one seeks to learn about the active processes of the production and use of artifacts. An understanding of the physical techniques and processes involved in tool manufacture is basic and necessary to an archeologist's ability to reconstruct the patterns of formation and deposition of data (wasteflake dispersal at a given site, for example). Such knowledge can also be used to provide the basis for inference about specialization and other social characteristics of a given cultural group.

At present the overwhelming majority of experimental studies in archeology are still imitative or replicative. Ascher's comments made over fifteen years ago are still relevant:

> The importance of the imitative experiment is limited to the kinds of problems in which they can be executed. The fact that these problems, dealing mostly with subsistence and technology, cover a relatively narrow range in the total cultural spectrum, does not diminish their utility, for the bulk of the archeological data consists of evidence relevant to these areas. The importance of the imitative experiment, therefore, is best judged in terms of its contribution to the solution of those kinds of problems for which there are archeological data and which, because the data exist, are most often handled by the archeologist (1961:793–94).

Much archeological evidence relates directly to subsistence and technology. Therefore it is natural that in these areas many situations arise in which imitative or replicative experiments are possible. When one thinks only of the array of stone and bone tools man has manufactured and used over the last few million years, there is an obvious and infinite source for experimental investigation in this area alone.

It is therefore clear why a large number of imitative experiments deal with lithic materials. For example, Speth (chapter 1) designs and carries out an experiment to discover principles of fracture of a siliceous material. He proceeds in a rigorous manner and can quantify his results. It is readily apparent, in such cases at least, that the archeologist may tightly control a number of variables. Speth chooses the raw material with meticulous regard for its structural properties so that generalizations can be made that will be useful in further lithic research. The glass selected has properties common to all glasses used in toolmaking but lacks the impurities and structural imperfections which usually characterize such materials. Speth also rigidly controls the impact velocity, the energy of the impact, and the angle of impact on the percussion surface. The entire procedure is designed to determine the physical structure of glass fracture rather than the cultural manner of percussion flaking. In this way Speth adds to the basic knowledge necessary before one can make precise statements about how prehistoric peoples worked similar materials. Obviously, Speth's work can be reproduced and this is an important feature in all experimentation; the more powerful experiments are those which are susceptible of replication. The other articles in part I all deal with replication in one form or another. Crabtree (chapter 2) considers stone tool use; Erasmus (chapter 3) wants to know how long it takes to build a "monument"; Puleston (chapter 4) tries to discover two particular functions of some holes in the ground and Weaver (chapter 5) tries to see how kiln walls bend. Each author controls a particular variable to add power to the concluding statements and generalizations which he draws from his work. The imitative and replicative examples included here are most easily perceived as "experiments" and attention to their structure will enable comparison with less easily recognizable experimental studies.

It is important to note that in most experiments the evidence is negative; the experiments demonstrate what could not have been done to produce the perceived results and can not "prove" what in fact did occur. Such an experiment, in effect, limits the range of alternatives which may be responsible for a given phenomenon. The strength of imitative experimentation lies not in providing a final and single magical proof of a hypothesis, but rather in the elimination of improbable hypotheses and narrowing and sharpening the definition of the "information." Puleston's article, for example, provides an excellent explicit discussion of this point. In sum, the highest probative reliability in any experiment is concentrated upon the negative, the elimination of non-knowledge.

A second class of experiment in archeology seeks to test the validity of methodological assumptions by applying them to known data or known results. Part II deals with this sort of experiment. The "knowns" in this case serve as controlled experimental variables. Guilday (chapter 6), in a pessimistic but highly valuable test of methods for archeologically estimating population from faunal remains, utilizes written records to provide controls. He knows the duration of the site's occupation and has at least partial control over population and diet.

It is important to note in Guilday's article that the variables under control are known sets of data, and that historical archeology can often function in one sense as a laboratory for the discipline by providing excavation situations with readily controllable variables. Frequently historic archeology allows a rigorous control of the time and space variables so important to archeological interpretation and explanation. This is evident in the Deetz and Dethlefsen article (chapter 7). Most obviously the dates on gravestones provide relatively precise time control, and given such a situation the authors can test the archeological assumptions themselves. Each of the authors in part II uses a controlled content in one way or another toward this end.

A third class of experiment can be termed "contextual." Here the archeologist tries to define and quantify the precise way in which a site is formed and subsequently deteriorates over time. Each of the articles in part III deals with some aspect of this question. Jewell and Dimbleby (chapter 10), for example, actually build a model site which provides tight control of all foreseeable variables; the artificial site constructed by Chilcott and Deetz (chapter 13) follows in the same tradition. Time is controlled by knowledge of the construction and excavation dates; stratigraphy, location, and position of deposited artifactual materials are also known. Climatic control is provided through direct observation. Less rigorous, but no less ingenious, is Ascher's (chapter 11) observation of processes involved in site formation and subsequent change. While Jewell and Dimbleby have constructed a tightly controlled laboratory situation that, it is to be hoped, will yield results of direct use in a wide range of archeological situations, Ascher seeks confirmation of his suggestions directly by comparison of two "real" sites in the process of decomposition.

Ethnoarcheology represents the fourth class of experiment considered here, and all articles in part IV deal, in one way or another, with ethnographic data. As Gould (chapter 17) points out, there is a definite "archeological point of view" in the collection of ethnographic data which is generally neglected by social and cultural anthropologists in their approaches to field work. The collection of such information with special reference to archeological problems, Gould's "living archeology," serves a dual purpose. First, it provides the basis for explicit statements concerning the relationship of human behavior, its material correlates, and the physical environment in a functioning, observable social setting. Yellen (chapter 14) examines and defines the rules which !Kung Bushmen follow when they butcher large animals. In this way he provides information useful to both archeologists and social anthropologists.

Secondly, and more importantly, the information derived from living archeology provides the basis for experimental tests of archeological assumptions concerning the observed relationships with reference to past societies. Yellen not only describes !Kung butchering techniques but also extends his statements to archeological data in an attempt to examine frequently made and often implicit assumptions many archeologists hold.

If "living archeology" is comparable to ethnography, as Gould suggests, then ethnoarcheology is analogous to ethnology because it represents a higher level of generalization and is generally cross cultural, that is, comparative. Living archeology, in other words, is a part of ethnoarcheology as are documentary studies (ethnohistory) and informant interviews when these are directed to the interpretation and integration of archeological material. Ethnoarcheology can effectively widen the data base, given the caveat suggested by Gould (as well as by Freeman, 1968) and given the methodological rigor demonstrated by the other authors whose work is presented here.

As our discussion shows, we have tried to select articles which illustrate the entire range of what we call "Experimental Archeology." We realize that our list is far from complete and the choices which confronted us were difficult ones, for this book could easily have been double in length.

THE NATURE OF ARCHEOLOGICAL DATA

It is not an overstatement to suggest that one of the most influential figures in American archeology during the past decade has been, and continues to be, L. R. Binford. At least one of us (Macdonald) considers himself to be primarily "Binfordian" in his approach to archeology and believes that almost any statement in the field may be considered as a position with reference to Binford. That the challenge and excitement of archeology are largely a result of Binford's constant probing and prodding, however, in no way should be taken as a stance in total agreement with his views. One area, important to the discussion here, in which Binford can most reasonably be criticized is in relation to his statements on the nature of archeological data. According to his position, "the practical limitations on our knowledge of the past are not inherent in the nature of the archeological record" but rather "the limitations lie in our methodological naïveté" (Binford, 1968:23). Binford then goes on to state that the entire range of sociocultural phenomena, the totality of a given cultural system, is potentially discernible in the archeological record if only archeologists can construct the correct methodological strategy. This seems to us to be a misleading statement given the nature of archeological data.

Most archeologists are aware of the differential nature of preservation of cultural remains and more than one article in this volume deals with that point. For example, a "Lignic" period in the cultural development of Southeast Asia has been suggested. It is assumed that during this time the main emphasis of tool technology was on wood, and only "generalized" stone implements were used. On the basis of extensive use of wood in the area today and evidence of cultural development too complex to be supported by such a simple tool assemblage (mainly chopper-chopping tools) as represented by the recovered remains, one may guess that raw materials such as bamboo provided the basis for a sophisticated material culture consistent with the definable social complexity. The rapid decay of wood in a tropical rain forest environment, which thus removes a significant percentage of data from the archeological record, should also serve to dampen an overenthusiastic Binfordian approach. In other words, the stone tools recovered are in fact primary tools—those used to make other tools. The secondary tools, the result of primary tool activity, and probably tertiary tools as well, are not preserved. Thus, if the information about the Lignic period is correct, poor preservation and not methodological naïveté is responsible for our imperfect knowledge of Southeast Asian prehistory.

We do not suggest however that the problems stated above are insurmountable and that research should continue only in areas with ideal preservation. On the contrary, we feel that experiments along the lines of some articles presented in this book can at least offer us a range of interpretive choices so that statements with some degree of predictive or retrodictive power can be made.

In addition to problems of differential preservation we feel it has been cogently demonstrated that cultural remains in the archeological record are imperfectly patterned and that an experimental methodology can be effectively utilized to demonstrate processes and extent of deterioration of diverse archeological sites. Ascher (chapter 11) has shown, for example, that sites are rearranged and restructured continually and the assumption that a given site is a microcosm in material culture directly reflecting a total behavioral system is dangerous at best. We feel that one of the first analytical tasks of an archeologist faced with the interpretation of excavated materials from a given site must undertake is a consideration of the destructive processes to which the remains have been subjected. In this way limitations of the data can be made explicit, promising avenues of analysis determined, and possibly even interpretive boundaries set. Overoptimism is as dangerous as no optimism at all, hence we suggest a middle road.

D. W. Ingersoll and
W. K. Macdonald

REFERENCES

Ascher, R. A. 1961. Experimental archeology. *American Anthropologist* 63(4):793–816.

Binford, L. R. 1968. Archeological perspectives. In S. R. and L. R. Binford, eds., *New perspectives in archeology.* Chicago: Aldine, pp. 5–32.

Freeman, L. G. 1968. A theoretical framework for interpreting archeological materials. In R. B. Lee and I. DeVore, eds., *Man the hunter.* Chicago: Aldine, pp. 262–67.

Taylor, W. W. 1948. A study of archeology. *American Anthropologist* Memoir 69.

» Experimental Archeology «

» ONE «

Replication of Technology and Discovery of Function

Man stands unique in the animal kingdom for the amounts and variety of cultural debris which mark his passing. Other species may fashion simple implements from wood, construct nests and hives, or tunnel into soft earth, but these remains are rarely long preserved. While many classes of human artifacts are likewise susceptible to decomposition and destruction, tools, monuments, and utilitarian structures of stone may—and in some instances have—survived for millions of years and thus, as much from necessity as choice, constitute a central focus for archeological study. Likewise clay objects, either whole or in fragmentary form, preserve well in archeological deposits, and analyses of this material play a large role in reconstruction of human history over the last 10,000 years.

Archeology, like any other discipline, is shaped in large measure by the classes of data most readily available to it for study; it is therefore unsurprising that scientists, whose avowed aim is the study of man within a broad time frame, have devoted a lion's share of their time to the meticulous examination of his material remains. The danger which all too frequently arises is the confusion of ultimate goals and the methods used to reach them. Then objects may become ends in themselves rather than convenient or necessary means for approaching those ends. From two points of view the five articles in this part share common themes. Each deals directly with objects or the raw materials from which they are made, and each investigator employs an experimental technique of one kind or another. Yet in no two cases are the same questions being asked. As you read these articles keep this point in mind because, when all is said and done, the value of an experiment can only be as great as the question it was designed to answer, and experimental design must also be evaluated against a particular and immediate objective.

To retreat briefly from the broader levels of generalization, and to consider objects themselves, one may ask five basic questions. Each of the articles included here considers at least one of these questions. First, from what is an artifact made? What are the properties of the raw material? Different materials by their very nature lend themselves to different forms, and impose varying limitations. Secondly, how are these raw materials transformed into finished products? What specific kinds of techniques are necessary? Given these techniques, how much time and manpower are required? Third, what direct and immediate function does a particular object or class of object serve? Fourth, how does an object change in the course of use? For the archeologist, this last question is of special importance because many of the artifacts he recovers are worn out or broken, and may bear only slight resemblance to their original, unused forms. And finally one must consider how an object or group of objects was altered by natural processes of destruction between the time it was discarded or fell into disuse and the time of excavation or study.

JOHN D. SPETH

Experimental Investigations of Hard-Hammer Percussion Flaking

The worker of siliceous rock—like flint, obsidian, or glass—is bound within a mechanical straitjacket because the restrictive nature of the raw material itself imposes severe limitations on the final form a piece may take and on techniques which may be used to achieve it. Pieces of flint recovered from a beach or the surface of a dirt road often show shaping due to repeated knocking about by the waves or vehicle tires, and often they assume forms virtually indistinguishable from humanly produced counterparts. In order to study man-made lithic remains and understand something about the cultur-ally held norms in the minds or their makers, it is desirable to learn as much as possible about the raw materials from which they are made. One goal of the archeologist is to use stone tools to define distinct cultural units with the aim of tracing these entities across both time and space. To do this, one must make stylistic comparisons and focus on those attributes of the piece which reflect human choice rather than mechanical necessity (see the article by Pollnac and Rowlett in this volume for a more complete discussion of this point). In such an analysis both the final form as well as the culturally determined techniques employed to reach it should, ideally, be considered.

Speth creates a controlled laboratory situation where the "cause" (a falling steel ball) can be carefully varied, and the "effect" (the type and dimensions of the flake removed) may be quantitatively determined. If this kind of research is expanded to include additional variables, it should, through carefully used analogy, provide a greater insight into the different techniques employed by prehistoric stoneworkers. Finally, as Speth points out, in a

Reprinted, with minor editorial changes, from *Tibiwa* 17 (1), 1974, pp. 7–36. Used by permission of Idaho State University.

*carefully controlled experiment one can study the interdependence of differ-
ent attributes. Must long flakes, for example, always be thick? This permits the
archeologist to focus on the most important attributes, to eliminate redundant
ones, and to simplify his analysis.*

The analysis of prehistoric flaked stone tools, commonly referred to under
the general rubric of "lithic analysis," is an important part of modern archeological research. The number of articles and monographs devoted entirely or
largely to the description and classification of flaked stone tools is almost
overwhelming. Over the years many typological systems have been devised,
and with the advent of high-speed computer routines for classifying lithic
materials which make possible the use of ever-increasing numbers of attributes, archeologists are faced with a veritable deluge of "relevant" attributes
and competing classificatory schemes. The selection of appropriate attributes
for analysis is clearly becoming one of the most fundamental problems faced
by the archeologist.

Many of the attributes and combinations of attributes appearing in lithic
studies today are selected largely because they have been in use for so many
years that they have come to be regarded as standard or "all-purpose"; their
omission would render the analysis incomplete and inadequate. For example,
it has become traditional in the study of Middle Paleolithic industries to
separate the lithic material into flakes and blades using an arbitrary value of
the length/width ratio as the dividing point (length/width = 2). This dividing
value has been used for years with little concern for whether or not the
underlying distribution curve of the ratio is normal, skewed, bimodal, or flat.
What is the theoretical justification for using this particular dividing point?
Why not use a different value? In fact, why use the length/width ratio at all?
Why not use some other ratio such as length/platform width, or perhaps a
three-dimensional index which in some way incorporates the thickness of the
flake as well? Clearly, there are an infinite number of possible attributes,
ratios, and indices that can be used. The selection of an attribute merely
because its inclusion in the analysis has become traditional is a questionable
practice. It is somewhat disconcerting, therefore, to observe in many recent
lithic studies the proliferation of arbitrarily selected and often redundant
attributes and ratios; this trend apparently stems from the widespread desire
on the part of prehistorians to make archeology a more quantitative science.
Merely increasing the total number of recorded attributes or refining the
methods by which they are measured will not lead to a significant improve-

ment in the explanatory value of the resulting typologies. The choice of the most relevant attributes cannot be based on arbitrary or traditional criteria. There will be no universal set of attributes which can be applied meaningfully to all problems. Some problems will be concerned more with mechanical variability, others with functional variability, and still others with stylistic variability. The attributes needed for each type of problem may be quite different. The archeologist, therefore, must first develop a clear understanding of the kind of variability that will be appropriate to his specific problem. Once this has been determined, he must then proceed to select those attributes which will permit him to quantify this variability in the most effective and least redundant manner. Ultimately, the selection process must be guided by a coherent body of theory which clearly and systematically relates the attributes to the particular problem with which the archeologist wishes to deal.

Such a body of theory is notably absent in the study of flaked stone tools produced by hard- and soft-hammer percussion. This is most unfortunate because percussion flakes constitute the bulk of the material recovered by the archeologist for more than 90 percent of the known span of human cultural evolution.

This paper will be directed specifically toward the selection of those attributes which are needed to quantify the mechanical variability of flakes produced by hard-hammer percussion, and toward an experimental investigation of the interrelationships between several of these attributes. Percussion flaking has already attracted the interest of prehistorians for decades, and a considerable amount of data are available in the literature. One particularly valuable source of information has been the direct ethnographic observation of percussion flaking techniques used by "native" or "primitive" peoples. Most notable are the descriptions of techniques employed by the Australian Aborigines and by the American Indians. These studies are familiar to most archeologists and need not be reviewed here (an extensive bibliography can be found in Bordaz 1970 and Hester 1972). Unfortunately, the making of flaked stone tools by native peoples has all but ceased throughout the world. As the questions posed by the archeologist become more sophisticated and complex, he is forced to rely more and more on other, less direct sources of information. Perhaps the most common approach today to the study of percussion flaking is the experimental one in which the archeologist starts with a piece of flint or obsidian and attempts to duplicate the stone tools and debris found in prehistoric sites. Valuable contributions have been made by Baden-Powell (1949), Bordes and Crabtree (1969), Crabtree (1966, 1967a, 1967b,

1968, 1970), Ellis (1939), Knowles (1953), Pond (1930), Semenov (1964, 1968), Warren (1914), and by many others. These studies have clarified and greatly augmented the data obtained by direct ethnographic observation, providing archeologists with an understanding of the general behavior of flint-like materials and indicating the range of possible and most probable techniques used in the past. Experimental investigations of this sort have given archeologists a *qualitative* sense of the complex interrelationships between the parameters of impact and core geometry and the various attributes of flake size and shape. Thus, for example, the prehistorian knows that size and shape are profoundly influenced by the size of the hammer, the distance from the point of impact to the edge of the core, and the shape of the core. But the *quantitative* interrelationships are not known, nor is it possible as yet to specify which attributes must be recorded and how these must be measured.

MODEL MATERIALS IN LITHIC ANALYSIS

The highly complex situations which arise from the use of irregular pieces of nonhomogeneous raw material, irregular hammers, uncontrolled impact angles, variable impact velocities, and so forth make it extremely difficult, if not impossible, to isolate the quantitative interrelationships between any given attribute and a known set of core and impact parameters. These difficulties, however, can be avoided to a great extent by experimental investigations which make use of model materials under controlled laboratory conditions. With a few notable exceptions (Crabtree 1967a; Faulkner 1972; Kerkhof and Müller-Beck 1969), this approach has received very little attention from archeologists. The apparent reluctance on the part of many prehistorians to use model materials in lithic studies is difficult to understand. One need only glance at the literature of such fields as hydraulic, mining, aeronautical, or civil engineering to appreciate the tremendous value of investigations using models. Perhaps many archeologists believe that for such studies both model and prototype must have identical properties and differ only in scale. And since the prototype, flint, is readily available in manageable sizes and forms, downscaling is unnecessary, and hence models are unnecessary. Such a view on the part of prehistorians is unfortunate. Model materials are often used precisely because their *physical* or *mechanical* properties are less complex or are better understood than those of the prototype material. For example, plaster of paris and concrete are often used in experiments in mining and hydraulic engineering because their properties can be analyzed much more rigorously than rocks under comparable laboratory conditions. Obviously, the ultimate goal is a firm understanding of the behavior of the prototype material under natural conditions; but to achieve this, one must begin with a systematic analysis of the simplest case and then gradually work toward an understanding of the more complex "real" situation.

There are many materials which exhibit regular conchoidal fracture, making them possible candidates for model materials in the study of percussion flaking (Crabtree 1967a; Faulkner 1972). These include glass, epoxy resins, plaster of paris, concrete, porcelain, and others. Glass, however, is by far the best material. Faulkner (1972:6–12) has discussed in detail the reasons for such a choice. He notes that both glass and flint-like materials are:

1. *elastic:* they recover completely from deformations once a force or load producing these deformations has been removed.

2. *brittle:* they continue to behave elastically (no plastic flow) as the force which produces deformation is increased, right up to the point where they fracture.

3. *homogeneous:* their properties are independent of direction within the body of the material.

4. *rigid:* they have a relatively high resistance to being deformed (rigidity and strength are not synonymous; chalk, for example, is relatively rigid but weak).

Two other important similarities of glass and flint-like materials should also be mentioned. First, both tend to be relatively strong when subjected to compressive (pushing) forces and weak when subjected to tensile (pulling) forces (i.e., they both have high compressive strengths and low tensile strength). This factor greatly influences their fracture behavior; fracture always occurs in tension at relatively low stress values, even when the force applied is compressive (Shand 1958:46). Second, both glass and flint-like materials have similar, low values of Poisson's ratio (about .25 or lower), an elastic constant which expresses the ratio between the lateral contraction and the longitudinal extension of a specimen in tension (Speth 1972:52; Shand 1958:39). Poisson's ratio, under certain circumstances, may also have a profound effect on the fracture behavior of these materials (see Speth 1972:51–53). The reader seeking more detailed discussion of these terms should refer to Speth (1972), Faulkner (1972), or to any standard textbook on rock mechanics, stress analysis, or the strength of materials (see, for example, Cottrell 1964; Jaeger 1964; Jaeger and Cook 1969; Moore 1954; Timoshenko and Goodier 1970).

Thus glass and the materials most commonly used in flaked stone tool production have similar mechanical properties. Glass is much closer, however, to the "ideal" or "perfect" brittle elastic solid and therefore makes an excellent model material. By using glass one can eliminate the ever-present problems in lithic analysis of obtaining specimens of uniform shape, size, composition, and texture; and at the same time one can retain the crucial mechanical properties which seem to have made flint-like materials desirable to prehistoric peoples.

THE SPALLING MODEL

In an earlier paper, I presented a model which attempted to show that an important mechanism in the production of a hard-hammer percussion flake is a process known as *spalling,* a type of fracture that results from the reflection of stress waves at a free surface of the core (Speth 1972). The essentials of the spalling model will be outlined briefly below.

When a brittle elastic solid such as flint or glass is struck by a hard hammer and the impact is of short duration, a compressive stress wave is produced which travels out from the point of impact with a spherically expanding front and at a very high velocity (Cunningham and Goldsmith 1959:162; Dally, Durelli and Riley 1960:33–34). When the impact is normal to the surface of the core, the maximum amplitude of stress in the wave lies directly along the axis of impact and decreases outward in all directions away from the axis. In the immediate area of impact, a small conical crack, known as a *Hertzian cone,* is formed. The cone penetrates only a short distance into the material, and it does not appear to be the principal mechanism responsible for the formation of a percussion flint. Relatively little happens beyond the impact area until the stress wave reaches the nearest free face of the core (a surface bounded only by air).

To visualize what happens next, it will be necessary for the moment to assume that the wave approaches the free surface with a plane rather than with a spherical front, and that the direction of propagation of the front is normal or perpendicular to the surface. Later in the discussion, I shall return to a consideration of the behavior of the more complex, but also more useful, spherical wave model.

The incident compressive pulse is reflected at the free surface in a manner analogous to the reflection of light. The angle of reflection is equal to the angle of incidence. But a very important change occurs in the nature of the reflected pulse. If the incident pulse is compressive, the reflected pulse will be tensile. The incident pulse puts the material through which it passes into a state of stress by pushing it together; the reflected pulse relieves this stress by passing back through the material, pulling it apart again. Thus, during the process of reflection, the outgoing tensile pulse overlaps with and cancels the compressive stress of the incoming pulse. The magnitude of the *net* stress in tension at any point near the free surface is given by the algebraic sum of the stress in compression and in tension at that point; it will be a continuously changing quantity which is largely a function of the shape of the pulse and of the distance the pulse has traveled from the surface back into the body of the material. If reflection continues to completion, the reflected pulse will have the same magnitude of stress as the incident pulse, but it will be entirely tensile. Reflection may be interrupted, however, before it has been completed. To illustrate how this may happen, consider a material such as flint which is capable of withstanding a considerably greater stress in compression than in tension. Flint has a compressive strength of perhaps as high as 50,000 psi (pounds per square inch) and a tensile strength of only about 1000 psi (Speth 1972:52). Suppose the material is struck by a hard hammer which produces a compressive stress wave with an amplitude of 3000 psi. The pulse will travel through the flint, producing little or no damage until it reaches a free surface and begins to reflect in tension. As reflection progresses, the stress in tension will increase while the stress in compression will decrease. If allowed to go to completion, the reflected pulse should have a tensile stress of 3000 psi. But this does not happen. As soon as the net stress in tension exceeds 1000 psi the tensile strength of the material, a fracture will develop at the location where this first occurs. This is a spall fracture; the distance from the free surface to the plane where the fracture develops is the thickness of the spall or flake. The formation of a flake by spalling is illustrated in fig. 1.1.

From this discussion, one can see that the thickness of a flake, produced by a pulse which is normally incident on the free surface, is dependent largely on five parameters: (1) the shape of the pulse (e.g., saw-toothed, triangular, half-sine, normal, or exponential); (2) the amplitude or magnitude of stress in the pulse; (3) the wavelength of the pulse; (4) the form of the wave front (e.g., plane, spherical or cylindrical); (5) the tensile strength of the material. Mathematical expressions relating the thickness to these parameters have been derived for various pulse shapes and are available in the literature (Rinehart 1960). Most of these expressions are based on a model which assumes that the wave propagates along a plane front rather than along a spherical front;

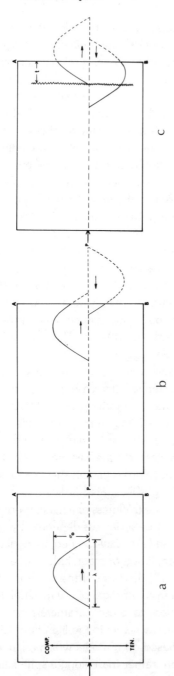

Figure 1.1 Reflection of half-sine shaped pulse at free surface of core.
[a] compressive pulse of wavelength λ and stress amplitude σ₀ leaves area of impact *P* and approaches free surface *AB* (wave considered to propagate along plane front).
[b] pulse begins to reflect at surface in tension.
[c] net tension of reflected pulse exceeds both compression of incident pulse *and* critical tensile strength of material at distance *t* from free surface, resulting in spall fracture.

they are therefore of limited direct applicability in the study of percussion flaking. But they do serve the important function of illustrating that at least one crucial attribute of flake size, the thickness, is directly and predictably dependent on a small and clearly specifiable set of parameters.

Turning now to the more useful spherical wave model, it can be shown that flake length and width are functions of the thickness and of the distance d from the point of impact to the free surface (fig. 1.2). The figure shows a

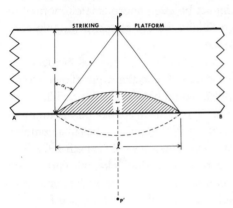

Figure 1.2 Relationship between length and thickness of flake (shaded area) produced by spherical stress wave when axis of impact is normal to free surface of slablike core opposite point of impact (referred to in text as *normal case*). P, point of impact; P', mirror image of P; PP', axis of impact; r, radius of spherical wave; d, thickness of core and distance from point of impact to free surface; λ, flake length (or width); t, flake thickness; AB, free surface of core; α_1, angle of incidence of wave front along radius r.

slablike solid struck at point P, such that the axis of impact is normal to the free surface AB. Henceforth in this article, this model will be referred to as the *normal* case. A stress wave travels out from P and is reflected in tension at the free face AB. The reflected pulse produces a flake of thickness t. The flake takes the form of a spherical segment of radius r with its center of curvature at P': the mirror image of P. The spherical shape of the flake can be attributed largely to three causes: (1) the wave initially has its highest amplitude of stress along line PP', the axis of impact; (2) the amplitude of the wave decreases with increasing radius (divergence); (3) as one moves away from line PP', the angle of incidence increases and, as will be discussed below, the amplitude of the reflected wave decreases (Kolsky 1963:188).

By using the Pythagorean theorem, one can show that

$$\left(\frac{\lambda}{2}\right)^2 = 2dt + t^2 \tag{1}$$

or

$$\lambda = 2(2dt + t^2)^{1/2} \tag{2}$$

where λ represents *both* the length and the width of the flake (i.e., the diameter of the base of the spherical segment) (Speth 1972:47–48).

The limitations of this model in archeology are apparent. We have been dealing with the special case in which the axis of impact is perpendicular to the free surface. To fulfill this condition, it has been necessary to use a model which assumes that a slablike solid is struck on one surface and the flake is removed from the face opposite the point of impact. Only if the platform angle is very acute will the axis of impact be even approximately normal to the free surface. Thus, in percussion flaking we are almost invariably concerned with a form of oblique incidence.

Oblique incidence is analytically more complex than normal incidence. It was possible to assume in the latter case that, if reflection were allowed to go to completion, the reflected tensile pulse would have the same amplitude of stress as the incident compressive pulse. In oblique incidence this assumption is no longer tenable. The amplitude of the reflected pulse varies in a complex manner with the angle of incidence and with Poisson's ratio (Speth 1972:50–53). In order to calculate the thickness of a percussion flake, this variation in amplitude must be taken into consideration. The relationships become complex and few expressions are available as yet in the literature (see Rinehart 1960:59). And there is no information comparable to that for normal incidence concerning the manner in which the flake's length or width is related to the thickness.

An additional factor must be considered when dealing with oblique incidence. For materials such as flint and glass, which both have average values of Poisson's ratio below 0.27, there is a range of angles of incidence within which the incident compressive pulse does not become tensile when it is reflected; within this range (between approximately 60° and 80°), no spalling will occur (Speth 1972:51 and fig. 1.9).

To avoid confusion, the reader should note that the angle is generally measured in such a way that when the direction of propagation of the wave is perpendicular to the free surface (normal incidence), the angle of incidence is 0°, not 90°; and when the direction of propagation of the wave is parallel to the free face (glancing or oblique incidence), the angle of incidence is 90°, not 0° (see Speth 1972:51 and fig. 1.8).

Much of the theoretical discussion concerning the variation in amplitude of the reflected pulse with the angle of incidence has been based on a plane wave model. When one deals with such a model, the value for the angle remains constant no matter how far the wave travels along the free surface from the point ot impact. When one ignores losses in energy owing to work done on the material by the passing wave (attenuation), the amplitude of stress in the reflected pulse will be the same at any point along the surface. When one deals with a spherical wave model, however, there are an infinite number of values for the angle of incidence (fig. 1.3). As the wave front first

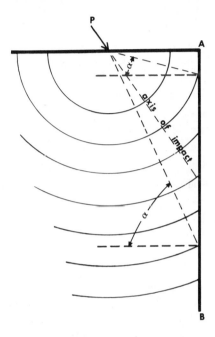

Figure 1.3 Oblique incidence of spherical wave on free surface of core. Spherical wave, produced by impact at point, *P*, strikes free surface *AB* at variable angle of incidence α (value of angle depends on distance traveled from source).

reaches the surface, the radius from the point of impact to the surface will be perpendicular to the latter. As the wave expands further, however, the radii to the points where the front just reaches the surface will be oblique to the latter; the angle of incidence becomes greater the farther out the wave has traveled from the source. Thus for a spherical wave model, "the" angle of incidence refers to the angle formed by a specific radius of the wave front (e.g., the axis of impact) with the free surface of the core. Because the angle is a continuously changing quantity, the amplitude of stress in the reflected wave will be different at each point along the surface. Unlike the plane wave case, the amplitude also varies with the radial distance the wave has traveled from the source (divergence) and with the angular distance away from the axis of impact.

For the spherical model with which we are concerned in hard-hammer percussion flaking, spalling can continue only so long as the angle of incidence of the expanding front remains less than about 60°, and so long as the net amplitude of the reflected pulse remains at least as great as the tensile strength of the material. This should place observable limits or constraints on the overall proportions of the flake. To take full advantage of the 60° spalling range, the flintknapper will strive to keep the axis of maximum stress amplitude within this range. This can best be accomplished by employing a core with an acute platform angle.

Spalling in normal incidence (as exemplified by the model in fig. 1.2) should not be considered as a completely different process from spalling in oblique incidence. Rather, normal spalling can perhaps be considered as a special, considerably simplified case at one extreme of a continuous range, the other extreme of which is spalling at the maximum degree of obliquity permitted by the value of Poisson's ratio. As already indicated, this range in flint and glass should lie between 0° and about 60°. Since the angle of incidence is directly affected by the platform angle, one may expect a percussion flake removed from a core with a very acute platform angle to approach in form the ideal spherical segment of the normal case.

As noted above, mathematical expressions relating the attributes of flake size and shape to various parameters of impact and core geometry are available to date only for flakes produced by a normally incident stress pulse. Comparable expressions are not yet available for the related but more complex case of spalling in oblique incidence, with which we are concerned in percussion flaking. From the theoretical considerations we have discussed, however, it is now possible to present a tentative list of what appear to be the major factors governing the mechanical variability of flake size and flake shape. Ultimately, all of these attributes, and probably others not included here, will have to be considered in order to develop suitable mathematical expressions for hard-hammer percussion flaking. These attributes include:

1. *Tensile strength of material*—the tensile strength may be determined experimentally.

2. *Stress amplitude of reflected pulse*—the amplitude is largely a function of:

   a. *Hammer velocity* (Speth 1972:45).

   b. *Mechanical properties of core and hammer*—these properties include Poisson's ratio, the density, and an elastic constant which measures the stiffness of the material known as Young's modulus of elasticity (see discussion in Speth 1972 and Faulkner 1972).

c. *Shape of wave front*—a spherically expanding front may be a reasonable model for waves produced by impact with a hard, rounded hammer (Cunningham and Goldsmith 1959:162; Dally, Durelli and Riley 1960:33).

d. *Angle of incidence*—the angle of incidence which the wave front, expanding along the axis of impact, makes with the free surface of the core may be particularly important and is probably dependent largely on the angle of impact (indicated by the symmetry and orientation of the Hertzian cone) and especially on the platform angle of the core.

e. *Divergence*—the amplitude of a spherically expanding stress wave decreases owing to the purely geometrical effects of the distance traveled from the source, such that the amplitude is inversely proportional to the square of the distance (Rinehart 1960:115).

f. *Attenuation*—attenuation is the lengthening and flattening of the pulse which results from work done on the material by the passing wave; the amount of attenuation per unit distance may be determined experimentally (Rinehart 1961:716, 1964a:91)

3. *Shape of stress pulse*—a symmetrically shaped pulse (e.g., half-sine or normal) may be the most reasonable model for waves produced by impact with a hard, rounded hammer (Glathart and Preston 1968:99).

4. *Wavelength of stress pulse*—the wavelength is largely a function of:

   a. *Radius of contact of hammer* (Speth 1972:45).

   b. *Mechanical properties of core and hammer* (see 2b above).

   c. *Velocity of wave propagation*—the velocity may be determined experimentally.

   d. *Attenuation* (see 2f above).

5. *Distance from impact point to free surface*—the greater the distance, the greater the effects of divergence and attenuation (see 2e and 2f above).

6. *Geometry and size of core*—two different aspects of the geometry must be considered:

   a. *Geometry of free surface*—the geometry of the face from which the flake is removed (e.g., flat, polygonal, or curved) will have a pronounced influence on the locus of fracture.

   b. *Geometry and size of core*—the overall size and shape of the core will determine the nature and timing of reflections from distant faces of the core; these may interfere with and alter the locus and form of the spall fracture, especially in the later stages of its development (see discussion below).

7. *Support conditions* — the manner in which the core is supported (rigidly affixed to another solid, clamped, hand-held, and so forth) may have an important influence on the form of the flake.

Although we do not as yet have theoretically derived mathematical expressions relating these attributes to those of flake size and flake shape, we do at least now know which attributes are important; this makes a direct experimental investigation of the relationships highly desirable.

EXPERIMENTAL PROCEDURE

This section describes a preliminary series of simple experiments, using glass as the model material, which was designed to investigate the interrelationships between several impact parameters and particular attributes of size and shape of flakes produced by hard-hammer percussion. In these experiments steel balls were dropped by an electromagnet onto massive glass prisms. By varying only the drop height, the ball diameter, and the distance from the point of impact to the edge of the prism—while holding the angle of impact, the mechanical properties of the prism, and the geometry of the prism constant—a number of interesting and important relationships have been observed.

The particular choice of glass specimens used in these experiments was dictated largely by the following considerations. First, it was decided to use specimens which had flat exterior surfaces; these are analytically less complex than those having curved surfaces. Second, specimens were needed which had an acute platform angle (Speth 1972:54). Optical prisms, obtained from World War II surplus tank periscopes, were the only specimens available at the time in sufficient quantity (at least 100) which fulfilled these conditions. These prisms are triangular in cross section (45°–45°–90°); each measures 5.75 in. (14.605 cm.) in length by 2.188 in. (5.56 cm.) in width (the hypotenuse of the triangle in section) by 1.094 in. (2.778 cm.) in height (the height perpendicular to the hypotenuse of the triangle in section). The edges of the prisms are slightly rounded. These bevels had no detectable influence on the experimental results, but they did prevent impacts very close to the edges. All impacts were made on the largest face of the prism, that is, on the face opposite the 90° angle. Henceforth this face will be referred to as the striking platform. The angle between the striking platform and the lateral faces of the prism is very acute (45°). Although this value falls below the mean angle of 60° to 70° commonly observed on prehistoric percussion flakes, it still lies within an acceptable range (Barnes 1939:109). The use of these specimens provides an opportunity to test the hypothesis offered above that flakes produced from cores with very acute platform angles should approach in form the ideal spherical segment of the normal case. This hypothesis is dramatically supported by the flakes produced in these experiments (a more detailed discussion of flake form will be given below).

In these initial experiments, the geometry and size of the core could not be systematically varied. In future and more extensive studies, specimens will have to be specially fabricated so that these important, complex variables can be included.

Each prism was clamped in a heavy, box-like wooden frame with the striking platform facing up and horizontal. The frame was positioned so that the specimen was situated directly beneath the electromagnet. The ends of the prism fit snugly into triangular notches cut into opposite sides of the frame; wooden pressure bars could be locked into position holding the prism securely at each end. This arrangement left approximately the mid–three-quarters of the specimen free of any obstruction. Clamp effects interfering with the fracture process were observed only when impacts were close to the ends of the prism; in such cases the resulting flakes became slightly asymmetrical. Deviations in flake form resulting from clamp effects will be discussed in greater detail below. The overall design and mounting of the frame was intended to minimize vibration resulting from impact.

The interior of the frame was completely padded with sponge rubber to prevent the flakes from disintegrating when they struck the walls. After each impact the padding was removed and cleaned to salvage any debris which may have been produced during the impact.

The electromagnet was attached to a massive steel drop tower by a series of movable arms so that its position could be accurately adjusted in three dimensions. This arrangement made it possible to move the magnet to any desired height and location over the striking platform of the prism. Some difficulty was encountered at first in devising a system that would make it possible to hit a very small target on the glass. This problem was finally overcome by winding the magnet over a steel rod which had a very tiny hole (≈ 1 mm) drilled longitudinally through the center. The rod was milled to a point with the hole passing directly through the tip. A very thin plumb line could then be passed through the hole and the point of the magnet lined up directly over the desired target. The line was then removed and voltage applied. The steel ball could be suspended from the point of the magnet with its center directly over the same target. Considerable accuracy was achieved in this manner. This technique also eliminated another problem. When the steel ball was suspended from the point of the magnet, it oscillated back and forth like a pendulum before it came to rest over the target. When the voltage was removed, the ball dropped with virtually no spin. This eliminated problems of friction which might arise from impacts by a spinning ball.

The Basic Percussion Flake

The percussion flakes produced in these experiments were virtually identical in form for all ball diameters and all drop heights (figs. 1.4, 1.5, and 1.6).

Figure 1.4 Photograph of fracture surface of typical flake showing prominent central spherical segment or lens, striking platform with Hertzian ring crack, and lateral wings. Other important features visible on flake include lance-like fractures extending out laterally from area of cone, two intersecting sets of "ripples" on surface of lens, and slight elongation of left wing owing to clamp effects.

The flake consists of a prominent lens-like spherical segment bounded laterally by relatively thin "wings." Both the wings and the central "lens" are truncated by the striking platform. The wings attain their maximum width at or slightly beneath the platform. The transition from the lens to the wings is smooth but quite abrupt, giving the flake, in transverse section, a profile reminiscent of the classic mathematical curve, the "Witch of Agnesi" (fig. 1.5b). In transverse section below the base of the Hertzian cone, the sphericity of the central portion of the lens is almost perfect. In longitudinal section, however, the sphericity is somewhat distorted by the cone, which produces a slight bulge (the bulb of percussion?) just below the platform. Also at the distal

Figure 1.5 General form of typical flake
[a] fracture surface of flake showing prominent central spherical segment or lens, striking platform with Hertzian ring crack, and lateral wings.
[b] striking platform of flake (note small bevel at edge of platform).
[c] section of flake (note hinge and small lip at distal end).

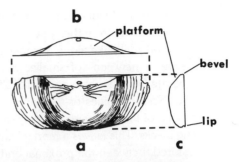

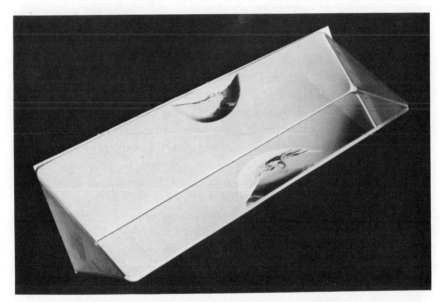

Figure 1.6 View of striking platform of glass prism showing two attached, partially formed flakes. Central lens or spherical segment is clearly developed in both, but wings have not yet formed. Sheet of white paper has been placed against back face to facilitate photography.

end of the flake, the fracture terminates by turning smoothly but abruptly outward toward the dorsal face and then slightly upward toward the striking platform, forming a smooth, rounded, hinge-like fracture. Just before the fracture reaches the dorsal face of the flake, however, it turns again sharply away from the platform leaving a small lip on the dorsal side of the hinge (fig. 1.5c).

Thin, small flakes produced by an impact very close to the edge of the striking platform almost invariably broke into several smaller pieces in a distinctive and highly consistent manner. The entire ventral face of the central lens, extending from the cone to the terminal hinge, separates from the body of the original flake along a somewhat rough and irregular spherical surface, leaving a new lens of smaller radius. The upper parts of the wings also separate from the main body of the flake along more or less the same surface. The thin extremities of the wings totally disintegrate into dust. The ventral surface of the cone also disintegrates, perhaps by the destruction of multiple ring cracks. This leaves a marked gap, almost a small crater, when the flake is restored, between the proximal end of the original lens and what remains of the cone. At slightly greater impact distances, only the upper parts of the wings separate from the flake. This suggests that the disintegration of thin flakes takes place according to the following general sequence: (1) the primary flake forms; (2) the upper parts of the wings detach from the flake, and the cone may disintegrate; (3) if the impact is sufficiently close to the edge of the prism, the ventral face of the lens separates from the body of the flake.

Asymmetrical flakes resulted from impacts very close to one of the clamps supporting the ends of the prism. The wing which formed nearest to the clamp became somewhat narrow and elongated. In very large flakes, both wings formed near the clamps and, as a result, both became slightly elongated. The dimensions of the flake other than the maximum width of the wings, in particular the dimensions of the central lens, do not seem to be significantly affected by the clamps. Archeologists have often noted that pressure exerted by the palm or fingers of the hand supporting the core may influence the final form of the flake (Are Tsirk: personal communication; Hodges 1964:101; Oakley 1964:41). It seems quite probable that the clamp effects observed in these experiments represent a comparable phenomenon.

While the clamps seem only to have a minor influence on the symmetry of the wings of certain flakes, the interference of waves reflected at distant surfaces of the core may have a much more profound effect on the spalling process. Compressive and tensile stress waves travel at a velocity nearly three times greater than the maximum propagation velocity of a crack (Rader 1967:161–62). If one postulates that the crack begins at the point of impact and then extends progressively downward into the core, it would be left behind very quickly by the advancing wave front. In relatively small cores, such as were used in these experiments, there would be ample time for waves to reach distant surfaces and return to interfere with the later stages of crack formation. The dimensions and overall geometry of the core would then be significant factors in determining the size and shape of a percussion flake.

There is an alternative explanation, however, for the formation of a spall fracture in which stress waves, reflected at distant surfaces of the core, may play only a minor or negligible role. As the wave travels outward and is reflected in tension along the free surface from which the flake will be removed, it travels so fast that it forms only a series of small, unconnected cracks rather than a single, continuous fracture. Thus the basic outline of the flake will be completely delineated by small cracks before the front has had time to reach other surfaces of the core and return to interfere with the fracture process. Part of the wave is trapped within the material behind the cracks, imparting a velocity to the flake which may be sufficient to complete the fracture. The proximal end of the flake will have the highest velocity; thus the final fracture, linking the smaller cracks, will extend downward from the striking platform. It is at this stage, after the form of the flake has already been established, that waves returning from other faces may also play a minor role in linking the smaller cracks. These waves may also cause the final fracture path to oscillate back and forth slightly, giving rise to the ripples often observed on the fracture surface. This type of spall fracture is well known in metals (O'Brien and Davis 1961) and also in Plexiglas (Rinehart 1964b). In metals the fracture surface is generally irregular and quite unlike the smooth surface observed on the flakes in the present experiments. It is possible, however, that in brittle materials, such as flint and glass, the irregularity expected by linking a large series of small cracks may be visible only at extremely high magnification. An interesting macroscopic analogy exists for this phenomenon of smoothly linking a series of adjacent small voids, namely the modern technique of rock blasting known as *smooth blasting* or *presplitting* (see Langefors and Kihlström 1967:296–303 and especially fig. 10:9b). In this type of blasting, a relatively low concentration of charge is detonated in a drill hole in rock. If a line of closely spaced, uncharged holes is drilled near the charged one, the blast may produce a single, smooth crack which links all of the holes. Almost no cracking will develop in other directions.

The experimental results of the present study appear to be entirely compatible with this type of spalling model. In particular, the form of the relationships between attributes of the central lens, such as length and thickness, are extremely consistent, regardless of the overall dimensions of the flake, or of the lateral position of the impact along the edge of the prism. These observations suggest that reflections from distant faces may have relatively little influence on the fracture process. If this type of spalling is, in fact, involved in percussion flaking, then the geometry of the face from which the flake is removed may be considerably more important than the size and geometry of the entire core in determining the *shape* of the flake.

The overall size of the core, however, probably does have an important influence on the *size* of the flake. One of the peculiar properties of brittle elastic solids is a tendency for the tensile strength of the material to increase markedly as the size of the specimen decreases (Lundborg 1970:22). The tensile strength is a critical attribute in determining whether or not a spall fracture will develop and also in determining the distance from the free surface of the core to the plane of fracture (see general discussion of spalling above).

Experiment I—Variable Drop Height and Constant Ball Diameter

In this experiment, a large series of flakes was produced by releasing a ⅝ in. (1.5875 cm.) diameter ball from eight different drop heights (4.331 in. [11 cm.]; 5.906 in. [15 cm.]; 7.874 in. [20 cm.]; 11.811 in. [30 cm.]; 19.685 in. [50 cm.]; 27.559 in. [70 cm.]; 31.496 in. [80 cm.]; 39.370 in. [100 cm.]). At each drop height numerous impacts were made, varying only the distance between the point of impact and the edge of the prism. This distance, referred to here as the *platform thickness,* was measured from the ventral edge of the Hertzian ring crack to the dorsal surface of the flake along a line perpendicular to the latter. The platform thickness determined in this manner can be converted readily to the distance or thickness measured in the plane of the striking platform by dividing the former by Cos 45° (0.7071).

The relationship between platform thickness and flake length is shown in a composite graph (fig. 1.7) for each of the eight drop heights. The length was measured from the top of the cone to the distal end of the flake along a line parallel to the dorsal face. The curves have been fitted by hand to give the reader a clearer visual impression of the form of the relationship. For any drop height, as the distance away from the edge of the prism increases, the flake length also increases. Each curve approaches a peak or maximum, which represents the largest possible flake length that can be obtained for a given combination of hammer size and impact velocity. If the platform thickness increases further, the flake length plunges very rapidly back toward zero, denoting a limiting value for the distance or platform thickness beyond which no flake will be produced. It is interesting to note that many of the flakes produced by impacts approaching the limiting value were completely formed but remained attached to the prism. In a few cases, the impacts were so close

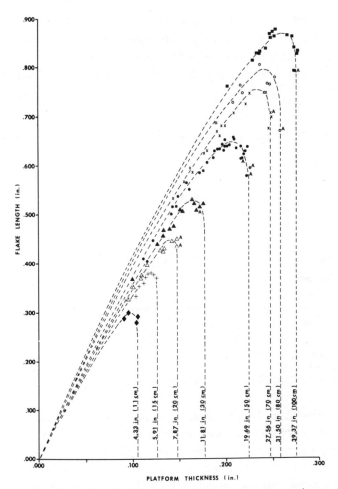

Figure 1.7 Flake length (in) plotted against platform thickness or true impact distance (in) for eight different drop heights (height indicated by number on vertical portion of curve). All impacts were made with ⅝ in (1.588 cm) diameter ball. Curves have been fitted by hand. Flakes marked with *A* were fully developed but remained attached to prism.

to the limit that the flakes were only partially formed; these flakes invariably lacked wings, which apparently are the last part of the flake to develop (fig. 1.6). The precise form of the curve in the vicinity of the origin could not be determined because flakes that were produced by impacts very close to the edge of the prism totally disintegrated and could not be measured accurately.

The eight drop heights were converted to impact velocities ($V = 2gh$), and then were plotted against (1) the limiting or terminal value of platform thickness [fig. 1.8]; (2) the terminal or maximum possible values of flake length [fig. 1.9]; (3) the terminal values of lens thickness (i.e., the maximum possible flake thickness) [fig. 1.10]. The composite graph of lens thickness

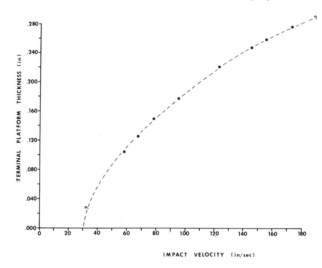

Figure 1.8 Terminal or limiting value of platform thickness or true impact distance (in) for a given impact velocity plotted against impact velocity (in/sec). All impacts were made with ⅝ in (1.588 cm) diameter ball. Curve has been fitted by hand.

plotted against flake length for each of the eight drop heights has been omitted here, but the curves are very similar to those shown in the composite graph for platform thickness versus flake length (fig. 1.7).

As the impact velocity decreases, the maximum distance at which a flake can be produced also decreases (fig. 1.8). The relationship is nonlinear; that is, the lower the impact velocity, the more rapidly the terminal platform thickness decreases. When velocity is plotted on a logarithmic scale (not shown), the curve becomes considerably more linear; this makes it possible to estimate in a very approximate manner the lower limit of velocity, the point where the curve reaches the horizontal axis. This occurs at an impact velocity of about 30 to 35 in./sec. The curves for maximum flake length (fig. 1.9) and for terminal flake or lens thickness (fig. 1.10), plotted against impact velocity, are also nonlinear and are very similar in form to that for terminal platform thickness.

Width has not been included in this analysis. The distance from the cone to the lateral margin of the lens is approximately the same as the length of the

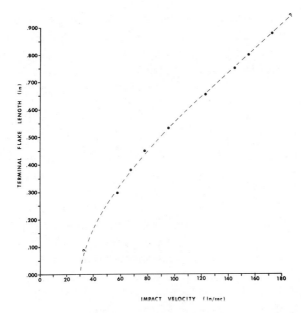

Figure 1.9 Terminal or maximum possible flake length (in) for a given impact velocity plotted against inpact velocity (in/sec). All impacts were made with ⅝ in (1.588 cm) diameter ball. Curve has been fitted by hand.

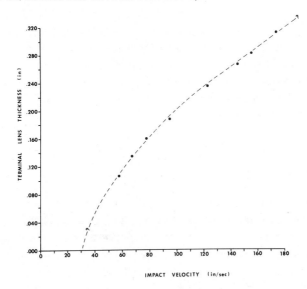

Figure 1.10 Terminal or maximum possible flake or lens thickness (in) for a given impact velocity plotted against impact velocity (in/sec). All impacts were made with ⅝ in (1.588 cm) diameter ball. Curve has been fitted by hand.

flake. This is to be expected because we are dealing with a spherical segment. The wings, however, extend the width considerably, and occasionally asymmetrically, beyond the lens. It was difficult to measure them accurately. In addition, the reason for the development of the wings is unknown at present. Thus, to avoid unnecessary complexity, the width has been omitted from the present study.

Experiment II—Constant Drop Height and Variable Ball Diameter

In this experiment, balls of six different diameters ($\frac{5}{16}$ in. [0.794 cm.]; $\frac{8}{16}$ in. [1.270 cm.]; $\frac{10}{16}$ in. [1.588 cm.]; $\frac{11}{16}$ in. [1.746 cm.]; $\frac{12}{16}$ in. [1.905 cm.]; $\frac{14}{16}$ in. [2.223 cm.]) were dropped from a constant height of 19.685 in. (50 cm.). For each ball size, numerous impacts were made, varying only the platform thickness. The relationship between platform thickness and flake length is shown in a composite graph (fig. 1.11) for each of the six different ball sizes. The curves are very similar to those observed for constant ball diameter and variable drop height in Experiment 1 (fig. 1.7). For each ball size, there is a maximum possible flake length and a limiting distance or platform thickness. Again, flakes produced close to the limit often remained attached to the prism.

Terminal platform thickness, maximum flake length, and terminal lens thickness are each plotted against ball diameter in figs. 1.12, 1.13, and 1.14, respectively. Superficially the curves are similar to those for impact velocity, but they are less curved and none of them appear to be linear when plotted on lognormal or log-log scales. No attempt, therefore, has been made to estimate the smallest ball size which will produce a flake from a 50 cm. drop height. The form of these graphs would perhaps be somewhat clearer had a larger range of ball diameters been used.

DISCUSSION

One particularly interesting prediction of the spalling model is that fracture will cease when the angle of incidence α of the stress wave on the free surface of the prism exceeds about 60° (fracture is very likely to stop at a smaller angle if the net stress amplitude drops below the tensile strength of the material). In fig. 1.2 above, the angle of incidence of the wave along line PP' is 0° (i.e., the wave front is normal to the free face). As one moves away from line PP', however, the angle of incidence increases. The angle α_1 of the wave front along line r represents the maximum angle beyond which no spall

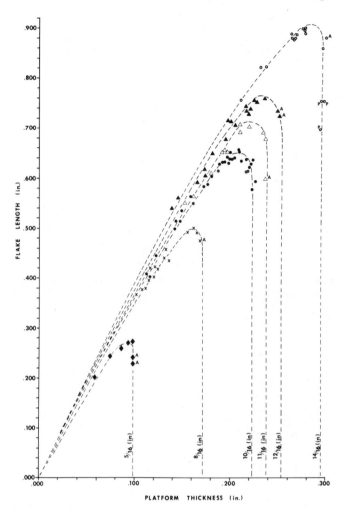

Figure 1.11 Flake length (in) plotted against platform thickness or true impact distance (in) for six different ball diameters (diameter indicated by number on vertical portion of curve). All impacts were from height of 19.69 in (50 cm). Curves have been fitted by hand.

Flakes marked with *A* were fully developed but remained attached to prism.
Flakes marked with *P* were only partially developed.

fracture will occur; this is the critical angle which, according to the spalling model, should not exceed about 60° in flint or glass.

To test this prediction, the observed values of angle α_1 were determined for all of the flakes produced in Experiments I and II. The angles were calculated in the following manner. First, the flake length was considered to be equal to

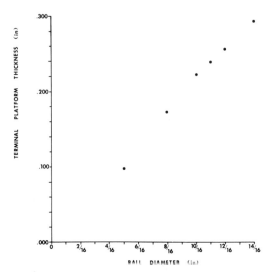

Figure 1.12 Terminal or limiting value of platform thickness or true impact distance (in) for a given ball diameter plotted against ball diameter (in). All impacts were made from drop height of 19.69 in (50 cm).

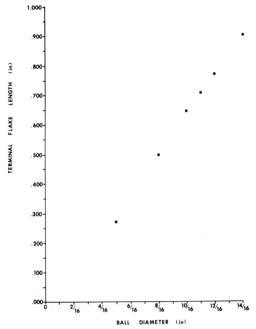

Figure 1.13 Terminal or maximum possible flake length (in) for a given ball diameter plotted against ball diameter (in). All impacts were made from drop height of 19.69 in (50 cm).

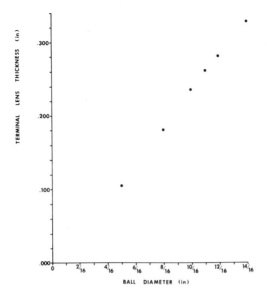

Figure 1.14 Terminal or maximum possible flake or lens thickness (in) for a given ball diameter plotted against ball diameter (in). All impacts were made from drop height of 19.69 in (50 cm).

one-half of the chord length of the spherical segment or lens. The thickness of the lens was considered to be equal to the height of the segment. Given these two values, the radius of the spherical segment can be calculated directly. To check whether these assumptions were reasonable, the radii of a large sample of flakes were determined visually using a chart of the type frequently employed by archeologists to find the radius of curvature of rim sherds. The values obtained by the two techniques were sufficiently similar to justify using the radius calculated directly by the chord method.

According to the model shown in fig. 1.2 above, the distance d from the point of impact to the free surface of the prism should be equal to the radius r of the spherical segment minus the lens thickness t (the height of the segment). Using the radius determined directly from the flakes by the chord method, and subtracting the lens thickness, the resulting values of d were found to be considerably greater than the actual or true distance from the point of impact to the free surface (represented on the flakes by the platform thickness). Thus, there are two distances which can be observed on the flakes: (1) the *true impact distance,* represented by the platform thickness; (2) an *imaginary impact distance* (referred to as d_i) which can be obtained empirically from the dimensions of the lens, and which represents the dis-

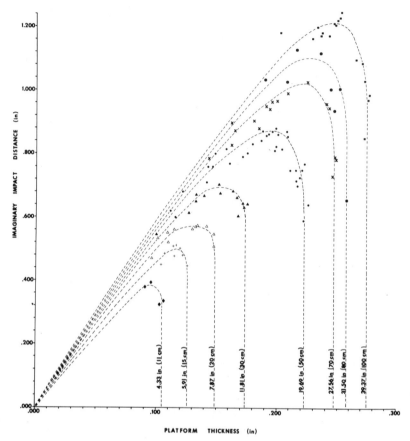

Figure 1.15 Imaginary impact distance d_i (in) plotted against platform thickness or true impact distance (in) for eight different drop heights (height indicated by number on vertical portion of curve). All impacts were made with ⅝ in (1.588 cm) diameter ball. Curves have been fitted by hand.

tance from an imaginary point of impact to the free surface. The relationship between the two distances is clearly nonlinear (fig. 1.15) and resembles the composite graphs discussed above. As the true impact distance increases, the imaginary impact distance increases to a maximum; it then drops back rapidly toward zero when the platform thickness approaches its limiting value (the figure shows the curves obtained for each of the eight drop heights; the curves obtained for the six ball diameters are similar and have been omitted here).

The discovery that the platform thickness is not identical to the impact distance, determined directly from the observed radius of curvature of the lens, may be an important clue to the relationship between normal spalling and the oblique spalling of percussion flaking. It is possible that the true and imaginary impact distances will be identical only when the free surface of the core is parallel to the striking platform—that is, when the platform angle is equal to 0° (the slab-like model shown in fig. 1.2). As the platform angle moves toward about 90° and the axis of impact becomes increasingly more oblique (and probably also closer) to the free surface, the true impact point and the imaginary impact point separate and begin to behave, with respect to each other, in the complex, nonlinear manner described above (fig. 1.15).

I am unable, at present, to offer a theoretical explanation for this peculiar behavior, other than to suggest that it may be attributable, in some way, to changes in the behavior of the spherical wave front in response to the increasing obliquity and proximity of the impact axis to the free surface. A suitable, empirically derived mathematical transformation, however, may eventually make it possible to treat spalling in oblique incidence in much the same way as spalling in the normal case as shown in fig. 1.2.

Let us return now to the prediction of the spalling model that the maximum angle of incidence α_1 should not exceed about 60°. Once the imaginary impact distance d_i and the radius r have been determined, the value of α_1 (with respect to d_i) can be calculated directly (Cos $\alpha_1 = d_i/r$). The highest value obtained was about 50°; this result provides interesting support for the utility of the spalling model in the analysis of hard-hammer percussion flaking.

The full 60° spalling range can only be used if the net stress amplitude of the reflected pulse remains above the tensile strength of the material over the entire range. One may expect, therefore, that there should be a positive correlation between impact velocity and the maximum observed value of the angle of incidence for a given velocity; this hypothesis is also supported by the experimental results, as shown in fig. 1.16.

The general relationship between angle α_1 and the true impact distance or platform thickness is shown in fig. 1.17 for three of the eight drop heights, and in fig. 1.18 for three of the six ball diameters. The curves have been fitted by hand and should be regarded as approximations. In both figures, as the platform thickness increases, the maximum angle of incidence increases, slowly at first, then very rapidly as the platform thickness approaches its limiting value.

CONCLUSION

Several interesting results have emerged from this study. In particular, three fundamental predictions of the spalling model have been confirmed: (1)

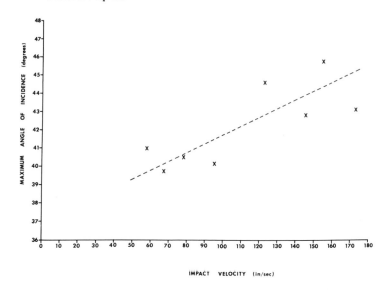

Figure 1.16 Maximum observed value of angle of incidence α_1 for a given impact velocity plotted against impact velocity (⅝ in diameter ball). Plot has been fitted by hand.

flakes produced from cores with very acute platform angles should approach in form the ideal spherical segment of the normal case illustrated in fig. 1.2 above; (2) the outer margin of the spherical segment will be formed before the angle of incidence of the incident wave front, with respect to the imaginary impact point, exceeds about 60° (the specific limiting value of the angle is fixed by the value of Poisson's ratio for the material); (3) the maximum observed value of the angle of incidence for a given impact velocity approaches 60° as the impact velocity is increased.

These results lead to the important conclusion that the spalling model does have explanatory value in the analysis of percussion flaking. The model, which is needed to develop precise mathematical expressions for the complex case of oblique incidence of particular interest to archeologists, is far from complete. Nonetheless, it has been possible to specify from theory the principal attributes which will have to be considered in order to develop suitable expressions. Preliminary direct experimentation, in which certain of these attributes were systematically varied while others were held constant, has clearly confirmed that regular and predictable relationships do exist; and it has provided some idea of the general form of several of these relationships.

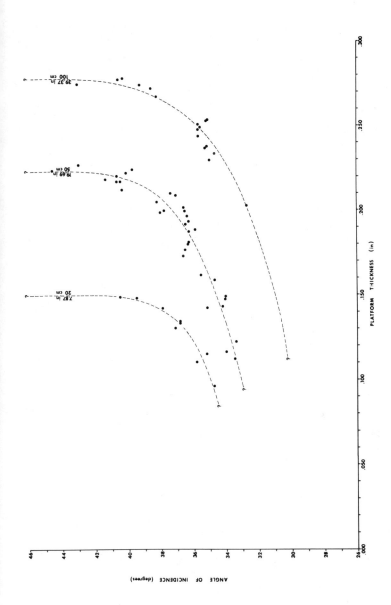

Figure 1.17 Angle of incidence α_1 plotted against platform thickness or true impact distance (in) for three different drop heights (height indicated by number on vertical portion of curve). All impacts were made with ⅝ in (1.588 cm) diameter ball. Curves have been fitted by hand.

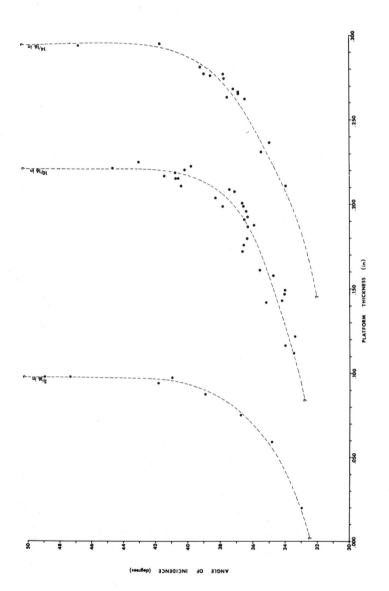

Figure 1.18 Angle of incidence α₁, plotted against platform thickness or true impact distance (in) for three different ball diameters (diameter indicated by number on vertical portion of curve). All impacts were from height of 19.69 in (50 cm). Curves have been fitted by hand.

As a sobering reminder to archeologists, however, the theoretical and experimental results of this study indicate that the relationships are exceedingly complex, multivariate, and nonlinear. Archeologists haphazardly measuring innumerable attributes on flakes and then searching for correlations may find correlations if they are lucky, but I seriously doubt that, *in the absence of theory*, they will ever be able to explain their results meaningfully.

ACKNOWLEDGMENTS

I am particularly grateful to Are Tsirk of the Department of Civil and Environmental Engineering, Newark College of Engineering, for his invaluable suggestions and criticisms of the manuscript. I assume full responsibility, however, for the errors and problems which remain in the final version of the paper. I would also like to acknowledge the useful comments and suggestions offered by Richard E. Blanton and Daniel G. Bates. And finally, I would like to thank Francis P. Conant, William Sawyer, Heather Blanton, and Stanley Willard for their assistance in preparing and photographing the figures and glass specimens.

REFERENCES

Baden-Powell, D. F. W. 1949. Experimental clactonian technique. *Proceedings of the Prehistoric Society* 15:38–41.

Barnes, Alfred S. 1939. The difference between natural and human flaking on prehistoric flint implements. *American Anthropologist* 41:99–112.

Bordaz, Jacques. 1970. *Tools of the old and new stone age.* Garden City, N.Y.: Natural History Press.

Bordes, François, and Don Crabtree. 1969. The Corbiac blade technique and other experiments. *Tebiwa* 12:1–21.

Cottrell, A. H. 1964. *The mechanical properties of matter.* New York: Wiley.

Crabtree, Don E. 1966. A stoneworker's approach to analyzing and replicating the Lindenmeier Folsom. *Tebiwa* 9:3–39.

—— 1967a. Notes on experiments in flintknapping: 3. The flintknapper's raw materials. *Tebiwa* 10:8–25.

—— 1967b. Notes on experiments in flintknapping: 4. Tools used for making flaked stone artifacts. *Tebiwa* 10:60–73.

—— 1968. Mesoamerican polyhedral cores and prismatic blades. *American Antiquity* 33:446–78.

—— 1970. Flaking stone with wooden implements. *Science* 169:146–53.

Cunningham, D. M., and W. Goldsmith. 1959. Short-term impulses produced by longitudinal impact. *Proceedings of the Society for Experimental Stress Analysis* 16(2):153–62.

Dally, J. W., A. J. Durelli, and W. F. Riley. 1960. Photoelastic study of stress wave propagation in large plates. *Proceedings of the Society for Experimental Stress Analysis* 17(2):33–50.

Ellis, H. Holmes. 1939. *Flint-working techniques of the American Indians: an experimental study.* Ohio Historical Society, Columbus.

Faulkner, Alaric. 1972. *Mechanical principles of flintworking.* Ph.D. Dissertation, Department of Anthropology, Washington State University.

Glathart, J. L., and F. W. Preston. 1968. The behavior of glass under impacts: theoretical considerations. *Glass Technology* 9:89–100.

Hester, Thomas R. 1972. *Lithic technology: an introductory bibliography.* University of California Archaeological Research Facility, Berkeley.

Hodgos, Henry. 1964. *Artifacts.* London: John Baltor.

Jaeger, J. C. 1964. *Elasticity, fracture and flow.* London: Methuen.

Jaeger, J. C., and N. G. W. Cook. 1969. *Fundamentals of rock mechanics.* London: Methuen.

Kerkhof, Frank, and Hansjurgen Müller-Beck. 1969. Zur bruchmechanischen Deutung der Schlagmarken an Steingeraten. *Glastechnische Berichte* 42:439–48.

Knowles, Sir Francis H. S. 1953. *Stone-worker's progress.* Oxford: Oxford University Press.

Kolsky, H. 1963. *Stress waves in solids.* New York: Dover.

Langefors, U., and B. Kihlström. 1967. *The modern technique of rock blasting.* 2d ed. New York: Wiley.

Lundborg, Nils. 1970. Fracture of glass by spherical indenters. *National Aeronautics and Space Administration Technical Translation* TT F–12,750.

Moore, Mark B. 1954. *Principles of experimental stress analysis.* New York: Prentice-Hall.

Oakley, Kenneth P. 1964. *Man the tool-maker.* Chicago: University of Chicago Press.

O'Brien, J. L., and R. S. Davis. 1961. On the fracture of solids under impulsive loading conditions. *Metallurgical Society Conferences* 9:371–88.

Pond, Alonzo. 1930. Primitive methods of working stone. *Logan Museum Bulletin* 2.

Rader, Dennis. 1967. On the dynamics of crack growth in glass. *Experimental Mechanics* 7(4):160–67.

Rinehart, John S. 1960. On fractures caused by explosions and impacts. *Quarterly of the Colorado School of Mines* 55(4).

—— 1961. Effects of transient stress waves in rocks. In *Mining Research,* pp. 713–26. New York: Pergamon Press.

—— 1964a. Fracturing by spalling. *Engineer's Digest* 25:89–92.

—— 1964b. Transient stress wave boundary interactions. In *Stress waves in anelastic solids*, edited by H. Kolsky and W. Prager, pp. 193–206. Berlin: Springer-Verlag.

Semenov, S. A. 1964. *Prehistoric technology*. Bath: Adams and Dart.

—— 1968. *Razvitie tekhniki v kamennom veke*. Leningrad.

Shand, E. B. 1958. *Glass engineering handbook*. 2d ed. New York: McGraw-Hill.

Speth, John D. 1972. Mechanical basis of percussion flaking. *American Antiquity* 37:34–60.

Timoshenko, S. P., and J. N. Goodier. 1970. *Theory of elasticity*. 3d ed. New York: McGraw-Hill.

Warren, S. H. 1914. The experimental investigation of flint fracture and its application to the problem of human implements. *Journal of the Royal Anthropological Institute* 44:412–50.

» 2 «

DON E. CRABTREE

The Obtuse Angle as a Functional Edge

The names archeologists give to tools may be extremely misleading because they often imply function. In point of fact no one knows what purpose a hand axe served, whether a "cleaver" was used to cleave, or a "chopper" to chop. Terms of this kind provide such handy, descriptive labels that efforts to replace them with nonfunctional substitutes have met with failure. In fact it is much easier to discuss similarities and differences between tools than to discover the uses to which each was put.

Since most forms of stone tool cannot be observed in actual use, the most straightforward and simple way to determine their original function is to make copies and then attempt to employ them in a variety of ways. While absolute proof will always be lacking, one may then argue by analogy to suggest a range of likely functions which hopefully can be buttressed by a variety of data. Crabtree's line of reasoning is worthy of note. He starts with the observation that wear marks are sometimes seen on the obtuse angled edges of some excavated specimens. This leads him to determine, through trial and error, a range of jobs to which such edge configurations are uniquely suited and these conclusions, in turn, give rise to furthur speculations on classes of Paleolithic tools which may have served these functions. The basic problem he faces, then—given that absolute proof is not possible—is how to support his contention. First he notes the position and configuration of small striations, the patterns of wear, which appear on his own experimental tools, and then compares them to prehistoric counterparts. In a like way similarities in the worked materials may also be assessed.

As often happens in experimental work of this kind, the conclusions may extend well beyond the problem as it was first conceived, and lead to additional questions. One type of question concerns methods required to produce oblique-angled tools. A second deals with the separation of "tools" *themselves from the lithic debris or* débitage, *which is a natural byproduct of their manufacture. The ability to discover such forms depends directly on knowledge of where to look and what to look for. And Crabtree suggests that archeologists should shift their attention away from exclusive examination of acute-angled edges which have long been recognized as efficient for cutting and shaping softer materials. As good experiments should, this one raises as many questions as it answers.*

The interpretation of the diverse functional uses of stone tools has to date been based principally on a theoretical analysis of their wear patterns (Bordes 1968, Semenov 1957). This has been our most reliable archeological guide, but actual functional experiments will give more substance to the theory. Questions must be posed and answered, among them: What materials was prehistoric man forming, altering, or modifying with his stone tools, and at what angle did he hold the working tool? Were the stone tools held only in the hand when performing these tasks or were they affixed to a handle or holding device by fitting and wedging? Were they adhered to other materials with vegetable resin, or were they lashed to stocks and shafts? Many stone artifacts have been placed in typological categories which imply function. Some are correctly typed because of actual observation and ethnographic accounts. Others are functionally typed based on theory or on the industries of a particular site which place similar implements bearing certain technological characteristics into useful typological categories. However, this tends to associate various shapes with specific functions, when in reality they could have been multipurpose tools. As a result, artifacts not conforming to these categories are said to be nondiagnostic and are often discarded as débitage, lithic debris, flakes, exhausted cores, or general manufacturing byproducts. The most reliable source of implied function is a careful analysis of the wear pattern on the edges or ridges of lithic implements.

The use of obtuse-angled edges or ridges of artifacts as working edges has generally been overlooked or ignored in the past, whereas recent evidence reveals functional scars and wear patterns on these angles. The results of functional experiments indicate that these obtuse angles provide additional diagnostic traits. The obtuse edge of a tool will often show polish when it is used continually on homogeneous materials. Striations or scratches on the obtuse edges are the result of abrasive contamination, while occasional minute step fractures are due to improper holding, too much pressure, or the nonhomogeneous nature of the material being worked.

We know from experiments and from archeological evidence that the acute angle of a flake or blade is an excellent cutting edge for yielding materials, but we have failed to consider the functional value of the obtuse angle of more than 90° and less than 130° (fig. 2.1). (The obtuse angle of more than 130° has proven so far to be too flat to have functional value.) Experiments in function reveal that the obtuse angle on stone tools can perform tasks which are impossible to complete with stone tools having acute-angle edges of 90° or less. That the obtuse angle can be used as a cutting edge has been a revealing experience and has opened the door to further experiments to determine the diverse uses of such edges.

Experimental results show that the obtuse angle on stone tools made of material even as fragile as obsidian can be used to remove spiral shavings from dry bone with accuracy and control, and the tool will still retain its cutting edge. For example, the obtuse angle of a stone tool may have been used for the elaborate carving of lintels of extremely hard wood (sapodilla) in Mayan temples in Yucatán; obtuse angles may also have been used for the modification of other resistant materials such as bone, horn, antler, and ivory. When the acute angle edge is used to work this type of resistant material, the tool will either break or the edge will dull before the task is completed.

I made replicas of obtuse angle tools and then used them in many ways—for cutting at different angles, holding in different positions, and cutting and working a variety of materials. I compared both the cutting tool and the material being worked with archeological specimens in order to evaluate the striations, polish, and functional flake scars. In each experiment, both the tool and the material being cut or formed were the same as those employed in prehistoric specimens.

It is essential that the worker modify the same materials as those which were available aboriginally—whether by gouging, planing, or chopping—in order to verify the manner of holding and function. Some implements having acute-angle edges, such as the obsidian blade, require light force for cutting soft materials. The thumb and index finger furnish sufficient force for these light cutting tasks; but when the obtuse angles of tools are used for cutting, more force is required—much the same principle as our modern lathe. The acute angle can be used to work softer material while an obtuse angle is used to work more resistant material. The angle of the tool edge must correspond to the resistance of the material being worked. During the functional experiment, the worker must keep in mind the brittle nature of the stone tool and must be familiar with the tool's strong and weak areas. These tools cannot be twisted or used in a levering way, and must be kept in correct alignment with

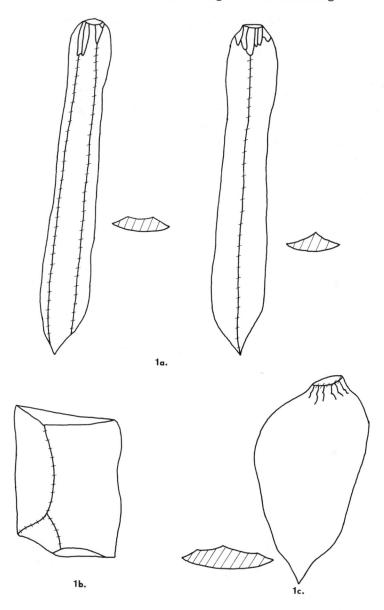

Figure 2.1 [a] Prismatic blades, with obtuse-angle ridges indicated by hatching [b] Obtuse angle ridges on a segment of blade [c] Obtuse angle edge on lip of flake

the opposing resistance of the material being worked. Skill in using any hand tool requires practice and reasoning, which necessitate continued experimentation. Even when experiments yield good results, they may not compare to the work of a skilled aboriginal workman.

One source of an obtuse-angle cutting edge is a blade scar ridge on a polyhedral core (fig. 2.2a). The parallel blade scars are slightly concave between the ridges, making the ridges satisfactory obtuse-angle working edges. The core is used as one would use a draw plane—holding the

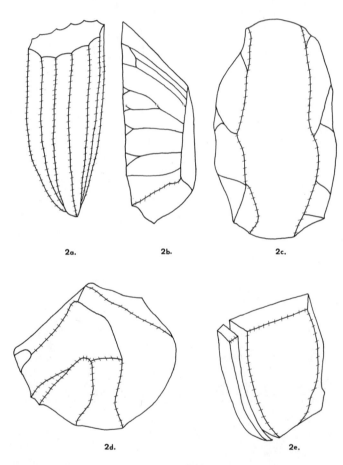

Figure 2.2 [a] Polyhedral blade core showing obtuse-angle ridges [b]–[e] A variety of cores exhibiting usable obtuse-angle cutting edges

proximal and distal ends of the core with the right and left hands. The modern draw plane or draw knife can only be pulled toward the user, but the obtuse-angle edge on a polyhedral core can be pushed or pulled. The polyhedral core is drawn at a slight angle rather than at right angles as one would use a modern plane. When used in this fashion, the depth of the cut may be accurately adjusted by a slight change of angle of the bearing surface. The obtuse angle of the cutting edge is far stronger than an edge of 90° or less. When soaked antler is worked, shavings three inches long may be removed with a single pass of the core. I know of no single-edged metal tool that will remove material with the speed of the obsidian core. The cuts are very clean and smooth and show no bruising of the surface being planed. When the core planer is used on very hard wood, the finish is excellent and the core can be used to produce flat surfaces. It is surprising how durable the obtuse-angle edge can be. Use flake scars along the edge generally result from the tool's being held at the wrong angle; lack of homogeneity occurs from contamination of the material being planed rather than from function. When the obtuse angle of the core is used repeatedly on resinous wood, resin will build up and impair the cutting action. The resin then must be scraped off or removed with solvent, or a new blade must be detached from the core to expose two new sharp cutting edges, or the entire polyhedral core can be rejuvenated by removing a series of blades around the perimeter to expose new obtuse-angle cutting edges.

The surprising and excellent results of using the obtuse angles of a core as a shaping and forming tool for antler, hardwood, and bone prompted me to look for similar angles on other artifacts to use in cutting experiments. Similar experiments with both burin blades and cores resulted in only moderate success. When the burin core was used in the manner of an engraving, the core slipped and its corners broke after a few passes. This generally occurred when the tip was lifted upward to terminate the cutting action. After a minimum amount of work on hard material, the right-angle edges of the burin core would crush because minute step flake scars formed on the margin. However, when the burin blade was removed at more or less than a 90° angle to the margin of the core, both acute and obtuse angles were formed on the core's edge. The acute angle was excellent for working soft woods, while the obtuse angle was good for working more resistant materials. Failure to correctly use an angle of 90° or more is probably due to a lack of understanding of the proper use of the many prehistoric styles of burins.

The natural facets on quartz crystals can also be used as forming tools but are neither so efficient nor so effective as the artificially made obtuse angles on cores and other tools. The natural facets on the crystal are plane surfaces, while those made by removing a blade or flake from a core leave concave surfaces between the obtuse angle ridges, giving a sharper cutting edge.

If the crystal is made into a blade core by removing blades longitudinally, the obtuse angles of the blade scars are a far more efficient cutting tool than the natural facets. However, the bruises found on the natural obtuse angles of a quartz crystal from Bandarawela, Ceylon, may well be the result of function (Allchin 1966, fig. 30).

Another functional experiment involved the use of a strangulated blade (fig. 2.3a). (In archeology this strangulated blade has been classified as a

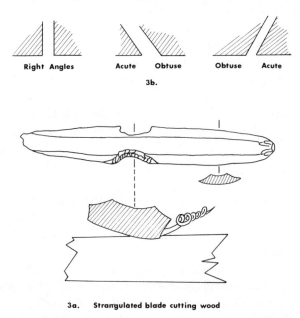

Right Angles   **Acute   Obtuse**   **Obtuse   Acute**

3b.

3a.   Strangulated blade cutting wood

Figure 2.3 [a] Strangulated blade cutting yield material [b] Right-angle, acute-angle, and obtuse-angle cutting edges

spokeshave.) Obsidian archeological specimens from the El Inga site in Ecuador were brought by Carl Phagan to the 1970 Idaho State University Flintworking Field School. We made replicas of the originals from obsidian. We attempted to use it by placing the concave edge on a wooden shaft and pulling the ventral side of the blade toward the worker. This removed only a slight amount of the wood and left a very irregular cut on the shaft. When additional pressure was applied to the blade, it broke. We then noticed striations on the ventral side of the El Inga specimen between the two opposing concavities which constituted the strangulation. These striations gave us a clue to the manner in which the implement was held and used. The striations indicated that the slightly convex ventral side of the blade was placed flat on the wooden shaft after being shaped. The convex surface acted as a bearing and aided the adjustment of the depth of the cut being made. When we used the strangulated blade in this manner, it made a flat, smooth cut and required little force to remove a clean shaving. Both concavities served well as cutting surfaces. The opposite concavity on the blade permitted the worker to tilt back the blade to terminate the cut. When used in this manner the blade did not break, because little force was necessary to remove shavings from the material being worked.

Further functional experiments with the strangulated blade showed that the angle of the cutting edge of the blade could be made acute for soft materials or obtuse for cutting harder materials (fig. 2.3b). If the cutting edge was too acute or was used improperly, use flakes were removed from the ventral side of the blade rather than from the concave portion of the strangulation. Many tools other than blades exhibit an obtuse angle, and these can be simply and rapidly made or resharpened. Often a new working edge is exposed by the removal of a single flake. It is possible to misinterpret this single sharpening flake as a tool when it is only a reconditioning or resharpening flake.

Robert Heizer showed me obsidian cores from Papalhuapa, Guatemala, which were formed by blade removal but which also showed evidence of function on the obtuse-angle ridges. The blade scar ridges on the cores were dulled, which indicated that they could have been used as planes, wedges, reamers, drills, anvils, or pointed percussors for making soft stone figures, and some could have been sectioned to be used as preforms for ear plugs. This site is important because it is near the source of raw material and should illustrate many manufacturing steps which can be related to ethnographic accounts. A preliminary report of this site has been published by John A. Graham and Robert F. Heizer (Graham and Heizer 1971). In 1970, Dr. Junius Bird, from the American Museum of Natural History, gave me a collection of six obsidian cores from Oaxaca, Mexico, which all showed signs of wear on the obtuse-angle ridges. Obsidian polyhedral cores from the Metro excavations in Mexico, D.F., shown to me by José Luis Lorenzo in 1970, displayed apparent use of blade scar ridges. Included was one core which indicated that the distal end was used as a drill or reamer until the core was worn to a smooth cylindrical shape. I collected obsidian polyhedral cores from Teotihuacán, Puebla, Colima, and the coast of the State of Nayarit, all of which bear evidence of the use of blade scar ridges as cutting and forming edges. Through personal communication with Denise de Sonneville Bordes (1970), I learned that she has noted evidence of functional scars on the dorsal ridges of blades from the Upper Paleolithic of Southern France. Personal examination of a blade from the Clovis site at Murray Springs, Arizona (1966), showed intensive wear and polish on the dorsal ridge while the lateral margins were still quite sharp. This suggests that the ridge was used as a cutting implement *before* the blade was detached from the core. When the ridge became dulled, a blade was detached from the core to expose two fresh useful ridges. The core, with multiple obtuse-angle ridges, would have been an ideal implement for rapidly shaping the shaft wrench made from the long bone of a mammoth found at Murray Springs (Haynes and Hemmings 1967). Occasionally cores are noted which are not exhausted for further blade detachment, but their ridges bear evidence that they were used for shaping tools while the core was still of adequate size for a specific function.

Functional polish appearing on some aboriginal artifacts presents problems of use analysis. Use polish is frequently observed on scraping and agricultural tools, which usually have acute-angle working edges. Scraping generally rounds or polishes the working edges, conceivably because of the abrasive nature of sandy soils on wet hides. The polish noted on agricultural tools could well be the result of continual digging and tilling, but polish and edge rounding also appear on tools which have acute- and obtuse-angle working surfaces. A tool with a rounded polished edge ceases to cut or plane and will only function when an excess of force and energy is applied by the worker. However, the rounded polished edge will work well as a burnisher. It is difficult to understand why prehistoric man would use an edge until it acquired a polish when a more functional edge could be established by detaching a flake to expose a new, sharp edge.

Diverse functional experiments were performed over a considerable period of time—cutting antler, bone, grass, hardwood, etc.—using tools with both acute- and obtuse-angle edges. Yet there was never a sign of polish on the edge, and use flakes were detached only when the tool was used improperly.

Because of the durability of the stone tool and the amount of use and abuse necessary to establish functional polish or scars, criteria for determining function must be approached with caution. Many tools may have performed their task and been abandoned before they exhibited any functional scars or polish. To wit—the axe. When an axe is used, most dulling occurs from misuse rather than from chopping clean wood.

OBTUSE-ANGLE BURIN

The success of using the obtuse angle for forming and shaping by the planing technique prompted me to experiment with slotting implements. An obtuse-angle burin appeared to be the logical tool for cutting strips from antler and bone to make harpoons, needles, awls, and similar implements.

It is a simple task to make a burin by modifying a thin, flat flake from a right angle to an acute angle by either percussion or pressure (fig. 2.4a–c). However, establishing an obtuse angle on the burin becomes an apparently impossible task (fig. 2.4d). When the worker is making an acute-angle burin, he can strike off a spall having an obtuse angle. But this spall is the bulbar part, so even though the spall is obtuse it has a rounded edge that will not cut. An effort was made to produce an obtuse-angle burin by detaching a flake with an edge of less than 90° (burin spall). The platform had to be tilted to receive the force; but when pressure was applied the tool would slip, and if percussion was used the percussor would ricochet. At this time it appears mechanically impossible to make an obtuse-angle burin by either pressure or percussion using the established technique.

Because of this failure I mentally reviewed aboriginal collections examined in the past which may have contained this characteristic. I recalled that Dr. Fred Johnson of the Peabody Institute had shown me a handful of such flakes from the Arctic. They resembled broken ostrich shell and had margins with double edges of 90°. One margin of these flakes had an obtuse angle and the other margin had an acute angle. Both edges of all margins were 90° to the dorsal and ventral sides of the flakes. This seemed abnormal, since snapped flakes or blades generally have one edge of the margin with a 90° angle while the other edge has been rounded by the breaking or snapping process, and such a process does not produce a margin with a double 90° angle. A question of manufacturing technique therefore arose. Dr. George Agogino had also sent me a flake assemblage from the Lindenmeier site. It contained a number of flakes with the same type of fracture as the Arctic specimens. Ruthann Knudson also had a similar assemblage of flakes from the Claypool site in Colorado. A number of them had double 90° cutting edges. These were termed pseudo-burins, because the fracture force was different from the

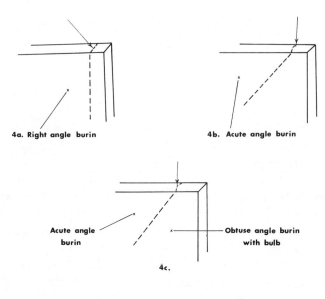

4a. Right angle burin   **4b. Acute angle burin**

Acute angle   Obtuse angle burin
burin   with bulb

4c.

CONVENTIONAL BURIN BREAKS

4d.   OBTUSE ANGLE BURIN ATTEMPT
Force will not remove burin spall

Figure 2.4 [a] Right-angle burin [b] Acute-angle burin [c] Acute-angle burin with obtuse-angle burin spall [d] Obtuse-angle burin attempt. Force will not remove burin spall

force applied to make normal burins (they are struck or pressed off longitudinally from the edge of the flake).

The shattered flakes of the Peabody collection had the appearance of the débitage of a broken window pane supported by its casing and broken by the force of a thrown rock or ball. The breakage was caused both by the support of the casing and by the force of the projectile. Fractures resulting from this type of breakage commonly have double 90° edges on one margin.

Using the support and projectile principle, an experiment was performed to replicate this style of fracture. An indentation was made in a soft stone to resemble a "nutting stone" (fig. 2.5a). The flake was then placed over this concavity and a punch of pointed stone or antler was placed on the flake and aligned with the concavity. The punch was dealt a sharp blow causing the flake to shatter. The force applied to the punch over the nutting stone concavity produced the desired double 90° edges. This type of intentional fracture will produce flakes with edges at right angles to the ventral and dorsal surfaces of the original flake. It will also cause the flake to break geometrically into pieces resembling triangles with both obtuse and acute angles (fig. 2.5b–c).

5a.   **Punch applied to flake resting over concavity in 'nutting' stone**

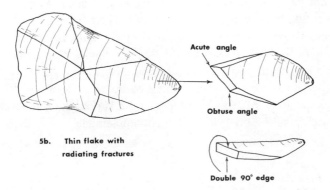

Acute angle

Obtuse angle

5b.   **Thin flake with radiating fractures**

Double 90° edge

Figure 2.5 [a] Punch applied to flake resting over concavity in "nutting stone" [b] Thin flake with radiating fractures [c] Segment of fractured flake showing acute-angle and obtuse-angle cutting edges and double 90° edge

The use of the concavity and the punch may be only one of several ways to produce this distinctive style of fracture. The pseudo-burins must be selected from the flake shatter, which is composed of both acute- and obtuse-angle burinlike objects. When the pseudo-burins are affixed to a handle with adhesive (fig. 2.6), the obtuse angle of the pseudo-burin will outlast and outcut burins of 90° or less when used on hard materials.

Figure 2.6 Obtuse-angle burin mounted in wood handle with adhesive

Because of the infrequent appearance of the classic burinations of tools from Middle America, the unidentified pseudo-burin may have been used to accomplish the same function as the conventional burin.

In conclusion, limited experiment and limited examination of Paleolithic implements indicate that more lithic debris should be retained and intensively examined and should not be discarded as nondiagnostic. It is entirely possible that distinct technological traits, characteristic modes of use, manners of holding or hafting, and the nature of the material being worked can be defined by this lithic debris. We also may find multipurpose implements. It has been a revelation to find that for some tasks a thin, sharp, acute-angled edge will not perform as well as an obtuse-angled edge. Aboriginal tools bearing an obtuse-angle working edge may not fall into the categories of well-defined types. Some may be asymmetrical or without definite form, but a careful study of the wear patterns on the obtuse angles may determine the amount and type of function, and how these tools were used.

My functional experiments were hampered by the lack of the aborigine's imperative know-how in using lithic tools, and it is doubtful if today we can ever approach his functional skill with stone implements.

ACKNOWLEDGMENTS

I wish to thank the National Science Foundation for its continuing support of my experimental work in lithic technology. Also, I am indebted to Dr. Earl H. Swanson, Director of the Idaho State University Museum; my wife,

Evelyn, for her suggestions and typing of the rough drafts; and the following people, who helped in preparing this article for publication: Guy Muto, Mae Jones, and Christine Lovgren. The illustrations are by James Mielke.

REFERENCES

Allchin, Bridget. 1966. *The stone tipped arrow*. London: Phoenix House.

Bordes, François. 1968. *The old stone age*. New York: McGraw-Hill.

Graham, John A., and Robert Heizer. 1971. Contributions of the University of California Archaeological Research Facility. No. 13, June 1971. University of California, Department of Anthropology, Berkeley.

Haynes, C. Vance, and E. Hemmings. 1967. Mammoth bone shaft wrench from Murray Springs, Arizona. *Science* 159(3811):186–87.

Semenov, S. A. 1957. *Prehistoric technology*. London: Cory, Adams and Mackay.

CHARLES J. ERASMUS

Monument Building: Some Field Experiments

Assumptions make up part of the basic intellectual baggage of any scientist. Some are realized and stated for what they are; others are so deeply ingrained that their validity goes unchallenged and one unconsciously accepts them as given truths. Herein lies the danger because such ingrained assumptions elude objective assessment. Most archeologists, for example, have assumed that enormous amounts of labor were required to construct the monumental Mayan ceremonial centers: those imposing and majestic stone-faced temples and enclosures. Therefore, a highly centralized state or political authority again appeared likely, since a good deal of coercion must have been necessary to organize workers and keep them at their task. Yet because Erasmus doubts that the Maya had reached a state level of political integration, he is led to posit the eminently reasonable question: Just how much work is required to erect edifices of this type?

Consider how Erasmus attacks the problem. The first, and probably the easiest, part involves direct experimentation. Using local labor, he determines how much earth and rock fill a man can dig and haul in a day, how long it takes to make the mortar, to dress, and to construct stone facing. He can then estimate the total number of man-days involved. Other guesses must then follow. These include the size of the effective community, population density, and the number of years actually involved in the construction of one monumental center at Uxmal. What Erasmus arrives at is the number of man-days per year a family must contribute. He himself points out that the number of estimates and guesses one makes along the way (how long, for example, was

Reprinted, with minor editorial changes, from *Southwestern Journal of Anthropology* 21 (4), 1965, pp. 277–301. Used by permission of the editors.

a working day?) preclude a high degree of accuracy, but one can, he argues, set an upper limit on the work a family must contribute each year. The final stage of the argument is the most original of all: By ethnographic comparison, he shows that this amount of communal work is well within the bounds commensurate with a chiefly society and need not require a centralized state level of organization.

The argument proves nothing at all. It does, however, shift the burden to those who would disagree, and neatly pulls the rug from under one widely held implicit assumption. It also shows that the experimental approach need not be limited to what might seem the more immediate and "simple" of archeological concerns.

While collecting information on peasant federations in Mexico during the summer of 1964, I employed some peasants to excavate and carry earth and rock, and collected data on stone masonry and stone sculpturing. The purpose of this activity was to obtain a measure of the man-days of labor invested in the construction of Maya ceremonial centers. I wanted to know how many man-days of labor went into a cubic meter of fill or masonry and into a square meter of sculptured stone veneer, so that I could then divide these figures into estimates of the volume of fill and masonry and of the area of sculptured walls of a ceremonial center.

Having thus determined the total labor investment in a ceremonial center with a known time duration, I intended to compute the average annual man-day investment. This figure, compared with population density estimates, could help fix the number of man-days per year invested by each household. This annual household labor contribution could then be compared with those known for communal projects in societies of varying degrees of organization to estimate the extent of associated political development. Here I present my findings.

Upon my return from Mexico I discovered that David Kaplan (1963) had anticipated my results in one of the most sensible articles on pre-Hispanic Mesoamerican civilization that has been published in the last decade. Kaplan feels that the traditional tendency for anthropologists to associate highly centralized political systems with imposing monumental ruins has involved unwarranted assumptions as well as circular causal reasoning: a highly centralized state is necessary to perform the imposing construction chores, yet the latter are necessary to produce a centralized state. Because such public works are usually built as "accretions over long periods of time" rather than all at once, because the populations concerned had sufficient "leisure" time to participate without making "full-time laborers" a requirement, because the engineering and architecture were really quite "technically simple" despite the artistic embellishments, because monument building may "function as a system-maintaining mechanism of a weakly organized polity" rather than as the manifestation of a strongly organized one, and because ethnographic evidence indicates that pre-state–level societies in many parts of the world were capable of mobilizing sizable work parties for communal projects, Kaplan believes much of the Mesoamerican monument construction could have been performed by people at a "chiefdom . . . level of socio-political integration." He defines the chiefdom category much the same as Service (1962:170–74) does. It lacks the coercive quality of the "state" and depends for integration on a redistributive economy and the vestiges of primitive kinship systems.

The data I shall present appear to support Kaplan's major thesis, although much more experimental work needs to be done. Most of his arguments are sound with the possible exception of the survival-value reasoning implicit in the "system-maintaining" function of monument construction for weak polities. This tired old efficient cause of the Michigan evolutionist sect is unnecessary and beside the point here. I much prefer Kaplan's alternate efficient causes—"the desire for public approval and prestige, duty to the community, religious sentiment, pleasure and pride in craftsmanship. . . ." Not all of cultural development is evolutionary in the cumulative sense of, for example, degrees of specialization or levels of integration. Much is "involutional"—variation within monotony (Goldenweiser 1936). The involutional developments are substitutive rather than cumulative. Many societies at a level of sociopolitical organization similar to the Mayas might have built pyramids and temples if they had had such easy-to-use building materials so readily available. Instead they developed their potlatching or head-hunting or yam displays. I am not returning to cultural relativism; I am simply pointing out that the involutional side of social behavior which misled us into relativism should not be forgotten in our return to evolutionary considerations. The Mayas were living on a great natural erector set—their rocky limestone peninsula—and they chose to play with it.

Most of the concern with the "decline" of Maya civilization, reawakened by Betty Meggers's (1954) provocative paper on limiting environments, is obviated by the realization that the word "decline" involves anthropological values based on a strong professional commitment to prehistory and its material artifacts. Although the Mayas did a lot for archeology before they "declined," the inhabitants of Yucatán were probably at much the same level of "socio-cultural integration" when the Spaniards encountered them as they had been for the previous millennium.

The centralized political organization which many authorities seem to feel is a concomitant of ceremonial centers is invariably associated in some fashion with the problem of food production. Morley and Brainerd (1956:140) took considerable pains to show that a Maya slash-and-burn farmer could support himself and his family with little more than 48 days of farming and had a surplus of "nine to ten months—during which the ancient Maya ceremonial centers were built. . . . With so much free time, the Maya Indian for the last two thousand years has been exploited—first by his native rulers and priests, next by his Spanish conquerors, and more recently by private owners in the hemp fields." There is a weakness in this line of reasoning which creates a "surplus" of leisure to explain the "exploitation" or power by which community labor is organized. Through some form of curtailment, "surplus" food production linked to "surplus" leisure also becomes a cause of the cultural "decline." Although the availability of labor is certainly a necessary cause, it is hardly a sufficient one. The similar view more recently presented by Dumond (1961:312) argues strongly for the relative efficiency of swidden farming in readily producing a food surplus above subsistence needs and thereby making possible "areas of population concentration" within "low-density populations" essential to the "centralized, stratified" social system indicated by Maya achievements. Ursula Cowgill (1962:283) also argues convincingly that the productivity of swidden farming in the southern Maya lowlands was sufficient to support a population of 100 to 200 people per square mile and would have left "something close to half the total labor supply" available "for construction of the monumental ruins of the Classic Period." In Altschuler's (1958) elaboration of the basic argument, the surplus was enough to encourage the growth of a priest class but not enough to meet their increasing demands, and social disorganization and peasant revolts ensued.

George Cowgill (1964:154) resembles Kaplan in emphasizing the voluntary participation and "community pride" of the Maya peasants in their "ritual system" and "the glories of their temples and leaders, a situation not unlike that underlying elite displays of wealth in Polynesia or on the Northwest Coast of North America." He favors Mexican invasions with forced resettlement as the explanation of the Maya "collapse." Thus his explanations of both development and decline imply such historical-causal incentives as prestige-seeking through community development and conquest in addition to the limiting causal condition of labor availability. It is my feeling that the results of the field experiments and data collecting to be presented here fit better with the position of David Kaplan and George Cowgill than with any other.

In the past I have been guilty, as have many others, of relying heavily on the surplus labor arguments. Calculating the quantity of man-days per year available within a five-mile radius of three hypothetical ceremonial centers under conditions yielding different population densities, I have argued (1961:127) that an impressive number of man-days can result even with swidden farming. With irrigation, the possibilities are staggering. But before "force" or a highly centralized state organization can be deemed necessary, the labor demands on the individual household must be estimated by some means. To show that the Mayas only had to farm two or three months of the year and had plenty of spare time for community development, given social differentiation and increasing power at the top, is to present a picture of bored aboriginals wandering aimlessly through the brush in search of a power structure to put them to work. Oddly enough this view very much resembles the modern ones on "seasonal" or "disguised" unemployment used to justify the bureaucratic leadership and expense involved in community development projects by which politically unsophisticated peasants are forced and cajoled into playing charades for the demonstration of Parkinson's Law. At least the Mayas picked their own game.

H. Ian Hogbin (1939:148) is the only ethnographer I know of who has estimated the man-days of labor which household heads donate to communal work tasks in a society at the "chiefdom" level. His descriptions of Wogeo clan organization and the redistributive generosity of a Wogeo chief, whose ability to distribute produce to his followers depends on his extensive fields farmed with their help, seem to qualify this New Guinea group for the chiefdom classification. According to Hogbin, most of the *kokwal*'s followers "spend an average of one day in eight in his service." Although we are left with some doubt as to the extent of the qualification "most," this rough estimate is better than none and indicates that about 40 to 45 man-days of service per annum is not burdensome for people at this level of sociopolitical integration. Although the Wogeo kokwal "has the right to demand help in agriculture and other work from his followers," his "authority is very largely dependent upon his wealth." In short his is a prestige entrepreneur in a conspicuous giving (Erasmus 1961:101–34) situation where the demands made by the generous "big man" involve the exchange of favors rather than the employment of coercion. Although Hogbin's estimate is not precise enough to determine exactly whom he includes within the kokwal's labor force, I am conservatively assuming that he is referring to adult males at the head of their own immediate families of procreation.

Once a "state" level of sociopolitical integration is reached and the authority figures have power to discipline as well as to reward or withhold rewards, the man-days per year family heads must allocate to those who control the power can readily quadruple. Stenton's (1951:137–38) research into the manorial records of feudal England indicates that from a third to a half of a man's year could be demanded for service on his lord's demesne. Reconstructing the pre-land–reform work services on thirty haciendas in southeastern Bolivia during the summer of 1963, I found the number of man-days of work required of each serf was within the same range. And as in medieval Europe, when peasant discontent led to minor flareups in Bolivia prior to the agrarian revolution in 1952, they were suppressed by military action.

However, the feudal-like conditions in Medieval England and modern Bolivia were by no means *extremely* coercive. Normal manorial and hacienda conditions involved a very paternalistic relationship between the master and his serfs. Compare this to the 500 days of labor service on state land demanded of each household on Ukrainian kolkhozes immediately following the Second World War (Belov 1955:178–79). In this last case, the entire family had to work at least part of the time on the kolkhoz demesne.

The scale of 40–150–500 man-days per year provides a rough measure of the degree of centralized power in any political structure employing corvée labor. But it helps only in fixing the minimal rather than maximal amounts. Dr. Edgar V. Winans has assured me in personal communication that in some very sophisticated African kingdoms no more than 40 days of labor service per annum are required of family heads. Our own society, too, is certainly at a much higher level of sociopolitical integration than a chiefdom, yet if we estimate that 20 to 25 percent of the average wage-earner's salary goes into taxes, we are giving only 52 to 65 work-days per annum to the state. (A monetary tax, however, involves inputs of coercion and/or voluntary support far different from a labor tax. The former does not interrupt the daily and annual work routine of the household whereas the latter does.) Moreover, under unusual circumstances involving messianic or nativistic religious movements people can voluntarily render high amounts of labor service to a communal enterprise. Ceremonial service in corporate peasant communities can consume enormous amounts of time, and the family investment in community service in an Israeli kibbutz actually surpassed that of the Ukrainian kolkhoz, since both members of each conjugal union were expected to work full-time for the community (Spiro 1956:11–18, 222–31).

Despite the rough quality of our scale we can better appreciate its significance by examining the evidence presented in the accompanying chart (fig. 3.1) designed to show how many man-days of labor per year each male

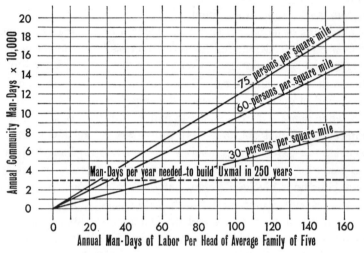

Figure 3.1 Relation of annual household and community corvee labor costs at different population densities.

household head would have to contribute to communal labor projects, given varying community labor requirements and population densities within a five-mile radius of a Maya ceremonial center. The center chosen is Uxmal[1] and the dotted horizontal line represents the estimated annual labor requirements for monument construction at Uxmal during its 250-year (Morley and Brainerd 1956:264) occupation period.

[1]Uxmal was chosen for my calculations because it is the closest ceremonial center to Tikul where all the experiments were carried out for rock excavation and carrying, etc. I picked Tikul for these experiments because it was handy to Mérida; my time was limited. Moreover, since Tikul is a town where lime manufacture has been a cottage industry for many years, it was a place where I could obtain reliable data on the subject. Finally, Uxmal seemed a desirable selection because this imposing center had a relatively brief occupation period of 250 years; if relatively low per annum labor inputs applied here, it seemed reasonable to suppose that they would not be higher elsewhere.

Vectors have been drawn on the chart for three different population densities—30, 60, and 75 persons per square mile. To determine the community (defined as the population within a five-mile radius of the ceremonial center) labor potential per annum for varying household inputs at varying population densities, select the desired household input on the abscissa, read up to the desired density vector, then follow back to the left-hand ordinate for the community potential. Where the density vectors cross the dotted line, read down to see the annual average household input necessary at that density to build Uxmal in 250 years.

Using even the minimal population density estimate of 30 inhabitants per square mile, the average annual labor input per household necessary to build Uxmal is not very much above the annual communal labor contribution for Wogeo. With the much more realistic figure of 75 persons per square mile, which I shall justify, the annual household requirement would be only 25 man-days per year. If future investigations support my findings, there is certainly no reason to assume that the constructions of the Mayas required a highly centralized political structure that was either disharmonic with swidden agriculture or that "declined" when monument-building ceased to amuse them.

In the remainder of this article I shall present my evidence. I shall begin with the experiments in excavating and carrying earth and rock.

The excavation and carrying of earth was done at Las Bocas, Sonora, a village I have known and visited often over the years. Four young Mayo[2] Indian men were employed to help determine how much earth a man could move in one day.

Most writers when estimating the amount of fill a man can carry a day do not specify distance, and when they specify time they specify an eight-hour day. The latter can be a somewhat ethnocentric calculation. In my experience, collective work parties in Latin America begin in the cool hours of early morning and last until the heat of midday. During this period five or six hours of intensive labor can be performed before exhaustion sets in or the heat becomes unbearable. It is not likely that the kind of voluntary and semi-festive labor that went into the construction of ceremonial centers would have involved more than five hours of extremely heavy work in a single day. At Las Bocas, the productivity of the two men carrying earth dropped markedly

---

[2]The Mayo Indians of Sonora and the Maya Indians of Yucatán should not be confused; the similarity of the names is coincidental.

during the sixth hour. For this reason only a five-hour morning work period was used in Yucatán for excavating and carrying rock and the sixth hour of the Sonora experiment was excluded from my calculations.

In the Sonora earth-carrying experiment two pairs of workers were employed, one man in each pair to excavate earth and the other to carry. The same man in each pair acted as carrier during the entire work period. The productivity of the man digging was not measured in this experiment, since his assignment was simply to keep his carrier supplied. The first carrier transported his dirt from excavation point to fill 50 meters, and the second 100 meters. Each carried the dirt in a 5-gallon can held on his shoulder; this was the method they chose. The cans of earth weighed 28 kilograms (including 1 kilogram for the can and its hardwood handle) and had a capacity of 1263.5 cubic inches (20,709 cubic centimeters). The first man completed 206 trips in five hours, and the second man 116 trips in the same time. The work began at 6:30 a.m. at a temperature of 84°F (29°C). By 9:30 the temperature was 101° (40°), and by 11:30 it was 110° (43°). The men were working in full sun. They deposited their fill in separate piles, each in the shape of a cone around a center pole on which heights had been marked and from the base of which stakes had been driven at measured intervals in four directions. Thus, symmetrical cones of fill resulted whose volumes were readily computed to be 3.62 and 2.05 cubic meters. The number of trips per hour dropped during the first five hours from 44 to 38 in the first case and from 26 to 20 in the second. (The sixth hour resulted in only 28 and 18 trips respectively.)

Table 3.1 shows the results of the earth-carrying experiment as it was conducted for a full six hours. The "ideal" weights and volumes are computed from the exact volume and weight of the contents of the cans and the number of trips. The "actual" weights and volumes are calculated from the volumes of the cones, which indicate that the first carrier averaged .0154 cubic meters or 20.15 kilos of earth per trip and the second carrier .0152 cubic meters or 19.94 kilos per trip. (The men averaged approximately 21 kilos each, with the weight of the can included.) There is a discrepancy between the "ideal" and "actual" figures in table 3.1 because the cans were not filled to capacity. Although the carrier going the longest distance between excavation and fill carried less earth per trip, he made up for this difference by covering a greater total distance. Table 3.2 shows the adjustments made to derive the amount of fill carried in the first five hours. Adjusted total weights and volumes are computed from the average amounts carried per trip.

TABLE 3.1
Earth-Carrying Experiment—(Six Hours)

	Total Trips	Total Distance (kilometers)	Total Weight Carried (kilograms)		Total Volume Carried (cubic meters)	
			Ideal	Actual	Ideal	Actual
Carrier I (50 meters)	234	23.4	6318	4716	4.84	3.62
Carrier II (100 meters)	134	26.8	3618	2672	2.78	2.05

TABLE 3.2
Results of Earth-Carrying Experiment Adjusted for Five Hours

	Total Trips	Total Distance (kilometers)	Total Weight Carried (kilograms)	Total Volume Carried (cubic meters)
Carrier I (50 meters)	206	20.6	4151	3.17
Carrier II (100 meters)	116	23.2	2313	1.76

In a separate experiment at Las Bocas, earth was excavated by shovel and by digging stick. Five-gallon containers were again used for measuring volume; the man with the digging stick used his hands to fill the cans. I agreed to pay the workers according to the number of cans produced, but the speed of their work so exceeded my expectations that I had to halt the experiment after thirty minutes. During that time the man with the metal shovel filled 46 cans and the man with the digging stick 19 cans (a surprising 41 percent of the first). I doubt, however, that these men could have maintained more than 75 percent and 66 percent respectively of their productivity over a five-hour period. Thus, a five-hour man-day of digging would conservatively produce 7.2 cubic meters of earth by shovel and 2.6 cubic meters by digging stick, a ratio of slightly less than 3 – 1.

The experiments made in Yucatán on the excavation of building stones are crucial for the conclusions here. Had I not personally observed these experiments I would not have believed that so much rock could be so rapidly pried from the surface of such a small area. Again two men were employed to excavate, one with the iron crowbar used today for this purpose and the other with a heavy hardwood post he chose for the experiment. Both men were Maya Indians, living in the town of Tikul (just across the Puuc Mountains from

Uxmal), who were skilled at excavating surface rock. The Maya who used the wooden bar understood the purpose of the experiment and like all the other men who participated in the various excavation, carrying, and masonry projects he became very much interested in the problem. The initial reaction of workers to the idea of excavating with wooden tools or to carrying rocks was usually one of amused incredulity. But once the objective was explained, interest in the project grew high. The Mayas are understandably proud of their past and are interested in any kind of investigation related to it. I definitely felt that there was a desire on the part of the Maya workers to excel at their tasks as well as to earn the high wages I was paying. This fact was borne out by the tendency for effort to increase during the last hour of the carrying experiment rather than to decrease as it did in Sonora.

The man excavating rock with an iron crowbar dug up roughly 5 tons of rock in an area of 30 square meters in five hours. The area was measured exactly, but the amount of rock is an estimate based on the average weight of a sample of seventeen rocks carried by donkey-cart to the freight scale at the Tikul train depot. The total weight of the seventeen rocks was 517 kilos, constituting those carried by one of the men in the rock-carrying experiment to be described. Thus, the average rock weighed about 30 kilos, and the number of rocks excavated was two hundred (the amount which was contracted for and which actually took the excavator only four and one-half hours). Allowing for a possible bias in the sample caused by the carrier picking stones of convenient carrying weight, I have reduced the total estimated weight of the 200 stones to 5000 kilos or roughly 5 tons.

The experiment took place in a field several years in fallow some two kilometers from Tikul. One readily understands why all Maya structures even today are made of stone and why stone walls are so common everywhere. In fact stone walls serve two purposes: keeping animals out of fields and ridding fields of excessive rock content. Obviously the rocks used in constructing Maya monuments, especially in the case of fill, were not difficult to obtain.

The man who excavated rock with a hardwood post for five hours excavated one-third the quantity of rock of the first man. Thus, the amount of stone excavated in one man-day of labor with only primitive tools would be about 1700 kilos.

Four men were employed to carry rock from the point where the first man had excavated the five tons (see table 3.3). Each man carried to a different terminal point along the same course: man A 250 meters, B 500 meters, C 750 meters, and D 1 kilometer. As in the Sonora earth-carrying experiment a

TABLE 3.3
Rock-Carrying Experiment

Carriers	Total Trips	Total Distance (kilometers)	Total Weight (kilograms)	Weight per Trip (kilograms)
A 250 meters	34	17	950	28
B 500 meters	20	20	500	25
C 750 meters	15	22.5	517	34
D 1000 meters	11	22	250	23

time was logged under each man's name as he completed a trip. The work began at 6:15 a.m. and ended at approximately 11:15. It was a cloudy morning and the temperature had risen from 70° (21°) at 6:15 to 80° (26°) by 9:00 a.m. when the sun came out. From 9:30 until 11:30 the temperature ranged between 102° (39°) and 105° (41°). Men A and C were locally deemed "pure" Maya Indians, and B and D mestizos. The "pure" Mayas consistently carried heavier loads. Age was not a significant factor since A was the youngest (20 years) and C was the oldest (55 years). The tumpline method of carrying was used by all but A, who carried his loads on top of his head. Only C's rocks were transported by donkey-cart to Tikul for exact weighing, after which the loads carried by the other three were estimated.

A comparison of tables 3.2 and 3.3 indicates that 21 kilometers (13 miles) is the average distance covered in five hours by a man carrying a heavy load half of the time. The average was somewhat reduced by A, who was slowed down for two reasons: first, balancing heavy rocks on the head does not result in the same sure-footed pace as the tumpline method; second, the first 100 meters of the course traversed by all four men was over uneven ground in the brush and the rest along a level path. A therefore was walking nearly half the time over more difficult terrain. Finally, the more numerous the trips, the greater the amount of time consumed in loading.

The dotted curve on fig. 3.2 shows the amount of rock or earth (by weight) which a man could ideally carry in five hours if we take 21 kilometers as a constant distance and 25 kilograms (average per trip for all six carriers) as a constant load. The solid line indicates the actual results obtained in the experiments. The lines are clearly exponential and indicate that the distance

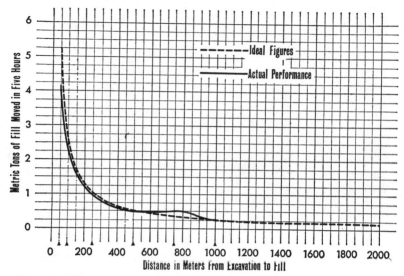

Figure 3.2 Relation of load to distance for human carriers.

between excavation and fill can make a big difference in the man-days invested in any given volume of fill.

To decide what average distance must be used in the case of Uxmal, it is necessary to introduce our estimate of the total amount of fill at that center— 850,000 cubic meters. At 1½ tons of rock per cubic meter (a very liberal estimate, see below), 1.275 million tons of rock would be required. Since we have already seen that a minimum of five tons of rock can be removed quite readily from 30 square meters (by taking only the most easily extracted and leaving the rest), a maximum of 7.65 million square meters is needed.

Uxmal covers an area 1200 meters long (from the "North Group" to the Chimez Temple at the southern end) and about 600 meters wide. By extending the area 950 meters farther in all directions, a total area of 7.75 million square meters resulted, of which about 100,000 square meters were covered by the buildings and terraces. This extended area is what would have been needed if only the most quickly excavated surface rock within a 950-meter radius of all buildings was used—again an extremely liberal estimate.

The average distance traveled for rock within 950 meters of a structure would be much greater than half the distance, since the areas between concentric circles of 100-, 200-, 300-, etc., meter radiuses increase with the size of the radius. Although the ratio of weight carried to distance traveled increases exponentially with *decreases* in the radius, as fig. 3.2 indicates, this fact does not compensate for the increase in area. A distance of about 750 meters would therefore be average. However, since the 7.75 million square meter area is a very liberal estimate and since the one carrier in the experiment whose total load was carefully weighed (Carrier C) was able to carry 517 kilos over a 750-meter course in five hours, 500 kilos per man-day seems a conservative and convenient estimate of the labor investment for rock-carrying at Uxmal.

As will be shown, 1440 kilos of rock are used per cubic meter of masonry. Since the stones used in masonry are broken and carefully fitted to reduce the amount of mortar, an estimate of 1500 kilos of rock per cubic meter of fill would be considerably higher than the true amount. With this liberal estimate, each cubic meter of fill would have required an investment of about three man-days of labor for the rock content and about one man-day for the dirt content (500 kilos). The estimate for dirt is based on the volume of mortar in a cubic meter of masonry and the weight of local *sascab* (see below) so often used in fill. Figures for masonry rather than fill are being used because exact measurements of weight and volume were obtained for masonry in the construction of a test wall described below. Any difference in the weight of a cubic meter of fill in which the proportion of dirt to rock was higher than the proportion of mortar to rock in our masonry figures is negligible within the limits of our maximal estimates.

We have already seen that one man can excavate more than 1.5 metric tons of rock in a day with a wooden bar; one excavator could thus supply the three men necessary to carry the cubic meter of stone. One man excavating earth with primitive tools could supply at least four men; therefore only .25 man-days per cubic meter would be required. The number of man-days per cubic meter of fill can now be estimated at 3 for rock carrying, 1 for earth carrying, 1 for rock excavating, and .25 for earth excavating—a total of 5.25.

My rough but, I believe, liberal estimate of the amount of fill in the terraces and buildings of Uxmal totals 850,000 cubic meters.[3] At 5.25 man-days per cubic meter *the number of man-days invested in fill totals about 4.5 million.*

[3]The basic measurements of all terraces and building dimensions used for estimating fill and masonry volume and sculptured areas are derived from Holmes (1895:82–100), Morley and Brainerd (1956:293–98), Ruz (1963), and Seler (1917). The structures for which adequate measurements are available include the most important: the Pyramid of the Magician, the Great Pyramid, the Nunnery Quadrangle, the Ball Court, and the House of Doves. Excavations have been inadequate for the Cemetery Group, the House of the Old Woman, the Chimez Temple, the West Group, the Terrace of the Monuments, the Northwest Group, and the North Group; but the Morley-Brainerd map (1956:Plate 49) provides the basic dimensions from which reasonable interpolations can be made, especially since we are after liberally estimated, *maximal,* labor-input figures.

To compute the man-days invested in a cubic meter of masonry, a test wall was constructed by a Maya stone mason with the 517 kilos of rock carried by C in the previous experiment. The volume of the partial wall constructed with this rock and the amount of mortar used in its construction were carefully measured, and the mason himself was timed. The results showed that this mason uses about 1400 kilos of rock, 100 kilos of lime, and 300 kilos of sascab per cubic meter of masonry.

Sascab is the native name for a material which authorities have defined as "powdery lime breccia" (Brainerd 1954:28), "a native marl" (Pollock et al. 1962:92), and "an unconsolidated form of calcium carbonate" (Littman 1957:135). In his 1958 (p. 175) analysis of this material, Littman has called it "a form of weathered limestone deposited in a cavity in preformed limestone by surface or subterranean water." Around Tikul sascab is so common that it seems practically a subsoil. In family backyards one frequently encounters small sascab mines, which supply the family's own needs for house construction and remodeling. It takes the place of the sand in our mortar; and, as in sand and cement mortars, it is usually mixed with lime at a 2–1 ratio by volume. As is the case with cement and sand, a dry mixture of lime and sascab loses up to 30 percent of its volume when moistened with water.

The excavation of sascab was not observed or timed, but informants estimated 750 to 1000 kilos could be excavated in one man-day. Since it would undoubtedly be mined close to the construction (the modern practice and quite possibly one means by which the ancient *chultunes*, or water storage cisterns, were formed in the Puuc area), transportation time would be minimal. One-half a man-day per cubic meter of masonry for sascab content would seem maximal. As for the rock content, the maximal estimate would be four man-days per cubic meter if we use our previous figures.

The man-day investment in the lime content of a cubic meter of masonry is again calculated from informant descriptions of lime manufacture, which was not personally observed. The crude open-air procedure of burning lime, which is still used and is probably the native method, produces 8¼ tons from some 12½ tons of rock and some 6¾ tons of green firewood. The transportation costs in the case of the rock would be much lower for lime manufacture than for fill or masonry, however, since the lime would be manufactured at the source of the raw materials. The best stone for making lime is not always as handy as the rock used for fill and masonry, and its source could conservatively be placed at one kilometer from the construction. Today at Tikul (15,000 population) it is not necessary to go more than three kilometers for the best stone, even though lime manufacturing was an important cottage industry there for many years and exhausted closer sources. At Pustinich, informants claimed they went only one kilometer. Since the lime product rather than the rock itself would be carried to the construction, 100 kilos would require a maximal .25 man-days of labor.

As in the case of the rock it would probably not be necessary for the firewood to be carried very far. In a region in which only a sixth of the land at most was being farmed at any one time (see below), 83 percent of the area was covered with heavy growth. Since green firewood is preferred for making lime (it burns more slowly), there would be less foraging for broken limbs, and the wood nearest to the pyre would do. It seems unlikely that the lime-makers would have had to go more than 500 meters for their firewood, a maximum of about 13 man-days of transportation for the 6¾ tons of firewood necessary to produce 8½ tons of lime. To these 13 man-days, of course, would be added the man-days necessary to cut the wood. With steel tools a *tercio* (30 kilos) of firewood can be cut in less than 90 minutes. Informants estimated it would take five hours—more than three times as long—to cut a tercio with stone tools. I did not check this estimate, for stone tools are no longer in use. Even if some had been provided for an experiment, the woodcutters would have needed several weeks of practice to develop skill in using them. The five-hour estimate is handy because it is the length of the man-day constant in these construction figures. Therefore, 225 tercios (6750 kilos) of firewood would involve 225 man-days of woodcutting. Thirty man-days would be necessary to stack the wood properly in the pyre and ten man-days to fragment and stack the rock on top of it. (Today, fifteen and five man-days of eight hours are required for these tasks.)

Including the fifteen man-days necessary to excavate the 12½ tons of rock for burning, the number of man-days invested in the production of 8¼ tons of lime would total about 300. The 100 kilos of lime in a cubic meter of masonry is 1.2 percent of 8½ tons and therefore represents about three and one-half man-days out of the 300 total.

Two native Maya building contractors in Tikul independently calculated for me the labor time invested in the stone walls of the new houses they were completing. Both estimates came very close to 20 hours per cubic meter. Another contractor building an elaborate stone wall in front of a merchant's home gave figures that indicated 40 hours of construction time per cubic meter. The mason who built the experimental wall for me with 517 kilos of stone worked fast and crudely, but at the rate of 10½ hours per cubic meter.

Converting these figures into five-hour man-days we have a range of 2 to 8 man-days and a mode of 4. The maximal rate was for work being remunerated on an hourly basis, the modal rate on a contract basis, and the minimal under test conditions in which the mason was endeavoring to impress me with his speed. Four man-days per cubic meter therefore seems the most reasonable rate for our purposes.

The labor investment in a cubic meter of masonry can now be itemized at 4.5 man-days for the excavation and transportation of rock and sascab, .25 man-days for transporting the lime, 3.5 man-days for lime manufacture, and 4 man-days for construction, a total of 12.25 man-days. To compute the total volume of masonry at Uxmal, I have included all terrace walls and estimated their average depth at 33 centimeters. In the case of all buildings or super-structures the amount of masonry was liberally computed at one-half their gross volume.[4] Equally liberal estimates were interpolated for the unexcavated structures. With these measures, *the masonry at Uxmal totals about 40,000 cubic meters and represents approximately half a million man-days of labor.*

At this point it should be noted that Littman's (1960:409) chemical and microscopic analysis of Uxmal mortars indicates that little burned lime was used. In his opinion "it seems highly probable that the mixtures used for mortars, plasters, and stuccos were composed of sascab or a similar material . . . stone chips, the by-product of quarrying or stone-dressing operations and only sufficient burned lime to facilitate rapid setting." Certainly, then, much less than the $1-2$ proportions of lime–sascab mixtures of present-day mortars were employed by the Uxmal inhabitants. Considering the great amount of labor involved in lime manufacture with only primitive woodcutting tools, it does not seem surprising that the lime content was kept low. Such a conclusion, though, is not consistent with Brainerd's (1953:94) observation that $\frac{1}{16}$th of the volume of lowland Maya structures is lime. But given Littman's later and more careful analysis, it would seem that the $1-2$ lime–sascab ratio used in our masonry figures is probably more than enough to cover not only the lime in the mortar but also any used in plasters or washes on the surface.

---

[4]Carole Lockhart, using the plans of three measured structures at Chichén-Itzá (Structures 3C9, 4D1, and 7B3 in Ruppert 1952:44, 92, 146), found that one-third to one-half of the gross volume of Maya buildings was masonry and fill (walls, facades, etc.) and one-half to two-thirds was room space. Within the walls themselves she estimated that at least a third was fill. To be on the conservative side I have not distinguished between masonry and fill within the buildings and have calculated them as solid masonry less one-half their total volume for room space.

Time estimates on cutting and sculpturing local limestone were obtained from two gravestone cutters in Mérida. For a stone with a face approximately 1000 square centimeters and a depth of 30 centimeters, the first artisan calculated two days to cut and square the stone and to sculpture a design that would cover the face. The second artisan estimated one day for the cutting and two for the design. In both cases the estimates were for cutting and sculpturing with metal tools. The second informant believed that with primitive stone tools it would take three times as long to cut the stone (a total of three days) but only one more day than with metal tools to make the design (total of three). In his opinion, the slower work of chiseling the face would not be increased nearly so much with stone tools expertly used as would the job of cutting the original rectangular block. Of course, his estimate on the cutting is for gravestones, which are expertly squared, as compared to the more roughly finished blocks at Uxmal.

The Maya stone mason at Tikul who made the test-wall for me earlier (see above) became so interested in the investigation that he voluntarily sculptured with metal tools a rock facing of approximately 1000 square centimeters, to see how long it would take. He had never attempted rock sculpturing before and did the job quite inexpertly with a small metal pick. However, in eight hours he achieved a pleasing Maya design that covered the entire face although it was relatively shallow compared to most Maya stonework. The three-day estimate of the professional stonecutter does not, therefore, seem too unrealistic. As a conservative estimate, three man-days per 1000 square centimeters of plain masonry veneer and an additional three man-days per 1000 square centimeters of sculptured masonry veneer would seem appropriate.

It should be noted that an eight-hour day is being calculated in this case instead of the five-hour day used in all the other estimates. The reason is obvious. This work is not so physically exhausting as is heavy carrying and lifting. Instead, like many creative efforts—and as happened in the case of my Tikul stonemason friend—it can so absorb the craftsman that he tends to resent interruptions and hardly notices the passage of time. It seems so likely that Maya stonecutters may have worked from early morning to late afternoon that the man-day estimates for stonecutting based on the modern eight-hour day are probably conservative.

It should also be noted that our estimates on stonecutting were for stones 30 centimeters deep, a depth which seems close to or above that of the average veneer stones on the Uxmal structures. Thus, we arrive at an estimate of 30 man-days per square meter of building exterior in which cut veneer stones were used and an additional 30 man-days per square meter for those which were sculptured as well.

In estimating the total areas of cut and sculptured stone, the same surfaces were used as for the masonry calculations. This is undoubtedly a partial duplication in most cases, but maximal labor input estimates are desired. Moreover, this overlap can absorb shortages in estimates resulting from the absence of good measurements on the surfaces of the earlier structures which were in some cases covered over by the later ones. Thus, *for about 75,000 square meters of cut stone of which some 10,000 square meters were sculptured, roughly 2.5 million man-days were expended.*

The total labor input for the Uxmal ceremonial center including fill, masonry, stonecutting, and stone sculpturing totals 7.5 million man-days by these liberal estimates. For the brief period of 250 years (Morley and Brainerd 1956:264) in which Uxmal was occupied, *an average of 30,000 man-days per annum* was expended on ceremonial construction. To decide what this expenditure cost the average household, population density estimates must be considered.

Although the absence of water in the Puuc region accounts for the meager population there today, the Mayas of late Classic times had apparently solved their water problem with plastered cisterns or *chultunes*. The Morley and Brainerd (1956:264–65) estimates indicate that far more than 75 persons per square mile could have been supplied with drinking water in this fashion. Since rainfall was the source of the water and the cisterns were man-made, any limits placed on the population density for this reason alone, before a great deal more archeology has been done, would be arbitrary. I am assuming, therefore, that the Mayas had enough water for their needs or they would not have been there at all, and I will concern myself with the population limitations which might have been imposed by food production.

According to the estimates I gathered from storekeepers and peasant family heads around Tikul, a family of five[5] consumes 3 to 4 kilos of corn (the Maya food staple) per day or 1100 to 1460 kilos a year. These figures are higher than Benedict and Steggerda's (1937:173) carefully gathered statistics, which gave a range of 2.5 to 3.5 kilos per day or 900 to 1300 kilos per year for a family of five, and Steggerda's (1941:127) calculation of 3 kilos per day

---

[5]Five persons was the size of the average Maya family before wonder drugs. (See Morley and Brainerd 1956:139–40.)

(1095 per year). They are closer to Ursula Cowgill's 1962 (p. 277) estimate of 1.7 pounds of corn per person per day or 1400 kilos per year for five, and this may indicate the Mayas were slightly more prosperous in the 1960s than they were in the 1930s. Inasmuch as these various estimates are reasonably close, 1300 kilos of corn per annum for a family of five seems a liberal consumption estimate.

Steggerda's (1941:127–30, 149) production and consumption statistics, used by Morley and Brainerd (1956:140) and based on 265 households in northern Yucatán, indicate that the average Maya family in the 1930s had an average plot of 10 acres, which produced 168 bushels of shelled corn. Of this, about 62.5 percent was sold to purchase clothes, gunpowder, jewelry, etc.; about 12.5 percent was fed to livestock; and about 25 percent was consumed by the family. The latter amounted to about 1085 kilos, or 25 *cargas*. Assuming that this one-fourth of the total production came from one-fourth of the total plot, the average family needed only 2.5 acres for subsistence, from which it harvested 10 cargas per acre or 1 carga per *mecate*.

A carga, according to my informants, equals 42 kilos. Steggerda (1941:110, 240) actually weighed five cargas and found they varied between 41.5 and 44 kilos and averaged 43 kilos. A mecate is an area of land 20 meters to each side. There are 25 in each hectare and, therefore, about 10 to an acre. At Tikul, the peasants I talked with felt that 1 carga of shelled corn was the production expected from 1 mecate of first-year land and ½ to ¾ of a carga for the second year. Thus, my own casually collected production estimates agree closely with Steggerda's figures. Ursula Cowgill (1962:276) obtained production figures of 1120 kilos of corn for 2 acres, one of which was first-year (655 kilos, or 1.5 cargas per mecate) and the other second-year (465 kilos, or 1 carga per mecate).

Taking the liberal consumption estimate of 1300 kilos (30 cargas) per annum per family and the minimal production estimate of 1 carga per mecate, the subsistence needs of a family of five in cultivated land would be 3 acres, or 30 mecates. This comes very close to the 35 mecate maximum which peasant informants at Tikul felt they could handle by themselves. Beyond that the weeding chores become too great and additional labor must be hired. However, informants claimed that in Quintana Roo, where the forests are much higher and the land rich and more weed-free, one man can handle considerably more than 35 mecates and that production is as high as 3 cargas per mecate the first year. It seems very safe to assume, therefore, that our estimates are truly minimal and that when the Puuc was occupied fewer than

3 acres of cultivated land would actually have been necessary to support a family. Inasmuch as the Mayas plant beans, squash, and other vegetables in the same fields with their corn, 3 acres of cultivated land can be considered a liberal estimate of the amount needed per family aboriginally.

Assuming that half of the cultivated lands of each family were newly cleared each year and half were in their second year, and assuming that land was left in fallow 12 years before replanting (the modern practice), each family would have needed a total of 21 acres to subsist. To estimate the number of families supported by the land in the vicinity of Uxmal, I shall conservatively limit the Uxmal radius of influence to five miles (eight kilometers). My informants at Tikul claimed that eight to ten kilometers (2 to 2½ hours) is the maximum walking distance today between fields and house, and when a man's milpa is farther away than this, he prefers to live in temporary quarters on his plot. This practice gives some measure of the local notion of "convenience" with regard to the location of farms and habitation sites and possibly therefore of ceremonial centers. Moreover, since Uxmal is nine miles northwest of the smaller center Kabah (Morley and Brainerd 1956:294), the five-mile radius seems a reasonable one for separating Uxmal's ceremonial jurisdiction from Kabah's. If we conservatively estimate that only half of the 78 square miles (50,240 acres) within this five-mile radius was cultivable and that it was divided among the families it could support under minimal production conditions, the immediate environs of Uxmal could easily have been inhabited by some 1200 families (6000 persons), about 75 persons per square mile.

Today Yucatán has a population density of about 35 per square mile (*Estudio* 1961:68), about 5 per square mile more than it did thirty years ago (Morley and Brainerd 1956:265). Despite this low figure for Yucatán as a whole, the *municipios* (counties) of Muna and Oxkutzcab to the north and south of the Puuc area have population densities of 60 to 80 per square mile, and Tikul to the east has a density of about 100 (*Estudio* 1961:72). It does not seem unreasonable to suppose that even in aboriginal times the areas immediately around ceremonial centers were much more densely populated than the peninsula as a whole.

By a conservative estimate of the voluntary community labor contribution of each family at 40 man-days per annum (chiefdom level), the 1200 families in the jurisdiction of Uxmal could have contributed 48,000 man-days each year, more than 1.5 times the average amount we computed would have been necessary each year (30,000 man-days) to build Uxmal over 250 years. However, the work was probably not performed in equal amounts each year but rather was aimed over short periods at the completion or modification of a particular structure. Until the excavations at Uxmal result in exact measurements of the temple structures superimposed one upon another (as in A. Ledyard Smith's [1950] model report on Uaxactun), it is useless to try to estimate the man-day investments in each stage. The largest building complex at Uxmal which appears to have been built according to one preconceived plan is the Nunnery Quadrangle, a structure requiring some 650,000 man-days of labor. Without exceeding 40 man-days per family per year the Nunnery could have been built in thirteen and one-half years. With a little enthusiasm (80 days per year), it could have been finished in less than seven years.

While traveling in rural Colombia in the early 1950s, I frequently encountered churches and public buildings under construction by community work groups. Each *vereda* (hamlet) within the municipio met a predetermined quota of *jornales* (man-days) per year, and the work often lasted over a period of several years. Such long-term projects were frequently instigated by the local Catholic priest. In a sense the work was redistributive, for the church buildings or the access roads so constructed were for the benefit of all. And the sanctions ensuring popular support were largely religious—fear of denial of marriage services, proper burial, etc. Church and state in Colombia, however, were mutually supportive, and the "good families" in any rural area could also exercise some economic sanctions to help ensure the "voluntary" support of the peasant labor force.

Although the Maya ceremonial centers could have been constructed at very light annual labor costs for the average household even with a small population, the planning and thought that went into the construction of buildings, the elaboration of calendars, and other achievements nevertheless mark Maya society as an unusual member of the chiefdom class. The crucial question is whether this kind of planning and this kind of esoteric elaboration of a priesthood subculture would have required any more "force" than the labor contributions. Brainerd (1954:41, 70–75) was obviously fascinated by the problem of Maya political structure and did not feel it was highly authoritarian. It puzzled him that there were no "economic motives and controls" such as crop irrigation to explain Maya social organization, and he wondered "if the chances of archaeological sampling may not have influenced our concepts of the development of civilization." In his analysis of the scenes of social life on the Bonampak murals of Classic times, he finds no evidence "that authority or status among the priests" was "concentrated in one individual," and he finds "no suggestion of regimentation or autocracy." He does see "much evidence of hierarchy of rank," but among the individuals with simpler headdresses and wearing apparel "there is not the slightest formality nor servility in their bearing; they are shown gossiping with one another and with the functionaries." Thus Brainerd concludes "that the concepts of a nobility, of some distinction between religious and secular authority and of captive slaves used for sacrifice, were a part of the Maya pattern of their time and place. The impression is also given of considerable camaraderie, at least among the favored group who dominate these paintings. The Bonampak murals seem to bear out inferences drawn from the Maya economy and settlement pattern, that repressive authority was not characteristic of the classic Maya."

The most elaborate social and cultural manifestations of the chiefdom type were, by their very nature, the most vulnerable to eclipse through contact with stronger "state" societies. Our sample of chiefdoms in the ethnographic literature is therefore skewed toward those which were least interesting to colonizing powers after 1492. The gap in our knowledge of the kind of societies which were transitional between the chiefdoms and the early states can now be filled only indirectly by ethnohistory and archeology. It would seem that continued archeological study of the Maya may help us to better understand what precisely were the potentials for elaboration within the chiefdom type.

Although it is not my intention in this article to discuss the problems of monument building for the entire Mesoamerican area, I cannot help sharing the same feeling of curiosity Brainerd (1954:18) evinces when he wanders from the Mayas to the Teotihuacanos while discussing the labor costs of pyramids and "large substructures." The fact that the Pyramid of the Sun at Teotihuacán was not the product of a long series of accretions as were Mayan substructures (Millon and Drewitt 1961) makes the explanation of its size in terms of social organization much more challenging. If one accepts Brainerd's estimate of one million cubic meters as the volume of the Pyramid of the Sun and assumes that the topsoil within a radius of one kilometer of the pyramid was removed to a depth of 33 centimeters to provide the fill, one arrives at the figure of 3 million man-days of labor, which was his estimate. Brainerd arrived at this figure by assuming that a man would carry 1500 pounds (680 kilograms) of earth per day, but he did not indicate distance or time. Given the same 500 kilogram figure from my experiments for a five-hour day carrying over an average distance of 750 meters, and given the weight of

Sonoran earth (sandy and heavy and therefore skewing toward conservative estimates) as 1300 kilograms per cubic meter, about 2.5 million man-days would have been required to scoop off the 1000 meter radius of topsoil. This is so close to Brainerd's figure that we might as well round ours off to his three million.

Three million man-days is a respectable amount of labor for one job. But the valley of Mexico can sustain much more productive agriculture (per unit of land) than Yucatán. Sanders' (1957:51–84) production figures suggest that a family of five could have supported itself with less than one acre of *chinampas*,[6] less than one and a half acres of "humid" land, or about two hectares (one in fallow) of "hill" land. Within the 2500 square miles immediately surrounding the complex of Mexican lakes shown in Coe's (1964:91) map of the Valley of Mexico as it was in the summer of 1521, we can speculate that even as far back as 600 A.D. as much as 20 square miles of chinampas, 20 square miles of "humid" lands, and 200 square miles of "hill" lands might have been cultivated. This amount and type of cultivated land could have supported 50,000 families (250,000 people), giving an overall population density of about 100 per square mile. But most of this population would have been within 40 miles of Teotihuacán. Fifty thousand heads of family donating only 40 days per year for ceremonial constructions could have provided 2 million man-days of labor in one year. At that rate the Pyramid of the Sun could have been built in a year and a half without taxing the labor of any one family more than it would have been taxed in Wogeo.

Organizing the labor force of such a large area would perhaps present some problems, but I personally doubt that it would have been as difficult to bring together a relatively large population to perform a job yielding spectacular results within a year's time as it would have been to get a smaller population to struggle with it for twenty years (Wolf 1959:94). It is also very possible that religious movements stimulated by intergroup contacts go back long before 1492 and that such movements could sustain considerable participation within an area the size of the Valley of Mexico. It is also argued that a great deal of organization and planning went into chinampa agriculture, and these factors must surely have been operative during the Aztec period when saltwater flooding became a problem and required large-scale projects for

[6]Production estimates which I collected from *chinamperos* at Xochimilco during the summer of 1964 indicated that only half an acre or less of intensively cultivated *chinampa* might have supported a family in subsistence crops (mainly corn) transplanted from seed beds. These estimates were from elderly informants; no one today transplants corn.

drainage, dikes, and freshwater aqueducts (Coe 1964:98). But much more work must be done before we can be sure this form of agriculture did not grow by slow, unplanned accretions at an earlier period. If anthropologists had found the Ifugao terraces in ruins, would they have considered them the result of a great state organization with a master plan?

ACKNOWLEDGMENTS

The field work on which this paper is based was supported by a University of California Faculty Research Grant. I also wish to express my gratitude to Miss Carole Lockhart, my research assistant supported by the Federal Work-Study Program, who patiently checked and rechecked my calculations and saved me numerous embarrassments. Whatever embarrassments are left, however, are all mine. Much more measurement of this kind will have to be done before anyone can claim the last word. This paper was written while I was the recipient of a Haynes Foundation Summer Fellowship for Faculty.

REFERENCES

Altschuler, Milton. 1958. On the environmental limitations of Mayan cultural development. *Southwestern Journal of Anthropology* 14:189–98.

Belov, Fedor. 1955. *The history of a Soviet collective farm.* New York: Praeger.

Benedict, Francis G. and Morris Steggerda. 1937. The food of the present-day Maya Indians of Yucatán. Washington, D. C.: *Carnegie Institution of Washington Contributions to American Archaeology* 3:155–88.

Brainerd, George W. 1953. The Maya civilization. *The Masterkey* 27:83–96.

—— 1954. *The Maya civilization.* Los Angeles: Southwest Museum.

Coe, Michael D. 1964. The chinampas of Mexico. *Scientific American* 211(1):90–98.

Cowgill, George L. 1964. The end of classic Maya culture: A review of recent evidence. *Southwestern Journal of Anthropology* 20:145–59.

Cowgill, Ursula M. 1962. An agricultural study of the southern Maya lowlands. *American Anthropologist* 64:273–86.

Dumond, D. E. 1961. Swidden agriculture and the rise of Maya civilization. *Southwestern Journal of Anthropology* 17:301–16.

Erasmus, Charles J. 1961. *Man takes control: cultural development and American aid.* Minneapolis: University of Minnesota Press.

Estudio Económico de Yucatán y Programa de Trabajo. 1961. Ediciones del Gobierno del Estato, Mérida, Yucatán.

Goldenweiser, Alexander A. 1936. Loose ends of a theory on the individual, pattern, and involution in primitive society. In R. H. Lowie, ed., *Essays in anthropology presented to A. L. Kroeber,* pp. 99–104. Berkeley: University of California Press.

Hogbin, H. Ian. 1939. Native land tenure in New Guinea. *Oceania* 10:120–65.

Holmes, William A. 1895. *Archaeological studies among the ancient cities of Mexico.* Part I, *Monuments of Yucatán.* Publication 8, The Field Columbian Museum Anthropological Series 1, 1.

Kaplan, David. 1963. Men, monuments, and political systems. *Southwestern Journal of Anthropology* 19:397–410.

Littman, Edwin R. 1957. Ancient Mesoamerican mortars, plasters, and stuccos: Comalcalco, part I. *American Antiquity* 23:135–39.

—— 1958. Ancient Mesoamerican mortars, plasters, and stuccos: The composition and origin of sascab. *American Antiquity* 24:172–76.

—— 1960. Ancient Mesoamerican mortars, plasters, and stuccos: The Puuc area. *American Antiquity* 25:407–12.

Meggers, Betty J. 1954. Environmental limitations on the development of culture. *American Anthropologist* 56:801–24.

Millon, René and Bruce Drewitt. 1961. Earlier structures within the Pyramid of the Sun at Teotihuacán. *American Antiquity* 26:371.

Morley, Sylvanus G. and George W. Brainerd. 1956. *The ancient Maya.* Rev. ed. Stanford: Stanford University Press.

Pollock, H. E. D., Ralph L. Roys, T. Prokouriakoff, and A. Ledyard Smith. 1962. *Mayapan, Yucatán, Mexico.* Washington, D.C.: Carnegie Institution of Washington Publication 619.

Ruppert, Karl. 1952. *Chichén-Itzá: Architectural notes and plans.* Washington, D. C.: Carnegie Institution of Washington Publication 595.

Ruz, Alberto. 1963. *Uxmal, official guide of the instituto Nacional de Antropologia e Historia.* Mexico: Instituto Nacional de Antropologia e Historia.

Sanders, William T. 1957. Tierra y Agua (Soil and Water), a study of the ecological factors in the development of Meso-American civilizations. Ph.D. dissertation, Harvard University, Cambridge, Mass.

Seler, Eduard. 1917. *Die Ruinen von Uxmal.* Berlin: Verlag der Königlich Preussischen Akademie der Wissenschaften.

Service, Elman R. 1962. *Primitive social organization: An evolutionary perspective.* New York: Random House.

Smith, A. Ledyard. 1950. *Uaxactun, Guatemala: Excavations of 1931–1937.* Washington, D. C.: Carnegie Institution of Washington Publication 588.

Spiro, Melford E. 1956. *Kibbutz: Venture in Utopia.* Cambridge: Harvard University Press.

Steggerda, Morris. 1941. *Maya Indians of Yucatán.* Washington, D. C.: Carnegie Institution of Washington Publication 531.

Stenton, Doris Mary. 1951. *English society in the early Middle Ages, 1066–1307.* Baltimore: Penguin Books.

Wolf, Eric. 1959. *Sons of the shaking Earth.* Chicago: University of Chicago Press.

DENNIS E. PULESTON

An Experimental Approach to the Function of Classic Maya Chultuns

The most complex experiments are not necessarily the most useful or definitive ones. This article provides a case in point. One often finds, associated with lowland Mayan sites, a particular type of chultun or underground chamber dug into solid rock. Since the early part of this century, when they were first described, attention has centered on the possible functions they may have served, and over the years ten possible uses have been suggested. These range from latrines, to water reservoirs, to storage places for maize or other food. What Puleston attempts to do is choose between alternatives, and then judge the probability that the most likely of them is correct. Through extremely simple experiments several possibilities may be quickly, easily, and decisively eliminated. For example, he pours 400 gallons of water into one chultun and notes that after 8 hours it has completely drained into the porous limestone. In a similar way, he shows that most agricultural products quickly rot in the naturally damp, humid chultun air. In retrospect, it is surprising that no one attempted such simple tests before and published the results; they seem so obvious after the fact.

Characteristic of experiments of this type is the ease with which hypotheses can be disproved and the extreme difficulty in gathering conclusive evidence to back positive assertions. Puleston suggests that chultuns were used to store seeds of the ramon tree. Experiment shows that these alone of the foods tested were well preserved in the damp underground conditions. Correlation of the distributions of ramon trees and house mounds at Tikal suggest that the trees were indeed cultivated; nutritional analysis demonstrates the high food

Reproduced, with minor editorial corrections, by permission of the Society for American Archaeology from *American Antiquity* 36(3), 1971.

value of the seed; the destructive effect of rodent predation makes it all the more likely that food would be stored in a safe place, quite probably below the ground. Thus Puleston may set his hypothesis forth as the most likely until and unless a better one comes along.

Puleston's work illustrates another important, and for the archeologist, a heartening fact: it is possible to discover behavior patterns for which no modern counterpart exists, which had previously been unknown, and gone unrecognized. In historic times the ramon provided an incidental food at best, whereas before 900 A.D. *it likely served as a staple food source at least at one Mayan site.*

Experimentation in archeological research can supply data of much greater potential than is generally realized. A useful review of past experimental work is found in Hole and Heizer (1969:184–86). In a stimulating earlier paper on the same subject, Ascher (1961.794) points out that imitative experiments, in vogue half a century ago, "are now seldom performed by professional archaeologists." It is to be hoped that, with the advent of what is sometimes called the "Age of Models," experimentation will come back into fashion, as archeologists become more inventive in their search for ways to overcome the limitations of excavated archeological data.

In the study of alternative functions of ancient Maya *chultuns* at Tikal, Guatemala, an experimental approach has proved particularly useful as a means to test hypotheses, after it became obvious that excavation was not going to produce the information needed to evaluate a whole range of possibilities suggested by the archeological data.

HISTORICAL BACKGROUND

Speculation as to the function of curious subterranean chambers found in the Maya lowlands begins with John L. Stephens' (1843, 1:231) examination of chultuns at Uxmal and Labná. While he was inclined to believe that they were water cisterns, he found himself at odds with Don Simón, a local landowner, who held that they were for food storage. Clearly, at this stage excavation data were needed. Ethnographic analogy could offer little in the way of clarification, at least on a local level, for no nineteenth-century Maya group made regular use of such underground chambers. Stephens (1843, 1:228) himself reports that at the time of his visit, "neither Don Simón nor any of the Indians knew anything about them." In fact, it was not until he reached Tikal that he found people who even referred to them as "chul-tunes," or thought that they had been wells (Stephens 1843, 1:284).

The etymology of the word chultun is of little help either. According to Tozzer (1913:190) it means simply, "excavation in stone," deriving from *tsul*, to clean, and *tun*, stone.

The first archeological investigation of Yucatecan chultuns was carried out during the years 1888 to 1891 by E. H. Thompson. In his definitive study, *The Chultunes of Labná* (1897), Thompson investigated some 60 chultuns at Labná, an impressive sample even by today's standards. He concluded that chultuns as he knew them were for water storage. This conclusion was based on well-reasoned evidence including: (1) the frequency of the occurrence of chultuns at sites at which natural wells or *cenotes* were absent; (2) their location on terraces and beside buildings where they could catch the most water; (3) their bottle-shaped form with depths of more than 6 m beneath the orifice; (4) the discovery of a thick lining of polished stucco or plaster on the insides of the chultuns which he assumed would make them waterproof. Several of these points are illustrated in fig. 4.1a. It should be noted that while the illustration shows a rather elaborate, vaulted, masonry chultun built in artificial fill, many, and probably the majority, of these cistern chultuns were excavated directly out of the limestone bedrock. These bedrock cisterns, without masonry or vaulting, were also lined with a heavy layer of plaster (Thompson 1897:77).

The assumption that the plaster lining made the chultuns waterproof remained untested until several chultuns, including at least one at Uxmal, were replastered and allowed to fill with rainwater by the enterprising chief inspector of archeological monuments for Yucatán, Eduardo Martinez (Blom 1936:184). The water obtained from one of these restored chultuns at Uxmal was used to sustain Blom's field crew at the site in 1930. This was the first application of the experimental technique to the problem of chultun function. Since that time other chultuns of this type have been restored with their circular catchment-basins, and are currently in use at Kabah, Sayil, and possibly other sites, as well as Uxmal. In former times, it is clear that whole terraces, sometimes some distance from the chultun, were used for catchment. At Chichén-Itzá a chultun was found with a masonry drain leading to it from a whole group of buildings (Morley 1928:306).

Ethnohistorical sources appear to confirm this picture provided by the archeological and experimental data. In 1579, Juan Gutierrez Picon (Rela-ciónes de Yucatán 1898–1900, 2:159) reported that on one of the larger

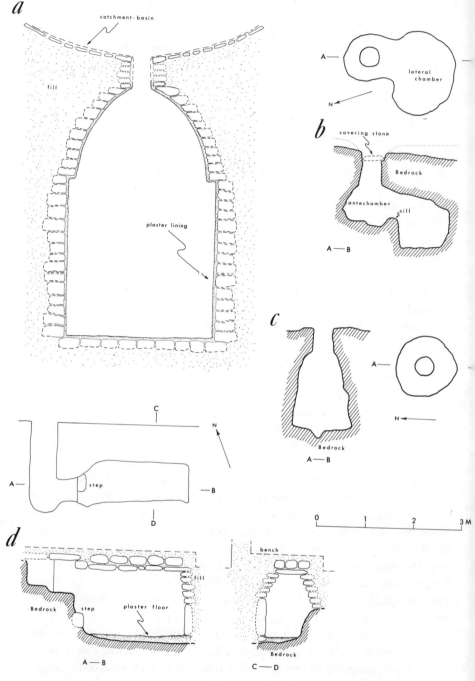

a

catchment-basin

fill

plaster lining

A ——

lateral chamber

N

b

covering stone

Bedrock

antechamber

sill

A —— B

c

A ——

N

Bedrock

A —— B

C

N

A ——

step

—— B

D

0   1   2   3M

d

bench

fill

Bedrock

step

plaster floor

A —— B

Bedrock

C —— D

Figure 4.1

buildings at Tiquibalon (Ekbalam [Tozzer 1941:60]) there were artificial cisterns which were used to collect rainwater, as well as silos which were used for storage of maize. The nature of the latter is yet to be determined, and while it is unlikely that they are identical in form to the cisterns it is curious that they have not been recognized archeologically. The reference suggests that there may have been substance to Don Simón's argument and that at least some chultuns or perhaps vaguely similar subsurface chambers were used for food storage. Charney (1887:302) in his visit to Ekbalam almost 300 years later describes what seemed to be water-storage cisterns on what is probably the same platform. Apart from complicating factors of this nature, however, Thompson's hypothesis regarding the water-storage function of the northern cistern chultuns has not been seriously contested by anyone other than O. F. Cook, who will be mentioned below.

The problem which concerns us now is the unintentional amplification of the designation "chultun" in the nineteenth century to include superficially similar holes-in-the-ground found only in certain parts of the southern Maya lowlands.

These southern chultuns differ in many ways from the cistern chultuns found in Yucatán and Campeche. Instead of deep bottle-shaped chambers, most of the southern ones have fairly small lateral chambers which often can only be reached from the surface by passing through a smaller and shallower antechamber (fig. 4.1b). It is this form which will be the principal subject of discussion in what follows, though it must be mentioned that a small percentage at Tikal have turned out to be bottle-shaped (fig. 4.1c); and an even smaller percentage are cylindrical pits. Unlike the comparatively huge cistern chultuns of northern Yucatán, however, the latter two forms are rarely much over 2 m. deep and show no evidence of stucco or plaster lining. The bottle-shaped pits are quite similar to the bell- and bottle-shaped pits found in the Guatemalan and Mexican highlands. Shook (1951:96) and Borhegyi (1965:9) have suggested these pits were used for storing food.

Unfortunately, the important subsurface differences between these southern chultuns and those described by J. L. Stephens (1843) and E. H.

Figure 4.1 Chultuns and a "burial vault" from the Maya lowlands: [a] section of cistern *chultun* at Labna, built in an artificial terrace (after Thompson 1897, Fig. 2); [b] section and plan of a lateral-chambered *chultun* at Tikal (Ch. 5C-1); [c] section and plan of pit *chultun* at Tikal (Ch. 6F-5), a covering stone may or may not have been present; [d] two sections and plan of Burial Vault 17, beneath Str. AA60a, at Mayapan (after Smith 1962, Fig. 16,e). All drawings are to the same scale.

Thompson (1897) were not recognized by the first archeologists to come into this region. These early explorers rather naturally assumed that the virtually identical appearances of the orifices from above ground indicated a corresponding similarity with respect to subsurface features.

Maudslay, who visited Tikal in 1881 and 1882, seems to have been the first to at least partially excavate and describe a southern lowlands chultun. In a paper he read before a meeting of the Royal Geographical Society in 1882 (Maudslay 1883:195), he described his investigation of what was certainly Chultun 5D–1 (Carr and Hazard 1961) located near the center of the Great Plaza of Tikal.

> In the plaza I found a small hole in the ground about eighteen inches across, cemented round the rim, and I set some men to work to clear it out, but as only one man could work at a time, he could only pass up the earth in small baskets-full. I was not able to clear it properly, but enough earth was removed to show me that it led to two circular subterranean chambers, six to eight feet in diameter. The sides of these chambers were not cemented, and it seems probable that they were used for the storage of food. . . .

He went on to consider the possibility that the chambers were used for water storage, but he clearly favored the food-storage hypothesis. It is ironic that he subsequently abandoned this perceptive and original assessment. Approximately 13 years later, in 1895, when volume 3 of his major work was published, he again refers to the chultun but makes no mention of food storage. He states merely that he found two "cisterns" and equates them morphologically and functionally with the "chaltunes" found to the north in Yucatán (Maudslay, 1889–1902, 3:49). The influence of Thompson's work on the Labná chultuns, along with the fact that he had not removed all the earth from the two small chambers, apparently convinced him that he had seen only the uppermost portions of a much deeper double cistern of some kind. Though his conclusion regarding the identity of the southern chultuns was soon shown to be erroneous, the name unfortunately stuck. The term chultun has continued to be used in unmodified form, camouflaging and confusing the essential differences between at least two very different and obviously functionally distinct constructions. It was next picked up by Maler (1911:5) who mentions finding a "chultun or rain-well" on his way into Tikal in 1895.

With the first complete excavations of lateral-chambered chultuns by Tozzer at Yaloch, Chorro, Nakum, and Holmul in 1909–10, their distinguishing characteristics were fully recognized for the first time. In a brief note published in *Science* (1912:669) Tozzer notes: (1) the predominance of lateral chambers in these chultuns; (2) their abundance in this region in contrast to the limited occurrence of water-storage chultuns in the north; (3) their association with small mounds; (4) their abundance in areas far from the ceremonial centers; (5) their occurrence in areas with abundant supplies of permanent water. The important observations relating to abundance and distribution were also recorded on a map which appeared with the Peabody Museum report on Nakum (Tozzer 1913, Pl. 31). In the text of the same report, Tozzer (1913:91) expanded on the distinctiveness of the southern chultuns, noting further that they (6) are not located so that water can drain into them, usually being "found on ground slightly higher than that of the surrounding country" and (7) frequently lack any signs of plaster on the porous limestone walls. Most of these observations apply to the small bottle-shaped pits also found in this region (fig. 1c), and though Tozzer (1913:192) distinguished these from the more elaborate of the northern water cisterns, noting that they lacked masonry walls and were not vaulted, he did not remark on their lack of plaster and comparatively small size. This oversight led him to confuse them with the bedrock variant of the cistern chultuns mentioned above.

The only plaster found in a chultun-like feature at that time in the southern lowlands was in a series of comparatively huge chambers discovered by Thomas Gann at the site of Santa Rita in northern British Honduras. One of these unusual features, described by Gann (1900:691), was entered by a half spiral staircase. The main chamber was found to be 18 feet long by 10 feet broad and lined with a layer of hard plaster. In this respect, these enigmatic chambers seem to be something like the northern cistern chultuns, and Gann referred to them as "underground rock-hewn reservoirs." We shall leave these apparently unique features now to return to the discussion of the more typical chambered chultuns excavated by Tozzer.

On the basis of the points mentioned above, Tozzer felt that it was unlikely that the chambered chultuns he had investigated were water cisterns, and reviving Maudslay's original assessment now suggested that they may have been for "the storage of maize and other foods . . . as they are generally dry and would be suited for such a purpose." As time went on, more lateral-chambered chultuns were excavated, this time by Thomas Gann in British Honduras. Gann (1918:83) echoed Tozzer's opinions on function, stating that they were probably used for the storage of maize and other provisions, with occasional secondary use for burials.

Thus, up until sometime during the Carnegie Institution–sponsored excavations at Uaxactun, the food-storage hypothesis seemed to be gaining acceptance. Wauchope (1934:151), in confirmation of Tozzer's and Gann's observations, noted that the interior of Chultun 53 at Uaxactun was not plastered and suggested that it has "probably been used for storage." In an article that appeared in 1935 in *Science* (1935:615), O. F. Cook went so far as to suggest that all chultuns, including the bottle-shaped ones of northern Yucatán, were used for food storage and went even further by stating that he believed the food stored in them was the nut-like seed of the ramon tree. The Uaxactun studies, however, shifted the emphasis away from food storage by producing a more comprehensive list of possible functions as well as some rather startling experimental data. Ricketson (1925:390) includes in a list of possible functions their use as water cisterns, storage places, burial chambers, ceremonial chambers, and places suitable for fine weaving where moist conditions were required to make the strips pliable. Sweat bathing, originally suggested by Maudslay (1889–1902, 2:25), was added to this list in the Uaxactun report on Group E (Ricketson and Ricketson 1937:123). O. G. Ricketson (1925) seems to favor the latter possibility, suggesting that hot rocks could have been dropped into the chultun to produce steam by pouring water on them. Blom (1936:128) favors water storage. A. L. Smith (1950:85), while stating that function remained problematical, favors the hypothesis that the orifice served as an efficient means of getting through the hard, 0.5 m. thick layer of caprock so that the Maya could mine the soft limestone marl below. Schufeldt (1950:227), who also felt that chultuns were the result of mining for marl, offers the thoughtful suggestion that the small orifice allowed mining to go on with minimal disturbance of valuable topsoil. Bullard (1960:362) states his preference for a storage function. Pollock (1956:540), in a discussion of a small bottle-shaped chultun found at Mayapan, suggests that they might have served as drains or refuse pits. He also mentions, as does Haviland (1963:505) apropos of the lateral-chambered chultuns of Tikal, the possibility that they functioned as latrines. Finally, Ursula Cowgill (Cowgill and Hutchinson 1963:41) poses the novel idea that most chultuns were not man-made at all but rather the creations of uprooted palm trees, which "in some cases the ancient Maya may have modified. . . ."

Most of these possibilities, along with the Uaxactun experimental data alluded to above, tended to draw attention away from food storage. The experiment, which seems to have occurred accidentally, rather dramatically disproved Tozzer's contention that chultuns were "generally dry" and therefore suitable for the storage of maize. The incident that produced these data seems to have occurred as follows. Blom, at the end of the 1924 field season at Uaxactun, decided to cache in a convenient chultun a number of spades and machetes for use in some future season. These were prepared for storage by greasing them with vaseline and tying them up in burlap before sealing them into the chultun with the usual covering stone. Twenty-one months later, in 1926, Ricketson returned to Uaxactun and has provided us with the following graphic description of what he found when the chultun was reopened.

> The horn handles of the machetes were cracked and broken and in some cases the horn had completely fallen from the tang. The blades of the shovels were represented by thin areas of rust; their wood handles could be broken between the fingers. The steel blades of the machetes still existed, but were rusted and quite unfit for use (Ricketson and Ricketson 1937:172).

This striking demonstration of the high humidity prevailing in chultuns had an obviously negative effect on the likelihood and popularity of the food-storage hypothesis.

INVESTIGATIONS AT TIKAL

It was in the face of this bewildering array of possible functions and data that systematic excavation and investigation of chultuns was begun at Tikal. The problem was to assemble clues from wherever possible in an attempt to elicit the primary function of the lateral-chambered chultuns. Over 220 chultuns have been found in the central 9 km^2 of Tikal. Of these, a sample of about 60 has been excavated. Between 80 percent and 90 percent of these have lateral chambers.

Some of the clues which eventually led back to the food-storage hypothesis have already been presented (Puleston 1965). While there is not room to discuss them in light of supportive data here, they will be so presented in a forthcoming report on the chultuns of Tikal. Summarizing briefly, they include the following: (1) the large number of chultuns found at the site and their apparent broad distribution in time, suggesting some basic and wide-spread function; (2) the distribution of chultuns all through the residential areas of the site in contrast to their virtual absence in the ceremonial nucleus, suggesting a secular rather than ceremonial function; (3) their frequent occurrence on higher ground where they would less likely be flooded by rainstorms; (4) the use of lidlike covering stones, as if a specific effort had been made to "protect" the contents of the chultun; (5) the frequent use of a raised sill between the antechamber and the main inner chamber, suggesting that in the event of rain it was desirable to keep water from trickling into the inner chamber (fig. 4.1b); (6) the fact that most chultuns were left empty and did not contain burials or ceremonial deposits; (7) the lack of any evidence of plastering apart from two obviously aberrant situations in which well-preserved plaster floors were found. These examples clearly demonstrated that if chultuns had been plastered the material could be expected to survive in fairly good condition. Finally, there is the evidence provided by (8) the discovery in Chultun 3F–6 at Tikal of five large, widemouthed vessels, apparently left *in situ*. Although these vessels are somewhat atypical, fragments of what may have been storage vessels have turned up in two or three other Tikal chultuns.

On the basis of points (3), (4), (5), and (7) above, it seemed safe to eliminate the possibility of water storage, as Tozzer had. Goaded on, however, by a colleague's suggestion that the limestone might be self-sealing once it became wet, in 1965 we performed the simple experiment of pouring 400 gallons of water into a chultun and observed the results. Within three hours there were only 100 gallons left and before eight hours were up the last of the water had completely drained away into the obviously very porous limestone.

Furthermore, the excavation data argued strongly against burial chambers as a primary function. Only one out of six or seven chultuns seems to have been so used. Even in those cases where they were used for burials it was often clear that they had served some other function first. A ceremonial function also seemed very unlikely in light of the apparent irregularity of the orientation and location of chultuns, the scarcity of ceremonial deposits in them, and their overall frequency and distribution. In view of the cramped conditions often found in chultuns, time-consuming human activities such as weaving and sweat bathing seemed unlikely. The backaches produced by even relatively short spells of crouching in the smaller chultuns while excavating or drawing provided convincing experimental data. Furthermore, no good evidence of rocks used for steam production, as suggested by Ricketson (1925), could be found, nor could we come up with an explanation as to how hot air and steam could be kept in the chultun when the lid was removed to drop in more rocks and let in the air necessary for breathing. With the discovery by Christopher Jones in 1964 of what was clearly a sweathouse, much like those identified by Satterthwaite (1948) at Piedras Negras, the likelihood of this explanation declined. The "necessity" of finding some kind of evidence for sweat bathing at Tikal, with chultuns as the most likely candidates, was no longer present. Smith's marl-extraction hypothesis seemed unlikely when considering the fairly regular size and shape of chultun chambers and the need of an explanation for the floor sills and covering stones. Nearby quarries, as pointed out by Bullard (1960:362), would have been a more convenient source for marl. Finally, the latrine hypothesis was rejected since it also provided no explanation for the lateral chambers and sills. Ethnographic data on modern Maya Indians (Steggerda 1941:18) suggest that the disposal of human feces was left to vultures and dogs. Even supposing that such customs have changed since Classic times it seemed unlikely that latrines would be secondarily used as burial chambers. No evidence of the expected deposits was found in excavation.

This series of eliminations left us with the food-storage hypothesis again, which actually seemed to fit the clues we had assembled fairly well. Food storage was certainly a basic, secular activity which would not require long periods of sitting in the chultun and yet would require them to be capable of being entered and sealed. Having spent the night in a maize storage house at Uaxactun in 1963, we could well appreciate the utility of rodent-proof underground storage. Our quarters literally swarmed with rats during the night and their annual toll on the stored crop must have been significant. While we could not be sure these were not introduced species, native rodents such as *Heteromys* are known to be granary pests (Walker 1968:746). Other native rodents including *Orzomys* (?) and another unknown species, possibly *Heteromys,* have been trapped with baited traps in storehouses and habitations at Tikal by Peter Puleston. The only problem that nagged us was the question of why chultuns did not seem to be used in the Petén in historic times. Apart from this, however, it all seemed to make good sense and all that apparently remained was to demonstrate that though chultuns may have been unfavorable for the storage of metal tools at Uaxactun, they were fine for the storage of certain Maya foods in certain ways. Which foods though and in what way? Experimental studies seemed an obvious course.

EXPERIMENTAL CONSTRUCTION OF A CHULTUN

Initially, we had intended to use a Maya chultun for our experiments but later decided against it in favor of constructing and using our own. This not only eliminated the possibility of uncontrolled variables accruing from the age of the Maya chultuns, but it also afforded an opportunity to study the techniques of their construction and the use of stone tools. Accordingly, in 1965 a number of stone tools of the types called biface ovate and biface elongate were hafted Polynesian fashion to wooden handles and used to excavate our own lateral-chambered chultun out of the limestone bedrock (fig. 4.2).

Summarizing very briefly: information resulting from this exercise included the following: (1) Flint tools were entirely adequate for cutting through

Figure 4.2 Starting the experimental *chultun* antechamber. Stone tools were found to be entirely adequate for cutting through the limestone caprock. At about this stage we had to start using the bit-ended tool. (Photograph by Francis P. Bowles.)

the hard surface layer and that it would have been quite easy for us to expand our orifice if our only concern were the extraction of the softer marl below. (2) Tools of different kinds were needed to construct the chultun. While the adze-hafted tools were adequate for most of the work, we had to devise a long-handled bit-ended tool to dig out the deeper portions of the narrow antechamber. (3) Tool marks on the walls of our chultun corresponded well with similar marks observed on the walls of ancient chultuns in respect to width, length of stroke, angle of stroke, etc. (4) The amount of time and labor required to excavate a chultun with stone tools was relatively small. In all, it required approximately 30 hours of work with the assistance of someone to haul out basketfuls of marl when work got going in the inner chamber. More time was required to cut out a circular covering stone, which was accomplished with the help of wooden wedges.

EXPERIMENTAL FOOD STORAGE

In the following season of 1966, we assembled an assortment of vegetables including maize, beans, squash, *yuca* or cassava (*Manihot esculenta* Crantz), *camote* or sweet potato (*Ipomoea batatas* [L.] Poir), *macal* (*Xanthosoma* sp.), and potatoes. The potato, of course, was not a Maya food and was included only for comparative purposes. Two varieties each of beans and sweet potatoes were used while maize was tested fresh on the cob, dried on the cob, and as dried kernels. Samples of all these vegetables were placed in the chultun, a control series was also stored above ground. This aboveground series was divided in two, half being stored on a screened-in porch which provided protection from rodents and some insects, while the other half was stored at the mercy of these vermin in an unprotected outbuilding. All the samples were examined, weighed, and photographed every two weeks for a period of eight weeks and finally at the end of eleven weeks.

Measurements of the humidity in the chultun, taken on June 5, 1966, indicated a figure of 100 percent. No difference was observed between the wet- and dry-bulb readings even after vigorous fanning. While the humidity of the chultun microenvironment must go up and down to some degree, it is unlikely that it is ever low for very long. The temperature in the chultun during the day in June fell in the range of 75°–80°F (20°–27°C).

With the ensuing activity of storage fungi and rodents, developments over the eleven weeks were fairly rapid both above and below ground. Below ground, the maize in all forms did very poorly. The fresh maize decomposed first after sprouting vigorously. It was followed by the shelled maize which seemed to be particularly susceptible to the attacks of fungi at the base of the kernel where it attaches to the cob. By the end of eleven weeks the shelled maize, along with the dried maize still "on the cob," suffered from a heavy infestation of mites. Only 10 percent of the dried maize on the cob was judged edible.

The beans fared little better. After a short time, they became soft as if they had been soaking in water and soon afterward succumbed to vigorous growths of fungi and mite infestations. The latter included specimens of the species *Tyrophagus putrescentiae* (Schrank). The one exception to this was a sample of black beans which had been placed in a deep but open glass jar. For some reason, although the beans became soft, they remained edible when beans on raised ceremic dishes decayed rapidly. One green squash, while it lasted longer than the aboveground controls, decomposed suddenly and completely sometime after the eighth week. The root crops produced ambiguous results. The potatoes and macal survived with minimal spoilage but underwent continuing if gradual weight loss. The yuca was 95 percent decayed by the end of eleven weeks. One variety of sweet potato became covered with fungi (*Rhizopus,* a common cause of rot in sweet potatoes) early in the experiment while the other variety did not. Both varieties sprouted but were still apparently edible at the end of the experiment.

Meanwhile, above ground, the depredations carried out by rodents and insects were impressive. By the end of eleven weeks virtually nothing remained of the maize, yuca, or sweet potatoes. The beans which had been placed in glass jars where only certain flying insects could get at them were virtually untouched. The root crops, and particularly the decaying yuca, were heavily attacked by the larvae of an as yet unidentified species of microlepi-doptera and a beetle, *Colopterus posticus* (Er.), Nitidulidae. Apart from the mites and some weevils (evidently *Sithophilus zeamais* Motsch.) which seem to have come in with the maize, no such attacks took place in the chultun.

In conclusion then, while the chultun apparently offered valuable protection from vermin, it evidently could not be used for the storage of maize, beans, or squash. Even the root crops did not do particularly well.

In light of the high humidity and temperature of the chultun microenvironment, these results probably could have been predicted. Maize, in the lowlands today, is stored under the driest, best-ventilated conditions possible. This is often in cribs in a storehouse located in the center of the milpa (fig. 4.3). Modern Yucatecan storehouses and granaries have been described by Wauchope (1938:133, 136).

Christensen and Kaufmann (1969:25) indicate that primary factors in the growth of storage fungi on grains include temperature, length of time in storage, and moisture content of the stored grain. Since the latter remains in equilibrium with the relative humidity, the higher the humidity, the higher the moisture content of a particular grain will be. The actual ratio between humidity and moisture content, and at what level of the latter fungi can begin to be a problem, varies from one crop to another. For maize, a moisture content of a little over 15 percent, which can be produced by a relative humidity of only 75 percent at 60°–77°F (20°–25°C), is perfect for some of the most common storage fungi. A temperature of 85°–90°F (29°–32°C) is ideal for the most rapid growth of the most common storage fungi. Optimum conditions for both mites and fungi tend to be about the same, and they seemed to characterize the conditions found in Classic Maya chultuns.

In respect to root crops, chultun storage did not seem to be particularly beneficial. Some, like the macal, would obviously do better if simply left in the ground and used when needed. The roots of the yuca are best "left in the ground, as they decay quickly when harvested" (Bailey 1935:1991). The

Figure 4.3 Maize storehouse situated near the center of a milpa at Tikal 1967. Maximum contact of dry, circulating air under these conditions helps keep moisture content of the maize, preventing the growth of gungi.

tubers of the sweet potato apparently rot in conditions of excessive humidity and temperature and are best stored for the wet season by harvesting and drying; otherwise they may be left in the ground and used as needed (Netting 1968:74). A certain amount of experimental work has been done with artificial storage of sweet potatoes, and it is worth noting that under conditions of high humidity (85 percent), best storage temperatures fall in the range of 55°–60°F (13°–15°C) (Cooley and others 1954). This is 20 degrees (F) cooler than that recorded for the chultun, and it is perhaps for this reason that drier storage conditions are preferable for sweet potato storage in the tropics. Finally, the possibility that chultuns were used for storage of root crops seemed unlikely in view of the fact that such an evidently popular innovation as the chultun did not continue to be used into historic times by groups who still consumed a fair amount of this type of food as indicated by Bronson (1966:258). These points in combination with the marginal performance of root crops in the experiment left us with the feeling that the raison d'être for lateral-chambered chultuns was still eluding us.

In the following year, 1967, we made one more try with maize, parching it in a fire as the Navajo do before storing it underground. The results were disastrous. The parched maize (*Aspergillus glaucus?*) began to mildew vigorously long before the unparched samples showed the first signs of fungi.

THE RAMON

Then, in that same year, in the course of another study, we discovered the phenomenal correlation between the present distribution of the ramon tree (*Brosimum alicastrum* Sw.) and the remains of Maya house platforms, suggesting that these trees were the descendants of trees cultivated, in the vicinity of their homes, by the Classic Maya of Tikal. Subsequent recognition of the high nutritional value of this dense carbohydrate food, coupled with the discovery of the staggering productivity of the trees, all served to confirm the potential significance of this crop for ancient Maya subsistence (Puleston 1968). The appropriateness of a test run for ramons in the chultun was self-evident by the end of the 1967 season. The fact that O. F. Cook (1935) had anticipated by more than 30 years the possibility of this relationship between chultuns and the fruit of the ramon tree remains a credit to his insight.

Thus, in 1968, a new series of fruits and vegetables including the ramon were stored in the experimental chultun with a single protected control above ground. The results of this experiment confirmed our suspicions beyond our expectations. After nine weeks, the previously tested vegetables produced much the same results as before (figs. 4.4, 4.5). The corn and beans were quickly reduced by fungi and mite infestations. The manioc rotted quickly while the sweet potatoes and potatoes sprouted but did not rot seriously within the period of the study. A few new fruits including avocados (*Persea americana* Mill.) and *zapote mamey* (*Calocarpum mammosum* [L.] Pierre) became inedible within three weeks. The ramon seed, however, after nine weeks gave *every* appearance of being as fresh as when it had been put in (fig. 4.6). Though some of the seeds had produced short sprouts, they were unaffected by fungi or mites. The seeds remained hard and did not soften up as the beans in the jar had. These seeds were left in the chultun at the end of the summer, and as of July 1969, after thirteen months of underground storage, they were still in excellent condition and completely edible (fig. 4.7) though the wicker baskets they had been placed in were reduced to a brown debris.

Why does the ramon preserve so well under conditions which are so destructive to so many other foods? The answer may lie in the very low water content of the seeds. Ramon seeds have a measured water content of only

Figure 4.4 Dried black beans after 3 weeks of storage; in the *chultun* (square); above ground, unprotected my screening (circle); and above ground protected by screening (triangle). Note extensive growth of fungi on the *chultun* sample and discoloration of the decaying basket.

Figure 4.5 Dried, shelled, yellow maize after 9 weeks in the *chultun*. Dissected kernels reveal the extent of internal decay. Note the solidified mass of decayed maize at the top.

Figure 4.6 Undried ramon seed after 9 weeks in the *chultun*. Dissected seeds reveal their excellent condition, one out of hundreds that decayed is at the top. Most of the seeds had begun to germinate.

Figure 4.7 Ramon seed after 13 mo. in the *chultun*. The seeds are still firm and completely edible. Sprouting seems to have been retarded.

6.5 percent as compared to 10.6 percent for dried maize and 12 percent for dried beans (Leung 1961). In this regard, certain parallels can perhaps be drawn between ramons and acorns as used by the Indians of California. The great importance of acorns in these cultures is attributed to the fact that, of all the available wild foods, acorns were the most amenable to storage because of their low water content, which is reported to be 9 percent (Baumhoff 1963:161). Thus, even with a relative humidity of 100 percent the equilibrium moisture content of ramon seed does not seem to come up to a level that would permit the growth of fungi. The possibility of the existence of a natural antibiotic in the seed might also be considered. The astonishing ability of these seeds to resist decay is not coincidental and probably represents a selective adaptation by the fruit to the highly humid microenvironment of the forest floor where the seeds eventually must germinate.

MAIZE STORAGE

At this point, a very real problem remains to be dealt with which leads from the statements of Landa, and possibly others, as well as the previously referred to sixteenth-century report on Ekbalam. Landa states that *"el maiz y las demas semillas"* were stored by the Yucatecan Maya in *"muy lindos silos y trojes"* *(Relaciónes de Yucatán* 1898–1900, 2:322) (Tozzer [1941:96] translates *silos* as "underground places" which in the light of sixteenth-century usage is apparently correct [Corominas 1954, 4:224–27]) and that they gathered great quantities of maize and made granaries *(trojes)* and kept it in underground places *(silos)* for the barren years (Tozzer 1941:195). The apparent inconsistency of these statements with the experimental data reported above suggests that underground storage in northern Yucatán may have been somehow more conducive to the storage of maize than in the chultuns of the southern lowlands. In fact, it is curious that Landa's "fine underground places" for maize storage have never been identified archeologically. Though an obvious place to start would be Ekbalam, an intriguing case can be presented for the possibility that they have already been discovered. In the course of the excavation of residential and associated structures at Mayapan, chambers were frequently found beneath, or rather within, the structure platforms (fig. 4.1d). Some of these could be entered from above, others from the side by means of lateral openings in the sides of the platforms or benches, and in several instances by means of stairways that passed down through the floor from inside the structure. Many of these contained burials, and on this basis, A. L. Smith has suggested that all were intended for this purpose. Those which did not contain interments (about 18) he classifies as burial vaults, "apparently prepared for future interment of the dead but never so used" (Smith 1962:232). In view of the fact that so many of these chambers were found to be empty, however, alternative hypotheses seem to exist in the possibilities that use of the chambers for interment was secondary rather than primary, and at least two functionally distinct chamber types, which happen to occur at the same locus, have been lumped together in a single category. The strong possibility exists that the majority of these chambers, constructed in aboveground deposits of dry fill and beneath a plastered platform with a structure on it, may have provided a comparatively dry storage place. This, in combination with the drier climate of northern Yucatán (Vivo 1964), may have made it possible to store maize "underground" in this region. The practice of locating granaries within structure platforms seems to be confirmed by the description of the silos at Ekbalam mentioned earlier, but experimental work on storage under these special conditions in northern Yucatán would seem to be in order.

SUMMARY

Usage of the term chultun has been confusing. At least two distinct functions may be attributed to morphologically distinct archeological features that fall under this term. In the northern lowlands deep, plaster-lined, bottle-shaped pits constructed of masonry in artificial fill or excavated directly out of the bedrock appear to have functioned as cisterns. These remain to be distinguished archeologically from possibly similar silos, mentioned in historical sources, that were apparently used for the storage of maize in Postclassic northern Yucatán. The function of shallow, lateral-chambered excavations in the limestone bedrock of the southern lowlands has not been so obvious. Of the many hypotheses presented, the results of extensive excavation and experimental studies appear to be most consistent with the suggestion that they were used for food storage. Maize does not appear to be amenable to storage under these conditions, however. Of a series of experimentally stored foods, the hard seed of the ramon (*Brosimum alicastrum*) did best, remaining entirely edible for at least 13 months. This fact, in combination with a high correlation between large numbers of ramon trees and the remains of Maya housemound settlement, and the prevalence of Classic and apparently Preclassic chultuns in certain parts of the southern lowlands, suggests that this fruit may have held a position of considerable significance in the subsistence systems of the Preclassic and Classic Maya over a good part of this region.

Subsurface food storage does not appear to have been restricted to the southern lowlands. Historical sources indicate fairly clearly that large quantities of maize were stored in artificial silos within structure platforms. Chambers within structure platforms, which could not have been used for water storage, have been discovered in archeological contexts at Mayapan. Though many of these contain burials, many others do not. Experimental work is needed to show that maize can in fact be successfully stored in this region under these conditions.

CONCLUSIONS

In respect to the lateral-chambered chultuns of the southern lowlands, it appears that O. F. Cook's hypothesis (1935) that they were used for the storage of ramon seed is viable. The hypothesis lends itself to an explanation of why lateral-chambered, bedrock chultuns are not in use among the Maya today and apparently have not been made or used in that form since the time of the collapse of Classic civilization, ca. 900 a.d. This explanation is that for some reason the fruit of the ramon ceased to be an important staple for the Maya after this time. The continued use of somewhat similar subplatform chambers in the northern lowlands may be associated with the storage of better-known crops.

By way of conclusion, I wish to point out the key role that experimentation can play in the construction and testing of hypotheses when dealing with problems of function. It offers a potent means of getting beyond what would otherwise be dead ends in archeological research if only archeological data were used as evidence.

ACKNOWLEDGMENTS

This is a revised version of a paper presented at the 34th annual meeting of the Society for American Archaeology, May 1969, Milwaukee, Wisconsin. It is with pleasure that I extend my thanks to the following for their assistance with the material presented in this paper: the staff of the Department of Entomology of the Smithsonian Institution (Karl V. Krombein, chairman) for insect identifications and particularly R. E. Werner and W. A. Connell for the identifications used here; E. W. Baker of the U. S. Department of Agriculture for identification of the mites; Clyde M. Christensen of the Department of Plant Pathology, University of Minnesota, for his tentative identification of the stored food fungi from colored slides; my brother, Peter Puleston, for his information on small mammals from Tikal; Francis P. Bowles for assistance in construction of the experimental chultun; my wife, Olga Puleston, for assistance with the storage experiments; and finally Bennet Bronson, William A. Haviland, and W. R. Coe for their helpful comments on the first draft of this paper.

REFERENCES

Ascher, Robert. 1961. Experimental archaeology. *American Anthropologist* 63:793 – 816.

Bailey, L. H. 1935. *The standard cyclopedia of horticulture.* New York: Macmillan.

Baumhoff, Martin A. 1963. Ecological determinants of aboriginal California populations. *University of California Publications in American Archaeology and Ethnology* 49:155 – 236.

Blom, Frans R. 1936. *The conquest of Yucatán.* Boston: Houghton-Mifflin.

Borhegyi, Stephan F. 1965. Archaeological synthesis of the Guatemalan highlands. In Gordon R. Willey, ed., *The handbook of Middle American Indians*. Austin: University of Texas Press.

Bronson, Bennet. 1966. Roots and the subsistence of the Ancient Maya. *Southwestern Journal of Anthropology* 22:251–79.

Bullard, William R., Jr. 1960. Maya settlement pattern in northeastern Peten, Guatemala. *American Antiquity* 25:355–72.

Carr, Robert F., and James E. Hazard. 1961. Map of the ruins of Tikal, El Peten, Guatemala. *Museum Monographs, Tikal Reports* 11.

Charney, Désiré. 1887. Ma dernière expédition au Yucatán, 1886. *Tour du Monde* 53:273–320.

Christensen, Clyde M., and Henry H. Kaufmann. 1969. *Grain storage, the role of fungi in quality loss*. Minneapolis: University of Minnesota Press.

Cook, O. F. 1935. The Maya breadnut in southern Florida. *Science* 85:615–16.

Cooley, J. J., L. J. Kushman, and H. F. Smart. 1954. Effect of temperature and duration of storage on quality of stored sweet potatoes. *Economic Botany* 8:21–28.

Corominas, J. 1954. *Diccionario crítico etimológico de la Lengua Castellana*. Editorial Gredos.

Cowgill, Ursula M., and G. E. Hutchinson. 1963. El Bajo de Santa Fe. *American Philosophical Society, Transactions* 53, pt. 7.

Gann. Thomas. 1900. Mounds in northern Honduras. *Bureau of American Ethnology* 19 *(Annual Report)*:655–92.

—— 1918. The Maya Indians of southern Yucatán and northern British Honduras. *Bureau of American Ethnology, Bulletin* 64.

Haviland, William A. 1963. Excavation of small structures in the northeast quadrant of Tikal, Guatemala. Ph.D. dissertation, Department of Anthropology, University of Pennsylvania. Ann Arbor: University Microfilms.

Hole, Frank, and R. F. Heizer. 1969. *An introduction to prehistoric archaeology*. New York: Holt, Rinehart and Winston.

Leung, Woot-Tsuen Wu. 1961. *Food composition table for use in Latin America*. Institute of Nutrition of Central American and Panama, Guatemala City. C. A. and Interdepartmental Committee on Nutrition for National Defense, National Institutes of Health, Bethesda, Maryland.

Maler, Teobart. 1911. Explorations in the Department of Peten, Guatemala: Tikal. *Peabody Museum of American Archaeology and Ethnography, Harvard, Memoirs* 5:1–91.

Maudslay, Alfred P. 1883. Explorations in Guatemala, and examination of the newly discovered Indian ruins of Quiriquá, Tikal and the Usumacinta. *Royal Geographical Society, Proceedings* 5:185–204.

—— 1889–1902. Archaeology. In *Biologia Centrali-Americana or contributions to the knowledge of the flora and fauna of Mexico and Central America.* Vols. 1–4, edited by F. D. Godman and O. Salvin. R. H. Porter and Dulau.

Morley, Sylvanus Griswold. 1928. Report of Karl Ruppert on the outlying sections of Chichén-Itzá. *Carnegie Institution of Washington, Yearbook* 27:305–7.

Netting, Robert McC. 1968. *Hill Farmers of Nigeria: Cultural ecology of the Kofyar of the Jos Plateau.* Seattle: University of Washington Press.

Pollock, H. E. D. 1956. The southern terminus of the principal sacbe at Mayapan—Group Z–50. *Carnegie Institution of Washington, Department of Archaeology, Current Reports* 37:529–49.

Puleston, Dennis E. 1965. The chultuns of Tikal. *Expedition* 7(3):24–29.

—— 1968. Brosium alicastrum as a subsistence alternative for the Classic Maya of the central southern lowlands. M.A. thesis, Department of Anthropology, University of Pennsylvania.

Relaciónes de Yucatán. 1898–1900. In *Collección de documentos inéditos relativos al descubrimiento, conquista y organización* de las antiguas posesiones, *Españolas de ultramar.* 2d Series, Vols. 2(1) and 13(2). Establecimiento Tipógrafico.

Ricketson, Oliver G. 1925. Burials in the Maya area. *American Anthropologist* 27:381–401.

Ricketson, Oliver G., and Elizabeth B. Ricketson. 1937. Uaxactun, Guatemala, Group E 1926–1931. *Carnegie Institution of Washington, Publication* 477.

Satterthwaite, Linton. 1948. An unusual type of building in the Maya Old Empire. *26th International Congress of Americanists* (Seville, 1934) 1:243–54.

Schufeldt, P. W. 1950. Reminiscences of a chiclero. In *Morleyana, A collection of writings in memoriam, Sylvanus Griswold Morley—1883–1948.* School of American Research and the Museum of New Mexico.

Shook, Edwin M. 1951. The present status of research on the pre-Classic horizons in Guatemala. In Sol Tax, ed. *The civilizations of ancient America,* pp. 93–100. Chicago: University of Chicago Press.

Smith, A. Ledyard. 1950. Uaxactun, Guatemala: excavations of 1931–1937. *Carnegie Institution of Washington, Publication* 588.

—— 1962. Residential and associated structures at Mayapan. In Mayapan, Yucatán, Mexico, by H. E. D. Pollack and others. Pt. 3, pp. 165–320. *Carnegie Institution of Washington, Publication* 619.

Steggerda, Morris. 1941. Maya Indians of Yucatán. *Carnegie Institution of Washington, Publication* 531.

Stephens, John L. 1843. *Incidents of travel in Yucatán,* Vols. 1–2. New York: Harper.

Thompson, Edward H. 1897. The chultunes of Labná. *Peabody Museum of American Archaeology and Ethnology, Harvard, Memoirs* 1:73–92.

Tozzer, Alfred A. 1912. The chultunes of northern Guatemala. *Science* 35:669.

—— 1913. A preliminary study of the prehistoric ruins of Nakum, Guatemala. *Peabody Museum of American Archaeology and Ethnology, Harvard, Memoirs* 5:137—201.

—— 1941. Landa's relación de las cosas de Yucatán: A translation. *Peabody Museum of American Archaeology and Ethnology, Harvard, Papers* 18.

Vivo Escoto, Jorge A. 1964. Weather and climate of Mexico and Central America. In Robert C. West, ed., *Handbook of Middle American Indians*. Austin: University of Texas Press.

Walker, Ernest P. 1968. *Mammals of the world*. Baltimore: Johns Hopkins Press.

Wauchope, Robert. 1934. House mounds of Uaxactun, Guatemala. *Carnegie Institution of Washington, Publication* 436. *Contribution to American Archaeology* 7.

—— 1938. Modern Maya houses, a study of their archaeological significance. *Carnegie Institution of Washington, Publication* 502.

G. H. WEAVER

Archaeomagnetic Measurements on the Second Boston Experimental Kiln

More often than not, the archeologist works with discarded objects: pieces that were either broken or worn down and thus thrown away by the last person to use them. Most stone tools and pottery fragments fall in this category. Alterations which occur during use deserve consideration for two reasons. On the one hand, study of wear may provide important clues to the original use of the object. In recent years, for example, increasing attention has been devoted to wear marks on stone tools (see chapter 2) as a way to discern function. On the other hand, transformations which take place during use may introduce bias that complicates later analysis. If one actually constructs and then employs a copy under controlled conditions, it is sometimes possible to determine the types of bias which may arise, and to correct for them. This article illustrates just such an approach.

Two physical properties of the universe combine to make archeomagnetic dating possible. First, the magnetic poles of the earth shift over time. Secondly, if materials containing iron—and these include most clays—are heated beyond a certain temperature, they are magnetized to the then present position of the pole. This thermo-remanent magnetism (TRM) may be later measured and its direction determined. Then, on the basis of known and dated polar shifts, a good estimate of when heating occurred can be made. One main difficulty is that the object must remain unmoved from the time it is heated until the TRM is measured. Thus, pottery is rarely usable, while fixed earthen kilns, dug into the ground and abandoned after use, provide an excellent source for study.

When the direction of TRM is measured on different parts of the same kiln, however, slightly different readings are obtained; and Weaver wants to know why. He postulates that cracking and movement of the kiln wall during the

Reprinted, with minor editorial changes, from *Archaeometry* 5 (1962). Used by permission of Cambridge University Press.

cooling process after firing is complete may be responsible for the observed TRM scattering; thus, he and his colleagues construct a kiln to test this hypothesis. The results are not conclusive: While Weaver notes that wall tilt is not the culprit, systematic error did occur, and the cause must yet be discovered.

The relationship between kilns and magnetic poles reflects the relationship between the archeologist and the natural scientist. All too often one thinks of expertise and information flowing in a single direction: from outside archeology into it. But often, the street may be traveled in both directions. Magnetic pole shifts allow age determination of some archeological remains. When one starts from objects susceptible to historic or other kinds of absolute dating, however, the process may be stood on its head and a sequence of pole shifts actually constructed on the basis of cultural remains. In fact, most knowledge of magnetic shifts over the last two thousand years comes from this source.

The second experimental kiln at Boston was welcomed by the magnetic dating department of this Laboratory as an opportunity to conduct field experiments designed to test the hypothesis of "Kiln Wall Fall Out" (Harold 1960). Harold observed a sinusoidal dependence of the magnetic directions of samples from some ancient kilns upon the azimuthal positions[1] of the samples within the kiln. He ascribed this variation to systematic wall movements. The first Boston experimental kiln showed a variation of magnetic directions in accordance with this hypothesis, so the effect is not necessarily related to the age of a kiln, or to the fact of its burial over a long period of time. Thus, if the walls of a kiln do fall outwards in the hypothesized way, they may be expected to do so during the cooling of the kiln. This article describes the attempts made to detect wall movement in the second Boston kiln and discusses the relevance of the observed movements to the scattering of the thermo-remanent magnetic directions of samples from the kiln.

FIELD EXPERIMENTS

Preliminary magnetometer surveys were made at various sites in Boston to ensure that the kiln was built in a magnetically undisturbed region. The chosen site was surveyed in some detail with a compass and a dip circle to determine the direction of the magnetic field in which the kiln would cool. The

---

[1]The azimuth is defined by the bearing of a sample from the center of the kiln; magnetic north being taken as zero.

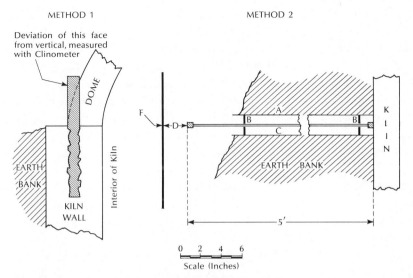

Figure 5.1 Apparatus for detecting kiln wall movements.

mean declination measured 9.1°W ± 0.2°[2] and the mean inclination was 67.9° ± 0.2°. Intensity variations of only 25γ (i.e. .05 percent of the total field strength) were observed over a region of about 50 feet diameter and enclosing the kiln. When the hole for the kiln had been dug, a magnetometer traverse showed a disturbance of about 5γ due to the hole and associated banks. The magnetic field is seen to be quite sufficiently uniform for the present purposes; any nonuniformities appearing during the experiment were caused by the kiln.

Two types of apparatus were used to detect wall movements and are shown diagramatically in fig. 5.1. For method 1, eight square-section Sindanyo rods were fixed vertically into the lip of the kiln at equal intervals all round. The parts of the rods in the clay were keyed to prevent movement independently of the walls. Radial angular displacements of these rods from the vertical were measured using a clinometer. The apparatus for method 2 was more elaborate. Asbestos drainpipes (A) some four feet long, were fitted with centralizing discs (B) through which a ½″ diameter aluminum rod (C) could slide. On each end of the rod a piston was fitted, preventing the rod from being withdrawn from the tube and also providing an area of about a square inch to bear against the outside of the kiln wall, it being felt that a

[2]This disagrees with the Ordnance survey declination of 8.1 ± 0.2 for the Boston region in 1962. The Ordnance survey value is based on an empirical extrapolation formula and the results of a limited magnetic survey of Britain in 1948. It takes no account of local distortions of the field.

smaller area would dig into the wall. This assembly was laid horizontally through the bank surrounding the kiln. In use, the aluminum rods were pressed gently against the kiln wall and the distance (D) between the outer end of the rod and a fixed point (F) measured with a ruler. The fixed points were lengths of 1″ diameter copper pipe driven about 4 feet into the ground and supported by a wooden stake. Nine sets of this apparatus were used, making measurements in three horizontal planes, about 6″, 2′0″, and 3′3″ below the lip of the kiln and at three stations around the kiln, at approximately east, northwest, and southwest azimuths.

At least 1° of wall tilt is necessary to produce a detectable systematic dispersion of thermo-remanent magnetic (TRM) directions. The clinometer used for method 1 had a sensitivity of .1° so movements of the lip of the kiln were detectable with sufficient precision. Method 2 can respond to various movements, for example shrinkage, bulging due to internal forces such as the load, or tilting at a uniform angle over the whole height of the wall. Assuming the latter case, with the axis of tilt at the base of the walls, a 1° tilt would correspond to a movement of about 2 mm at the bottom plane (some 9″ above the floor) and about 10 mm at the top of the walls. Measurements were made to 1 mm accuracy and a careful check was kept on the relative positions of the fixed points (which did not move during the experiment).

Measurements were made by both methods from immediately before the prefiring of the kiln, throughout the pottery firing, and during cooling, until sampling was started. Only the latter results are of direct concern to TRM directions, but it was felt to be of general interest to have a complete history of wall movements and a comparison between the prefiring and pottery firing. The results are tabulated in tables 5.1 and 5.2.

Figure 5.2 shows the relative movements of the lip of the kiln. Zero on this graph is not necessarily vertical, but merely the position of the rods at the beginning of the experiment. The curves have been smoothed so that major trends are shown without confusion by small experimental errors; this smoothing process nowhere involves a difference of more than 0.2° between the indicated and measured values. The most noticeable feature of the graph is the almost uniform outward tilt of about 2° during the main firing. This seems likely to be the result of the outward thrust of the dome. A similar movement was seen at the beginning of the prefiring; but after the dome had collapsed, and prefiring was continued without a dome, the movement was mainly inward. During the final cooling an inward tilt of about ¾° was observed except in the section of wall over the flue (rod 1), which had come loose and continued to fall out.

TABLE 5.1

Movements of the Lip of the Kiln Measured by "Method 1" (positive angles represent outward tilt)

Deviation (degrees) of rods from vertical at various times

		Hours				
	0	16	30	50	70	140
Rod 1	−1.1	−0.4	+0.1	+0.3	+2.3	+2.9
2	−3.3	−3.1	−2.7	−2.8	−1.3	−1.0
3	−3.6	−3.8	−4.2	−4.2	−3.2	−3.5
4	−2.2	−2.1	−3.2	−3.0	−1.8	−2.2
5	−3.6	−3.6	−4.1	−3.7	−3.2	−3.7
6	−7.5	−7.1	−6.6	−6.3	−5.8	−6.1
7	−4.3	−4.7	−5.2	−5.0	−3.9	−4.7
8	−3.7	−3.4	−3.7	−3.7	−2.4	−2.7

Changes in deviation (degrees) of rods from vertical over various periods

			Hours		
	0−16	16−30	30−50	50−70	70−140
Rod 1	+0.7	+0.5	+0.2	+2.0	+0.6
2	+0.2	+0.4	−0.1	+1.5	+0.3
3	−0.2	−0.4	0	+1.0	−0.3
4	+0.1	−1.1	+0.2	+1.2	−0.4
5	0	−0.5	+0.4	+0.5	−0.5
6	+0.4	+0.5	+0.3	+0.5	−0.3
7	−0.4	−0.5	+0.2	+1.1	−0.8
8	+0.3	−0.3	0	+1.3	−0.3
Mean	+0.13	−0.17	+0.15	+1.15	−0.21

The results from the horizontal rods (Method 2) are summarized in fig. 5.3, where sets of wall profiles, deduced from the measurements, are drawn. In this diagram the walls are assumed to have been vertical at time zero. This assumption is not necessarily true but would not invalidate the diagram for showing relative movements even if it were untrue. The vertical scale is about $\frac{1}{40}$th of the horizontal scale, thus emphasizing the distortion of the walls. It appears that the walls have bent at about the pottery floor level. The bulging is outward at the northwest and the southwest stations, and inward at the east station, suggesting a slight movement toward the flue. Most of the distortion at the front of the kiln (N.W. and S.W. stations) occurred when the kiln was hot, though the sudden changes at 66 hours in the "N.W. bottom" and the "S.W. middle" positions may be caused by pieces of earth falling into the way of the rods. During cooling the walls recovered toward their original position. By assuming that bending has been entirely about the middle plane a rough assessment of the tilting occurring during this period may be made and the expected deviations of TRM directions calculated.

Table 5.3 tabulates the movements during cooling and makes a generous estimate of the dispersion of TRM directions which might be caused by this movement.

When the kiln temperature was down to about 30°C (86°F)—after cooling for three days—orientated samples were taken for the measurement of TRM directions. Forty samples were taken from three levels around the walls, and from the floor of the furnace chamber. Figure 5.4 shows the positions from which samples were taken. Sampling closer than 9″ from the nickel alloy thermocouples was avoided so that their magnetic effect on the sampled material was negligible. (At 9″ distance a specimen thermocouple deflected a

TABLE 5.2

Wall Movements Measured by "Method 2"

Changes in the Distance (D) between the outer end of the aluminum rod and the fixed point. Distances measured in millimeters. (Positive distances represent outward movement.)

Time (hours)	Position								
	NW top	NW middle	NW bottom	SW top	SW middle	SW bottom	E top	E middle	E bottom
0 (Datum)	0	0	0	0	0	0	0	0	0
3	0	+1	0	0	−1	−1	+1	+1	+1
5	0	0	0	0	0	0	0	+1	+1
7¼	0	0	0	0	0	0	0	+1	+1
8¼	0	0	0	0	0	−1	0	+1	+1
9½	0	0	0	−1	0	−1	0	+1	+1
11	0	+1	0	0	0	−1	+1	+1	+1
12	0	+1	0	0	0	−1	+1	+1	+1
13	0	+2	0	0	0	0	+1	+2	+2
14	−1	+2	0	−1	+1	−1	+1	+2	+2
16½	−2	+2	+1	−3	+1	0	0	+2	+2
18¾	−2	+2	+1	−2	+1	0	+1	+2	+2
20	−1	+3	+1	−1	+1	0	+2	+3	+2
21¼	−2	+3	0	−2	+1	0	+2	+4	+3
22¾	−1	+3	0	−1	+1	0			
25	−5	+3	0	−3	0	0	+2	+3	+4
27¼	−6	−1	0	−5	−4	0	+1	+3	+3
30¾	−8	−3	−1	−6	0	+1	0	−4	+1
41½	−9	−2	−1	−5	−3	+1	−1	−7	−1
44¾	−9	−3	−1	−5	−3	−5	−1	−8	−2
49½	−8	−2	−2	−5	−2	−4	−1	−8	−2
52½	−8	−2	−5	−5	−4	−3	−1	−8	−1
54½	−8	−2	−3	−5	−3	−4	−1	−8	−2
56½	−8	−1	−1	−4	−4	−4	−1	−8	−1

TABLE 5.2 continued

Time (hours)	Position NW top	NW middle	NW bottom	SW top	SW middle	SW bottom	E top	E middle	E bottom
59¼	−7	0	0	−3	−3	+1	0	−7	−1
61¼	−5	+1	+1	−1	−3	−1	+1	−6	−1
62¾	−5	+4	+12	0	−1	+4	+2	−5	−1
66¼	−4	+7	+14	+2	+16	+4	+4	−1	+1
67¾	−4	+10	+2	+3	+11	+1	+5	−1	+1
69¼	−3	+7	−1	+3	+9	+2	+5	−1	+1
72	−3	+7	−2	+3	+5	+3	+4	−2	+1
74	−4	+6	−1	+3	+5	+3	+4	−3	+1
77	−5	+5	−3	+2	+4	+2	+3	−3	0
79½	−5	+5	−3	+2	+3	+3	+3	−4	0
82	−5	+4	−3	+2	+1	+2	+2	−4	−1
84¼	−6	+3	−3	+2	+1	+3	+2	−4	−1
86¼	−6	+3	−3	+2	0	+2	+2	−5	−1
88¼	−6	+4	−3	+1	0	+3	+2	−5	−1
90	−6	+4	−3	+1	−1	+3	+1	−5	0
93	−5	+4	−3	+1	−1	+4	+1	−5	0
96½	−6	+3	−2	+2	0	+4	0	−4	−3
99	−7	+3	−2	+1	0	+5	+1	−5	−3
101	−6	+2	−1	0	+1	+5	0	−5	−3
102½	−8	+2	−1	0	0	+4	0	−5	−2
116½	−10	+2	0	−2	+2	+3	−1	−5	−2
121½	−9	+1	0	−2	+2	+3	−2	−4	−1
126	−10	+1	0	−2	0	+3	−2	−4	−1
141	−10	0	0	−2	−1	+2	−3	−7	−2
144	−10	0	0	−2	−2	+3	−3	−6	−2
193			+1			+2			−1

compass by ¼°.) The Curie points of Chromel and Alumel used for the thermocouples are about 120°C (248°F) and 350°C (662°F) respectively.

The quality of the material was generally much better than that of the 1961 kiln, mainly owing to the absence of any organic matter intentionally mixed into the clay. The furnace-chamber floor was badly cracked, perhaps because of the close proximity of the water table. The floor samples did not prove very reliable, partly because of this.

LABORATORY EXPERIMENTS

The directions of the TRM were measured on the spinning magnetometer after four weeks' storage aligned with the earth's magnetic field in the same

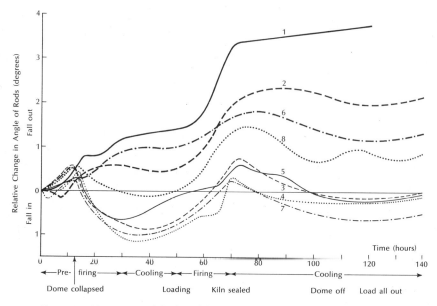

Figure 5.2 Movements of the lip of the kiln.

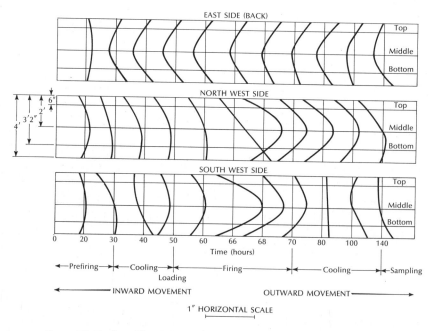

Figure 5.3 Wall profiles deduced from "Method 2."

TABLE 5.3

| | Wall Tilt During Cooling | | Maximum Dispersive Effect | |
| | At Lip, by | From Wall | | |
Position	Vertical Rods	Profiles	Declination	Inclination
N	0.7° in	—	0°	−0.7°
NE	0.5° in	—	1.0°E	−0.3°
E top	0.6° in	0.4° in	1.2°E	0°
E bottom	—	0.7° in	1.7°E	0°
SE	0.4° in	—	1.8°E	+0.3°
S	0.7° in	—	0°	+0.7°
SW top	0.2° in	0.8° in	1.2°E	−0.6°
SW bottom	—	1.5° in	2°W	+1.0°
W	1° out	—	2°E	0°
NW top	0.6° in	0.5° in	1°E-1°W	±0.4°
NW bottom	—	1.2° in	2°W	−0.8°

way as when in the kiln. (This allows the viscous magnetism acquired during transport to be reorientated in its original direction.) A measuring procedure which allows a direct determination of the size of the viscous component was used. The viscous magnetism changes its intensity according to the law $\delta V = k \log t/t_0$ where t_0 is an arbitrary time at which δV is taken to be zero and k is a constant for the material. The viscosity of the samples is indicated by the coefficient k expressed as the percentage change of the total magnetic moment of the sample per logarithmic cycle of time. Over a long period of time the viscous magnetism can produce a shift of several degrees in the direction of the magnetic moment though in this case no such opportunity for a large shift has arisen unless the effects of transporting the samples in a steel vehicle have been drastically underestimated.

The declinations, inclinations, total magnetic intensity, and viscosity of the samples are tabulated in table 5.4. The mean directions and the Fisher index at the 95 percent confidence level for the separate layers and for all the samples together are to be found in table 5.5. The known field direction lies within the confidence limits for all groups.

The declinations and inclinations for layers A, B and C are plotted against the azimuthal positions of the samples in the kiln (fig. 5.5). There is no obvious correlation of these curves with the predicted dispersions of table 5.3, or with the sinusoidal variation characteristic of the "wall fallout effect," except to a small extent for layer B samples.

To establish any such sinusoidal correlation quantitatively, a correction was applied to each sample depending on its azimuth, the size of the correction being varied to simulate gradually increasing amounts of wall fallout. Fisher indices were calculated for the corrected results (table 5.6).

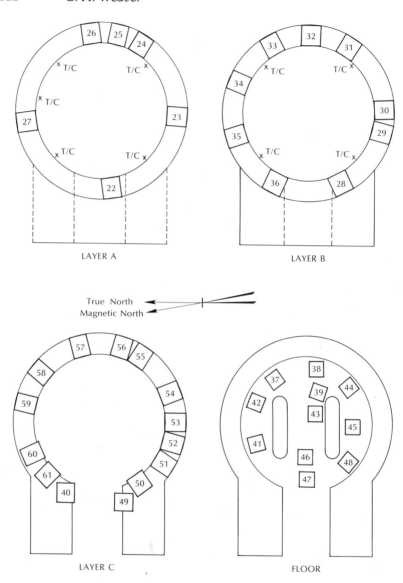

Figure 5.4 Distribution of the samples in the kiln. Layer A: 9 in. below lip of kiln; B: 3 in. above pottery floor; C: Base of walls. Floor: floor of furnace chamber.

TABLE 5.4
Direction of TRM

	Sample	Declination (D)	Inclination (I)	Intensity (e.m.u.)	k%
Layer A	22	2.9°E	65.3°	2.48	0.4
9″ below lip	23	10.2°W	68.3°	1.83	0.5
of kiln	24	6.1°W	67.5°	2.45	0.9
	25	9.3°W	64.6°	3.39	0.5
	26	14.4°W	67.5°	4.35	0.2
	27	11.2°W	69.9°	5.41	0.5
Layer B	28	11.7°W	67.4°	2.46	0.9
3″ above	29	9.2°W	68.8°	1.26	0.6
pottery	30	8.9°W	66.4°	1.20	0.5
floor	31	14.1°W	66.6°	2.11	0.5
	32	14.9°W	67.2°	0.94	0.7
	33	21.1°W	69.0°	1.06	0.5
	34	13.2°W	69.3°	1.36	0.7
	35	5.4°W	69.0°	0.27	0.8
	36	3.7°W	69.1°	1.79	0.7
Floor of	37	8.8°W	67.6°	0.072	2.4
furnace	38	12.8°W	63.2°	0.66	0.8
chamber	39	8.1°W	65.2°	0.14	1.3
	40	1.6°E	66.8°	1.20	0.6
	41	7.6°W	65.4°	0.046	—
	42	24.2°W	62.3°	0.017	—
	43	6.6°W	69.7°	0.35	0.9
	44	9.9°W	66.7°	0.21	1.0
	45	14.3°W	66.7°	0.13	0.3
	46	8.3°W	64.9°	0.50	0.9
	47	7.7°W	62.9°	0.46	0.9
	48	31.9°W	63.8°	0.24	1.1
Layer C	49	3.1°W	67.2°	1.96	0.4
Base of	50	4.2°W	63.9°	1.91	0.6
walls	51	16.9°W	67.8°	0.72	0.1
	52	8.5°W	64.5°	0.94	0.5
	53	8.2°W	65.7°	0.60	0.1
	54	4.4°W	69.6°	0.50	0.1
	55	7.2°W	69.2°	0.61	0.1
	56	6.1°W	66.2°	0.30	0.9
	57	3.0°W	67.2°	1.94	0.8
	58	17.0°W	67.3°	0.94	0.8
	59	13.1°W	69.5°	0.34	0.6
	60	11.1°W	77.1°	0.65	1.3
	61	0.2°W	73.9°	0.73	1.0

TABLE 5.5

Layer	Number of Samples	95% Fisher Index	Mean Declination	Mean Inclination
A	6	2.54°	7.9°W	67.3°
B	9	1.44°	11.4°W	68.2°
C	14	2.02°	7.2°W	68.4°
Floor	11	2.32°	13.0°W	65.5°
All Samples	40	1.07°	9.9°W	67.4°

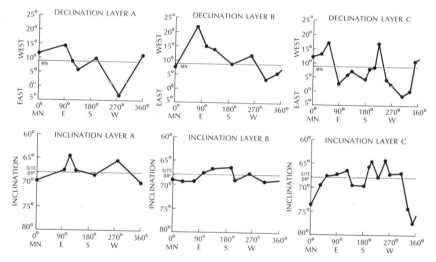

Figure 5.5 Variation of magnetic vectors with azimuth.

TABLE 5.6
Correction Amplitude (degrees of "wall fallout")

	0	2	4	6	8
Layer A	2.54°	2.22°	2.14°	2.33°	2.73°
Layer B	1.44°	1.13°	1.07°	1.31°	1.73°
Layer C	2.02°	1.84°	1.75°	1.78°	1.90°

TABLE 5.7
Directions of TRM After Thermal Washing

	After Washing to 100°C				After Washing to 250°C			
Sample	Declination (D)	Inclination (I)	Intensity e.m.u.	Change in Intensity (%)	Declination (D)	Inclination (I)	Intensity e.m.u.	Change in Intensity (%)
Layer B								
28	11.3°W	67.3°	2.37	4.3	12.0°W	67.4°	2.19	11.3
29	8.8°W	69.2°	1.21	4.9	9.7°W	69.4°	1.10	13.7
30	8.9°W	66.2°	1.15	4.7	9.8°W	66.5°	1.05	12.6
31	13.0°W	67.2°	2.02	4.7	11.3°W	67.7°	1.90	10.5
32	15.4°W	67.0°	0.89	5.6	13.8°W	67.1°	0.81	13.8
33	21.0°W	69.0°	1.00	5.5	21.7°W	70.2°	0.92	13.1
34	12.6°W	69.4°	1.30	4.9	12.3°W	69.5°	1.18	13.2
35	5.3°W	68.0°	0.26	6.4	3.4°W	69.8°	0.22	19.9
36	2.3°W	67.3°	1.73	3.5	3.2°W	68.8°	1.66	7.6
Layer C								
40	2.3°E	66.3°	1.14	5.0	3.1°E	66.9°	1.02	14.7
49	14.5°W	67.9°	1.86	3.6	12.4°W	67.3°	1.60	18.3
50	3.0°W	64.1°	1.81	5.0	4.5°W	64.0°	1.68	11.8
51	14.7°W	67.7°	0.68	5.7	16.2°W	68.0°	0.60	17.3
52	8.6°W	64.3°	0.88	6.3	9.1°W	63.7°	0.71	24.7
53	6.8°W	65.6°	0.56	6.3	8.4°W	65.9°	0.47	21.5
54	4.7°W	68.6°	0.46	6.3	3.4°W	68.9°	0.40	19.3
55	6.0°W	67.8°	0.56	7.8	7.1°W	68.6°	0.48	20.3
56	5.3°W	66.3°	0.27	8.8	3.2°W	65.3°	0.22	26.2
57	4.1°W	67.1°	1.84	5.3	2.4°W	67.3°	1.74	10.2
58	16.8°W	67.3°	0.88	6.4	17.5°W	67.7°	0.75	19.9
59	13.5°W	68.8°	0.31	8.7	15.4°W	69.0°	0.27	21.9
60	8.2°W	77.2°	0.61	6.9	14.6°W	79.4°	0.51	22.1
61	1.8°E	74.9°	0.68	5.9	4.3°E	72.2°	0.61	16.4

The minimum Fisher indices occur with a correction amplitude of about 4°—i.e., the results are scattered as they would be if 4° fallout occurred all around the kiln. However, the wall movements were nowhere as great as 4°, and there was not even an outward tilt on the whole, so the systematic error demonstrated by the minimum Fisher indices cannot be attributed to this effect.

That the above systematic error is not the only cause of dispersion is clear, not only by inspection of fig. 5.5 but also from the fact that the Fisher index does not fall to zero for any correction amplitude. Among the wall samples values of declination ranging from 3°E to 21°W are found and inclinations spread from 63° to 77°. Wall movements are again unable to account for this

TABLE 5.8
Fisher Indices after Thermal Washing

	Thermal Washing Temperature °C	Correction Amplitude (degrees)				
		0	2	4	6	8
Layer B	100	1.48°	1.28°	1.32°	1.60°	2.02°
	250	1.52°	1.28°	1.28°	1.52°	1.91°
Layer C	100	2.06°	1.89°	1.83°	1.83°	1.96°
	250	2.28°	2.13°	2.05°	2.07°	2.17°

wide, random scattering, nor is an accumulation of experimental errors in sampling and measuring a feasible source. Local distortion of the magnetic field by thermocouple metals is ruled out since layer C is quite as badly scattered as the others and all these samples were over 18″ from the thermocouples. If the dispersion is due to a low-temperature magnetic component it can be removed by "thermal washing," that is by reheating the samples to some chosen temperature and cooling them in zero magnetic field, when the "soft" magnetic grains are left in random directions giving zero net moment. Layer B and layer C samples were subjected to this treatment by heating them first to 100°C (212°F) and subsequently to 250°C (482°F). The new directions and intensities are given in table 5.7.

It will be seen that thermal washing has not affected the dispersions as measured by the Fisher index (see table 5.8), remains at approximately 3° to 5° correction amplitude showing that the systematic error has not changed, and the actual values of the minimum Fisher indices show that thermal washing has certainly not reduced the random dispersion.

Measurements of specific magnetization, magnetic susceptibility, and iron oxide content were made upon specimens for various depths into the kiln wall. The material for measuring specific magnetization made up a single complete wall block; a different wall block was used for iron oxide content and magnetic susceptibility.

Fig. 5.6 shows these quantities plotted against the position of the specimens in the wall. The iron oxide determinations were made spectroscopically and are subject to errors of about ±20%. The high iron content of the region 1″ to 2″ is well outside these limits; there seems no obvious explanation for this inhomogeneity. The susceptibility was measured at 2000 c/s using a simple inductance bridge circuit (Reid 1962). The sharp change in susceptibility at 2″ to 3″ into the walls can only partly be ascribed to the change in iron oxide content, as this varies by less than a factor of two between the back of the wall

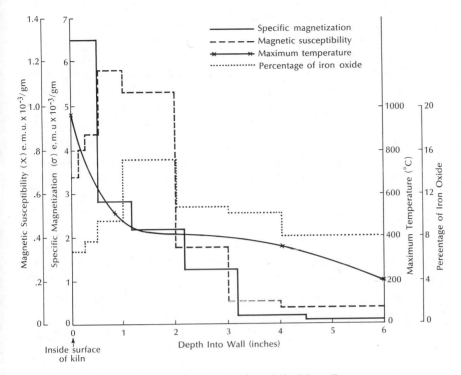

Figure 5.6 Variation of magnetic properties through the kiln wall.

and the maximum iron content region. A much stronger influence is provided by the change in mineralogical state of the iron oxide from hematite to the much more magnetic reduced iron oxide, magnetite. A reducing environment is provided by the organic debris in the clay; in fact, this part of the wall is quite black with carbon, resulting from charring of organic matter. Le Borgne (1960) has shown that the reduction proceeds rapidly above a critical temperature around 350°C (662°F) to 400°C (752°F). Reference to the maximum temperature curve shows that the sharp rise in susceptibility occurs in this temperature range. Reduction of only a small proportion of the iron oxide would account for the observed change in susceptibility. The lower susceptibility closer to the inside surface probably reflects the lower iron oxide content rather than any further mineralogical change. This part of the wall is a reddish color only because the carbon has been burnt out completely.

Owing to the complexity of the magnetic properties of mixtures of iron oxides, and the critical dependence of the specific magnetization on the maximum temperature reached (particularly if this temperature is close to the Curie point), it is not possible to correlate the curves for specific magnetization and susceptibility. The general form of the specific magnetization curve is as expected, with the highest magnetization occurring where the material has been heated to the Curie point. The sharp drop after ½" is consequent on the lower maximum temperature. Beyond 3" the TRM is very slight in spite of the slow change in maximum temperature through this part of the wall. This again demonstrates the mineralogical change occurring at a critical temperature. It seems possible that this strong gradient of magnetic properties across the wall might be the cause of the dispersions of thermo-remanent directions.

CONCLUSIONS

The inferences to be made from this experiment are not conclusive; indeed, measurements on a single kiln could scarcely hope to be so. The known facts are summarized below.

1. During cooling the walls tilted by an amount not exceeding 1½°.

2. Any tilt which occurred was not uniform with azimuth.

3. The TRM results show a systematic error compatible with 4° wall fallout but not explained by any observed wall movements.

4. The TRM results show dispersion which is random with respect to azimuth and strongly predominates over the systematic error.

5. Thermal washing to 250°C (482°F) has shown that the dispersive effects are not limited to the low temperature components of the TRM.

It appears then, at least for this kiln, that wall fallout makes no significant contribution to TRM dispersion. This alone does not rule out the possibility of wall fallout in other kilns, however; indeed this experiment indicates that wall movements are feasible. The more telling observation is that a systematic error *did* occur in spite of the lack of wall fallout.

REFERENCES

Harold, M. R. 1960. *Archaeometry* 3:45.

Le Borgne, E. 1960. *Ann. des Geophysiques* 16:159.

Reid, P. M. 1962. Oxford University Thesis (Chemistry Part II).

» TWO «

Experiments with
Quantitative Methods and Theory

For the archeologist, collecting enough data to work with is rarely the problem. Rather, the reverse is more often true; one is confronted with large numbers of assemblages, potsherds, stone tools, animal bones, or the like. The problem then is to simplify, to organize, and to reduce a mass of raw information into a unified and consistent whole. The approach or method one employs depends both on the nature of the material itself and on the questions one wishes to ask. This fit between a body of data, the techniques used to analyze it, and the kind of answers one hopes to obtain is more complex than first meets the eye. Invariably, in the course of analysis, a number of implicit and explicit assumptions must be made. A first and very basic one involves the completeness of the information itself. The archeologist realizes that the materials he digs out of the ground represent only a portion or sample of the total number present over the span of time the site was occupied. He must work with incomplete data and hope to take this factor into account. The first question he must ask is whether the data are so insufficient that speculation becomes meaningless. The following article by Guilday (chapter 6) deals with just this kind of problem.

A second question must then be asked. What kinds of variables of a cultural, chronological, or geographical nature go into shaping the assemblage or groups of assemblages under consideration. The answer, quite obviously, sets a limit on the kinds of questions which may be asked. It can, however, raise another kind of difficulty as well when more than one variable is involved. Similarities and differences between assemblages, for example, may be caused by any of the three factors mentioned above, acting alone or in various combinations with one another. As the remaining three articles in this part show, assemblages may be compared on an objective basis, but one must still decide how to interpret the results. Are they significant, and if so, just what do they mean? To answer this most basic question, one looks carefully both at the results which emerge and at the techniques or methods used to reach them. Pollnac and Rowlett (chapter 9) concentrate on the former while Deetz and Dethlefsen (chapter 7) and Brainerd (chapter 8) focus their attention on the latter.

In all of these articles, the emphasis is as much or more on the methods themselves as on the results which emerge from their application. In those cases where the data employed can be subject to external control, through historical records or data inscribed on gravestones, the conclusions reached about the value and pitfalls of a particular method carry a greater weight than in those cases in which such control is lacking. And this again illustrates how an "experimental" approach to archeology may yield direct and practical results.

» 6 «

JOHN E. GUILDAY

Animal Remains from Archeological Excavations at Fort Ligonier

A reasonable estimate is often the best that an archeologist can hope for. The calculation of the minimum number of man-days of meat consumed at a site provides just that kind of educated guess made with a grain of salt and a hope that it falls not too far short of the mark. From excavated faunal remains, the minimum number of individuals for each species is determined, and a calculation of the amount of available meat may be made. One then assigns a figure for amount of meat an adult eats per day, divides this into the total available, and arrives at the number of man-days of meat present at the site. There are many reasons why this estimate will invariably be less than the true figure, but just how great the discrepancy may be is, in most archeological circumstances, impossible to ascertain.

The use of controlled data—in this case a fort whose occupation is documented—permits Guilday to put the man-day estimate to the test. He finds that this technique so grossly underestimates the amount of meat consumed that it is highly misleading and thus worse than useless. Guilday notes not only that archeological recovery of bones from butchered animals is poor—this has always been recognized as a problem—but also that much of the meat (salt pork) was butchered, boned, and salted elsewhere and carried to the fort in this prepared form. This observation underlines an often implicit assumption in estimates of this type: that meat was butchered at the site itself, and thus at least in theory the bones are capable of later recovery there.

Reprinted, with minor editorial changes, from Archaeological Investigation of Ligonier, 1960–1965, J. L. Grimm. Appendix by J. E. Guilday, Annals of Carnegie Museum 42 (1970):177–86. Used by permission of the Carnegie Museum. (The publication is in print and available from the Fort Ligonier Memorial Foundation, Ligonier, Pa. 15658, or the Carnegie Museum, Pittsburgh, Pa. 15213.)

Comparison of observed excavation results and historical documentation is not, however, all negative or precautionary in nature. While total amount of meat is impossible to estimate closely, the relative numbers of animals may be more accurately determined.

And finally one may note in Guilday's study that benefits accrue in both directions. He excavates Fort Ligonier, where documentary content is available to sharpen archeological technique; at the same time, however, his excavation serves to round out and fill in the written record which often states what people should do, and not necessarily what actually happened. Because of danger from Indians, hunting was forbidden. While some hunting was known to occur, analysis of faunal remains suggests that this practice was much more prevalent than expected, and that hunters ranged surprisingly far into the hostile countryside.

Fort Ligonier was a British Army relay station between Carlisle and Pittsburgh during the French and Indian War. It was garrisoned between 1758 and 1766 and played a prominent role in the Forbes campaign, which resulted in the founding of Pittsburgh, and in Pontiac's War, during which it was briefly besieged.

HISTORICAL INTRODUCTION

Problems of supply have preoccupied the minds of military field commanders in all wars. The vulnerability of supply lines to guerrilla attack or flanking maneuvers has always dictated caution in the advance. This was particularly true of the Forbes campaign, conducted as it was in unfamiliar mountainous terrain that was densely forested, roadless, removed from river transport, and subject to harassment by the Indian allies of the French for the full 100 miles from Bedford (Rays Town) to Pittsburgh (Fort Duquesne). Overland transport was confined to wagons and pack horses. The greatest detriment to horse transport, especially in forested regions, was the scarcity of forage. Hay was as big an item to a horsedrawn army as gasoline to a modern military force. Writing from Carlisle, Bouquet informs Forbes at the onset of the campaign (June 3, 1758): "I have spoken for all the meadows in this vicinity. . . . Some will be reserved for making hay. The rest is more than enough for the Light Horse, cattle, and all that may go through here."

Forbes, with the campaign underway, instructs Bouquet, now at Rays Town (Carlisle, August 2, 1758): "As you have Scythes and Sickles might not you cause make Hay all arround you & along the new road as they proceed."

Grasslands were one of the major attractions at Loyal Haning (Ligonier) in the eyes of men dependent upon horse supply. (G. Armstrong to Bouquet, Kicknepaulins, July 27, 1758): " . . . Loyalhaning a very pretty place, well waterd, & Grass in Abundance. . . ."

Bouquet complains to Forbes from Rays Town (August 8, 1758): " . . . In six weeks a frost may destroy the grass on which our cattle feed, and if we have no [salt] pork on what shall we live?"

The main food staples of the British Army in this era before the invention of canning and refrigeration were salt pork and flour. Salt pork, the solid meat of the hog barreled in brine, was prepared in the field by a preliminary soaking to remove excess salt. It could, on occasion, get monotonous. The advance detachment cutting road from Rays Town to Loyal Haning lamented (Stephen to Bouquet, Edmund's Swamp, August 12, 1758): " . . . There is not a Dear in this neighbourhood, & the Salt pork, has very near dryd up your Spring, at this Encampment."

Roadwork was fatiguing, and Stephens asks Bouquet for " . . . three or four Cross Cut saws to Seperate the numberless, damnd, petryfyd old Logs hard as Iron, & Breaks our Axes to pieces."

He prefaces this, wistfully we may assume, with " . . . There is nothing would have a greater Effect upon these Rocks, than the Essence of Fat Beef gradually mixt with a Puncheon of Rum, This would add weight to every stroke given them."

The simple expedient of driving cattle, sheep, and hogs with the army and slaughtering them as occasion demanded solved both the problems of transport and of preservation. But the scarcity of forage, the need of a guard of sizable proportions, and the difficulty of procuring suitable animals all added to the problem of livestock accompanying the army. Large movements of livestock, however, did accompany the armies of that era both in the field and in permanent army garrisons. Advance scouting of French-held Fort Duquesne by the British indicated (Bouquet to Forbes, Rays Town, August 20, 1758): ". . . many cattle and many sheep at Fort Duquesne."

It would not have been practical to over-winter livestock in this forested area where hay and forage were scarce and winters were long and hard. Colonel Bouquet suggested a plan that, because of rapid military developments, was never carried out. Bouquet to Forbes, Rays Town Camp, August 18, 1758:

> I thought that one of the easiest and least expensive ways of feeding the army
> in the fall and during the winter would be to send a thousand head of cattle to
> the other side of the mountains next month, besides the usual provisions, and
> to smoke the meat in large chambers constructed for that purpose.

Hunting, although practiced by individual soldiers, furnished no appreciable amount of food. It provided an occasional supplement and, doubtless, sport. Individual messes sent out their own hunters, and were allowed to consume all they could shoot, in such permanent garrisons as Rays Town (Bouquet's Orderly Book, Rays Town, June 29, 1758):

> The Hunters to parade every evening at Retreat Beating before the Virginia
> Regiment, and the Feild officer of the Day is to order what number he thinks
> Proper to hunt next morning, they are to keep all they kill to themselves.

Hides were a different matter (from Bouquet's Orderly Book, July 3, 1758):

> All the Dearskins that are Actually or shall be brought into Camp are to, be
> Delivered to the Artillery Store as soon as they are dried & stretched, as they
> are wanted to make Mockessons for the Men that go on party's—The Soldiers
> who hunt shall receive from Lieut. Lyon 5/. for Large Buckskin, & 4/. for a small
> one or a Doe Skin. . . .

The same order forbade sutlers from buying deerskins. But since the list of delicacies carried by the sutlers accompanying the Forbes expedition included such things as Madeira wine, rum, cordials, sugar, soap, tamarinds, candles, cheese, chocolate, stationery, tobacco, vinegar, mustard, salad oil, smoked beef, coats, blankets, and whiskey, we can surmise that there must have been considerable incentive to hunt at long-established Rays Town.

At the advance post at Loyal Haning hunting was officially forbidden as too dangerous (Bouquet to Burd, August 23, 1758): "Suffer (in the beginning chieffly) no hunters . . . to prevent their being taken. No gun to be fired." Such orders were not always obeyed, however. Bouquet informs Forbes from Loyal Haning on September 11, 1758, of two parties of soldiers who had gone hunting against orders and were attacked by Indians.

All this has implications in archeological interpretation. We might expect to find in the cultural debris at Fort Ligonier bones of both wild and domestic mammals in rather large quantities. Bouquet estimated the average live weight of the cattle at Ligonier at 300 pounds per head, and set the daily ration to include 1 pound of flour and 1 pound of beef (or its equivalent in salt pork). One cow would provide the daily ration for perhaps 100 men; one sheep for perhaps 20. Mercer to Bouquet at Loyal Haning, September 14, 1758 records:

> *14 waggons with Pork & 80 Packhorses wt Flour . . . sett off yesterday [for Loyal Haning]. . . . Tomorrow 100 Packhorses . . . will proceed with a further supply—together with 100 Bullocks [c. 10,000 lbs. dressed] & 200 Sheep [c. 4,000 lbs. dressed].*

Halkett to Bouquet (December 29, 1758) mentions 50,000 pounds (live weight) of hogs "on the road" from Winchester. Clark to St. Clair (December 15, 1758): " . . . They are to be drove to and slaughter'd at such places as the General or Commanding officer directs."

Live cattle, sheep, and hogs driven with the army and slaughtered at intervals were of major importance in provisioning such posts as Fort Ligonier. Accordingly, bones of these three species formed the largest percentage of the excavated bone refuse. Local hunting (orders notwithstanding) would appear to have been commonly practiced at the fort. The minimum number of deer recovered from the excavations was 16, as against only 6 for hog. A variety of wild birds and mammals (see table 6.1) also went into the military stewpot.

ANIMAL REMAINS

Archeological excavations produced 40,537 bones or fragments of bones. Preservation of the bone material recovered from the hilltop site of the Fort itself was generally good. Bone from the stream-bed excavation, although less fragmentary, was not so well preserved. Stream-bed bones were eroded and fragile, dark brown in color and often many were covered with a bright-blue, powdery (upon drying) patina of vivianite [ferrous phosphate anhydrate: $Fe_3(PO_4)_2 8H_2O$].

Bone was recovered from the following areas of the site. Stream bed (site of present administration building); a refuse area near the South Bastion; two ash pits in the powder magazine; the remaining bone in the powder magazine; a fire pit near the North Bastion; the area near the Bedford Gate; the area near the Spring Gate. All remaining bone was recovered from miscellaneous locations.

Cattle (*Bos taurus*)

Over one-half of the identified bones and most of the 37,000 unidentified bone fragments were cattle remains.

TABLE 6.1

Faunal List, Refuse Bone, Fort Ligonier

Total sample: 40,569
Identified: 4,783
Unidentified: 35,786 (all large mammal, probably cattle)

Species Mammalia	Mammals	Fragments 4497	Individuals 108	Stations 1	2	3	4	5	6	7	8
Bos taurus	cow	2730	24	560	1065	14	240	80	124	43	553
Ovis aries	sheep	1040	28	38	510	14	71	31	41	12	281
Sus scrofa	swine	202	6	15	64	1	32	5	19	10	51
Equus caballus	horse	75+	1	74+	—	—	1	—	—	—	—
Odocoileus virginianus	deer	150	16	45	24	—	25	24	10	—	47
Ursus americanus	bear	78	2	8	30	—	10	—	4	—	19
Procyon lotor	raccoon	10	3	—	8	—	—	—	—	—	2
Urocyon cinereoargenteus	gray fox	2	1	—	1	—	—	—	—	—	—
Lynx rufus	bobcat	3	1	—	2	—	—	—	—	—	1
Felis domesticus	house cat	1	1	—	—	—	—	—	—	—	1
Castor canadensis	beaver	3	2	—	3	—	—	—	—	—	—
Marmota monax	woodchuck	2	1	—	—	—	2	—	—	—	—
Sciurus carolinensis	gray squirrel	33	5	1	5	6	—	5	15	1	—
Sylvilagus, species?	rabbit	3	1	—	2	—	1	—	—	—	—
Rattus norvegicus	Norway rat	skeleton	1	—	—	—	1	—	—	—	—

		Total	MNI						
Aves	*Birds*	157							
Meleagris gallopavo	turkey	72	12	4	36	3	2	4	23
Gallus domesticus	chicken	27	3	—	8	3	—	—	15
Ectopistes migratorius	passenger pigeon	6	3	—	—	—	—	—	—
Anas, species?	mallard or black duck	1	2	—	—	—	—	—	—
Anas, species?	domestic duck	1	1	—	19	4	4	7	21
	Unidentified ducks	4	?						
Bonasa umbellus	ruffed grouse	1	1						
Corvus	crow	1	1						
	Unidentified bird	44							
Reptila	*Reptiles*	24	4						1
Terrapene carolina	box turtle	2	1	—	1	—	—	—	—
Chelydra serpentina	snapping turtle	4	1	—	4	—	—	—	—
Crotalus horridus	rattlesnake	15	1	—	15	—	—	—	—
Natrix, species?	water snake	17	1	—	17	—	—	—	—
Ancistrodon mokosen	copperhead	3	1	—	—	—	—	—	—
Pisces	*Fish*	105	2		5				
Aplodinotus grunniens	drumfish	5	1	—	5	—	—	—	—
Catostomidae	sucker	100	1	—	100	—	—	—	—

At least three of the animals were about 2½ years of age (lower fourth premolar just erupting) but the rest were fully adult, many senile with molars worn flat. They were not, even by the standards of the time, considered good beef cattle.

Bouquet to Forbes, Rays Town, August 25, 1758:

> We have 600 cattle here. . . . We received 300 yesterday from Virginia, small, lean and as poor as they could be. I have forbidden Hoops to take a single one more from that province, and to buy what he will need for salting in Pennsylvania where there are some in abundance all the time.

Bouquet to Sinclair, Loyal Haning, September 9, 1758: "Some of the Bullocks have weighed 170 w and in the General Computation Mr. Clarke Supposes them 300 w one with another. . . ."

Twenty horn cores were recovered during the excavation, the majority from the stream bed. The largest estimated horn was 15 inches in length and 10 inches in basal circumference. The smallest was 6 inches in length by 6 inches in basal circumference. The horn sheaths would add several more inches to their length. Most of the cores had been sawed or hacked from the head and presumably discarded.

As much of the animal was consumed as possible. In setting the ration Colonel Bouquet stated that the head of a bullock would be considered the equivalent of five pounds of meat, the heart two pounds. Limb bones were broken up, probably for marrow. Lower jaws always had the front teeth removed by chopping through the diastema, and had the ascending rami removed. Carcasses were treated much as they are today, i.e., split in half with axe or saw. Twenty-six animals were represented by cranial elements, 24 by limb elements.

Sheep (Ovis aries)

Hugh Mercer to Bouquet at Loyal Haning, Rays Town, September 14, 1758: ". . .Tomorrow 100 Packhorses . . . will proceed with a further supply—[of salt pork and flour] together with 100 Bullocks & 200 Sheep."

Most of the sheep remains were from adult animals. Some were extremely old with molar teeth practically worn out. One lamb of unknown age was represented by a single astragalus.

Axe marks were common on sheep bones and there is little doubt that they were slaughtered by the British army garrison.

Pig *(Sus scrofa)*

Clark to St. Clair, Carlisle, December 15, 1758:

> *Mr. Rutherford from Virginia has engaged to send a Number of hoggs to the amt. of 50.000 lb to Rays Town & ca. the one half is now ready to be sent, the other will soon follow. They are to be drove to and slaughter'd at such places as the General or Commanding officer directs.*

Note that the first mention of live pigs postdates the fall of Fort Duquesne. Pigs were apparently of secondary importance as a source of fresh meat. Salt pork, the mainstay of the army, was a different matter, but left no archeologically recoverable trace. A minimum of six animals were recovered. Based upon toothwear, three were 9–12 months of age, the other three much older.

Cattle, sheep, and pig bones were found at all eight stations of the excavation, the only three species of which this was true.

Parmalee (1960) in his discussion of the contemporary British Fort Loudon on the Tennessee River (1754–60) points out the almost complete dependence of that garrison upon cattle, pigs, and chickens in hostile Cherokee territory.

Virginia Deer *(Odocoileus virginianus)*

Though officially frowned upon during at least some periods of the occupation, hunting was carried on at the fort. Deer was the third most common animal in the bone refuse, and the presence of bear, raccoon, beaver, bobcat, and turkey—all local game species—strengthens the hunting assumption.

Note in table 6.2 that portions of the carcass—head, forequarters, hindquarters (as represented by mandibles, humeri, and astragali)—are in essential balance in the case of cow and sheep, but that hindquarter elements of the deer are over twice as common as forequarter elements or skull parts. This strongly suggests that, in many cases at least, deer were killed and dressed at some distance from the fort and only the hindquarters were brought in. There appears to have been no contemporary mention of venison in the military commissary stores or of local trade with the Indians. Quite the contrary, the Ligonier garrison is known to have suffered casualties from the Indians during hunting forays (Bouquet to Forbes, Loyal Haning, September 11, 1758).

Remains of one fawn, and antlers of at least seven bucks, were recovered. Antlers were crudely chopped from skulls in most cases.

TABLE 6.2
Minimum Number of Animals Based upon Skeletal
Elements Recovered in Cultural Debris, Fort Ligonier

Species	Skull	Forequarter	Hindquarter
Cow	26	25	21
Sheep	28	13	22
Pig	6	—	—
Deer	6	7	16

Norway Rat (*Rattus norvegicus*)

This skeleton was found in the powder magazine excavation (Station No. 4) and undoubtedly postdates the military occupation. A stable occupied that area in the late 1800s (J. Grimm, letter). The rat probably died in its burrow.

The specific identification, based upon dental pattern, is important in this case. The closely related black rat (*Rattus rattus*) had been present in the Western Hemisphere since early colonial times and plagued the army in 1758. " . . . the Rats are very prejudicial to us here also, yet not so bad as at Fort Loudon [Tennessee]." (Armstrong to Bouquet, Carlisle, June 17, 1758.) The Norway Rat, a more aggressive animal, introduced into the New World during the American Revolution, has displaced the black rat over much of Pennsylvania.

Horse (*Equus caballus*)

The approximately 74 horse bones recovered from Station 1 were part of one skeleton. The animal was a lightly built, medium-sized, light draft or riding animal. Its height at the shoulder (estimated from metacarpal length of 225 mm) was 14 hands. Its age, based upon toothwear, was in excess of 2 years. Unlike the associated cattle the animal had not been butchered.

Remains of a second animal are suggested by one terminal phalanx from Station 4.

Birds

Birds appear to have been quite incidental. Domestic chickens and ducks were present in small numbers. The turkey, grouse, wild duck, and passenger pigeon were undoubtedly shot as food.

Reptiles and Fish

The turtles and snakes may have been brought in as curiosities—a "Hey-you-guys, look-what-I-found" type of thing.

The drumfish, undoubtedly from Loyalhanna Creek, may have been eaten, but the one sucker was no more than 6″–8″ in length, little larger than a minnow.

Meighan et al. (1958) states,

> Attempts have been made (Cook 1946:6) to correlate midden deposit, population density, and food consumption from information derived from quantitative analysis. Although speculative in part, results so far obtained indicate that with further refinement this technique may prove of considerable value.

Fort Ligonier was garrisoned continuously from September 3, 1758, until the spring of 1766—approximately 2364 days. The size of the garrison varied from as many as 4000 men for a brief time during the Forbes campaign to a minimum of eight. In January of 1759 only 86 men were on duty, though a great many were in the hospital. In February of that year there was a garrison of 242; in March, 180; and in May, 379. About 55 men over-wintered in 1764 and from then until 1766 the garrison numbered 18 to 20 soldiers.

Placing estimates of usable meat at 100 pounds per cow, 20 pounds per sheep, 75 pounds per deer, and 100 pounds per bear, the amount of meat represented by the minimum number of animals recovered archeologically is about 4000 pounds. At standard field ration of one pound of meat per man per day, 4000 pounds would have sustained only two men for the length of time of the known occupancy, or the entire garrison at full strength for just one day!

Calculations such as these are patently ridiculous. The major portion of the meat ration (salt pork) left no archeological trace, troops were not on full rations at all times, the sample recovered is but a portion of the full archeological sample at the site, and the facilities for garbage disposal in the creek, where it would be lost to the archeologist, were excellent. Any attempt to assess length or intensity of occupation from this sample alone would have been futile. Such estimates based upon food remains recovered archeologically from Indian village sites have been attempted in the past. A certain minimum figure can be arrived at, but no matter how ingenious the calculations, the results may be as ridiculously wide of the mark as were the estimates of the Fort Ligonier occupation based upon food remains alone.

Qualitatively, however, a fair idea of the relative importance of the various meat animals in the military diet and the relative importance of hunting can be derived from the collection.

ACKNOWLEDGMENT

I wish to thank Jacob L. Grimm, Curator, Fort Ligonier Memorial Foundation, for allowing me to study the collection of items found during archeological excavations that preceded restoration of the Fort. Research was conducted under a grant from the Fort Ligonier Memorial Foundation.

REFERENCES

Cook, S. F. 1946. A reconsideration of shellmounds with respect to population and nutrition. *American Antiquity* 12(1):50-53.

Meighan, C. W., D. M. Pendergast, B. K. Swartz, Jr., and M. D. Wissler. 1958. Ecological interpretation in archeology: Part I. *American Antiquity* 24(1):1–23.

Parmalee, Paul W. 1960. Vertebrate remains from Fort Loudoun, Tennessee. *Tennessee Archaeological Society* Misc. Paper No. 6:26-29.

Stevens, S. K., D. H. Kent, and A. L. Leonard. 1951. The papers of Henry Bouquet, Part II: The Forbes expedition. Harrisburg: Pennsylvania Hist. and Mus. Committee.

7

JAMES DEETZ • EDWIN DETHLEFSEN

The Doppler Effect and Archeology: A Consideration of the Spatial Aspects of Seriation

The most reliable way to determine the relative ages of assemblages is to discover them in a sealed stratigraphic context, one above the other. Often, however, survey and excavation will yield a series of individual sites which can be set in chronological order neither by stratigraphic nor by absolute methods of dating. The technique of "seriation" was devised for problems of just this type, and over the last 25 years has been put to widespread use in both the New and Old Worlds. If one accepts at the outset several general principles about change in material culture, the technique can be developed, as it in fact was, in a logical and deductive manner. The basic assumption one must make is that stylistic changes—the preference for one pottery type or gravestone decoration over another—occur in a gradual and relatively constant manner within a given region. If this is the case, then those assemblages most similar to each other will also be separated by the smallest time differential. It then remains only to find some way to measure similarity, and Deetz and Dethlefsen employ a standard graphic or "Fordian" method to make the necessary comparisons.

Invariably, models of this kind simplify reality because all the variables that may affect patterning between assemblages cannot be taken into account. For this reason, bias in some varying degree is inevitable. Deetz and Dethlefsen ask the following question: If we suppose that two additional factors— which in the past were ignored—must be considered, how seriously can this

Reprinted, with minor editorial changes, from *Southwestern Journal of Archaeology* 21 (3):196– 206. Used by permission of the editors.

affect results which emerge from a standard seriation? The way they set about answering this question is noteworthy. They first construct a theoretical model which predicts what the expected effects should be. Next, they put these predictions to the test through use of controlled or experimental data — in this case gravestones —where "assemblages" may be conveniently dated by the information chiseled on their faces. In the end, they prove nothing, but the data they present tend to support their model rather than refute it. What is equally important, however, is the demonstration that the standard "Fordian" seriation method does give reasonable results and that confusion which derives from what the authors term the "Doppler effect" is not great enough to invalidate the method itself.

In their well-reasoned and lucid description of seriation methods employed in the lower Mississippi Valley, Phillips, Ford, and Griffin (1951:219–23) state the basic assumptions which form the foundation for their analytical procedure. These assumptions can be briefly summarized as follows:

1. Population was stable in the survey area.
2. The majority of sites were occupied only for a short time.
3. Cultural change in the area in question was gradual, and migration had not occurred.
4. Pottery types used in seriation would show a single peak popularity curve when measured through time.
5. Pottery type frequency curves would differ somewhat in each part of the area at any point in time.

Our purpose is to make explicit two additional assumptions and to suggest that their inclusion with the above might lend some small measure of sophistication to the seriation method. The suggestions offered here should not be taken as an adverse critique of seriation methods in general; we subscribe to the validity of this approach to chronological ordering. Our intent is to attempt a modest degree of methodological refinement.

The first of our additional assumptions is that any type used in seriation originated at a single locus and subsequently spread outward from that point. An artifact type used in seriation must occur at two or more sites, in order to have utility. This multiple occurrence can either be interpreted as evidence of the movement of the mental template which was responsible for its production—either through migration or through less dramatic, secondary diffusion processes—or as evidence of the independent formulation of this template at each site. The latter is extremely unlikely, and Phillips, Ford, and Griffin

(1951:229), aware of the role of diffusion in cultural process, select the former alternative as the only reasonable interpretation:

> *The groups of ideas to whose products have been tagged such names as Mazique Incised did not spring up simultaneously all over the area. They moved from one part to another, and that took time. For example, the idea of red slipping on clay-tempered vessels (Larto Red Filmed) apparently was moving from south to north through the region, while cord-marking on clay tempered pots (Mulberry Creek Cord-Marked) was moving from northeast to south. Naturally, the former is earlier to the south, and the latter to the north.*

The second assumption, anticipated in the above quotation, is that sites further removed from the locus of origin of any type will show the occurrence of that type, at a given frequency, later in time. A corollary to this proposition is that a type might still be present at some distance from its point of inception after it had disappeared from that point.

These two assumptions can be made more explicit through the use of a model in which rate of change and dimensions of spatial and temporal units are held constant (fig. 7.1). The model demonstrates the spread of a single type outward in two directions from a center, indicated as locus M on the horizontal space axis. Loci $N-P$ and $N'-P'$ are progressively more distant from locus M, and distance between all adjacent loci on the space axis are equal. The vertical axis of the model represents time, with each number unit, 1 through 10, representing a time segment of equal duration. As in all conventional seriation charts, the earliest time level is at the bottom.

The occurrence of the type through time is indicated by percentage bars at each locus, with a constant rate of change of 25 percent for each time unit indicated by the width of the bar. Thus, at each locus, identical patterns of increase and decrease of the type occur. However, since the type originates at M, and spreads from M to P in one direction, and to P' in the other, its appearance at a given frequency is later at each locus further removed from the center. For example, at M the frequency is 50 percent during time period 2 and reaches the same percentage at the next locus in each direction in time period 3, for it is diffusing one pace unit in each unit of time. Since the type originates at locus M, spreads to lock $N-P$ and $N'-P'$ moving one space unit per time unit, and goes through an identical increase and decrease of popularity at each locus, its maximum occurrence is later in direct proportion to its distance from the locus of origin. Thus, during time unit 8, although it has already disappeared at locus M, the type is still relatively popular at loci P and P', and progressively less popular at loci closer to M. This graphic

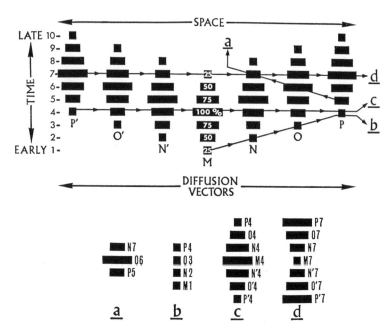

Figure 7.1 Model illustrating the spread of a single type from a point (M) outward in two directions.

presentation of the spread of a type through time and space should serve to make the two additional assumptions clear. While a constant set of circumstances such as this model represents would probably never occur in reality, the variables of space, time, and types of change of frequency are correctly shown as they relate to one another, and a clear presentation of certain phenomena is made possible.

The nonsimultaneity of inception, increase, decrease, and disappearance of any type in a given area permits the construction of a number of different developmental formulations from the same set of data. Depending on whether samples are taken from short-term occupation sites which become successively later in a direction running counter to the direction of diffusion (in the model P to M, P' to M) or from sites which are located such that they become later in an alignment running with the direction of diffusion (M to P, M to P'), quite different apparent rates of change are indicated for the type. In the former case, a rate of change greater than the true rate is indicated (fig. 7.1a); in the latter, a rate of change is obtained which is less than the true rate (fig. 7.1b). This difference between the apparent and true rates and between the types of change of frequency has a close parallel in the Doppler effect, a familiar phenomenon of the physical world. Anyone who has ridden on a train has noticed that the clanging of a station bell rises in pitch as one is approaching the source of the sound and drops sharply in pitch as one moves away from the bell. One perceives this shift in frequency because as one is approaching a fixed source of sound, more waves are encountered per unit of time than are actually being emitted, and an apparent increase in frequency (pitch) results. Conversely, as one moves away from such a source, the perceived number of wave maxima is lower than the true number emitted in any given time interval, and an apparent decrease in frequency results. The variable factor in this case is the observer; his motion combined with the outward dispersal of sound waves is additive as he approaches and subtractive as he departs from the source. The more rapid his motion, the greater the discrepancy between observed and true frequencies.

The model showing the spread of a single type through space, with constant spatial and temporal units, can be used to demonstrate that a Doppler-like process should be considered in seriation procedure. As shown above, if one should sample short-term occupancy sites at loci *M* through *P*, moving away from *M*, and if these sites are progressively later in time as one moves away from *M*, no change in the percentage of occurrence of the type from site to site will be indicated if one space unit is traversed for each time unit (fig. 7.1b). A constant percentage of occurrence results because the archeologist, the observer in this instance, is in effect moving through space at the same rate as the type is diffusing, one space unit per time unit. In this case, although the true rate of change is 25 percent per unit of time, the observed rate is zero. Should the observer slow down, moving only one space unit for every two units of time, the apparent rate is the same as the true rate, since the observer is effectively waiting at each locus for one time unit to pass, bringing the frequency at the new location to the same level as it was in the prior one during the previous time unit.

A sampling of sites which become later in time as one approaches point *M* (*P'* to *M*, *P* to *M*) produces a graph which indicates an apparent rate of change which is twice the true rate if one space unit is traversed in one time unit (fig. 7.1a). Increases of 50 percent per unit of time are indicated, while the true rate remains a constant 25 percent per time unit. In this case the increase results from the motion of the observer toward the source of diffusion. Increasing the rate of motion will make an even higher rate apparent, with two space units traversed in one time unit producing an apparent rate of change three times the true rate, or 75 percent per time unit. The close analogy between this phenomenon and the Doppler effect is obvious; and in a controlled model, such as the one employed here, the Doppler formula can be slightly modified and shown to be applicable. The Doppler formula, as it applies to sound waves from a fixed source, is:

$$f' = \left\{ \frac{v \pm v_0}{v} \right\} f$$

where f' is the frequency heard by the observer, v the velocity of sound in the transmitting medium, v_0 the velocity of the observer, and f the true frequency. In the numerator, the plus sign is used if the observer is approaching the source, the minus sign if he is moving away from the source. The analogous formula, applicable to diffusion as demonstrated by the model, is:

$$r' = \left\{ \frac{d \pm v_0}{d} \right\} r$$

where r' is observed rate of change (percent per unit time), d the diffusion rate (space units per time units), v_0 the observer's rate of motion (space units per time unit), and r the true rate of change (percent per time unit).

By passing through the model in various directions, a number of different formulations of rate and direction of change can be graphed from identical data. The differences are a function of differences in sampling direction in time and space. Crossing the model in the same time unit at a time when the type has reached its maximum occurrence at locus M produces a perfect "battleship-shaped" diagram, even though the spatial units are all in the same time unit (fig. 7.1c). A sampling of contemporary sites at a time when the type has nearly vanished at the center but remains as a popular type at more distant loci results in a wasp-waisted diagram, which if it were to result in the routine course of seriation would be considered as good evidence of improper chronological ordering of the sites in question (fig. 7.1d). The degree to which this effect is manifested is largely a function of the rate of diffusion of a particular style. The slower the rate, the less likely there is to be a pronounced skew resulting from direction of sampling. Furthermore, the cases demonstrated with the model assume a selection of sites in an order which would be somewhat improbable in practice. Nonetheless, there seems to be considerable heuristic value in demonstrating this phenomenon, if for no other reason than to suggest that imperfect alignments, which almost always result in the seriation of a large number of types, might result at least in part from this case. An awareness of this phenomenon might also lead to a more reasonable interpretation of certain evidence.

To move from a neat model, in which all variables are controlled and other quantities held constant, to the real world, where such control is rarely possible, is a constant problem in the application of theoretical constructs. Like most of the current body of archeological method, seriation has been devised and applied using data for which a rigorous measure of control has been impossible. Recent studies in the spread of gravestone design types in eighteenth-century New England have directed attention to a controlled laboratory situation in which to check a number of the basic assumptions of archeological method (Dethlefsen and Deetz MS). These stones and their designs are admirably suited to such a study; they were the products of nonspecialists who resided in small towns and provided stones for the immediate area; they are precisely dated and fixed in space, and their designs are integrally tied to the culture which produced them. The present article stems from an awareness of some of the more detailed aspects of the spread of style which the authors gained through working with gravestone designs in southern New England.

Between 1700 and 1800, colonial gravestones in eastern Massachusetts were decorated in three universally occurring design types: death's heads, cherubs, and urns shaded by willow trees. The death's head design was earliest, and was replaced by the cherub motif during the latter half of the eighteenth century, and was in turn replaced by the urn and willow design at the close of that century. The pattern exhibited by each of these styles as it increased and decreased through time is striking support to one of Phillips, Ford, and Griffin's assumptions—that the rise and decline in the popularity of a style or type will be in the form of a long single-peaked curve (1951:220). Figure 7.2 shows the distribution of the three universal styles and two local designs between 1700 and 1829 in the cemetery at Concord, Mass. The full single-peaked curve is seen to best advantage in the cherub and Roman motifs. The urn and willow design generally declined in popularity after 1829, although not at Concord. The death's head design is the earliest for which an adequately large sample can be obtained for proper quantification, and it is represented in the figure only during the later period of its existence.

In addition to the three design types which are universally distributed throughout the eastern Massachusetts area, a number of local styles exist and,

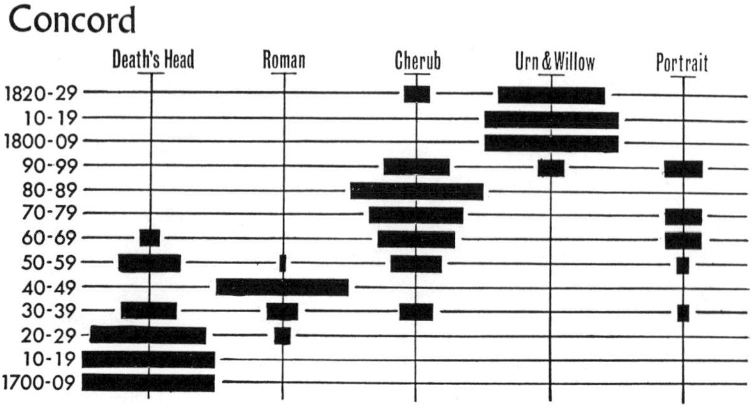

Concord

Figure 7.2 Stylistic change and succession in an eastern Massachusetts cemetery.

like the universal styles, exhibit single-peaked curves as they are plotted for temporal change in relative frequency of occurrence. Because gravestone designs follow the predicted developmental form and can be precisely plotted in time and space, they provide a tightly controlled set of data to demonstrate that the effect shown in the model has a close counterpart in reality.

The style selected for this demonstration is a distinctive local design, the so-called "Roman" motif. This design occurs in the Concord and Sudbury River drainages west of Boston. It occurred first in the third decade of the eighteenth century, and last in the seventh decade. All stones of this type in the Harvard-Groton-Lexington-Sudbury area are known to have been carved by Jonathan Worcester, a stonecutter who resided in Harvard, Massachusetts (Forbes 1927:77). Worcester seems to have copied this design from stonecutters in Essex County, Massachusetts, fifty miles northeast of Harvard. Here, designs very similar to Worcester's occur in a number of cemeteries during the first half of the eighteenth century, including some which date to the first decade, having been cut during the years just after Worcester's birth in 1707. Worcester's rendering of this design is very conservative; there is little variation between his earliest and latest stones. He died in 1754, and apparently left a large number of cut stones to his wife, since they continue to appear until the late 1760s. At least one entry in the probate records shows that stones of this type were being purchased from his widow. One such case was the purchase, by the executor of Josiah Burge of Westford, of an unspecified number of stones from the "widow Worcester" in 1756. Burge's stone, bearing Worcester's unmistakable design, can be seen today in the cemetery at Westford.

To demonstrate the Doppler analogue as it operates in gravestone-design distributions, five cemeteries were investigated and the percentage of the Roman motif calculated for each subsequent ten-year period in each cemetery, beginning in 1720 and ending in 1769. The study cemeteries are located at Harvard, Groton, Concord, Sudbury, and Lexington, Massachusetts. The five graphs for the design in each of the five cemeteries were then arranged in order according to their distance from Worcester's residence in Harvard. By positioning the cemeteries in this fashion, one is constructing a graph which is identical in its basic arrangement to the Doppler model (fig. 7.3a). The style

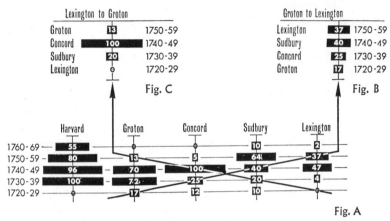

Figure 7.3 Frequency of Roman design, by decades, in study cemeteries.

can then be sampled in succeeding decades, moving first toward Harvard, then away from Harvard, in each case beginning in the 1720s and ending in the 1760s. If the effect observed in the model is manifested in this second construct, then relatively little change in popularity of the Roman style should be observed as one moves away from Harvard while moving through time (fig. 7.3b). By sampling the same set of cemeteries in identical time ranking but moving from Lexington, the most distant, toward the Harvard center, the result should be an apparent rate of change in popularity that exceeds the true rate (fig. 7.3c). Inspection of the graphs derived from this procedure shows such to be the case, with a high degree of agreement with the predicted results.

The cemetery at Harvard could not be utilized in the formulation because it is saturated with Worcester stones for three decades, a weighting of the data which results from Worcester's residence in Harvard. Frequency of the Roman design at Harvard is 80 percent or more during three decades from 1730 until 1759, a much greater popularity than observed in the other study cemeteries. The graphs are constructed, therefore, to have decade samples begin and end at Groton, the nearest of the four other cemeteries to the Harvard center. This produces a four-decade series through four cemeteries. The mean rate of change in these four cemeteries is 39 percent per decade and ranges from 61 percent at Concord to 38 percent at Groton and 29 percent at both Sudbury and Lexington. The mean rate of change along the Harvard to Lexington axis (fig. 7.3b) is 9 percent per decade, while the mean rate along the Lexington to Harvard axis (fig. 7.3c) is 62 percent per decade. Whereas four-decade samples are obtainable while moving with the direction of diffusion, only three decades, showing a rapid increase and decrease, can be graphed while moving against the direction of diffusion (fig. 7.3c). At no cemetery is there only a three-decade span of the Roman type.

It must be emphasized that the entity which is diffusing in this case is a preference for a certain style, since all of the stones were carved at Harvard and sent to more distant points for erection. At the two cemeteries further removed from Harvard, a significant percentage of stones was purchased and erected after this preference had disappeared in the two nearer cemeteries. At the most distant cemetery, Lexington, no Roman stones were erected during the 1720s, a time when they were being utilized in numbers at locations nearer the source of supply. The graph showing frequency of occurrence of the Roman type in the Harvard cemetery is of significance in this connection. Although the two nearer cemeteries have no Roman stones on graves of the 1760s, there was apparently an adequate supply, since they are present at Harvard during this decade in 55 percent of all cases. The pattern here seems to be one of people purchasing stones from Worcester's widow for use at Lexington and Sudbury after their use had ceased at Concord and Groton. Further insight regarding the more rapid disappearance of Roman stones after 1759 in Concord and Groton is provided by the historical record, which shows that in 1756, a new carver, William Park of Groton, had filled the vacancy in the Harvard area created by the death of Jonathan Worcester. Park's stones rapidly became popular and occur in great numbers in Groton, Harvard, and Concord, although they are less prominent in Sudbury and Lexington.

The progressive reduction in rate of change per decade of the Roman style recorded in cemeteries further removed from Harvard might be a manifestation of a more generally distributed effect—that of the damping action on the vigor of a style by distance. The great popularity of the Roman style at Harvard results from Worcester's residence in that town. As one observes its popularity at greater distances, there is an expectable reduction, which probably results from the inclusion of other styles radiating from other centers at these locations. The mean frequency of occurrence of the style between 1720 and 1760 at Harvard is 83 percent, at Groton 43 percent, at Concord 35 percent, at Sudbury 28 percent, and at Lexington 21 percent. Such a diminution in popularity is expectable, and it is accompanied by a reduction in rate of change, from 38 and 61 percent at Groton and Concord respectively, both equal to or greater than the mean rate, to a mean rate of only 29 percent per decade at Lexington and Sudbury, well below the mean for all four localities.

It has been shown that a simple formula can be used to state the relationship between diffusion rate, observer rate, and true and observed rates of change of frequency in the model used to demonstrate the effects of spatial location on seriation ordering. While the application of the model to the distribution of a gravestone style has shown the relationships indicated by the formula to hold in a general way, the inevitable irregularities in the gravestone data which result from sampling problems, differences in distance between cemeteries, and other imponderable factors might make any application of the formula to this corpus of data merely approximate. In spite of these problems, the formula was found to fit with remarkable precision. Computing the difference between true and apparent rates of change with an approaching observer, and solving for quantity r', produced a figure of 72 percent per decade as compared to a known apparent rate of 62 percent.[1] Similar results were obtained when r' was obtained for a receding observer, with an r' of 6.5 percent produced by calculation with the known apparent rate being 9 percent. Both solutions are certainly order-of-magnitude indicators at the very least.

It has been shown that a striking analogy can be drawn between the Doppler effect and certain aspects of the spread of a style or type through space and over time. An awareness of the existence of this factor in seriation ordering might aid in clarifying the relationships between different types at

---

[1] The following quantities were used: d = 6 miles per decade, v_0 = 5 miles per decade (mean distance between cemeteries), r = 39% (mean rate of change in four cemeteries).

different locations, and in explaining discrepancies which might emerge in different seriational arrangements from the same area. This effect might conceivably produce an impression of sudden intrusion of a type when in fact such a disruption did not occur. On the other hand, more gradual change within certain types might not indicate cultural conservatism but merely sampling direction. In both the theoretical model and its application, only one type was considered. Seriation, which proceeds normally using a quantity of types, can still achieve its stated purpose without introducing a spatial axis to formulations, but interpretation of results might be sharpened by taking this effect into consideration. Further refinement along the lines suggested in this paper might also eventually enable the prehistorian intentionally to sample his sites along a line known to represent a diffusion vector, thereby permitting the postulation of site interaction, rates of spread, and the existence of factors which either impede or accelerate the movement of a cultural idea. Factors of this type might include exogamy, endogamy, political boundaries, trade networks, linguistic areas, or any other cultural pattern which is known to affect social interaction. As such, consideration of this as yet unnamed but seemingly important effect in cultural reconstruction has at least potential importance.

ACKNOWLEDGMENTS

This is a revised version of a paper read at the November 1964 annual meeting of the American Anthropological Association, Detroit, Michigan. The authors acknowledge the valuable suggestions of William Mayer-Oakes, who was the first to perceive the analogy between the Doppler effect and the phenomenon of diffusion of gravestone styles.

REFERENCES

Dethlefsen, Edwin, and James Deetz. MS. Death's heads, cherubs and willow trees. *American Antiquity* (in press).

Forbes, Harriet. 1927. *Gravestones of early New England.* Boston: Houghton Mifflin.

Phillips, Phillip, James A. Ford, and James B. Griffin. 1951. *Archaeological survey in the lower Mississippi alluvial valley, 1940–1947.* Papers of the Peabody Museum, Harvard University, vol. 25.

8

GEORGE W. BRAINERD

The Place of Chronological Ordering in Archeological Analysis

Brainerd and the authors of the preceding article share a common concern: To what extent do orderings of units produced through seriation reflect a time variable? While Deetz and Dethlefsen use a visual seriation technique, Brainerd employs a statistical method for determining similarity between each assemblage and every other one; using these measures, units are then ordered within a matrix. To fully understand the mechanics of this approach see Robinson (1951) who collaborated closely with Brainerd in his work.

On a first, and most practical, level Brainerd tries to see how well the Robinson technique stands up, and he approaches the problem from two directions. He checks Robinson's ordering of a body of provided archeological data for internal consistency, by examining types not included in the original analysis to see how neatly they also form a meaningful pattern given Robinson's seriation. He next attempts a controlled experiment by applying the technique to data over which stratigraphic control exists. And to his satisfaction he finds that the "Robinson" and stratigraphic orderings give essentially the same results.

The second question Brainerd poses is more complex. Like Deetz and Dethlefsen he accepts the fact that seriation can provide a unidimensional ordering where units most nearly alike are placed closest together. Like them he realizes that time likely proves a major factor responsible for observed similarities, and like them realizes that more than one factor may cause similarity and difference. How can one tell if two variables—time and status of

Reproduced, with minor editorial changes, by permission of the Society for American Archaeology from *American Antiquity* 16 (4), 1951.

the user, for example—are both responsible? What happens, he asks, if some of the assemblages are, in fact, mixtures of two or more? What happens if the samples are not evenly distributed across the entire time span but are clustered in limited periods and absent in others?

Although the term was not in fashion when Brainerd carried out his work, he conducts, in fact, a simple simulation study. Because controlled data, such as tombstones, are not available, Brainerd constructs his own. He invents imaginary samples in which units are varied or biased just as he wishes them to be. By using a graphic technique, he can determine just what effects different kinds of bias can have, and with this knowledge in hand can return to analysis of actual archeological data to see if the "biased patterns" are reflected therein. And in recent years, archeologists have placed ever-increasing emphasis on simulation models of this type, and have employed them to study quite diverse kinds of problems.

The introductory section of this article is a defense of archeological artifact typology as a primary tool of analysis, and of mathematical and graphic working techniques in the chronologic placing of material. To the archeologists who approve of and constantly use these techniques I apologize for my verbosity but plead that in many reports the method of sequencing is given briefly and sometimes nearly apologetically. To those ethnologists who find in trait lists at best a superficial method of culture study I plead a special purpose for typology in archeological analysis.

TYPOLOGY IN ARCHEOLOGICAL ANALYSIS

During the past few decades there has been a growing and proper demand that archeologists extract from their artifacts more reconstructions of past cultures, more data that will add historical perspective to ethnology. Steward and Setzler (1938) presented an example of a well-reasoned plea for broader archeological interpretation. In sympathy with this demand there has been a laudable tendency among archeologists to provide more complete and carefully considered culture reconstructions. These reconstructions have usually taken the form of amplified descriptions of archeological phases or "horizons." The current forms of archeological typology have been under sharp criticism during the last few years. From these two critical trends has emerged in some minds the conclusion that archeologists should forgo the barren escapism of typology and proceed directly to the goal of culture reconstruction or, a less radical cure, that whatever typology is used should of itself provide a functional description of the culture. To my mind these proposals reflect a misunderstanding of the fundamental purpose of archeological typology.

The tracing of culture change through time by careful documentation is as major a responsibility of the archeologist as is culture horizon description; he is a culture historian as well as an ethnographer. Although his competence in the former field has been taken for granted by many, actual performance has often not been exemplary. Human migrations have certainly too often been invoked to explain culture change. Such major errors as the misunderstanding of the Basketmaker-Pueblo transition (Brew 1946:32–85) and of the interrelationship of the central and northern Maya groups (Brainerd 1948) have come from failures in historical reconstruction. Some errors of this type might have been avoided if more attention had been given to careful chronologic sequencing, to working through time as a continuous variable rather than by the limitation of description to successive chronologic cross sections. Other errors have been perpetuated unduly through the uncritical acceptance as fact of theoretical interpretations of culture sequence based on thinly distributed data.

The archeologist has a unique chance to determine empirically how preliterate cultures came to be as they were. His use of technical procedures in reaching an ever more finely drawn chronological scale needs no apology; these are prerequisite to his determination of culture change through time, a subject in which he should be able to work with unique authority.

The materials which come to the hand of the archeologist have invariably been made by man during an interval of time, and only after these have been sequenced can he write culture history, or even know when he has arrived safely at the way station of horizon description. Few archeologists would question the advisability of formulating horizon descriptions, both because of the insight these give into cultural configurations and the opportunity they afford for direct comparison with the richer horizon descriptions available from the ethnographers. But the techniques of close chronological placement, if not systematically explored and improved, can prejudice ·all future work toward culture reconstruction from archeological remains.

The prime working tool of the archeologist in the formulation of his time-space framework is typology. The effects of the time factor can be isolated by stratigraphic or seriational analysis of types. This procedure is a specialized archeological technique best applied in the first stages of the work.[1] The impatience of many ethnologists with detailed archeological typology is easily understandable. In studying a human group the ethnographer can follow the direct procedure of describing the organization, conventions, and techniques of a society, appending descriptions of the material results of its arts and crafts. The archeologist, attempting to apply inductive methods toward reconstructing cultures from their material remains, produces a monograph the bulk of which provides frustrating reading to the ethnologist. He finds the material culture descriptions unduly detailed, organized in an incomprehensible manner, and including data extraneous to even his most exacting needs and interests. Failing to realize the purpose of archeology typology, he is apt to suspect the archeologist of an interest in objects rather than in their makers.

There is adequate reason for nonfunctionally oriented artifact typology, even that of the most detailed sort, if it is objectively formulated and serves the purpose of construction of the necessary time space framework. If a chronologic sequence can be constructed by procedures unconnected with cultural interpretation, and if the process provides its own proofs of validity, it gains authority thereby. The cause and effect relationships subsequently reconstructed will then be supported by independent chronologic anchorage and are sure to be unaffected by circular reasoning on the part of the investigator.

Such an objective technique is completely feasible, as may be demonstrated by analogous techniques developed in geological sequencing and in chromosome mapping. Archeological types may properly be formulated, as indeed they usually are (Krieger 1944:277–79; Rouse 1939:25–26), by noting which objectively describable artifact traits occur often in combination in single artifacts. The frequencies in artifact collections of types thus formulated can serve as the working material from which chronological sequences may be built. Furthermore such objectively determined types may reasonably be assumed to represent cultural standards (Rouse 1939:18–23) which may be later utilized as parts of the cultural description.

The value of an initial typology should not be judged by what it directly tells

---

[1]Although these dicta will seem self-evident to most archeologists, they are far from universally accepted. The Midwestern Taxonomic system defers chronology for later consideration, while Taylor (1948:147) defers comparative and taxonomic studies until the "culture types" existing in the archeological material have been "separated inferentially on the basis of cultural cohesiveness." Although I do not completely understand his statement, this sequence of procedure would seem to favor the making of culture reconstructions before the establishment of the time-space framework.

of the culture to be investigated but by the sensitivity and reliability of the time-space framework which it can be made to yield. Time moves by imperceptible increments through the archeological sequence. The more finely drawn and objectively determined the chronology, the more delicate and authoritative can be the insight which it provides into the interpretation of changes undergone through time.

THE PROBLEM OF CHRONOLOGICAL ORDERING

The problem of objective and closely controlled determination of chronological sequences from frequencies of types in collections or samples is the subject of the experimental work here described. I have long felt that this type of determination can most logically be done by mathematical procedures using the largest possible number of types or trait assemblages. It is my contention that the reasoning so often advanced against necessarily simplified mathematical formulations of complexly interrelated cultural factors does not apply here to the extent of invalidating a chronological sequence. I believe this claim is borne out by the independent checking of sequences established by Robinson's (1951) ordering techniques.

It should perhaps be pointed out here that statistical treatments of chronological ordering are not subject to certain logical complexities, inconsistencies, and uncertainties of judgment inherent in the mathematical formulation of measures of similarity between regional cultures. Variations undergone by a culture through time, although likely as complex in their causation as the regional variations found in contemporary cultures, can be arranged in a linear order which is not varied by differences of emphasis or judgment. American culture of 1900 may be related to that of 1950 by use of a linear time scale which is in itself not subject to the questions of viewpoint and interpretation which enter so profoundly into an assessment of the relationship of, for example, modern English and American cultures. Variations in judgment as to the relative importance of kinds of cultural differences can profoundly alter estimates of similarity between contemporaneous cultures, but should not alter sequential orderings of artifact material along a time axis. Although the *sensitivity* of time differentiation in an archeological sequence is directly dependent upon the judgment of the typologist, its *ordering*, if objectively arrived at, should not be affected thereby.

If the above scheme of thought be acceptable we may start our problem with a described and tabulated mass of archeological material that has been segregated into the divisions which will be used as our criteria in the formation of a time-space framework.

The nature of these divisions does not bear directly upon the scheme of analysis proposed here; although those employed in this problem are of the commonly used hierarchic sort whose smallest division is often called a type,[2] the subdivisions used may equally well crosscut hierarchic classifications.[3] A single important qualification must be met by the sorting criteria used. Each must be of such complexity in number and organization of attributes that the presence of an artifact belonging to it suggests that its maker lived in the same cultural milieu as that of makers of all other artifacts classified into the same sorting group; thus all artifacts classified under one group must have been made at approximately the same time and place. This hypothesis is tested for each group by the subsequent analysis, and is empirically proved for various groups if the analysis is successful. These sorting groups will henceforth be called *types*.

Types are normally encountered in artifact *collections*. A collection is defined as a group of artifacts which were found together, and therefore are suspected of having been made at approximately the same time and place. The *types* associated in collections are listed quantitatively, and the frequency of occurrence of the various types defined in a collection of any size may thus be computed.

The analytic technique whereby collections of artifacts may be placed in a time-space framework is based on the concept that each type originates at a given time at a given place, is made in gradually increasing numbers as time goes on, and then decreases in popularity until it becomes forgotten, never to recur in an identical form.[4]

If, in a mass of cultural material from a single region, a series of artifact types follows the course outlined above, each originating more or less independently of another, the corollary may be drawn that if a series of collections comes from a culture changing through time, their placement on a time axis is a function of their similarity; collections with closest similarity in

[2]Such types are not so restricted in definition as Krieger's; they will, for example, not meet Krieger's qualification (1944:285) of having demonstrated chronologic or regional significance, since such proof is one of the byproducts of our procedure.

[3]Cf. Rouse's (1939:11–12) *modes,* and Brew's (1946:46) plea for "more" classifications.

[4]Cf. Rouse (1939:14–15). New types do not normally originate at identical times save by chance. If a series of collections shows mass displacement of types at a single time, cultural displacement by conquest or other means seems indicated. This corollary has been much overworked in the past (as in the Basketmaker-Pueblo I transition) by reconstructing from too widely spaced series of collections.

qualitative or quantitative listing of types lie next to each other in the time sequence. This corollary allows a "seriation" or ordering of collections to be formed which, if time is the only factor involved, must truly represent the temporal placing of the collection,[5] although determination of the direction early to late must be obtained by other means.[6] Stratigraphic excavations have abundantly confirmed this general disposition of artifact types through time in archeological deposits.[7]

ROBINSON'S ORDERING TECHNIQUE

I posed to Robinson the problem of obtaining a mathematical measure of similarity among collections which would depend upon the comparative frequencies of a considerable number of types common to the collections. Since the variation among the collections to be analyzed was suspected to be principally chronological, an objective method for the seriation or ordering of the collections on the basis of these measures of similarity was desired.[8]

My immediate need for this sort of method was to aid in the formulation of a more closely defined chronology for the Maya ceramics of the Puuc region in Yucatán. The numerous collections made by the Carnegie Institution in

[5]Spier (1917) first published a mathematical formulation of a chronological sequence using the above-described principle. The sequence arrived at by Spier seems to have been previously formulated by inspection by Kroeber (1916). Formulation of sequences by the principle of placing collections or artifact styles or types in order of closest similarity has been done, using a wide variety of techniques, by many workers, among whom Kidder (1915), Kroeber (1930), Olson (1930), Ford (1938), Rouse (1939), Beals, Brainerd, and Smith (1945) and Ford and Willey (1949) may be cited as examples. Several have qualified their orderings as provisional, awaiting establishment or disproof by stratigraphy.

[6]Spier knew historically which end of his sequence was late. Stratigraphic placement of two or more points will also give direction. A technique for this determination from the data of the seriation itself forms part of the present study.

[7]Nelson (1916) first demonstrated such a stratigraphic sequence to Americanists. Kidder (Kidder and Shepard 1936) was able to check his seriational results (1915) by later stratigraphic excavation.

[8]Robinson's (1951) statistical techniques show certain obvious similarities to those used in ethnological studies. He was unfamiliar with these at the time of his work. (See Driver and Kroeber 1932; also see Kluckhohn 1939, for a bibliography and evaluation of such studies.) Kroeber, perceiving the similarity in ordering of data between ethnological trait lists and the trait lists employed in archeological studies using the Midwestern Taxonomic system, applied the ethnological statistical method to a series of archeological sites, getting results similar to those made by previously used inspectional methods (Kroeber 1940). Similarities between this and Robinson's work are doubtless due to the fact that both techniques were formulated to demonstrate relationships based on mathematical measures of similarity. No former work on this basis has been oriented toward chronology; clumping, not seriation of collections in matrices, was attained by previous studies. Also, qualitative rather than quantitative trait distributions have generally been used by previous workers to compute measures of similarity.

Puuc ruins had failed to yield evidence of ceramic change when analyzed by my inspectional techniques, although considerable variation of types through the collections from single sites was evident. An accurate objective serial placement of these collections in chronologic order was desirable to allow the study of the development of the associated architecture and other facets of the culture as well as the ceramic development. Detailed results of the statistical analysis will be presented in other articles. This article is confined to method and theory.

Robinson (1951), a sociological statistician, showed an immediate enthusiasm for the problem, tempered only by considerable distrust of the sort of data furnished him. His delighted comment that the results are more definitive than any he has obtained in several years may perhaps be taken to demonstrate the ease of chronologic analysis as compared to that of the interaction of factors in contemporaneous society.

As may be seen from Robinson (1951), the linear orderings which he formed are based upon the relative degrees of similarity among a group of collections from an archeological site. The types or criteria used by Robinson in computing the measures of agreement were chosen by me from his field tabulations. The sum of these criteria normally constituted a high percentage of each collection but never the total collection.

The criteria of constant combination of attributes in the defining of types and of complexity of attributes in gauging their cultural validity had been adhered to in the making of the field tabulations. From types meeting these requirements were selected those suspected of showing significant variations in frequency among the samples. The criteria chosen belonged to various grades in a hierarchic classification; some were wares, some vessel forms, some rim shapes, since the classification had originally been made in that form. The base used for frequency computation was the sum of the criteria chosen, not the collection total.

It should be emphasized that the collections worked on by Robinson (1951) were not chosen as likely prospects but were, on the contrary, those which had failed to yield chronological sequences to my inspectional techniques. Robinson's results are thus free of any bias from hypotheses previously formed by me on other than statistical grounds. This is not a mathematical expression of a previously hypothesized ordering[9] but a *de novo* objectively determined sequence.

[9] Cf. discussion by Griffin (1943:334) on the procedure of workers under the Midwest Taxonomic System.

To determine whether or not chronology was the causative factor in the formation of his collection orderings Robinson (1951) repeated his technique on the Mani collections, which showed stratigraphic ordering, and has demonstrated that the distribution of individual types in the orderings obtained by his technique is that previously known as correct (1951, fig. 91). That his results checked accurately shows that his method will order collections correctly at least in certain cases when chronologic differences are present, but does not conclusively rule out the possibility of factors other than chronology causing a sequence in all instances. Certain irregularities of type frequencies in the Maya ceramic collections suggest quite definitely that factors other than chronology and sampling errors must be hypothesized to account for variation in single sites. In an effort to provide theoretical bases for the more accurate isolation and analysis of chronologic variation and thus to permit analysis of the remaining nonchronologic variation, the following series of tests was run:

The classification categories of the sites were graphed in Robinson's (1951) seriated order of collections. These graphs show the characteristic lenticular shapes previously established as characteristic in chronologic sequence. Included in these graphs are various categories not included in Robinson's computations. Figure 8.1 shows an abbreviated series of graphs of the Kabah pottery according to Robinson's ordering.

That these characteristic nodal curves are followed by several wares, types, and shapes concurrently suggests that the causative factor must have been linear in nature, and that it is correctly represented by the linear ordering furnished by Robinson (1951). Although it might be possible that varying frequencies of a single well-represented type, coupled with the inevitable and complementary frequency changes in all others, might yield an ordering by Robinson's technique, these graphs show concurrent changes in groups when computed on separate percentage bases, and thus their variations are not simply complementary to each other. Robinson made an additional check on the possibility of the ordering's being due to variation in a single type. Measures of agreement were recomputed for a site after eliminating the type showing the largest percentage variations in the series. The ordering was not changed thereby.

It is believed that the abovementioned linearity of causal factor may with certain reservations be used to isolate chronologically caused variation from variations produced by other causes. Factors such as regional differences in culture and social stratification suggest themselves as the likely causes of variation alternative to chronology. The regional variations in culture studied

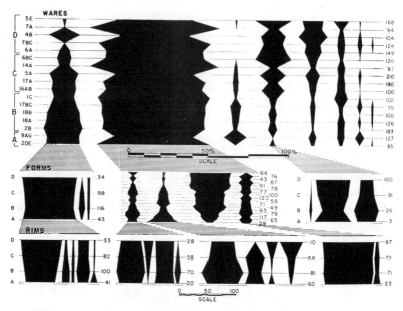

Figure 8.1 Ceramic frequencies in the Kabah ordering. The collections, which came from trenches dug within the site of Kabah, are in the order determined by Robinson's mathematical technique; late collections are toward the top, early toward the bottom. The upper percentage scale applies only to the upper graph, the lower scale was used to plot the two lower rows of graphs. Numbers of fragments in the groups considered are given to the right of each graph and should be used to judge the validity of frequencies in their groups. The upper graph shows frequencies of rim sherds of the 8 major wares found. Unslipped ware, first column, decreases through time. Thin Slateware and Thin Redware, columns 4 and 5 respectively, increase through time. The second row of graphs shows frequencies of vessel forms of certain of the wares, each computed with its ware total as 100 percent. When ware totals have been too small to provide statistically useful samples the collections have been grouped as shown into four sequent clusters, A, B, C and D. Note in the center graph, which shows Medium Slateware divided into jars, basins, basal break bowls, and hemispheroid bowls, that the jars and basins decrease in frequency through time, while the basal break bowls increase. The lowest row of graphs shows the frequencies of the commoner rim shapes of certain of the vessel forms shown in the middle row of graphs.

by Driver and Kroeber by techniques quite similar to those evolved by Robinson gave matrices which, as would be expected, show clumping rather than linear ordering. Regional cultural variation can confidently be expected to show other than a linear matrix patterning, since the geographic framework in which it evolved is of itself multidimensional.

The question of variation in pottery deposits due to social stratification in the site is a knottier one. In general a linear sequence running from coarse to fine pottery and based on wealth or social power might be conceived to occur in sites of complex societies, complicated by such variables as industries with special uses for ceramics and in Maya sites very possibly by special ceramics used in religious ceremonies. The graph shown for Kabah (fig. 8.1) may be inspected to decide whether chronology or social stratigraphy has caused our sequencing. It will be noticed that unslipped ware and Medium Slateware jars and basins decrease bottom to top while Thin Slateware, Thin Redware, and Medium Slateware basal break bowls increase. This sequence in general shows coarser wares and larger vessels at bottom with finer smaller pottery at the top, suggesting a possible basis of cultural stratigraphy for the seriation. Some of the changes through the ordering are not, however, thus classifiable. It is difficult to imagine why simultaneous frequency changes should occur in so many seemingly unrelated shapes and forms unless a chronological factor were dominating the sequence. Fortunately, inspection of collections dating before and after the occupation of Kabah bears out a chronological trend through time toward finer pottery; a factor other than chronology is not needed to explain it.

ANALYSIS OF ORDERED MATRICES

From the above analysis and similar analyses done on other sites it seems safe to assume that the linear orderings shown in Robinson's matrices are the result of chronology, and that strong deviations from a linear ordering are likely to have been caused by factors other than chronology. To aid in the judgment and interpretation of matrices I have found it advantageous to contour them in the manner of relief maps and to construct a series of matrices from geometric models to discover the significance of their "surface characteristics." Figures 8.2–8.8 are matrices contoured in this manner.

If contoured, Robinson's mathematical model (1951, table 16) would show a central ridge of high measures of agreement with sides of constant slope diagonal to the upper-right-hand and lower-left-hand corners. These two slopes are mirror images of each other about the diagonal of perfect agreement. The table may be said to be analogous to results from a series of short-term, unmixed collections showing a constant rate of ceramic change between each successive two. The collections may be visualized as successive points on a straight line, equidistant at one unit of measure apart. Measures of agreement between any two may then be obtained by measuring distance and subtracting it from a constant, in this case 7. For example, from point 2 to

point 6 measures 4 units. By subtracting these 4 units from the 7 above we
derive 3—the figure in Robinson's table.

Using the same geometric system we can compute and contour a matrix
from a group of points irregularly spaced along a straight line 200 units in
length (fig. 8.2). In this and the following matrices presented, we show only

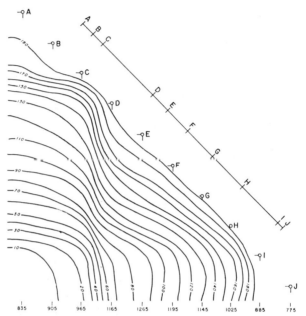

Figure 8.2 Geometric model of points irregularly spaced along a
straight line. Line is 200 units in length. Distances between points
have all been subtracted from 200, and resultant values contoured.

the lower left half; the other half is always mirror symmetric across the
diagonal axis. This matrix should be to some degree analogous to that given
by collections separated by varying degrees of chronologic (linear) change or,
more properly, by relative degree of ceramic change since such change is our
only measure of time lapse. Note that the contours all equally change
direction along lines parallel to the axes of the matrix both horizontally and
vertically between points C and D, the two most widely separated adjacent
points of the sequence. Also note that the sums of the matrix columns, shown
along the baseline, depart markedly from the smooth curve of those in
Robinson's (1951) table 16; the sums of close spaced points group closely,
those of widely spaced points show larger differences. This synthetic matrix

shows markedly similar characteristics, both in contour and column sums to the Mani matrix, in figure 8.8. The collections from this site, which occurred stratigraphically, show marked ceramic change among the major pottery wares at the points indicated: between 2G and 4F, between 4C and 4D, and between 4A and 1A. The ceramic collections at Mani would be expected to show these sharp changes since deposits some 2.5 meters deep document over 2,000 years of ceramic change, as compared to from 150 to 400 years in the other matrices illustrated.

Another synthetic matrix was plotted using a group of points having a random pattern in a plane. Linear arrangements in two directions were tried, oriented to align with widely separated points (fig. 8.3). These matrices should give some idea of the irregularity of contour to be expected if the best possible linear arrangement is made of a group of collections showing no close relationship to a linear (chronologic) pattern. All matrices from the Yucatán pottery are more regular than either of these, with the exception of Uxmal, thus indicating that Robinson's results are in most cases not merely artifacts of his technique as applied to nonlinear material. Graphing of the pottery types in the Uxmal collections in seriated order showed that even with this unprepossessing matrix (fig. 8.5), the ceramic changes of the major wares correspond in general to those of other contemporaneous sites. The irregularity of contour seems due to "wild" values of the fine wares, a suggestion of the strong intrusion of social stratigraphy into the total variation.

Fundamental to the working methods used in this study is the assumption that each collection consists of artifacts made during a shorter time span than that covered by the whole group of collections. The formation of chronological orderings verifies this assumption but does not sort from the data the results due to variable time span of deposit of artifacts included in a single collection. The results of the latter causative factor are obviously to be suspected of bulking large when the collections come from a concentrated area or site, when deposits are shallow, when the total time period is short, and when the analysis is carried to the ultimate degree of chronologic subdivision. All these factors apply to our material.[10]

The accurate determination of these chronologic variabilities in individual collections is of course possible only in the terms of relative amount of

[10]In most analyses of sherd materials from sites this problem is met by taking only the "pure" collections, that is, those collections showing most striking differences among them, to define chronologic phases, components, or horizons. The bulk of the material is then assumed to be "mixed" or "transitional" and its characteristics are used only to augment the detail of the descriptions taken from the "pure" collections.

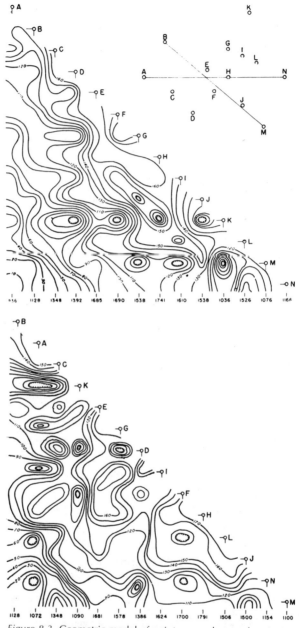

Figure 8.3 Geometric model of points spaced at random in a plane. A-N is 200 units in length. Matrices have been formed about two lines A-N and B-M. Distances between points have all been subtracted from 200, and resultant values contoured.

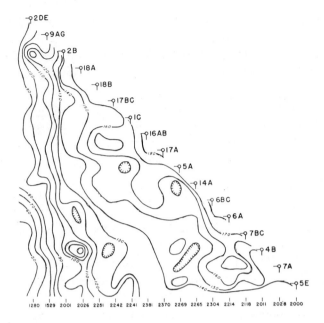

Figure 8.4 Contoured matrix of the final ordering of Kabah.

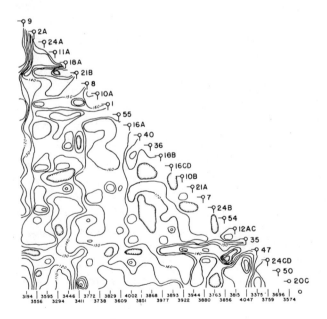

Figure 8.5 Contoured matrix of the final ordering of Uxmal.

ceramic variability in collections, since this variability is our only time indicator. In the analysis of collections for span of deposition of individual collections some separation between the causative factors may be possible: (a) the time during which the archeological deposit was laid down in its final position before excavation, (b) amount of admixture of earlier material through reuse of earth, and (c) that of later material introduced by animal and plant activities since deposition. The effects of factor (a) may be assumed in the main to be a mixture of artifacts more or less evenly covering a segment of the time span of the site. Factor (b) is more likely to cause a mixture of material from two markedly separated intervals of that segment of the time span preceding deposition, and factor (c) is likely to cause sporadic occurrence of small numbers of artifacts of later date in preponderantly earlier collections. Factor (c) is nearly certain to be the least active of these three in a long occupied site.

The effects of these factors on a linearly ordered matrix can be to some degree prophesied. In Robinson's synthetic model (1951, table 16) the measures of agreement of each collection rise steadily from a low value at each edge of the matrix to a high at each side of the diagonal. His model is analogous to a condition where each collection represents but a point on the time scale. If, on the other hand, the deposition of a single collection covers in an even manner the whole time span of the matrix, the inverted V figure formed by profiling its measurements of agreement with the other collections in sequence will be lower at the vertex and higher at the ends than are those of the short span deposits.

This diagnostic feature of long-term collections has been checked empirically by inserting into sequences synthetic collections formed by combining several collections in the sequence and computing new frequencies. A synthetic long-term collection when sequenced will fall into a position intermediate among that of its component collections, and will show lower measures of agreement with adjacent collections in the sequence, and higher measures with distant collections, than will shorter term collections. Relative "degradation of profile" is thus a measure of the time interval covered by the materials contained in the deposit, and a mathematical measurement of relative time spans of the collections in a matrix may eventually be feasible. The column total of measures of agreement in the instances tried fitted well into the even, nondisjunctive sequence of column totals as exemplified by Robinson (1951, table 16). Thus column total variability seems promising as a criterion in separating effects of mixed collections and variable period of depositions from those of variable spacing in ceramic change. Meanwhile much may be seen by inspection of contoured matrices.

Many profiles show multiple peaks. Multiple peaks in a degraded profile indicate the presence of materials which fit the sequence at the points indicated by the peaks. Thus a single profile may be checked for high points and the position in the matrix where such points fall will indicate the time level from which the mixed or long-term deposit has received material. The actual analysis of this condition is complicated by the fact that all collections in the matrix are sure to cover varying time intervals, and each measure of agreement is a function of two collections. In analyzing which of the two component collections has caused a given peak the column and row profiles should allow a judgment. Whichever profile shows a documented upslope adjoining the peak is the one to suspect as a mixed collection. An isolated high value in a profile suggests that its complementary collection at that point has caused it. In topographic terms spurs from the central ridge or independent ridges suggest that the collections whose profiles they follow are long term. In the making of any of the above analyses the column totals of measures of agreement should first be checked to assure that irregularity of spacing along the axis of ceramic change is not the causal factor.

It should be easy for the reader to gather from the above that the interpretation of the apparently chaotic topography of Robinson's matrices has not yet reached the ordered stage of an exact technique. It may be worthwhile for me to record, however, my conviction that the fault lies in the immaturity of my working methods rather than in any permanent intractability of the data. There is considerable evidence that the results of variable deposition span and of variable spacing of collections along the axis of ceramic change (the time axis) can be objectively, and quite precisely, separated. The proper understanding of these two variables and the consequent control of the errors introduced by them into the time scale should improve the precision of time placement of collections, and concurrently allow a closer separation of variability due to time from that due to such causes as social stratification and regional variation and trade.

Early in the course of this project it was noticed that in contoured matrices from several Puuc sites there is a tendency for the matrix to slope upward toward one end of the diagonal axis rather than parallel to the axis as would be expected, and that concurrently the other end of the axis shows a very sudden rise to high value from low values at edge of matrix (figs. 8.4–8.7). Graphing of the pottery sequences covered by the collections which formed these matrices, and comparison with stratified material, showed that the four examples were uniform in that the sharply rising end of the ridge is the early end of the sequence. Reading along the profiles of the individual collections

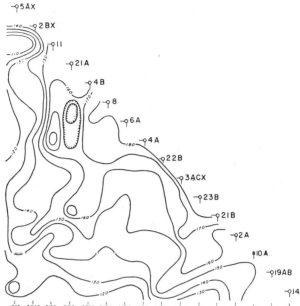

Figure 8.6 Contoured matrix of the final ordering of Sayil.

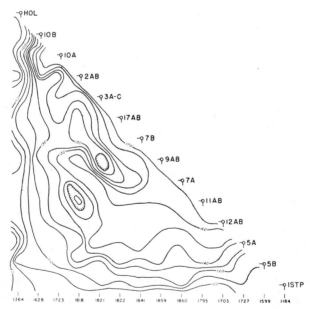

Figure 8.7 Contoured matrix of the final ordering of Holactun.

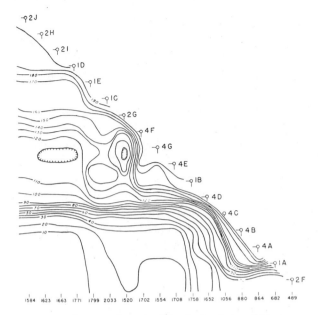

Figure 8.8 Contoured matrix of the final ordering of Mani.

reveals that those at the early end of the sequence show the characteristics outlined above as those of short-term deposits, a high peak value for adjacent collections, and low values for those further removed in the sequence. Collections at the late end of the sequence conversely show the degraded profiles of long-term deposits. Although this tendency is not striking it was sufficient to allow recognition of time direction before its causes were known.

The cause must be progressive mixing of deposits, for the factor (b) above acts with increasing strength through the depositional period of the site. This principle has been used by Kidder to hypothesize the priority of a phase from mixed deposits (Kidder, Jennings and Shook 1946:258). This phenomenon may be expected to show most strongly in groups of collections from a concentrated site showing continued occupation. Its value in giving time direction in sites where stratigraphy has not been obtained should be obvious.

SUMMARY OF RESULTS

The results of the work reported above may be summarized as follows. Of major importance is that Robinson has worked out a mathematically simple, objective technique for the chronological seriation of archeological collections. This technique requires no special system of classification and recording and thus is immediately applicable to large masses of tabulated material which, if not found stratigraphically, are often difficult to place by present techniques, and it allows their more accurate assignment in a chronological scale. Such assignment greatly increases the efficiency of archeological analysis, and there is sound reason for desiring this; archeological deposits are not inexhaustible. I believe that undoubtedly seriations formed by this technique will allow refinements in chronology greater than those currently possible, but it should be cautioned that the number of seriated steps is no direct measure of the number of chronological substages which may reliably be defined, since spans of deposition of individual deposits are very likely to overlap considerably with those of adjacent collections. It should also be cautioned that, as has so often been said of statistical techniques, this method will not give closer results than are inherent in the data put into it; although poor typology should not give erroneous orderings, it cannot be expected to give finely graded seriations. An additional caution should be given as to the type of material suitable for this technique. Since the seriation of collections depends upon relative degrees of difference between collections, orderings cannot be obtained from collections which do not share a number of their included types. Stratigraphy is the only valid method for the sequencing of completely disparate cultural materials, and, save in deposits where progressive mixing has occurred, it is the only device for obtaining time direction. Although stratigraphy has often been called the final proof of archeological sequence, it seems questionable whether possible errors due to redeposition do not render stratigraphy at times less reliable than are the internal evidences of concurrent culture changes upon which seriations depend. Stratigraphic placement supported by the evidence of finely graded concurrent cultural changes through the artifacts from a series of overlying deposits is certainly a final clincher; it is unfortunate that such deposits are found so seldom!

Robinson's statistical technique for chronological ordering is a tool ready for use. Although its results will need constant testing and evaluation, its underlying rationale is uncomplicated enough to allow most archeologists an adequate judgment as to the meaning of its results. Techniques for the utilization of the numerical data produced by the procedure are the present need and these must be evolved by archeologists. Beginnings in the recognition of the relative spacing of collections along the chronological axis and of the relative spans of deposition of individual collections are described in this article. These techniques when developed fully should allow a more precise separation of time-caused variation in archeological collections. A promising clue to the determination of early from late end of sequences found from nonstratified collections has also been described. Adequate understanding and analysis of the variation caused by time in archeological collections allows the close documentation of culture dynamics, and throws into sharper relief the nonchronologic variation from which the archeologist can in turn make more finely drawn and reliable inferences as to the functional relationships shown by his material.

REFERENCES

Beals, Ralph L., George W. Brainerd, and Watson Smith. 1945. Archaeological studies in northeast Arizona. *University of California Publications in American Archaeology and Ethnology* 44(1).

Brainerd, George W. 1948. Review: The Ancient Maya (Sylvanus Griswold Morley). *American Antiquity* 14(2):133–36.

Brew, John Otis. 1946. The archaeology of Alkali Ridge, southeastern Utah. *Papers of the Peabody Museum of American Archaeology and Ethnology, Harvard University* 21.

Driver, H. E. and A. L. Kroeber. 1932. Quantitative expression of cultural relationships. *University of California Publications in American Archaeology and Ethnology* 31:211–56.

Ford, James A. 1938. A chronological method applicable to the southeast. *American Antiquity* 3(3):260–64.

Ford, James A. and Gordon R. Willey. 1949. Surface survey of the Viru Valley, Peru. *Anthropological Papers of the American Museum of Natural History* 43, pt. 1.

Griffin, James B. 1943. *The Fort Ancient aspect.* Ann Arbor: University of Michigan Press.

Kidder, A. V. 1915. Pottery of the Pajarito Plateau and of some adjacent regions in New Mexico. *Memoirs, American Anthropological Association* 2 pt. 6:407–62.

Kidder, A. V. and Anna O. Shepard. 1936. *The pottery of Pecos.* Vol. 2. New Haven: Yale University Press.

Kidder, A. V., Jesse D. Jennings and Edwin M. Shook. 1946. Excavations at Kaminaljuyu, Guatemala. *Carnegie Institution of Washington, Publication* 561.

Kluckhohn, Clyde. 1939. On certain recent applications of association coefficients to ethnological data. *American Anthropologist* 41(3):345–77.

Krieger, Alex D. 1944. The typological concept. *American Antiquity* 9(3):271–88.

Kroeber, A. L. 1916. Zuni potsherds. *Anthropological Papers of the American Museum of Natural History* 18, pt. 1.

—— 1930. Cultural relations between North and South America. *Proceedings of the 23rd International Congress of Americanists,* pp. 5–22.

—— 1940. Statistical classification. *American Antiquity* 6(1):29–44.

Nelson, N. C. 1916. Chronology of the Tano ruins, New Mexico. *American Anthropologist* n.s. 18(2):159–80.

Olson, Ronald L. 1930. Chumash prehistory. *University of California Publications in American Archaeology and Ethnology* 28, no. 1.

Robinson, W. S. 1951. A method for chronologically ordering archaeological deposits. *American Antiquity* 16:293–301.

Rouse, Irving. 1939. Prehistory in Haiti, a study in method. *Yale University Publications in Anthropology,* no. 21.

Spier, Leslie. 1917. An outline for a chronology of Zuni ruins. *Anthropological Papers of the American Museum of Natural History* 18, pt. 3.

Steward, Julian and Frank M. Setzler. 1938. Function and configuration in archaeology. *American Antiquity* 4(1):4–10.

Taylor, Walter W. 1948. A study of archaeology. *Memoirs, American Anthropological Association,* no. 69.

9

RICHARD B. POLLNAC • RALPH M. ROWLETT

Community and Supracommunity Within the Marne Culture: A Stylistic Analysis

At first glance, the authors of this article seem to deal with a question quite distinct from the one posed in the two previous papers: They start with an archeologically defined culture, the Marne variant of La Tène from Western Europe, and attempt, with some success, to subdivide it into smaller regional units. In a broader context, however, their basic problem is to describe variation between units (in this case entire sites), search for some underlying pattern, and then determine what, if anything, observed regularities reflect. Pollnac and Rowlett can select roughly contemporaneous sites and thus minimize the chronological factor. They examine variation and regularity over space; Brainerd, and Deetz and Dethlefsen trace relationships over time, and the techniques they employ could, in fact, be adapted to Pollnac and Rowlett's quite different goals.

A complete understanding of the complicated procedure of factor analysis is not essential to grasp what Pollnac and Rowlett attempt to do; the research design itself is of most immediate interest. Evidence derived from linguistic and ethnographic analysis serves as a basis to predict what type of variation between sites one might expect to find if, in fact, the term "Marne Culture" had been applied to several related but distinct "supracommunities." From this it was possible to determine the general form isoloads produced by factor analysis must take to have significant cultural implications. Because the resulting configurations do meet explicitly stated expectations, the authors then conclude that their content is meaningful as well, and they conclude that the tripartite division of La Marne Culture observed reflects three distinct supracommunities.

In this instance—which is a realistic archeological situation—it is highly desirable to have some independent means to provide a second check of the validity of their results. The authors are aware of this problem, and in one sense they create their own experimental situation where some means of control is possible. By withholding certain elements from the factor analysis, they can later use them as a check to see if patterning of such variables as the location of craft centers, violated and unviolated graveyards, and chariot burials supports the general picture obtained by statistical means.

Given what seems a reasonable set of results, the authors, in conclusion, shift their emphasis to consider the method itself, and in effect they turn the tables and assess the method against the conclusions drawn from it. They break their first body of data down into two classes, one ceramic, the other nonceramic, treat each separately, and conclude that the more data included in a factor analysis, the more meaningful the results are likely to be.

Our purpose here is to analyze the Marnian variant of the La Tène Ia in order to determine whether or not a subdivision of this variant is justified. We shall explore the utility of the concepts of community and supracommunity in archeological investigations, and investigate the usefulness of style as an indicator of social interaction.

The Marne culture has long been recognized as constituting a distinctive variant of the widespread La Tène Culture of central, west-central, and east-central Europe. Although originally distinguished by a rather informal discussion of the evidence, the Marnian variant nevertheless does possess enough distinctiveness to be easily differentiated from other La Tène manifestations. Marnian sites are distinguished above all on the basis of fairly large cemeteries with consistent westward orientation of the graves, black earth grave fill (in an area where the prevailing soil color is light brown), almost universal burial of weapons with adult males, lineal village layout consisting of one or more parallel rows of houses, distinctive rectilinear carinated pottery with frequent incised or painted decoration, frequent chariot burials with occasional inclusions of trade vessels from the Etruscans or Greeks of Classical antiquity, as well as a myriad of special types of jewelry and fibulae which are exclusively or predominantly found in the Marnian district of northern Champagne.

The distinctiveness of the Marne Culture persists clearly through four chronological horizons (La Tène Ia through II) from about 480 b.c. to 100 b.c. There are hardly any students of prehistoric Europe who question the validity of the concept of a separate Marne Culture within the broader La

Tène world; indeed, there are those who implicitly treat the Marne Culture as one main sociocultural unit. Those who have worked closely with the Marne Culture, however, such as Bretz-Mahler (1957) or Rowlett (1967), have noted by inspection that certain cultural traits seem to occur more frequently in some parts of northern Champagne than in others, and that there may be other slight cultural differences within the easily perceived Marnian variant. However, virtually none of these elements are exclusively confined to one or the other geographic regions within the Marnian area. In determining whether there exists significant variation that clusters geographically within the Marne Culture, it would be helpful to know if any of the cultural traits tend to associate together. One can see, for example, that when the geographic distribution of the spatial relationship of village area to cemetery is plotted on a map (see fig. 9.9), the eastern Marnian district tends to have virtually all of those sites where burials are located among the houses; in the more northern parts cemeteries are adjacent to village areas; while on the western side cemeteries are so far away from settlements that it is seldom possible to recognize associations. The choice of cemetery location with respect to the areas of the living was assuredly a matter involving many other aspects of culture. Therefore, it seemed necessary to use some sort of multivariate analysis in order to determine if there is any consistent patterning in the varying distributions of cultural elements within the Marne Culture. To control for temporal differences, this study analyzes only data from the La Tène Ia (480–400 b.c.) horizon (Rowlett 1968).

One possible interpretation of the localized patterning of occurrence of cultural elements is that within the Marne Culture there were several suprasettlement interaction spheres that could be referred to as supracommunities. We have sought to determine whether or not archeologically definable supracommunities exist within the Marne Culture, and if they do, to determine which assemblage items best distinguish these groupings.

An important concept in our discussion is that of *community,* which we shall define as a geographically contiguous group of individuals with a characteristically higher degree of face-to-face interaction among themselves than with members of other groups. A *supracommunity* is a group of communities with a higher degree of interaction among themselves than with other communities. There are many levels of supracommunity grouping. For example, the Celts could be considered one level, and the Marne variant of the La Tène Ia a supracommunity grouping within the large Celtic group. Redfield's (1960) discussion of communities within communities provides an interesting theoretical discussion of this phenomenon as well as a number of excellent ethnographic examples.

A problem here, however, is one of determining supracommunity groupings from their archeological remains. Since these groupings are defined by different interaction patterns, the problem becomes that of interpreting the archeological record in terms of human interaction. What archeological materials can be thus interpreted?

Archeologists such as Deetz (1965), Longacre (1964), and more recently Whallon (1968) have discussed the interrelationships between the structure of sociocultural systems and the stylistic behavior of the material items associated with them. Whallon wrote that "the nature of the diffusion of stylistic ideas and practices, both within and between communities, will be determined by the nature of interaction among artisans" (1968:223). The influence of group identification on the distribution of stylistic elements is also well documented in the ethnographic literature. Fredrich Barth, for example, has listed features such as dress, language, house form, and general style of life as those which people use for group identification (1969:14). It would be superfluous to list the many examples in the literature which support Barth's statement. Style and group identification are so closely interrelated that the social theorist Duncan wrote that "style is a social identification" (1962:274). It must be pointed out, however, that although specific styles will tend to cluster within the boundaries of a group, they will also diffuse—although the diffusion will always be the result of interaction. This interaction can be of any form: visibility due to geographic proximity, trade relations, and even warfare are examples. The point is that the greatest clustering of styles will be within groups that possess some sort of self-identity, and that the nature and intensity of intergroup interaction will determine a group's stylistic similarity with other groups. The level of intragroup stylistic similarity is of course a function of intragroup interaction, and with regard to the above definition of community, we would expect to find greater stylistic similarity within communities at any given level than between them. We shall therefore examine the stylistic elements in the archeological record to determine the supracommunity groupings within the Marne Culture.

If style is to be used as the defining characteristic in this study, we may say that style is that aspect of an artifact which may vary without affecting the primary function of the artifact. There are artifacts whose primary function appears to be group identification, such as pins or medals which signal group membership. The overall class of these items can be considered to function primarily as adornment, and it is their variation that functions as group identification. Such items therefore fall within our definition of style.

The validity of our classification of an element as stylistic is an empirical matter which can be determined in the course of the analysis. We shall follow Whallon, and assume that if the selected attributes manifest patterns of behavior that can be systematically related to social, cultural, or individual factors rather than to function or the physical environment, the attributes and their behavior can be considered stylistic (Whallon 1968:224). It cannot be too strongly emphasized that the manifestation of style that is of interest here is a "time-place-group characteristic" and not an "individual uniqueness that sets an artist apart from contemporaries whose work is similar in the time-place-group level" (Paisley 1968:203).

We may now proceed to a discussion of the specific distributional characteristics of style which will permit us to infer supracommunity groupings and boundaries. It was explicitly stated above that we would expect to find greater stylistic similarity within communities analyzed at any level than between communities. Nevertheless, the distribution of stylistic attributes should not be viewed simply as a static clustering of attributes in time and space. The distribution must be viewed as the result of a dynamic process of differential levels of human interaction being affected by the total environmental complex, both natural and cultural. An analysis that will provide values indicating degrees of similarity is thus necessary. Methods for interpreting the distribution of cultural elements in terms of degrees of similarity have been discussed in the literature, and a review of the more pertinent of these discussions is in order here.

One domain of stylistic variation that has been vigorously investigated and plotted on maps is that of language dialects. Dialect geographers, in the course of their investigations and analyses, have discovered that dialect areas are defined by boundaries which correspond to an area where a large number of isoglosses run parallel and in close proximity on a map (Hockett 1958:473–76). This is in accordance with Maull's girdle method as used by geographers. This method consists of superimposing a number of regional boundaries and selecting as a geographical boundary an area "where more than a given number of boundaries approximately coincide" (Grigg 1967:493). In analogous analyses, some anthropologists (e.g., Driver, Kniffen, Gifford, and Kroeber) have noted that when the amount of shared cultural elements (some stylistic, some not) are plotted on Cartesian coordinates with distance on the other axis, the plot within a tribal area produces a gentle convex curve which falls away at the tribal boundary and then drops sharply beyond the boundary (Clarke 1968:374–80).

Finally, Wilhelm Milke (1949) presented an extremely significant analysis based on isoplethic maps of cultural similarity. He did this by first selecting a core site, calculating a coefficient of similarity of this site with all other sites within the area of interest, and then plotting these coefficients on a map of the area and analyzing it in terms of areas of equal similarity. From the geographical distribution of similarity coefficients he concluded that there is a general decrease in cultural similarity as the distance from the point of reference increases. He also noted that the rate of decrease differs according to the direction taken from the reference point, and attributed this to both topographical and cultural influences. More important for our purposes however is his observation that there were areas on the maps where isopleths ran very close together, indicating a rapid drop in the similarity coefficients of adjacent sites. He interpreted these areas as cultural boundaries and noted that they had the character of an extended barrier zone rather than a sharp line.

The varieties of analysis discussed above support the proposition that there is more cultural similarity within a group than between groups. Moreover, Milke's analysis of the spatial distribution of cultural similarities, especially his discussion of boundaries, provides a justification for the dynamic type of analysis that we deem essential. Most important, however, is that these analyses provide objective criteria for determining the boundary of a group. Nevertheless the above cited approaches do have some weaknesses. One problem, especially with Milke's analysis, is that the criteria for the selection of the point of reference site are not defined adequately. An analytical technique proposed in a more limited analysis of the Marne Culture has provided a solution for this problem (Rowlett and Pollnac 1972).

The information analyzed consists of 367 traits which are distributed in varying degrees among 77 archeological sites within the above described area. These sites are distributed in an area approximately 100 by 75 kilometers (fig. 9.1). The trait categories reflect mainly stylistic elements such as location of vessel in grave; vessel shape, color, and decorative motif; jewelry, knife, and scabbard styles; and chariot pit shape. The use of such a large range of cultural items in a stylistic analysis lessens the chance that we are delimiting merely single item trade areas rather than cultural groupings—a potentiality pointed out by Richard Bradley (1971).

The goal of the analysis of this data is twofold. First is to determine the degree and spatial distribution of the localized patterns of concurrence of

Figure 9.1 Location of Marnian La Tène Ia sites used in analysis. 1 cm. = 5 km.

stylistic elements in the Marne culture during the La Tène Ia, and second to determine which elements are patterned and thus responsible for the supra-community groupings that emerge.

Factor analysis with factor scores will produce all the needed information. We have used that method (1) to group the sites on the basis of patterns of occurrence of assemblage items, (2) to provide a value for each site that indicates its degree of association with the pattern or factor underlying each grouping of sites, and (3) to determine the assemblage items responsible for each grouping of sites.

For the most part, we shall use factor analysis in a deductive manner. Our hypothesis is that we shall find patterns in the data that will reflect patterns of human interaction corresponding to those predicted by the above theoretical discussion. The factor analysis of the data will be an empirical test of the above hypotheses concerning the spatiotemporal distribution of stylistic elements.

The first step was to correlate sites on the basis of assemblage items. A factor analysis of the resultant correlation matrix was then performed to determine the regularities that underlie its complex interrelationships. We used a common factor analysis model. Squared multiple correlations were used as the initial communality estimates, and iterations were performed on this estimate until the mean absolute deviation of the communalities was reduced to less than .0001. Since the primary goal here was to define the distinct clusters of relationships that were present in the data, the factors were rotated to orthogonal simple structure utilizing the varimax criterion. The first three factors rotated grouped the sites into three distinct groups. All of the factors beyond three accounted for very small increments of total variance explained and thus were considered irrelevant to our objective of determining the major groupings of sites.

The factor loadings for each site on each factor were then plotted on maps of the spatial distribution of the sites. The loadings for each factor were plotted on separate maps. The factor loading measures the degree to which a variable (in this case a site) is involved in a factor pattern. Its interpretation is similar to that of a correlation coefficient except that in this case the site is not being measured for its degree of association with another site, but is instead being measured for its degree of association with a cluster of sites that were defined on the basis of similarity of variation with regard to assemblage items.

The plotted factor loadings were then analyzed in a manner similar to that used for weather maps. Lines of equal factor loadings, which we call isoloads, were drawn, and the resultant configurations are presented in figures 9.2, 9.3, and 9.4.

At this stage of the analysis it is evident that we have resolved the abovementioned problem with Milke's technique. The problem of selecting a point of reference site was accomplished objectively as a byproduct of the analysis. Rather than selecting a site and correlating the other sites with it, we have determined the interrelationships of all the sites, mathematically defined a subset which is interrelated in a similar manner owing to the presence or absence of a subset of stylistic traits, and then determined how well each site fit into the pattern—the site with the best fit received the highest loading, the next best fit the next loading, etc.

The next stage in the analysis was to determine which stylistic traits were responsible for the various groupings. In order to do this we took advantage of the fact that one can calculate a score for each case on a factor. In this instance the cases are the stylistic traits. The regression estimate technique was used to calculate this score. The stylistic traits most strongly associated

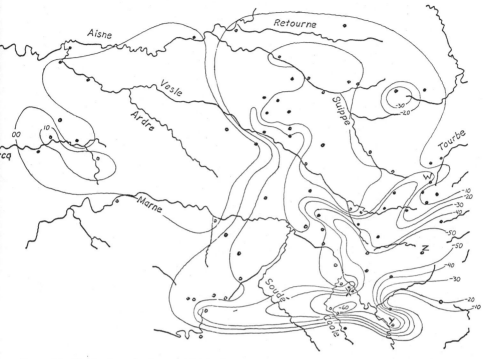

Figure 9.2 Distribution of orthogonal Factor I.

with each of the three factors can be found in table 9.1. The traits listed there are those which received a factor score in excess of one standard deviation from the mean on the related factor. If a trait received a high score on more than one factor, it is listed under the factor it received the highest score on. In several cases where a trait received an equally high score on two factors, it was listed under both of them. (A complete list and description of the 367 stylistic traits used in the analysis can be obtained from the authors.)

In interpreting the analysis it should first be pointed out that the three factors explained 8.1, 4.5, and 3.3 percent of the variance respectively, summing to 15.9 percent of the total variance in the data set. This low percentage of variance explained was not unexpected in light of the stylistic heterogeneity present in this area. Stylistic elements seemed to flow quite readily between the various sites. In another study, in which a hypothesis concerning residence pattern was tested, it was found that with regard to ceramic stylistic attributes, the degree of intracommunity heterogeneity was

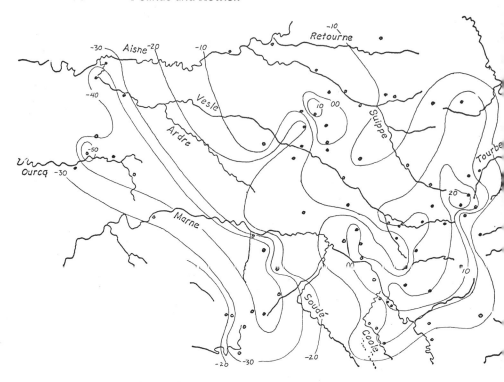

Figure 9.3 Distribution of orthogonal Factor II.

about as great as that within five adjacent communities in the Factor I area (Pollnac, m.s.).

As can be seen in the figures, this analysis neatly grouped the sites into three geographical areas. The configurations of the isoloads for the various factors graphically display a general decrease in stylistic similarity as one moves away from a point of reference. The rate of decrease in similarity differs depending on the direction taken from the point of reference, a phenomenon noted by Milke (1949) in his study of the distribution of cultural similarity cited earlier. This differential rate of change of stylistic similarity doubtless reflects a differential rate of communication which could be the result of either topographic or cultural factors. The partial correspondence of the isoloads with physiographic features such as rivers in the area leads one to infer that it is a combination of the two factors. Since the isoloads are in general clustered more tightly at the boundaries of the subcultural areas (we have used an absolute loading of .30 or higher to bound a subcultural area) it

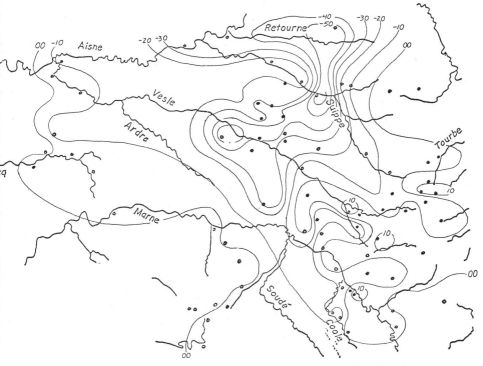

Figure 9.4 Distribution of Orthogonal Factor III.

can be inferred that communication was greater within rather than between the areas. This clustering at the boundary is more marked with Factors I and III than with Factor II, but this could be the result of the lower density of sites within the area bounded by Factor II. The sites which fall between the boundaries, such as those between the boundaries of Factor I and Factor III, can be considered as transitional sites—those which belong fully to neither group according to the criteria set up here.

Although the analysis presented thus far has conformed with our theoretical expectations, thus indicating a fair degree of external validity, the supracommunities defined may be composed of smaller supracommunities. The analytical technique used, that of orthogonal rotation of axes, is capable of defining distinct clusters of relationships, but when several clusters are correlated with each other, the orthogonal technique fails to define them. Oblique rotation to simple structure is the technique employed in order to more clearly define interrelated clusters of variables. With this technique we shall be able to

TABLE 9.1

Stylistic Traits Associated with the Three Orthogonal Factors.

Traits associated with Factor I

1. Vases chiefly to right, at foot.
2. A-3a vase with long flat upper shoulder.
3. Ac-1a elongated, footed cup.
4. a-1 squat vase with high flat upper shoulder.
5. ac-5a footless short cup.
6. A''-1a jar with high round shoulder and vertical rim.
7. a⁰-1a bowl with high round shoulder, vertical neck, and everted rim.
8. B vase with flat everted rim.
9. B vase with vertical rim.
10. Rimless B and b vases.
11. b-1a footed short vase with high, flat upper shoulder.
12. b₁-1a bowl with short, flat upper shoulder and rounded base.
13. c-4 bowl with flat bottom and flat everted sides.
14. c⁰-2a cup with foot, rounded body, and everted rim.
15. Ta⁰-1 tall triconic cup.
16. Tc⁰-2a rimless chalice.
17. Rectilinear conical cist predominant form.
18. Ceramic motif: vertical combed lines.
19. Ceramic motif: vertical wavy combmarks.
20. Ceramic motif: naturally limited vertical lines.
21. Ceramic motif: triple chevron.
22. Ceramic motif: double chevron.
23. Ceramic motif: inverted chevron.
24. Ceramic motif: dotted line.
25. Ceramic motif: reticular.
26. Ceramic motif: zig-zag lines.
27. Ceramic motif: step-up to right.
28. Ceramic motif: horizontal 3-rung ladder.
29. Ceramic motif: ladder motif with double line rung.
30. Ceramic motif: thick "X."
31. Ceramic motif: thin "X."
32. Ceramic motif: wide cordon.
33. Ceramic motif: assiette bottoms.
34. Thin red paint on ceramics.
35. Orange-yellow pottery at least 10 percent of ceramic colors.
36. Wide band painting technique on pottery.
37. Bracelet with continuous series of circumferentially incised lines.
38. Majority of twisted torc hooks in the plane of the torc.
39. Bird torcs & bird vases and other bird images (except on fibulae).
40. Knife with complete handle and rectangular pommel.
41. Knives with convex dorsal lines and short, riveted handles (D-1 and D-3c).
42. Organic scabbard.

Traits associated with Factor II

1. Cremations as well as inhumations.
2. Vases chiefly at head.
3. A-2b vase with drooping upper shoulder.
4. B-1a footed vase with rim and flat upper shoulder.
5. B⁰-1a vase with high rounded shoulder & rim.
6. C-4 vase with slightly convex sides.
7. Cylindrical cist predominant form.
8. Ceramic motif: single and stacked lozenges.
9. Ceramic motif: step-up to left.
10. Ceramic motif: vertical combed lines.
11. Ceramic motif: horizontal ladder with rungs marked by triple lines.
12. Over 33 percent grey pots.
13. Over 10 percent orange-brown pots.
14. Over 50 percent twisted torcs.
15. Plaque catch-plate on torcs.
16. Torc hooks perpendicular to plane of torc.
17. B-6 torc with conical endings with little ridges and bumps interrupting the smoothness of the cone.
18. C-3 torc with fine incisions on terminus.
19. Rectangle and triangle bracelet motif.
20. Pointed ended bracelet with flattened section and overlapping ends.
21. B-2-b bracket.
22. D-1-c bracelet.
23. Flat rectangular fibula terminal with incised "X" design.
24. A-2 fibula.
25. B-4 fibula.
26. C pendant—beads and stones.
27. E pendant—amber.
28. cobalt blue glass beads.
29. amber beads.
30. rings as amulets (E-4).
31. rings as amulets (E-7).
32. I-1 pendant wire.
33. Predominantly low-arc scabbard mouth.
34. Knife with short, stepped handle.
35. Bronzes decorated with a series of small circles.

TABLE 9.1 Continued

Stylistic Traits Associated with the Three Orthogonal Factors.

Traits associated with Factor III

1. Vases chiefly to left, not at foot.
2. A vases with rounded bellies.
3. a^0-1a bowls with high round shoulder and vertical neck.
4. A-1 vase with flat lower and upper shoulders and a flat everted neck.
5. A^0-2 vase with high rounded shoulder and neck curved outward.
6. A^0-3a spheroid jars.
7. B^0-3 vase with incurvate upper shoulder.
8. b^0-3 spherical pots.
9. Ta^0 chalice with flaring rim.
10. Tc^0 conical chalice.
11. Black piriform wheelmade urns.
12. More than 50 percent black pottery.
13. Ceramic motif in relief.
14. Ceramic motif: one horizontal line.
15. Ceramic motif: continuous horizontal ladder.
16. Ceramic motif: symmetrical rectangular meander.
17. Ceramic motif: nested serial lozenge.
18. Ceramic motif: pyramidal.
19. Ceramic motif: punctate decoration with relief margin.
20. Cross-hatched decoration on fibula bows.
21. F pendant—stones.

determine the internal structure of the supracommunities defined by the orthogonal rotation.

The oblimin oblique rotation criterion was applied to the primary factor loadings, yielding the simple loading oblique solution which is plotted in figure 9.5. In this figure, the plotted value represents the oblique factor upon which the site in question received its highest loading. We can see that once again the analysis conforms with the theory discussed above in that the factors are, in general, composed of geographically contiguous sites. A more refined analysis in which each factor was plotted on separate maps and analyzed also indicates that there are areas of rapidly changing similarity which can be interpreted as boundaries, as would be theoretically expected (see figs. 9.6 and 9.7 as examples). Moreover, the results of the oblique analysis confirm Rowlett's (1967:525) observation that the chariot burials were dispersed in such a manner that it was impossible to identify political power centers. If each chariot burial site represented the remains of a settlement that exercised some sort of authority, one would expect each to be associated with its own interaction sphere of communities. In view of the propositions presented above, we would expect this to be manifested in our analysis by a distribution of one chariot burial site per oblique factor. The distribution of the chariot burials as plotted in figure 9.8 clearly do not fit this expectation, thus supporting Rowlett's observation.

It should be noted that with an oblique analysis it is possible to calculate a correlation matrix of the rotated factors, since the factors are not necessarily

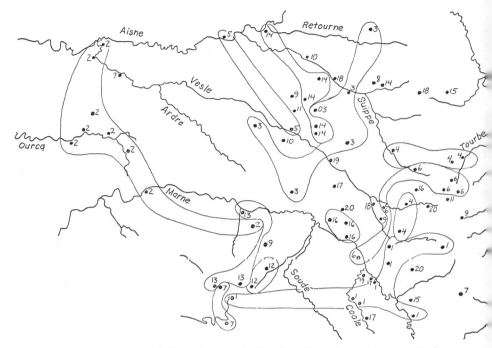

Figure 9.5 Distribution of oblique factors. Number plotted is the factor the site received its highest loading on.

independent. The correlation matrix of the oblique factors can then be factor analyzed to define second-order factors. The second-order factor analysis will delineate the clusters of obliquely defined supracommunities which are relatively similar in terms of the occurrence of stylistic traits. It is expected that the second-order analysis will result in clusters which are basically similar to the orthogonally defined clusters. The clusters will not be exactly the same, however, because the microareal patterning of stylistic attributes responsible for an oblique factor will probably be substantially different from the macroareal patterning that resulted in the orthogonal clusters. Nevertheless, we still expect that geographical proximity will play an important role in the interaction patterns that are responsible for the distribution of stylistic traits, even those traits responsible for the oblique factors, and thus predict that areal groupings will result that are similar to the orthogonal analysis.

The results of the second-order analysis presented in figure 9.9 are markedly similar to the orthogonal analysis, thus conforming to our expectations.

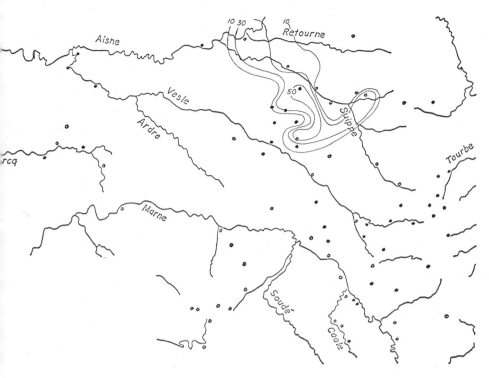

Figure 9.6 Distribution of Oblique Factor XIV.

The problem now is to determine whether the classifications described above have validity as cultural categories or simply as descriptive or empirical categories, as discussed by Taylor (1948:111–49). It should first be noted that the configurations of the isoloads meet the theoretical expectations discussed above. In addition, the location of the burials in relation to the dwelling units, a rather large-scale cultural trait, is related to the subgroupings which were determined on the basis of small-scale stylistic traits. Burial location was entered in only forty of the site reports, so this was not included in the factor analysis. These are, however, plotted in figure 9.9; the fit is not perfect but it is rather good.

There are also other configurations within the data set which are in accordance with theoretically expected distributions. Some of these are admittedly weak and based on incomplete data, but used in conjunction with the above justification of the analysis they lend a degree of external validity to the classification presented here that it hard to deny.

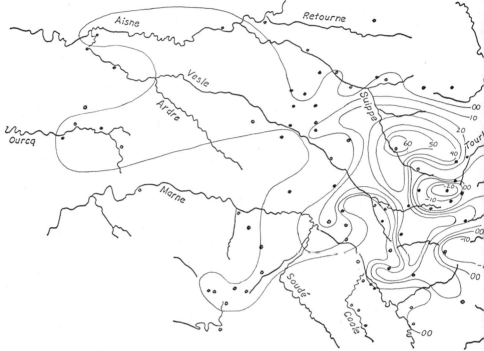

Figure 9.7 Distribution of Oblique Factor IV.

In part, this additional justification is based on the following propositions:

> *1. By contrast with core areas, the surrounding areas of relative heterogeneity represent transitional areas of less sociocultural stability (Lively and Gregory 1954:30).*
> *2. The area of relatively high sociocultural homogeneity displays more of the essential criteria of an integrated social system than the heterogeneous area, and therefore, possesses a greater potential for collective social action (Lively and Gregory 1954:31).*

If, in addition to the above two propositions, we accept the hypothesis that graves are more likely to be plundered by contemporaneous peoples (see Rowlett 1967 for justification for that assumption) in areas of lesser rather than greater sociocultural stability and social integration, we would expect to find that a greater percentage of burials would be violated within sites located where the isoloads run closely together—that is, close to the boundary of a supracommunity and in an area where there is the greatest stylistic variation as one moves through space.

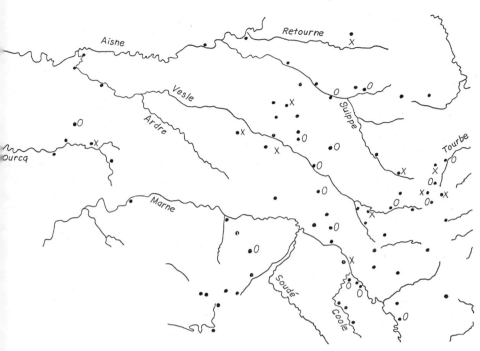

Figure 9.8 Distribution of Chariot burials.
X = intact chariot burial
O = violated chariot burial

The percentages of graves violated are plotted for sites for which the data are known in relation to the orthogonal and the second-order oblique factors in figure 9.9. Although good in some respects, the fit with the orthogonal analysis is rather questionable. With regard to the second-order analysis, the fit is in the expected direction. However, this should not be construed as being a definitive test of the value of one technique over the other because, as was noted above, the data concerning violated graves are incomplete.

Further support for our analysis is provided by the differential distribution of burials indicative of aristocratic warriors and graves associated with craftsmen. Poix (marked by *Z* in figure 9.2), a simple village with burials indicative of craftsmen, is in a relatively central area in Factor I where the isoloads are rather far apart. In accordance with the propositions stated earlier, this configuration of isoloads would indicate that social stability was probably a characteristic of the area around Poix, thus creating an ideal situation for the establishment of a village of craftsmen. When we turn to those sites manifest-

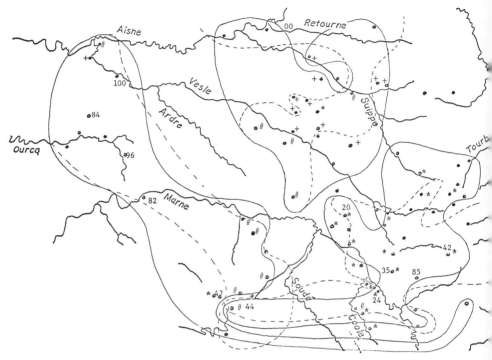

Figure 9.9 Distribution of orthogonal and second order factors.
----- = orthogonal analysis
_____ = second order analysis
  * = graves among houses
  + = houses adjacent to cemetery
  # = houses distant from cemetery
  numbers plotted are percentage of intact graves.

ing the greatest concentrations of chariot burials, such as the Somme Tourbe sites, Mairy, and La Chaussee (*W, X,* and *Y* respectively in figure 9.2), we find that they are in peripheral locations where the isoloads are rather close together—areas of contact with other subgroups and instability where we would expect to find such concentrations of warriors.

The evidence presented thus far provides a great deal of support for the claim that the three supracommunities with the Marne Culture have validity as cultural categories. The use of a wide range of cultural items in the stylistic analysis minimized the chance that we are delineating trade areas rather than communities. Nevertheless it would be informative to examine the structure of intersite stylistic similarity with respect to specific classes of artifacts. Here we shall conduct analyses within the ceramic and nonceramic categories only. Other potentially useful categories for such an analysis can be visualized (e.g., iron tools), but for the purposes of this article the two we have selected should be sufficient. It should be noted that 18 ceramic variables were added for this analysis. This resulted in 147 ceramic and 238 nonceramic variables.

Factor analysis was used, as it was above, to determine the patterns of interrelationships between the sites with respect to both the ceramic and the nonceramic stylistic variables. Common factor analysis was used and the configurations were rotated to orthogonal simple structure using the varimax technique. The factor loadings for each site were plotted and analyzed and can be found in figures 9.10–9.15.

The analysis of the 147 ceramic variables resulted in configurations which once again delineated a North, East, and West Group (figs. 9.10–9.12). The boundaries, however, are not so clearly defined, and the West Group (Factor

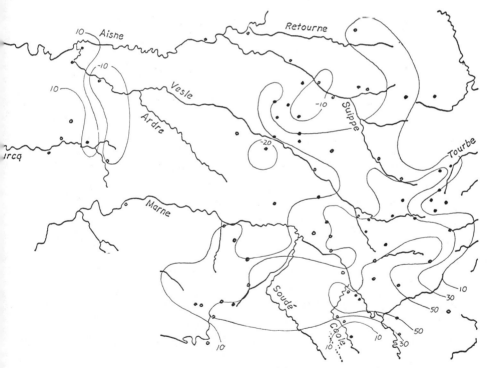

Figure 9.10 Distribution of ceramic attribute orthogonal Factor I.

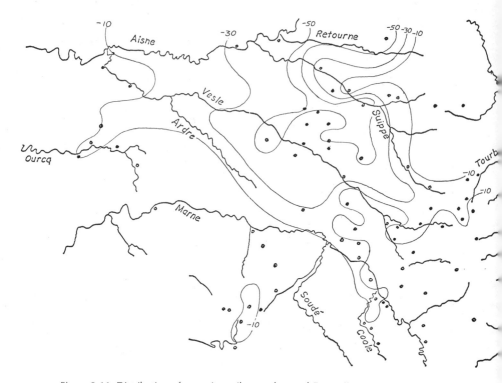

Figure 9.11 Distribution of ceramic attribute orthogonal Factor II.

III) intrudes more into the other groups. The analysis of the nonceramic data defines only a Western Group (fig. 9.13) and an Eastern Group (figs. 9.14 and 9.15). A North Group failed to appear even when factors were rotated beyond the point where the increase in the amount of explained variance ceased to be significant.

The analyses of the data in terms of the ceramic and nonceramic categories have thus resulted in configurations which are less clearly interpretable than the analysis of the categories combined. This suggests that in analyses of this type the stylistic analysis of a wide range of categories of artifacts will result in more valid configurations than an analysis restricted to one or two categories.

In summary, it can be seen that we have achieved our objectives of determining the geographical distribution of cultural similarity in such a manner that the boundaries of the supracommunities within the Marne

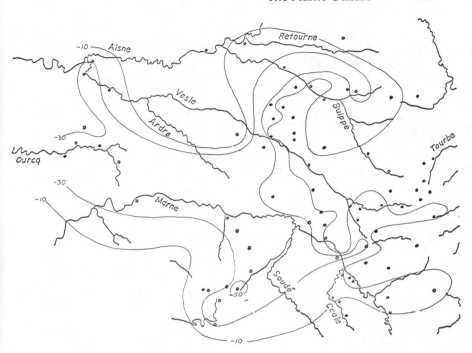

Figure 9.12 Distribution of ceramic attribute orthogonal Factor III.

Culture could be defined and have determined the stylistic traits responsible for these patterns. Isarithmic maps of the three orthogonal factors and the 20 oblique factors were constructed and their correspondence with topographical features was explored to determine whether the vectors representing differential rates of change in stylistic similarity from a reference point corresponded with any topographic features. Correspondence was slight but some was noted, thus leading to the inference that the variance in interaction inferred from these vectors was due partially to topography and partially to cultural factors.

The manner with which the analytical technique consistently led to theoretically expected results lends quite a bit of external validity to a technique already demonstrated to be internally consistent and thus argues for its continued application to complex problems such as the one presented here.

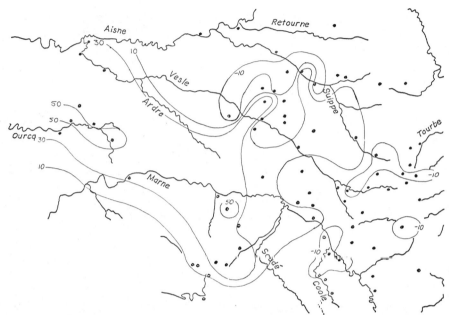

Figure 9.13 Distribution of non-ceramic attribute orthogonal Factor One.

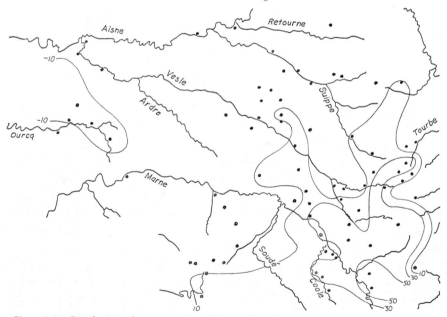

Figure 9.14 Distribution of non-ceramic attribute orthogonal Factor II.

Figure 9.15 Distribution of non-ceramic attribute orthogonal Factor Three.

REFERENCES

Barth, F. 1969. *Ethnic groups and boundaries*. Boston: Little, Brown & Co.

Bradley, R. 1971. Trade competition and artifact distribution. *World Archeology* 2:347–52.

Bretz-Mahler, D. 1957. "Observations sur quelques cimetières de La Tène I en Champagne," Bulletin de la Société Prehistoric Française 55:688–91.

Clarke, D. 1968. *Analytical archeology*. London: Methuen & Co.

Deetz, J. 1965. *The dynamics of stylistic change in Arikara ceramics*. Illinois Studies in Anthropology 4. Urbana: University of Illinois Press.

Duncan, H. D. 1962. *Communication and social order*. London: Oxford University Press.

Grigg, D. 1967. Regions, models and classes. In R. Chorley and P. Haggett, eds. *Models in geography*. London: Methuen & Co.

Hockett, C. 1958. *A course in modern linguistics*. New York: Macmillan.

Lively, C. E. and C. C. Gregory. 1954. The rural socio-cultural area as a field for research, *Rural Sociology* 19:21–31.

Longacre, W. 1964. Sociological implications of the ceramic analysis. In P. Martin, et al., eds. *Chapters in the prehistory of Eastern Arizona.* Publications of the Chicago Natural History Museum, pp. 155–70.

Milke, W. 1949. The quantitative distribution of cultural similarities and their cartographic representation. *American Anthropologist* 51:237–51.

Paisley, W. 1968. The museum computer and the analysis of artistic content. In *Computers and their Potential Application in Museums.* New York: Arno Press.

Pollnac, R. m.s. Relative homogeneity as an indicator of social process: an Old World Example.

Redfield, R. 1960. *The little community.* Chicago: University of Chicago Press.

Rowlett, R. 1967. *The East Group of the Marne Culture,* Ph.D. dissertation, Harvard University.

——— 1968. "The Iron Age North of the Alps," *Science* 161:123–34.

Rowlett, R. and R. Pollnac. 1972. Multivariate analysis of the Marnian La Tène cultural groups. In D. G. Kendall, F. R. Hodson, and P. Tautu, eds. *Mathematics in the historical and archeological sciences.* Edinburgh: Edinburgh University Press.

Taylor, W. 1948. *A study of archeology.* Carbondale, Illinois: SIU Press.

Whallon, R. 1968. Investigations of late prehistoric social organization in New York State. In S. Binford and L. Binford, eds. *New perspectives in archeology.* Chicago: Aldine Publishing Co.

» THREE «

The Site: After

Time deals harshly with the works of man and makes the archeologist's task all the more difficult. The natural forces of wind and rain, of bacterial action, erosion and sunshine, the accidental treading by human and nonhuman feet, and the not-so-accidental attention of scavengers work in two ways. First, they cause changes in position. Objects may be pushed downward into the ground, where they may or may not be more likely to survive. They may also be displaced horizontally and carried either to another portion of a site or removed from it completely. Secondly, most cultural remains are themselves transformed over time, and more often than not mechanical and chemical processes remove them completely from the archeological record. While some alterations, such as the transformation of Carbon 14, are slow and regular enough to permit chronological inferences to be made, change rarely works in the archeologist's favor.

Unfortunately the single most abrupt disruptive act may be caused by the archeologist himself and it is a truism to note that excavation by its very nature is destructive. Even with the greatest care small, fragile, and decaying bones may disintegrate, and tiny dirt-covered objects slip by unnoticed. Complex relationships between stratigraphic units become clearest after-the-fact through examination of wall profiles, and even careful measurement of position at the time of excavation does not ensure that proper stratigraphic context may be subsequently established. The article by Chilcott and Deetz (chapter 13) illustrates these points all too clearly.

The archeologist then finds himself two levels removed from the people and the processes he wishes to study. He must try to reconstruct from excavated remains how a particular site looked at the time of abandonment; only then can he attempt cultural reconstructions. The most crucial question one must pose is this: To what extent is the destruction, displacement, or removal of materials from a site random? If each object is equally susceptible, the net result is simply to increase the difficulty in making any interpretations at all. If, on the other hand, disruptive forces work in a nonrandom manner, a bias is introduced which makes it all the easier for an archeologist ignorant of those forces to reach an erroneous conclusion. One example may illustrate this point. The notion that Paleolithic man depended primarily on meat for sustenance derives, in large part, from the masses of animal bone recovered from archeological sites; but most ethnographically known hunters and gatherers depend primarily on vegetable foods, and it is interesting to reconsider the prehistoric record in light of this fact. One then realizes that in most cases plant remains have an extremely short archeological lifespan, and the likelihood is almost nil that direct evidence of plant utilization would be preserved in Early Man sites. On the other hand, given the right conditions, butchered animal bones remain intact for millions of years.

Problems of this kind readily lend themselves to a direct "experimental" approach. The range of natural forces which have shaped and distorted the archeological record over millions of years may be directly observed today. This is one of the limited number of cases where the law of uniformitarianism may be directly employed by the archeologist; the only constraint is the length of time one is willing to wait between setting the experiment up and reading the final result.

10

EDITED BY P. A. JEWELL • G. W. DIMBLEBY

The Experimental Earthwork on Overton Down, Wiltshire, England: The First Four Years

To construct an *"artificial"* site and excavate parts of it after varying intervals of time may provide the means toward more than one end. *Both Jewell and Dimbleby and Chilcott and Deetz (chapter 13) use the controlled context of a constructed site, but the questions they ask are not the same. Jewell and Dimbleby concern themselves primarily with the long-term changes a site and its contents may undergo. Their aim is to avoid errors in site interpretation and also to discover new and promising techniques of analysis.*

Some types of change seem to progress in a regular, orderly fashion, and the authors, with good reason, take pains to isolate them. If the direction of such processes can be determined, one may then extrapolate backward from the observed end-point and postulate, for example, that the flat shallow ditches that surround many ancient English sites once had straight deep walls. And if, by some good fortune, one can estimate the rate at which such changes take place, a means for absolute dating may present itself. Thus, the authors are much interested in measuring the rate at which animal and human bone lose their original nitrogen content over time.

Other types of site alterations which are neither unidirectional nor predictable in nature cause nothing but trouble. By working in a rigidly controlled context, for example, Jewell and Dimbleby can document the major mixing

This report is published with the aid of a grant from the Council of British Archaeology. Reprinted, with minor editorial changes, from *Proceedings of the Prehistoric Society* 32(11), 1966, pp. 313–42. Text and tables from pp. 326–35 have been deleted from this version. Used by permission of the society.

effect which moles may have on archeological deposits. Likewise, to their own surprise they note the extent of migration of pollen grains both upward as well as downward in a sealed deposit. Thus, from one point of view the artificial site may serve a negative but still essential function because it may isolate processes which both hinder and strongly bias interpretation. The best that the archeologist can do in such cases is to try to avoid such pitfalls once they are pointed out.

The Overton Down earthwork was constructed in 1960, the first of a series designed to study the changes which take place with time in a bank and ditch, and in selected materials buried within the bank. Full details of the construction of the earthwork are given by Jewell (1963), hereafter referred to as the *Basic Manual*. The experiment was designed to be sectioned at intervals of 2, 4, 8, 16, 32, 64 and, perhaps, 128 years, though, in the early stages particularly, observations will be made at more frequent intervals. We deal here with the results of the two- and four-year sections, together with such other observations as were made. It has not yet been possible to complete the analytical work on all the buried objects; deficiencies will be made up as far as possible in future reports.

METHODS OF EXCAVATION

The excavation of March 1961 was confined to the small amount of scree which had formed in the ditch during the first seven and a half months from construction. A cutting 30 inches wide was made 6 feet from the northwest end of the ditch; this section was left open.

For the excavations through the bank and ditch in September 1962 and July 1964 identical procedures were adopted. A bridge or gantry of steel scaffold-poles was erected over the bank (pl. 10.1, no. I) to cover the area of a transverse cutting 5 feet wide, the northwest side of which contained the relevant steel tube. This framework was supported laterally on the flat ground at the inner and outer tail of the bank, and on the central line by two steel putlogs driven vertically into the crest, 30 inches outside the sides of the cutting. Two carefully leveled horizontal tubes, with measuring tapes fastened to their inner faces, provided a datum-plane for the recording of the section, and a similar taped tube at ground level was used as a datum for the ditch.

The steel framework also provided a planked platform on each side of the bank, 3 feet from the ground, so that excavation of the outer layers could

No. 1

No. 2

No. 3

Plate 10.1 The Ditch, Overton Down Experimental Site: General Views

No. 1, March, 1961. After a mild winter; No. 2, April, 1962. After second mild winter; No. 3, March, 1963. After severe winter

proceed at two levels simultaneously. These were dismantled after the excavation of layer D, and the remainder of the scaffolding was removed when the sections had been drawn, to clear the site for photography.

The bank material was excavated with trowels, brushes, and buckets, and was dumped from wheelbarrows on to sheets of corrugated iron laid clear of the line of the section. The cutting was subsequently refilled to conform with the adjacent profile.

CHANGES IN THE BANK AND DITCH

As the bank and ditch have so far developed quite independently of each other, it is possible for the sake of convenience to consider them separately. The two sections are, however, fully represented in figs. 10.1 and 10.2.

The Ditch

March 1961 (7½ months after construction). Although the winter had been mild, scree had formed in the bottom angles of the ditch to a height of 10–12 inches up the walls, and extended up to 24 inches across the floor on either side (pl. 10.1, no. 1). The angle of repose was 35°–38° from the horizontal. The lowest level, resting on the chalk floor, consisted of a sprinkle of dark soil, derived from the topsoil at the lips of the ditch (pl. 10.3, no. 1). Above this the major part of the deposit consisted of fine chalk rubble interspersed with soil crumbs. Only the topmost 1–2 inches was of coarse clean chalk fragments, presumably detached by occasional frosts during the early months of 1961.

The sides of the ditch had been slightly but uniformly weathered above the scree level, to a maximum penetration of 1 inch. At the lips the soil had expanded slightly to produce a small overhang. At the northwest end the steps cut in the ramp were still discernible, though much degraded and crumbled by frost. By contrast the exposed floor of the ditch appeared to have suffered little from frost weathering. The small hollows in it were filled with a thin deposit of rainwashed chalk mud.

September 1961 (13½ months after construction). The main point of interest at this date was that the cutting through the ditch-fill, which had been left open in March, was showing a further accumulation of rubble, reaching a maximum depth of about 3 inches (pl. 10.3, no. 2). This shows that even during the summer slow disintegration of the ditch sides continued to occur.

April 1962 (20½ months after construction). Following another mild winter, unexpectedly marked changes had occurred in the ditch (pl. 10.1, no. 2).

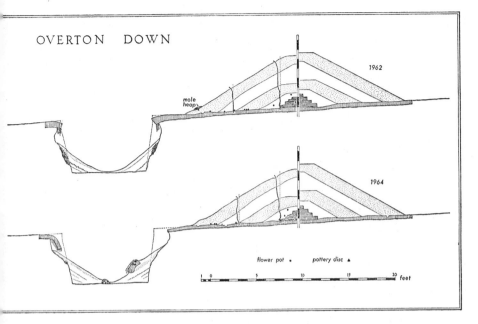

OVERTON   DOWN

1962

mole
heap

1964

flower pot •   pottery disc ▲

| 0   5   10   15   20
feet

Figure 10.1 Sections of the Overton Down experimental earthwork, 1962 and 1964.

Scree had accumulated to a vertical height of 36 inches and the chalk wall above this had disintegrated and collapsed to such a degree that the turf was deeply undercut, causing it to drop downward at the edges of the ditch. A series of measurements of this undercutting was taken in each face of the ditch at points opposite the posts in the bank (see *Basic Manual,* fig. 8). The results (in inches) were as follows:

Post Number	1	2	3	4	5	6	7	8	9	Mean
Northeast face	12	12	12	10½	11½	10	14	14	12	12
Southwest face	11½	12	12	10½	10½	10½	13½	11	12	11½

Although the northeast face receives the brunt of the wind and rain, and is exposed to greater temperature fluctuations, it had not decayed materially faster than the southwest face.

The cut edges of the turf had also eroded back 1–1½ inches, exposing many flints which were at the junction of the humic horizon and the underlying chalk. Some of them remained suspended in the mesh of grass roots (pl. 10.2, no. 1).

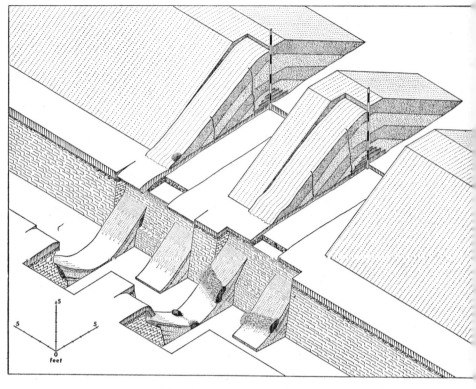

Figure 10.2 Isometric view of the sections cut in 1962 and 1964, Overton Down experimental earthwork.

The angle of repose of the silt remained constant at 35°–38° toward the top of the scree, but flattened toward the bottom, where the larger fragments of chalk and flint had rolled down. A strip about 18 inches wide, down the center of the ditch floor, was still substantially bare.

September 1962 (25½ months from construction). On August 7, 1962, after torrential rain, the first piece of undercut turf fell from the outer lip of the ditch and came to rest on the center of the floor. A second piece fell before the excavation began on September 10.

When sectioned (pl. 10.3, no. 3), the top of the scree in the ditch reached a vertical height of 40–42 inches. The lower margins had coalesced to give a parabolic profile and the center line of the ditch was lightly covered by rolled fragments of chalk and flint.

In section the scree showed alternating bands of coarse and fine chalk

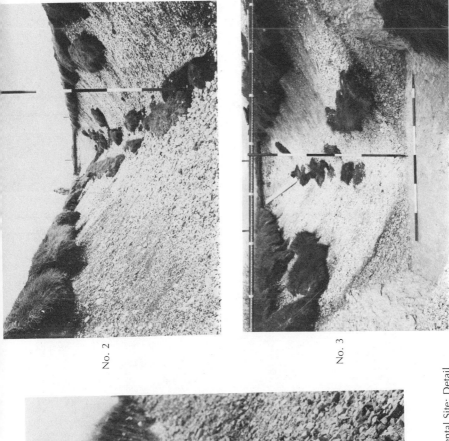

No. 2

No. 3

No. 1

Plate 10.2 The Ditch Overton Down Experimental Site: Detail

No. 1, April, 1962. Flints suspended by grass roots owing to undercutting and erosion of humus horizon; No. 2, March, 1964. Scree piling up against turves which fell in the winter of 1962/3; No. 3, July, 1964. Section through fallen turf, showing accumulation of scree

No. 1   No. 2

Plate 10.3 The Ditch, Overton Down Experimental Site: Sections

No. 1, March, 1961. First winter's accumulation; No. 2, September, 1961. In the background is the section of the previous March, now covered with material fallen during the summer; No. 3, September, 1962. Two years' accumulation, showing stratification; No. 4, July, 1964. The floor of the ditch is completely covered rubble, the latter mixed with soil crumbs and dust. These clearly represent deposition respectively in winter and in summer. The deposit in the first year had protected the sides of the ditch from all but superficial disintegration, to a height of about 18 inches. Above this the profile of the sides was markedly concave, the maximum undercutting being 12 inches horizontally. Toward the top the amount of erosion decreased, where the sides were partly shielded by the drooping overhang of turf and the thick fringe of rootlets hanging from it. The expansion factor for the material accumulated during these first two years was 1.62.

March 1963 (32 months from construction). The earthwork was inspected at the end of March 1963, after one of the severest of recent winters (pl. 10.1, no. 3).

In the ditch the scree rose to within 12 inches of the surface of the chalk—that is, to a vertical height of about 50 inches. This is some inches higher than the level recorded 16 months later, at the time of the second excavation, so that there must subsequently have been some downslope movement, probably as a result of heavy rain.

The most marked effect of the recent heavy snow was on the turf at the lips of the ditch, numerous pieces of which had broken away; the total fall amounted in all to about three-fifths of the lengths of the sides, excluding the ramps at either end. Most of these pieces measured from 1 foot to 3 feet in length, and up to 18 inches in width, and had slipped or rolled into the bottom of the V-shaped trough formed by the screes. A few larger strips, however, the longest measuring 10 feet, had come to rest at various distances down the scree slopes, and rubble was already beginning to pile up above them (pl. 10.1, nos. 2 and 3).

Though no precise measurement was made at this time, it was clear that this severe winter produced much less erosion and scree-formation than might have been expected. Even sixteen months later the amount of detritus formed during the second two years from construction, including this winter, was only about one-quarter of the volume formed during the first two, relatively mild, years (see table 10.1). This much lower rate of accumulation is partly to be accounted for, of course, by the progressive shrinking of the depth of exposed ditch wall, as the screes rise; but it is also probably due in part to the prolonged character of the frost and the presence of a protective blanket of snow. The effects of a series of isolated frosts of equal severity, but separated by thaws, would undoubtedly have been greater.

July 1964 (48 months after construction). At the time of the second

TABLE 10.1
Cross-Sectional Areas of Ditch Fill, Overton Down
Experimental Earthwork

	1962	1964
Volume of sides weathered	5.92	6.12
Volume of scree formed	9.56	11.60
Expansion factor	1.62	1.90

Volumes given in cubic feet, excluding "turf" (A1).

excavation, which began on July 24, the top of the scree in the ditch reached a vertical height of 48 inches where the overhanging turf had fallen away, and a few inches less where it had not (pl. 10.2, no. 3). Very little additional turf had fallen since the spring of 1963. The portions which had then come to rest with the roots downward were still more or less intact, and supported a strong growth of grasses. Those which had fallen grass downward were beginning to disintegrate into heaps of loose soil, which had been only rarely colonized by secondary vegetation.

Except where the slopes were broken by turf lumps, the angle of repose was around 32° from the horizontal, a lower angle than those previously recorded (pl. 10.3, no. 4). The uppermost 3 to 4 inches of the scree was markedly more fine-grained and earthy than the lower levels. The expansion factor of the accumulated material was 1.9. The layer of soil crumbs at the base, deposited during the first few months after construction, was still identifiable, though partially impregnated with calcium carbonate. A number of worms were recovered from the silt and the turf lumps, but evidence of their activity was less marked than in the bank.

The Bank: Morphological Changes

March 1961 (7½ months). At this early stage little apparent change had taken place in the bank, apart from some comminution of the surface of the chalk rubble (see below). This surface layer was still loose, and could easily be deformed by the weight of a person climbing up the slope of the bank.

April 1962 (20½ months). After the second winter's exposure the crest of the bank had sunk by 3–3½ inches. Though a superficial layer, ½–1 inch thick, remained loose, the underlying material had begun to consolidate into a crust, so that it was possible to walk up the slope of the bank with only slight distortion of the surface.

September 1962 (25½ months). The section of the bank (pl. 10.4, no. 2 and fig. 10.1) showed that after two years the profiles of all the constituent

No. 2

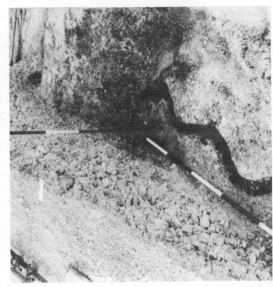

No. 4

No. 1

No. 3

Plate 10.4 Bank Sections, Overton Down Experimental Site

No. 1, September, 1962. The scaffolding erected for making the section; No. 2, September, 1962. The first section; No. 3, July 1964. The second section; No. 4, July, 1964. Mole run penetrating the turf core

layers had become somewhat rounded, and that the crest had sunk by 4 inches. Almost all this shrinkage is to be accounted for by the compression of the two innermost layers, A and B. A table of cross-sectional areas is given in table 10.2.

The base of the bank had spread laterally by about 9 inches at front and back, and grasses were beginning to grow through this recently deposited rubble. A number of molehills had also contributed to the accumulation of

TABLE 10.2

Cross-Sectional Areas (Sq. Ft.) of the Bank, Overton Down Experimental Earthwork

Layer	As Built	1962	% Shrinkage	1964	% Shrinkage
A Piled turf	3.6	2.7	25	2.3	36
B Soil and chalk	7.4	5.4	27	5.2	30
C Chalk rubble	15.6	13.4	14	13.5	12
D Chalk rubble	22.5	22.2	1	22.5	0
E/F Chalk rubble	29.6	26.8	9	24.2	18
Whole Bank	78.7	70.5	10	67.7	14

new material at the tails of the bank section. The buried polythene tubes (fig. 10.1) showed that there had been a downslope movement of the upper layers, amounting to 4–7 inches at the surface, and progressively less with increasing depth. The base of the outer polythene tube appeared to have been moved bodily toward the ditch for a distance of 4 inches. This movement is difficult to explain, even by the action of moles.

Surprisingly, after only two years, the rubble of the bank had consolidated sufficiently to allow the northwest side of the section to be cut back to a vertical plane, exposing the full depth of the steel tube. The expected collapse of the sides, for which ample allowance had been made in the design of the earthwork, did not take place, though it must be admitted that they stood unsupported only for a few hours before refilling.

When refilled, the excavated material only just occupied the volume from which it had been dug out; and subsequently the center of the refilled cutting has sunk by 1½ inches. The lack of any expansion is to be accounted for by the double handling of the chalk rubble during excavation and refilling, which reduced the average particle size and thus permitted a greater degree of interstitial packing.

March 1963 (32 months). Though the greatest effects of the severe winter were to be seen in the ditch, the bank also bore marks of it. Exposed flints on the surface of the bank were frost-shattered, and the top of the bank was spongy, with open frost cracks, presumably the result of frost-heaving.

July 1964 (48 months). The profiles of the constituent layers of the bank had become even more rounded (pl. 10.4, no. 3 and fig. 10.1), and the crest had sunk 6½ inches from its original height, an effect again due almost entirely to the continuing compression of the turf and soil core. The distortion of the buried polythene tubes suggested that some downslope movement of the upper layers had taken place since 1962, though at a reduced rate.

Little or no additional lateral spread of the base of the bank had occurred, presumably because the tails of the slope were becoming stabilized by a vigorous growth of grasses, itself doubtless encouraged by the soil deposited there by moles. It was noticeable that the upper margin of the grass-fringe acted as a barrier to the downward slip of the superficial layer of loose chalk gravel, leading to the formation of a distinct hump in the profile immediately above this point.

The chalk rubble was again sufficiently stable to allow the temporary cutting of a vertical face without collapse. In layers C and D the cementing of the rubble by redeposited calcium carbonate was well-marked.

The Bank: Textural Changes

Observations on the textural changes in the bank surface were of three kinds. First, comparative observations, based on both visual and photographic records, were made on the disintegration of the chalk and flint rubble. Secondly, the gravitational sorting down the slope of the bank was investigated by mechanical analysis, and this was augmented by the third approach, the changes in the distribution of acid-insoluble residues as time went on.

Disintegration of chalk and flint rubble. On completion of the earthwork the rubble of the bank consisted of chalk and flint lumps mainly in the 2–3 inch range, but with a uniform scatter of larger lumps of 3–4 inches. These lumps were angular and randomly distributed. Finer material was also present. At this time it was difficult to distinguish the flint rubble from the chalk, the sizes being comparable.

By October, only three months after construction, there had been a noticeable reduction in the size of the larger lumps, and in places it was possible to see the lumps breaking up (pl. 10.5, no. 1). As this was before the winter, frost was not responsible. Cracks, due to the mechanical disturbance in excavation and possibly to the release of compression, were opening up under the influence of wetting and drying and temperature fluctuations.

Plate 10.5 Bank Surface, Overton Down Experimental Site, showing early weathering

No. 1. Fragmentation of larger chalk lumps in first three months, October 1960. No. 2. Frost-shattered chalk after first winter

Frost action undoubtedly played some part during the winter of 1960–61, bringing about further reduction of the larger lumps (pl. 10.5, nos. 2–4), but thereafter there has been relatively little change, though, as noted above, frost-heaving occurred during the winter of 1962–63. Latterly flint nodules have become more conspicuous as their disintegration has been less rapid than that of chalk lumps initially of equivalent size.

The sections of 1962 and 1964 revealed clearly the reduction in size of the surface rubble compared with that lying deeper in the bank. This reduction in size affects the top 3 inches; below this no changes appear to have taken place.

By 1964 larger lumps of about 2 inches diameter were still to be found, but the mean size of the rubble, which was still angular, was between ½ and 1 inch, representing relatively slight change over the last two years. It is interesting to note that the two sides of the bank showed no consistent differences due to aspect (pl. 10.6, nos. 1 and 2); one is reminded of the same lack of differentiation in the weathering of the two sides of the ditch. On the other hand, rubble on the two ends of the bank was much smaller than that of the sides, the average maximum size being only 1 inch and the mean diameter about ½ inch (pl. 10.6, nos. 3 and 4). A possible explanation is as follows:

Downslope movement on the two sides of the bank has progressively uncovered a small but significant supply of large unweathered rubble which, spreading down the two sides, has provided as it broke up a supply of about 2-inch diameter rubble. In other words, it has maintained a high average maximum rubble size. At the ends of the bank, because of their triangular shape, such a supply of large-sized rubble produced by denudation is not available and therefore disintegration of the chalk *in situ* has proceeded at what we might term a normal rate. This smaller-sized rubble probably represents the true rate of disintegration in the four years that the bank has been exposed to atmospheric weathering.

Gravitational sorting. Samples were collected from the sloping face of the bank, on the side away from the ditch, in 1962 and 1964. On each occasion three large samples were collected, from the base, middle, and top of the sloping surface. The samples were subdivided for convenience of handling in the laboratory. To determine the size composition of the surface material in 1962, the subdivided samples were gently machine sieved for five minutes, while in 1964 they were sieved by hand for a similar length of time. This change in technique was adopted because of the variations between subdi-

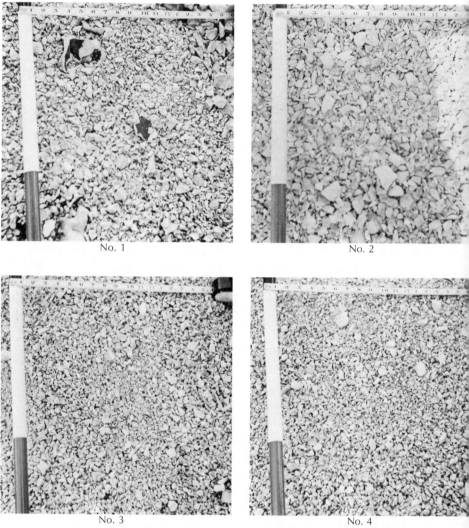

No. 1   No. 2

No. 3   No. 4

Plate 10.6 The Bank Surface, Overton Down Experimental Site, March, 1964

No. 1, The north-east side of the bank at Pole V; No. 2, The south-west side of the bank at Pole V; No. 3, The north-west end of the bank; No. 4, The south-east end of the bank vided samples in 1962. Variation was less in 1964 and it is thought that there was better separation and less mechanical disintegration than before. Before sieving in 1964, any aggregates of chalk particles were separated by gently crushing between the fingers; no aggregates had been noted in 1962.

The results for the two years, shown in table 10.3 and diagrammatically in fig. 10.3, are not, therefore, strictly comparable, but the results in both years show marked differences between the samples from the top of the bank slope

TABLE 10.3

Size Characteristics of Samples from Slope of Bank of Experimental Earthwork, Overton Down, Wilts.

	1962			1964		
	Base %	*Middle* %	*Top* %	*Base* %	*Middle* %	*Top* %
Passing No. 72 sieve	1.9	4.7	7.2	0.2	0.3	0.6
Retained on No. 72 sieve	1.6	1.8	8.3	0.3	0.4	1.6
No. 25 sieve	1.1	0.7	21.2	1.2	1.5	6.2
No. 8 sieve	1.5	0.6	14.1	2.6	3.0	8.3
⅛ in. sieve	8.6	3.7	18.5	13.5	14.9	22.5
¼ in. sieve	46.0	34.3	21.6	40.0	47.7	35.6
½ in. sieve	39.2	54.2	9.1	42.1	32.1	25.1

and those from the middle and base. The diagrams for samples from the base and middle are strongly skewed to the right, indicating the very considerable proportion of material in the coarser grades. The diagrams for the top samples show that a greater amount of finer material is present. There are, however, considerable differences between the top diagrams for 1962 and 1964; only the latter are skewed to the right, and then less markedly than in the base and middle diagrams. The top diagram for 1962 shows a relatively large amount of fine material and none of the characteristic concentration of material into the coarser grades. Visual inspection of the earthwork since it was built had indicated changes in the surface characteristics with time and some variations along the length of the bank; and it seems likely that the differences in the top diagram reflect real differences in surface features. In both years the analyses have reinforced the impression of a noticeable concentration of coarser material toward the base of the slope.

Among this coarser material there was a high proportion of flints. A crude estimate of the amount of flint is given by the percentage of acid-insoluble residue (material remaining after prolonged treatment with 10N HCl). For uniformity of comparison the results are given as percentages of total sam-

OVERTON DOWN EXPERIMENTAL EARTHWORK
CHARACTERISTICS OF SAMPLES FROM SURFACE OF BANK

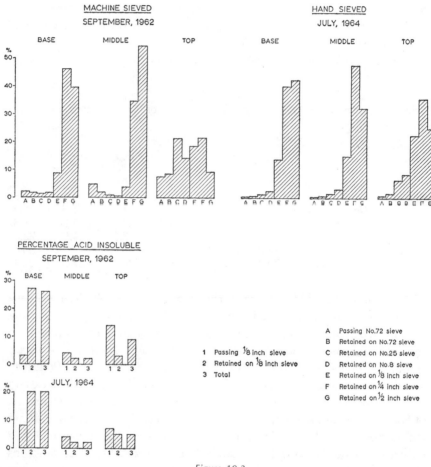

Figure 10.3

ples, and of material greater or less than ⅛ inch for each of the three sites on the bank surface in each year. The results in 1962 and 1964 were very similar, the outstanding characteristic being the large percentage of acid-insoluble material in the basal samples (table 10.4). At the base of the bank in 1962, 94 percent by weight of the material was greater than ⅛ inch, 27 percent of this being acid insoluble. The corresponding figures in 1964 were

TABLE 10.4

Percentage of Acid-insoluble Material in Samples from Bank of Experimental Earthwork, Overton Down, Wilts.

	1962			1964		
	Base	*Middle*	*Top*	*Base*	*Middle*	*Top*
Passing ⅛ in. sieve	3	4	14	8	4	7
Retained on ⅛ in. sieve	27	2	3	20	2	5
Total	26	2	9	20	2	5

96 percent and 20 percent acid-insoluble. At the top of the bank in 1962 only 49 percent of the material was greater than ⅛ inch and only 3 percent of this was acid insoluble. Of the finer material 14 percent was acid-insoluble. In the 1964 top sample the difference in the percentage of insoluble residue between the coarser and finer fractions was scarcely significant although the tendency for the finer material to contain more acid-insoluble residue was retained.

Field observations and the data reported above enable an outline to be given of suggested processes in the weathering of the bank surface. After construction, the effect of weathering would be to break up the material on the surface of the bank, largely by alternate freezing and thawing, by wetting and drying, and by solution of calcium carbonate from the chalk, leading to disaggregation. Although initially the flinty material in the bank was probably generally larger in size than the chalky material the greater percentage of flint present in the larger grades does suggest that the flint blocks have been more resistant than the chalk to disintegration. Under the conditions of creep, wash, and consolidation leading to the slow downhill movement of material at the bank surface, as shown by the bent polythene tubes, there would be a tendency for the larger material to roll, or slide, to the lower parts of the slope and there accumulate. If the movement of the larger material occurs sporadically rather than continuously, then we would expect to find a patchy distribution of larger material on the surface of the bank. On occasions, particular areas of bank surface would lose a considerable part of their larger material, and there would be a more even distribution of the various grades of material, as in the top sample collected in 1962.

As well as disintegration of material, some aggregation has also taken place, with the "cementing" of chalk particles by redeposition of calcium carbonate. This was noted in all the samples collected in 1964, and was especially common with material between ¼ inch and ⅛ inch in diameter, although it did occur on both larger and smaller particles. Usually this "cemented" chalk could be disaggregated by gently crushing it between the fingers, while its porous nature could be clearly seen. It is this material which should hold any water that is available for plant growth, and which would allow the colonization of weathering chalk surfaces by higher plants (compare Locket 1945–46, a, b).

In all the 1964 samples organic matter was also found. This consisted of remains of higher plants—fragments of leaves, stems, seed cases, roots, and fruits; fragments of mosses and other plants; and crumbs of humus. With the exception of the moss fragments which might have been derived from plants growing on the bank, although none had been seen in spite of careful search, this organic material had obviously been blown on to the bank from the surrounding area. There were a few fragments which seemed to have been burnt before being blown on to the bank.

The organic matter present was estimated by determining the amount of organic carbon present using the wet oxidation method of Walkley and Black (Walkley 1947). Determinations were carried out using as a blank a sample of chalk the surface of which had been carefully scraped to ensure that the sample was uncontaminated and as little weathered as possible. The results, shown in table 10.5, indicate the concentration of a considerable amount of organic matter in the fine fraction (< 2 millimeters) of all the samples from the surface of the bank. Values in all size grades are higher for base (maximum 3.1 percent) and top samples than for middle samples. Some of this organic matter will have been wind-carried, and snow also deposited fine material; but the outermost layer of the bank initially contained some organic matter derived from the ditch trimmings.

BURIED MATERIALS

Recovered specimens, residues or "altered" (see Biek 1963: 108 ff.) materials were examined by the appropriate specialists. It was not possible to assemble all the information in time for this article, so the overall picture is inevitably incomplete.

The following brief summary of conclusions to date should be read in conjunction with section VII, below, which suggests that even the turf core provided an aerobic, strongly biologically active environment. For details of the original materials, positions, and conditions the *Basic Manual* should be consulted. Such detailed descriptions as are available of the states of various

TABLE 10.5
Percentage of Organic Matter in Samples from the
Bank of Experimental Earthwork, Overton Down,
Wilts.

	1964		
	Base	Middle	Top
< 2 mm.	3.1	1.6	2.1
2 mm. — $\frac{1}{8}$ in.	0.7	0.4	0.9
$\frac{1}{8}$ in. — $\frac{1}{4}$ in.	not determined		0.6

materials after two and four years' burial are given after this summary, in the same order as in the original report.

Summary of Conclusions

Sheer thickness of material afforded some protection, as the inner layers of folded textiles were in better condition than the outer. In the chalk, cotton plain cloth was already much weakened after two years and was partially broken down after four. By contrast, the khaki twill showed no breakdown even after four years, though it was weaker weftway. Of the two wool cloths, though both were very weak after four years, the gaberdine was in better condition after two, but rather worse after four (pls. 10.7–10.9). The slight differences between the two linen specimens may reflect degrees of bleaching (not necessarily indicated by the original color of the cloth, owing to possible residual color from the raw flax fiber), or they may be within the degree of variation in replication. Linen appeared to be better preserved than the other textiles. In all cases there was discoloration, and black and brightly colored staining; and such evidence as there was all pointed to bacteria as the principal agents of degradation, especially on the vegetable fibers.

There is need for some care in interpreting the results. Sometimes there was evidence of considerable bacterial growth without much obvious damage to the fiber. Again, there was gross fungal growth on the wool specimens (pl. 10.10, nos. 1–4), but no work has yet been done to show whether this has been responsible for any of the observed weakening or staining.

There was no evidence of fungal activity or decay on the vegetable fibers. The fibrillation and rectangular cleavage are presumably the result of embrittlement due to removal of hemicelluloses and amorphous cellulose. This effect is normally associated with degradation by a nonfungal, probably chemical, agency or possibly with high moisture alone. It is thought to be similar to the state observed in wood after long periods of burial under conditions

214   *Jewell and Dimbleby*

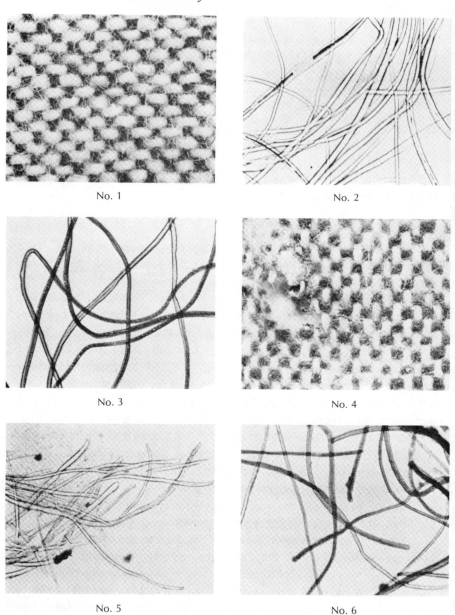

No. 1

No. 2

No. 3

No. 4

No. 5

No. 6

Plate 10.7 Buried Material, Overton Down Experimental Site: Woollen Contrast Cloth (1)

No. 1, Cloth before burial (×4); No. 2, Warp fibres before burial (×75); No. 3, Weft fibres (dyed) before burial (×75); No. 4, 1962. Cloth from upper (chalk) level (×4); No. 5, 1962. Warp fibres from upper level (×75); No. 6, 1962. Weft fibres from upper level (×75)

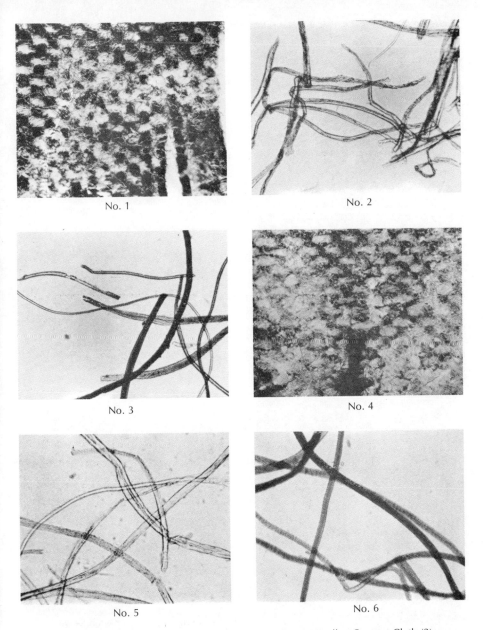

Plate 10.8 Buried Materials, Overton Down Experimental Site: Woollen Contrast Cloth (2)

No. 1, 1962. Cloth from lower (turf) level (×4); No. 2, 1962. Warp fibres from lower level (×75); No. 3, Weft fibres from lower level (×75); No. 4, 1964. Cloth from upper level (×4); No. 5, 1964. Warp fibres from upper level (×75); No. 6, Weft fibres from upper level (×75)

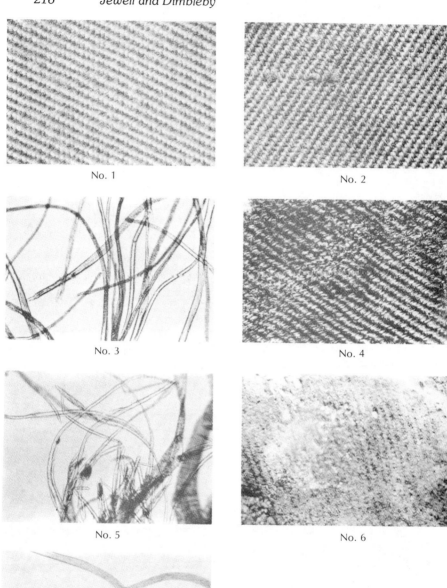

No. 1

No. 2

No. 3

No. 4

No. 5

No. 6

No. 7

Plate 10.9 Buried Material, Overton Down Experimental Site: Gaberdine

No 1, Cloth before burial (×4); No. 2, 1962. Cloth from upper (chalk) level (×4); No. 3, 1962. Warp fibres from upper level (×75); No. 4, 1962. Cloth from lower (turf) level (×4); No. 5, 1962. Warp and weft fibres from lower level (×75); No. 6, 1964. Cloth from upper level (×4); No. 7, 1964. Warp fibres from upper level (×75) where fungal degradation had presumably been inhibited by the very low oxygen tension, as in waterlogged and highly organic deposits (e.g. Preston, in Biek 1963a). In view of the predominantly fungal nature of the attack on the wooden billets (pl. 10.10, no. 5) it would be valuable to know whether the decisive factor here is not so much a lack of oxygen as an avoidance of the material by fungus, possibly due to a fungistatic environment created by bacterial or chemical concentration. Again, it is clear that there can be substantial removal of woody matter, as indicated by loss in density, without gross change in appearance.

Special mention has been made of the adhesion of some textile specimens, and not others, to the chalk and to themselves, as some significance may attach to this in subsequent attempts at interpretation. It might be supposed that solubilization and recrystallization of calcium carbonate would play a part in this effect, which could then be selectively influenced by the pH or some other property of the buried material. Thus cotton stored under moderately high humidity shows fungal attack at first and then bacterial attack, with a pH change as one supersedes the other. Slow solubilization and modification of, for example, starchy or mucic components could have similar effects. In this connection the precise nature of the "particulate matter" on the vegetable fibers (at present under investigation) may be of importance. A similarly "selective" effect was observed on the leathers.

In the turf, cotton could not be recovered even after two years, linen was found virtually unrecognizable, and wool was severely disorganized though it fared best, especially (again) in dyed cloth. Clearly here, as in the khaki cotton (in the chalk), biostatic protection had been given to the fibers by certain metal ions released from dyes, notably chromium which is, of course, so utilized in modern wood preservation.

In contrast to this general difference between levels of burial for textiles, there seemed to be no significant distinction between the same wooden billets or leather samples recovered from the two locations. After four years, there was a density loss amounting to about ⅓ for oak and ¼ for hazel. The charred specimens did not differ significantly in condition from the uncharred, but signs of attack were fewer and mainly at the edges and, sometimes (depending on the route and progress of decay), in the core—as would be expected from the nature and extent of the charred skin.

Leather had not been notably affected at all, after four years, but again perhaps slightly less in turf. Although keratin (wool protein) is more stable than collagen (skin protein) to bacterial attack, the tanning of the skin into

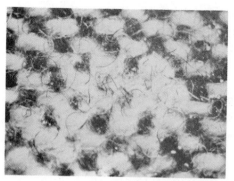

No. 1

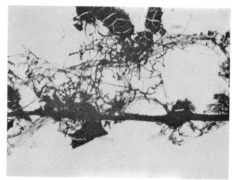

No. 2

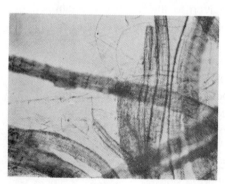

No. 3

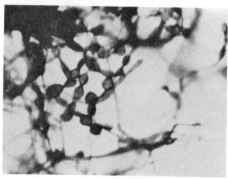

No. 4

No. 5

Plate 10.10 Buried Materials, Overton Down Experimental Site: Fungal Attack

No. 1, Fungal mycelium on woollen contrast cloth, from upper level, 1962 (×7); No. 2, The same, higher magnification (×115); No. 3, The same, higher magnification (×480); No. 4, Mycelia in area of pink discoloration, gaberdine, 1964 (×225); No. 5, Rotting of charred and uncharred hazel billets, upper level, 1962 leather gives the latter more resistance than the wool has. The main changes observed were some deformation (indentation and buckling) such as might be expected in a plastic material, and some stiffening which may be significant (o), as well as a little darkening of the lighter-colored specimens. Although plant roots had grown into the leather, biological attack seemed to be negligible even in the soles, which contained no chromium, and changes are probably due to physicochemical causes alone (a). The fully chrome-tanned, and (initial) chrome vegetable retanned, leathers were in very good condition. The rest seemed much the same, the oak-bark–tanned sole perhaps slightly the worst although it was (again) visually indistinguishable from the modern extract-tanned sole.

OTHER APPLIED MATERIALS

Lycopodium Spores

As described in the *Basic Manual* (pp. 23 and 34), *Lycopodium* spores were dusted over the ground surface to simulate pollen rain, and at the time of each section series of samples were taken in order to trace the movement of these spores.

At each time of sectioning three series of samples were taken, one under the turf stack (layer A), one under the chalk mound (layer C), and one at the edge of the chalk mound (layer E/F) (see figs. 30 and 31[a] of *Basic Manual).* Each series consisted of contiguous samples stemming from above the buried turf line and down through the buried soil to the chalk subsoil. Samples were generally at 1-inch intervals, except in the surface of the buried soil where they were at ½-inch intervals.

The samples were given standard treatment for pollen analysis and all the counts of *Lycopodium* spores in each series were made on the same quantitative basis. The total of spores counted in each series was used as the basis for calculating percentages per sample.

In the 1962 counts, the first series differed from the other two in that the bulk of the spores remained near the original surface, whereas the other two series showed some dissipation of the concentration both upward and downward. This would seem to imply an absence of mixing by earthworms and a minimal effect of downwash under the turf stack as compared with the positions beneath layers C and E/F. By 1964, however, the condition had changed: spores were now being moved both upward and downward even under the turf stack, though in a somewhat irregular pattern. This accords with the field observation that earthworm activity was considerable even in the turf stack by 1964. The other two series also demonstrate a continuance of this process, and movement in an upward direction is particularly remarkable. In fact, the pattern of sampling is apparently inadequate to cover this upward movement, and in the future the sampling pattern will have to extend much further up into the mound for each series.

Charcoal

As described on p. 34 of the *Basic Manual,* crumbled charcoal was spread on the soil surface beneath the bank to represent an occupational deposit, and it was intended that its movement be studied by recording its presence in the microscope preparations used for pollen analysis. It was found later that the soil already contained finely divided charcoal, so this method was not feasible. Other methods could be devised, but for the 1962 and 1964 sections no further attempt was made to trace the fate of the applied charcoal.

Pottery Pieces

On visits of inspection to the earthwork a note was made of the position of any numbered pottery discs that were exposed on the surface of the earthwork or in the ditch. It soon became clear, however, that some pieces were widely displaced and some were found on the grass well away from the earthwork, as far as the enclosure fence. Evidently the pieces had been thrown about by casual visitors to the site. Therefore, no further record was kept of these surface finds.

COLONIZATION BY VEGETATION

As the photographs show, the bank remained essentially bare of vegetation even after four years, and in the ditch the only living plants were those growing on the turves which had broken off and slid down the talus slope. While this is the overall situation, however, it should be recorded that there was a constant pressure by plants of the surrounding vegetation attempting to invade both the bank and the ditch, but for one reason or another successful establishment was not achieved.

The reasons for this lack of success on the bank may be guessed at, but specific investigations have not been made. During the spring of 1961 a number of seedling grasses did appear on the bank but they failed to survive the summer. It will be remembered that the surface of the bank contained material derived from the ditch trimmings (see p. 38 of the *Basic Manual),* including a small amount of the humic topsoil, and it is to be expected that this material could contain seeds. The seedlings occurred on both the windward and the sheltered side of the bank. Nevertheless, in later years, as the ungrazed grass within the fenced enclosure flowered freely, dead flower spikes were frequently found on the bank, though they had probably lost their seed before being torn from the plant. Other plant remains blown on to the bank included seeds of *Rumex acetosella* (Sheep's sorrel), roots of *Festuca ovina* (Sheep's fescue) and plants of the moss *Bryum capillare.* There was no evidence of further colonization by blown seed, even where the weathering surface, which was becoming more compacted (see above), was broken by rabbit scrapes. There was vigorous growth of grasses and some herbs around the margin of the bank, but these were clearly plants which had been rooted in the old soil and grew through the thin chalk cover. Vigorous mole activity, which disturbed the overlying cover, favored this growth.

From 1962 onward a green layer occurred about 1 inch below the surface. This was found to be due to the blue-green alga *Nostoc* and other members of the Cyanophyceae, which are often abundant colonizers of chalk in southern England. Scattered cells of several unicellular green algae of the Ulotrichales and Chlorococcales were also originally present, but in 1964 only one small green alga, probably *Chlorococcum* sp., could be identified. It was surprising to find this layer developing below the surface rather than at it; on the other hand, green algae are known to grow as much as 4 inches below the surface in flower pots—well below the reach of light. There is no question of this layer's having been buried; it followed the contour of the surface and had it ever been exposed it would have been noticed during inspections. Moreover, it occurred in a comparable position even at the crest of the bank where denudation rather than aggradation is taking place.

There is no indication as yet that the colonization of the bank surface is being encouraged by the growth of the blue-green algae. These algae are able to fix atmospheric nitrogen, but in view of the fact that this surface layer contains a certain amount of topsoil, nitrogen deficiency is probably not serious enough to prevent at least a light growth. On the evidence, it seems more likely that a physical factor, such as drought, is limiting plant colonization.

This conclusion is borne out by the fact that colonization of the ditch floor did begin in the first year, though it was overwhelmed by the scree formation of the second and third winters. The ditch bottom was pure chalk; the only influence of topsoil (that which fell into the angles of the ditch from the overhanging soil of the ditch edges) was covered by the first year's fall of scree. Several downland plants established themselves from seed, notably: *Festuca ovina, Holcus lanatus, Arenaria serphyllifolia, Euphrasia nemorosa* (flowered), *Plantago lanceolata, Thymus drucei.*

In hollows in the floor, green algae (Chlorophyceae) were present when conditions were damp and a moss, *Fumaria hygrometrica,* established itself.

On the scree slopes, which of course were unstable, colonization was minimal. A few grass seedlings and dicotyledonous seedlings briefly appeared where a scatter of topsoil had fallen from the ditch edge, again suggesting that the seeds were already in the soil. None of the plants became fully established and were soon overwhelmed by further scree movement.

BIOLOGICAL ACTIVITY

Perhaps the most significant of our observations about biological conditions in the ditch and through the bank are those on the activity of earthworms. Though the soil shows a well-developed earthworm mull, quantitative determinations of the earthworm population in November 1959 suggested that the population then was low (*Basic Manual,* pp. 72–73). This was borne out by the 1962 excavation, which produced little evidence of earthworm activity. The distribution of *Lycopodium* spores showed that the turf core was practically undisturbed by worms, though the two series from under layers C and E/F did show some slight movement which could have been due to worms. In the 1964 section, however, the situation had changed. Worm casts could be seen in interstitial spaces throughout the bank, and the *Lycopodium* spores were clearly being moved upward as well as downward. These spores were of such size to be ingested by the worms along with soil material and voided in the worm casts. By 1964 this process was taking place vigorously in the turf core as well as nearer the edge of the mound.

The downland turf is vigorously worked through by moles, and since worms are a staple component of their diet the observations on mole activity are of considerable biological significance. During the first two years a few molehills appeared along the margin of the bank, and in the 1962 section it was found that the buried surface was disturbed by mole runs for a distance of about a yard in from the edge of the bank. The severe winter of 1962–63, however, seems to have had a profound effect on mole activity. After the snow had melted, the surrounding downland was crisscrossed with numerous mole tracks which had been made on the surface of the turf. Moles do not hibernate, and presumably the ground was hard frozen so that they were driven to move at the turf/snow junction. By March 1963, the downland was dark with fresh molehills, and many new ones appeared along the margin of the bank. The fact that road-chippings from the interfaces of layers C and D, and D and E/F were thrown out shows that they were active for a distance of at least 6 feet into the bank.

The 1964 section exposed a mole run extending right into the turf core (pl. 10.4, no. 4) showing that the moles were exploiting the previously mentioned buildup in the earthworm population. The reasons for this buildup of population have not been investigated, but it is likely that an abundant supply of dead and decomposing vegetation is one factor, and a microclimate with constant humidity and equable temperature is another. Whatever the reasons, it is obvious that even in the center of the mound the oxygen supply is adequate to support vigorous aerobic activity.

This conclusion is confirmed by the condition of the buried materials. Deterioration due to bacteria was general and fungal growth was prevalent on some of the wool samples. The wood specimens were also being attacked by aerobic wood-rot fungi.

In the ditch filling, too, there was a similar increase of worm activity between the dates of the two sections, though not on the same scale as in the bank. Worms were found in the fallen turves, and these may have been the source of the population which was building up in the scree in the ditch. Perhaps the scree has to reach a certain thickness before it provides the environmental conditions favorable to earthworms.

ARCHEOLOGICAL IMPLICATIONS

Although the experiment is still in its early stages, certain tentative conclusions may be drawn which have a bearing on the interpretation of excavated ancient earthworks on chalk:

1. The development of the characteristic "trumpetmouthed" ditch profile, by the progressive weathering of sides originally both steep and straight, has been amply demonstrated. The original profile of ancient flat-bottomed ditches may thus by analogy be reconstructed at least approximately, and the lowest part of the excavated profile, preserved by the earliest scree, may be used as a guide to the original inclination of the sides.

2. It will be observed from the 1964 section that the slope of the inner

scree is already approximately in line with the front slope of the bank. From this it may safely be inferred that the future extension of the ditch profile across the berm will not undercut the bank, and will not lead to any sudden and massive slip of bank material into the ditch. Such a slip could thus occur only if the berm had been substantially narrower than its original width of 4 feet.

In excavated sites, therefore, it can be inferred that substantial deposits of bank-material found in the ditch-filling are more likely to have been transferred by human than by natural agencies, unless it can be shown that the original berm was very narrow. Calculation of the original width of the berm can be based (though necessarily with caution) on a reconstruction of the original profile of the ditch, referred to above, and on the apparent stabilization of the adjacent tail of the bank at an early stage in its history.

3. The activity of moles in removing substantial quantities of soil (and possibly small objects as well) from beneath a bank, and depositing them at the tail of the earthwork, may be of significance in two respects. First of all, it may account in large part for the thicker accumulation of soil normally found at the junction of the slope of an earthwork with the surrounding flat ground—a phenomenon hitherto ascribed to soil creep. Secondly, it may lead to the displacement, subsequently undetectable, of diagnostic finds. The 1962 section shows that a flowerpot sherd had been thus displaced from the buried ground surface to the top of the tail of layer E/F; and it is clear that more misleading displacements could occur, even if only occasionally, in the same way.

4. The presence of earthworms and their castings, derived from the soil core, in the chalk rubble layers of the bank appears to represent the early stages of a process whereby, in the course of time, soil could become widely diffused in deposits originally laid down as clean, soil-free chalk rubble. Such changes, after construction, have an obvious bearing upon the interpretation of the origin of the layers concerned, and underline the dangers of the assumption, all too commonly made, that the appearance and composition of a layer at the time of its excavation is an indication of its original state.

5. The apparently seasonal alteration of fine and coarse rubble layers in the ditch-filling, though by no means regular or easy to distinguish in section, seems to provide a basis for the more precise chronological interpretation of the early stages in the silting of chalk-cut ditches. This is a point toward which excavators could usefully devote in future a greater degree of meticulous record than has been usual hitherto.

6. The section of 1964 provides an object lesson in the dangers of dating a structure by the uncritical use of the contained finds. In the center of the ditch, resting on the floor, was a lump of turf which yielded, on dissection, two sherds of flowerpot and two numbered pottery discs. It is safe to say that in a few years at the most the disintegration of this lump, and the upward transport of part of its constituent soil by worms, would have left these four finds lying on or very close to the ditch floor, in a layer of earthy chalk rubble no longer identifiable as a turf fallen from the lip of the ditch. Both kinds of pottery would then have been regarded, by the usual canons of interpretation, as contemporary with each other and with the construction of the ditch.

In fact, however, only the flowerpot sherds are of this date. The numbered discs were inserted *into* the turf on both edges of the ditch, and thus represent sherds which could have been dropped centuries before construction.

From the pattern of development of the filling it follows that finds in the angles of the ditch-bottom, close to the wall, are more reliable as dating evidence; and that those near the center-line, even if found right on the bottom, should be treated with great caution.

7. The difference in the degree of comminution of the rubble on the ends of the bank as contrasted with the long sides suggests that a more or less conical structure such as a round barrow may, under identical conditions, develop a fine texture more rapidly than a long bank.

ACKNOWLEDGMENTS

The Research Committee is deeply indebted to those specialists who have dealt with the various buried materials; without their help this aspect of the work would have been fruitless. They are Mr. H. M. Appleyard (Wool Industries Research Association, Leeds), Mr. D. K. Barrett (Commonwealth Forestry Institute, Oxford), Dr. J. P. Garlick (Department of Anthropology, London), Mr. H. M. Hodges (Institute of Archaeology, London), Mr. A. H. Little (Shirley Institute, Manchester), Dr. W. R. M. Morton (Department of Anatomy, Queen's University of Belfast), Mr. E. F. Nattrass (British Leather Manufacturers' Research Association, Egham), and Dr. M. L. Ryder (A. R. C. Animal Breeding Organization, Roslin). In addition, we are grateful to Dr. B. A. Whitton (Department of Botany, Durham University) for examining and identifying the algae and higher plants found on the bank; and to Mr. Inigo Jones, until recently Warden of the Fyfield Down Nature Reserve, for his interest in the project and his careful observation on changes in vegetation.

To the list of Committee members published in the *Basic Manual* the following names should be added: Mr. L. Biek (Ancient Monuments Laboratory, Ministry of Public Building and Works), Mr. C. E. Everard (Department of Geography, Queen Mary College, London), and Mr. P. J. Fowler (Extra-Mural Department, University of Bristol), all of whom have contributed valuably to this report.

REFERENCES

Basic Manual

Jewell, P. A., ed. 1963. *The experimental earthwork on Overton Down, Wiltshire, 1960*. London: British Association for the Advancement of Science.

Other Reports

Ashbee, P. and I. W. Cornwall. 1961. An experiment in field archaeology. *Antiquity* 35:129–34.

Dimbleby, G. W. 1965. Overton Down experimental earthwork. *Antiquity* 39:134–36.

Jewell, P. A. 1959. Earthworms and archaeology. *The Times Science Review* (Winter 1959):18.

—— 1961a. An experiment in field archaeology. *Advancement of Science* 71:106–9.

—— 1961b. An experimental earthwork on Fyfield Down. *Wiltshire Archaeological and Natural History Magazine* 58:38.

Proudfoot, V. B. 1961. The British Association's experimental earthwork. *New Scientist* 11:596–98.

—— 1964. Experimental earthworks in the British Isles. *Geographic Review* 54:584–86.

—— 1965a. Bringing archaeology to life. *Advancement of Science* 22:125–33.

—— 1965b. The study of soil development from the construction and excavation of experimental earthworks. In E. G. Hallsworth and D. V. Crawford, eds., *Experimental Pedology*, pp. 282–94.

Technical References

Biek, L. 1963a. *Archaeology and the microscope*. New York: Praeger.

—— 1963b. Soil silhouettes. In D. Brothwell and E. Higgs, eds., *Science in archaeology*, pp. 108–12. New York: Basic Books.

Gansser, A. 1950. The early history of tanning. *Ciba Review* 81:2938–62.

Locket, G. H. 1945–46a. Observations on the colonization of bare chalk. *Journal of Ecology* 33:205–9.

—— 1945–46b. A preliminary investigation of the availability to plants of the water in chalk. *Journal of Ecology* 33:222–29.

Ryder, M. L. 1963. Remains derived from skin. In D. Brothwell and E. Higgs, eds., *Science in Archaeology,* pp. 529–44. New York: Basic Books.

Walkley, A. 1947. A critical examination of a rapid method for determining organic carbon in soils. *Soil Science* 63:251–64.

11

ROBERT ASCHER

Time's Arrow and the Archeology of a Contemporary Community

To simplify the problems which confront them, archeologists are wont to make assumptions they realize may not hold completely true. While no researcher would deny the disruptive forces which affect a site after it has been abandoned, one often prefers to believe that the occupants did not themselves contribute to this process. Objects that have outlived their usefulness, bones, and other debris are left where they have been discarded and are not sorted through, moved about, or picked up and used for other purposes. Or so one likes to think. For if these assumptions hold true, one may then attempt to reconstruct activities on the basis of artifact or debris type, association, and spatial distribution. As Ascher points out, all too rarely does such a situation occur. Disruptive effects are, however, minimized in sites occupied briefly and then rapidly covered by protecting sediments. But unfortunately such instances are rarely discovered because the amount of debris that marks their presence is usually slight, making them—from an archeological point of view—invisible. Only rarely do volcanos erupt and bury entire cities intact.

Ascher works within the controlled context of the ethnographic present, and this article could well have been included in the following section of this book. He notes three factors that cause "disorganization" in a Seri village which is in the process of becoming an archeological site. Because two of these—"smearing and blending" and "broadcasting"—follow a regular and likely predictable course and possibly relate in a systematic way to human behavior, the situation may be turned to the archeologist's advantage. And on this basis, Ascher suggests, it may be possible to guess which portions of

Reprinted from K. C. Chang, ed. Settlement Archaeology (Palo Alto, California: National Press Books, 1968), pp. 43–52. Used by permission of National Press Books.

*large sites were occupied before others, and which foods were most seasonal
in nature.*

*In passing, Ascher mentions how difficult it may be to distinguish between
the works of man and nature; the confusion of natural with human patterns
may lead to extremely serious errors in interpretation. Some researchers, for
example, have used bone accumulations in South African caves to argue that
early hominids were proficient in hunting and butchering. Others point to
hyenas, leopards, and other carnivores as the directly responsible agents.
While no one can directly observe Australopithecine behavior, African carnivores may be studied both in the zoo or field, and here the "experimental
approach" may make a direct and significant contribution to the understanding of man's past.*

More than 99 percent of human biological and cultural evolution happened before history was invented. What can be known about man's behavior before history, therefore, must be learned from the alterations he has
made to the natural world in shaping it to his purposes. Traces of man's
activity, in the shape of reordered matter, as well as occasional traces of man
himself, are the facts of prehistory.

The kind and amount of information we have about early human behavior
are strictly limited, for some of the things men did left barely discernible traces
and much of what men might have done could leave no traces at all.
Moreover, the acts that turned natural objects into archeological facts are
unintelligible to the uninitiated and far from easy for experts in the science
and art of prehistory to unravel. If the absence of certain facts circumscribes
possible knowledge of the past, facts that are available but formidable to
interpret pose a challenge. Thus, the initial question of prehistory can be
formulated: How can information be extracted from the results of behavior
stored in matter by men remote in both time and culture?

In interpretational astronomy, the evolution of remote stars is reconstructed
on the basis of their behavior in different phases of evolution. The astronomer
observes the relative brightness of stars, listens to stellar emissions, and draws
on the regularities of local physics to infer past astronomical phenomena. To
infer the past behavior of men or stars, in archeology or astronomy, descriptions of known behavior must be introduced. Surely, prehistorians know that
they must utilize the present to infer the past, but they do not know what of
the present should be observed, and too little is known about the regularities
that govern human behavior.

This article is concerned with the first problem: What of the present should be observed? I am interested in the notion that every contemporary community is destroying as well as renewing itself, and I believe that observations of this process are of heuristic value in making sense out of the remains of the distant past. In developing this idea, I shall first consider disorganization and its relation to archeology, and then, by way of example, extend the discussion to a particular community. I take for granted that the physical mass of part of a community, or of an entire community, as it moves through time and space, is as profitable a unit for study as is the standard artifact class or some similarly small unit.

DISORGANIZATION AND ARCHEOLOGY

"Inhabited" and "Ghost" Phases. Ordinarily, the existence of a community is equated with change in the direction of organization. In the terminology of the late Norbert Wiener (1954), a human community is a temporary island, pocket, or enclave of decreasing entropy in the midst of a universe where entropy is inevitably on the increase. From a distance—that is, from the long-term overview of a hypothetical giant—this picture is correct and comforting. A view from close to the ground shows that, in every community, disorganization and organization proceed simultaneously at different rates, and at different rates at different times. From the inception of any community, at every point in its "inhabited" phase, and during its gradual decline, people and nature in combination act as agents of disorganization.

As an example, consider what can happen in the familiar American automobile yard. One such yard, founded in 1956, is located on the outskirts of Ithaca, New York.[1] The yard holds the remains of 56 vehicles, 39 of which are passenger sedans, ranging in date of manufacture from 1935 to 1958. The distribution of all the vehicles is such that the older members, in an advanced state of decomposition, are toward one end of the rectangular yard, and the more recent, less decomposed, vehicles are at the opposite end of the yard. Table 11.1 shows the major missing parts of 10 Chevrolets, constituting one-fourth of the passenger sedan population. The data imply that ordering

[1]The data on the automobile yard were gathered by Mr. Thomas Greaves, a graduate student, and Miss Allison MacLeod, an undergraduate, during a project for a course in interpretive archeology at Cornell University in the spring of 1966. Subsequently, I worked at the yard with one of the students. I thank both students for permission to use the data. I also thank the owner of the yard, Mr. Nelson Eddy, for access to his property.

TABLE 11.1

Parts Removed from Ten Chevrolets in an Automobile Yard

Year of Manufacture	'36	'39	'41	'47	'48	'49	'50	'51	'52	'54
Block	+	+	0	0	0	0	0	0	0	0
Carburetor	+	+	0	0	+	0	0	0	0	0
Distributor	+	+	0	0	0	0	+	0	0	0
Starter	+	+	0	0	0	0	0	0	0	0
Fan	+	+	0	0	0	0	0	0	0	0
Radiator	0	0	+	0	0	0	0	0	0	0
Horn	0	+	+	+	+	+	0	+	0	0
Air Cleaner	0	0	0	0	+	0	0	0	0	0
Battery	0	0	+	0	0	0	0	0	0	0
Headlights	+	+	+	0	0	+	0	0	+	0
Windshield	+	+	+	+	+	+	+	+	+	0
Rear Window	+	+	+	+	+	+	0	+	0	0
Front Bumper	+	+	+	0	+	0	0	+	+	0
Grill	+	+	0	+	+	+	0	0	0	0
Hubcaps	0	0	0	0	+	+	0	+	0	0
Hood Ornament	0	0	0	+	0	+	+	+	0	+
Hood	+	+	+	0	0	+	+	+	+	+
Right Fender	+	+	+	0	+	+	+	+	+	+
Right Door	+	+	+	0	0	+	0	+	+	0
Front Seat Springs	+	+	+	+	+	+	0	+	+	0
Heater	-	0	0	+	-	0	0	0	0	0
Transmission	+	+	0	+	0	0	0	0	0	0
Differential	+	+	0	0	0	0	0	+	0	0
Right Front Wheel	+	0	0	0	0	0	0	+	0	0
Right Front Rim	0	0	0	0	0	0	0	+	0	0
Right Front Tire	0	0	0	0	0	0	0	+	0	0
Driveshaft	+	0	0	0	0	0	+	+	0	0
Radio	-	-	0	0	-	+	-	0	0	0

0 = Removed   + = Remains   - = Not Original Equipment

(manufacture of automobiles) is followed by reordering (accumulation of automobiles in the yard), and then by disordering and reordering (selective removal of parts and their use elsewhere), and so on.

Because the existence of a community is often erroneously equated with continuous unidirectional change, it is held that when ordering ceases, the community halts. The fault in this view is best revealed by considering "ghost" towns. Towns without people are thought to have taken on static form because nothing novel is added, but observations of such towns over even short periods show that change continues in the absence of people. In all "ghost" towns, natural agents are disorganizing matter that was once arranged in patterns by human effort. The fact that all change in "ghost" towns is in the direction of diminishing order, and that the agency is natural rather than human and natural, should not obscure the issue: a community vanishes only when all of the effort congealed in matter is totally disorganized. It is true that ordering ceases in the absence of man, but change in the direction of disorganization is continuous with him and without him.

For illustration, we return to the case of the automobile yard and consider one natural agent of decomposition, namely, rusting. An automobile begins to rust as soon as it is used, and rusting probably is a factor leading to its deposit in the yard. Various stages of rusting could be observed on the automobiles in the sample, as indicated in table 11.2. In early stages, the metallic surfaces turn reddish-brown and become rough and pitted; in later stages, the metal turns to a scaly, porous mass. As time passes the cars will fall apart and certain information that the automobile might be made to reveal about American culture will be gradually lost. An observer at some far future time will find nothing at all.

Archeological Phase. After the "inhabited" and "ghost" phases of a community's existence, the archeologist enters—to introduce yet another irregularity in the long-term unbroken curve of disorganization.

The romance some find in archeology derives from the notion that any turn of the shovel can yield the unusual or the unexpected. Although overstated, this notion is essentially correct. But high uncertainty, resulting from the limited predictability of the course of excavation, is more troublesome than it is romantic; the act of excavation, the disturbance of items suspended in the earth, itself produces disorganization. Specifically, disorganization is introduced because contexts, defined as purposeful arrangements in space and time, are not predictable, and awareness of them may postdate their destruction.

TABLE 11.2
Rust on Ten Chevrolets in an Automobile Yard

= Removed   1 = No rust
2 = Light rust
3 = Heavy rust
4 = Holes due to rust
5 = Material decomposed
6 = Material trace only

Year of Manufacture	'36	'39	'41	'47	'48	'49	'50	'51	'52	'54
Roof	3	4	4	3	2	2	3	2	2	2
Hood	3	—	—	—	2	2	—	1	—	—
Trunk	3	3	3	3	3	2	3	2	2	1
Right Rear Fender	4	4	4	4	—	4	4	4	4	3
Right Rear Wheel Well	3	4	4	4	4	4	4	4	4	2
Floorboard	6	5	6	3	4	4	4	4	3	4
Right Front Door Panel (Chrome)	3	3	3	4	4	3	4	2	1	1
Front Bumper	4	3	4	—	3	3	—	3	—	—
Trim	3	2	2	2	1	1	2	2	1	1
Grill	3	2	5	4	3	2	—	2	3	—
Instrument Framing	3	3	5	5	3	3	3	3	2	1

To understand this clearly, imagine the excavation of an ancient community that has become a buried cube of large dimensions. At the start of the excavation the perceptual field of the observer is limited to the surface of the cube lying parallel to the ground. The excavation begins by horizontally and vertically partitioning the cube into a number of smaller units, and proceeds by systematically observing, recording, and removing the contents of each unit. Each advance of the shovel uncovers a fraction of the cube; arrangement of all items with each other is possible only at the close of the work. Observations and recordings in any one arbitrary unit are guided by knowledge of other arbitrary units already excavated. It is impossible to observe and record everything, but everything must be removed. Thus, indicators of a context already partially destroyed by removal become evident as the excavation proceeds, when earlier failures in observation and recording can no longer be repaired.

There are, of course, difficulties beyond those inherent in excavation: the recognition of man's purposeful arrangements depends on *distinguishing between* the action of natural agents and the action of human agents. Generally, the elapsed time between the abandonment and the excavation of a community yields a good inverse relationship to the amount of information the excavation can be expected to produce. In areas where rain is heavy, and lightning storms are common, a few decades are enough to decay all contexts. In an even shorter period of time, more subtle changes can occur. Worms, for example, can alter the distribution of objects and produce novel arrangements, as was demonstrated in a series of elegant experiments by Charles Darwin and his son Horace (Darwin 1901). Indeed, the heavy use in archeological literature of the ambiguous term "feature" to describe any apparent patterning of objects is a tacit admission that the contributions of natural and human factors to an archeological matrix are often indistinguishable.

It is illuminating to review some archeological situations that have achieved notoriety. A feature common to most of these cases is an exceptional set of circumstances that have served to reduce the magnitude of the problems discussed above. In August 79 a.d., for example, a shower of ashes and pumice from erupting Mt. Vesuvius descended on Pompeii, suddenly and instantly terminating the "inhabited" phase of its existence and sealing it off from agents of natural disorganization. As we would expect, many of the instances similar to this involve the excavation of burials. In general, a burial is a below-ground, spatial-temporal arrangement of a corpse, usually with other matter; and if it is not a deliberate attempt at creating a durable context, it is nevertheless the ordering activity most resistant to disorganization. Burials that are particularly resistant to decay and rich in content, but have not been attractive enough to invite pilfering, appear with regularity in the annals of popular archeology.

But Pompeii and instances like it are clearly special cases. In most situations, disorganization is gropingly interrupted by the spade, and in every archeological situation observation is limited to the results of the process at one point in time. The path of disorganization from "inhabited," through "ghost," and on to archeological disturbance is irreversible, but it must be figuratively reversed when inferring past human behavior. This creative task can lead to alternate inferences, any one of which might be as plausible as any other. Ideally, the best solution is the one derived from the accurate retracing of the path of disorganization, but because so little is understood about the path, there is no sound basis for the elimination of any solution.

Information about the path of disorganization can be found in data that are becoming but are not yet archeological. Such data are present in every "inhabited" community. Since this is true, it should be possible and profitable to look at a contemporary community with the aim of learning how it starts to become the past as it moves from the present into the future.

TRENDS IN A COMMUNITY

Prehistoric man extracted energy from his environment by some combination of hunting, fishing, and gathering. This way of life set upper bounds on the development of, for example, the number of occupational specialties and the size of the population. Today, there are still a few communities with similar means of subsistence; by analogy, these communities parallel the kinds of communities that existed for most of human history. It is thus reasonable, in extending the discussion to a specific community, to select one that fits this general class—the Seri Indian community in the state of Sonora, Mexico (Ascher, 1961a; 1961b).

The Seri live on a strip of coastal desert, about 70 miles long and four miles wide, along the Gulf of California. Although the strip is arid, with an average rainfall of less than 10 inches per year, falling mostly in late summer, microclimatic conditions encourage the flowering of desert plant life. The Gulf forms a natural trap for fish and marine mammals, and the waters are rich in marine food. In spite of these resources, the scarcity of fresh water has constituted in the past, and at present is, the critical inhibitor to occupancy by large terrestrial animals, including man.

The Seri are fishermen; secondarily they gather the fruits of the desert; and to a lesser degree they hunt small game. The sea turtle is most important in Seri economy, but other products of the sea are also taken, including sea lions, crabs, clams, and several varieties of fish. Women and children gather the desert fruits; men do the fishing and hunting. The Seri utilize a number of camps in addition to Desemboque, the main base at the strip's northern extreme. In pursuit of food, fishermen and their families traverse the territory during the summer months, stop at camps, and eventually return to the main base.

Today, 400 years after they were first seen by Europeans, there are about 240 Seri. Until recently, the Seri camped on Tiburón Island in the Gulf, and sometime earlier their land included a large mainland region. The original occupancy, which occurred at least 500 years ago, stemmed either from Baja California, via the Gulf of California; or from the north, via an overland route or routes. There are no reliable figures of past population size, but former territory and length of occupancy suggest that there were once considerably more Seri than today.

Judging from independent studies, spaced at approximately 30-year intervals (Ascher 1962; Kroeber 1931; McGee 1898), Seri–Western relations have been sporadic, with the result that the Seri have been neither converted to Christianity nor displaced by Mexican interests. Major Seri–Western contact is between fishermen and Mexican entrepreneurs who have been purchasing fish and turtles in exchange for cash and equipment since the late 1930s. The strength of Western intrusion can be inferred from declining population alone, and the fact that Seri garbage includes rusty tin cans, worn-out factory-made shoes, and plastic containers is sufficient warning to those who would prefer to view them as a "Stone Age" people.

Now let us turn to a few trends viewed as systematic movements along the path of disorganization.

Smearing and Blending. The main base of Desemboque stretches one-fifth of a mile along a small bay, the limits of which, the Seri point out, form natural boundaries. In the 34 years since its founding, the community has been developing north to south along the Gulf frontage such that the entrance to almost every house faces the water. Two conspicuous features on the landscape are wattle-and-daub or cardboard-and-string houses and garbage mounds.

When Desemboque is overlaid with a checkerboard grid system of 25-foot squares, the varying extraorganic matter in the squares reveals a space-time sequence corresponding to the development of the community. Density, that is, is greater in units falling on the newer portions of the community and less in older areas. Another regularity emerges when the squares are compared in terms of uniformity of distribution of matter. The more recent sections of the community show discontinuous distributions, with large gaps, for example, separating house from house, garbage heap from garbage heap, and house from garbage heap. By contrast, on that portion of the landscape where daily activities of the community were once but are no longer held, there is less dense, but more equal, distribution of decaying matter.

The movement of the Seri community into the past, then, has the effect of smearing or blending. Clear delineations disappear. The rapid deposition of windblown sand in conjunction with degeneration of form by chemical decomposition is partly responsible for this effect. There are also contributing human factors in the first stages of smearing and at every stage in its progression. For example, a Seri, in walking from one point of the community to another, chooses the shorter path, oblivious of the ubiquitous heaps of fishbone and carapace that at least one non-Seri consciously avoided. The results of this combination of factors can be clearly seen in fig. 11.1, which depicts the oldest section of the community. In the future, Desemboque may well look like the 5000-year-old archeological midden shown in fig. 11.2.

Cycling of Serviceable Material. A. L. Kroeber, who visited the Seri in 1930, wrote (1931): "The Seri mode of life led to many instabilities with makeshifts often actually more in use, but finished or efficient types of artifacts seemingly latent and sporadically emerging in the stream of their culture." Kroeber's insight is understandable in terms of the recycling of scarce materials in an environment where scarcity is a universal descriptor. The material contents of the Seri community are ordered, disordered, and ordered again, and then again. The cycle cannot, of course, be repeated indefinitely; fresh materials or substitutes must sooner or later be found.

Laminated cardboard, parts from a 1931 automobile, sections of rubber tires, scraps of rubber, ocotillo poles—these and other materials with which the Seri build houses and harpoons—cycle in a spatial-temporal direction. For example, when a Seri dies, his house is dismantled, some of the materials are used to rebuild another house, and some are left behind. If the remaining materials are not necessary at the moment, they will surely be picked up and used at a later time. In this manner, serviceable material gradually catches up

Figure 11.1 The oldest section of the Seri community at Desembogue. Two houses once stood in the area depicted.

Figure 11.2 A five thousand year old archeological midden. Five thousand years from now, Desemboque will probably appear similar to the site shown here.

with the movement of the community, leaving in its wake rock, fishbone, and scraps of rubber and metal too small to be of use. In general, those materials that are adaptable, or potentially adaptable, tend to contract in space-time and to accumulate in the more recent areas of the community.

Broadcasting. What may be organization from one point of view becomes disorganization from another. In the course of one hour, a Seri may dismember a turtle and crack open the bones of some small land mammal. Hundreds of similar prosaisms broadcast the byproducts of human workmanship over the surface of the community. Such acts proceed at a much quicker rate than either cycling or smearing, and impart a past-to-present that can be read from both bottom-to-top and across the mass of unserviceable debris.

Let us consider an example. The Seri gather over a dozen varieties of shellfish; of these, half have long seasons, some have short seasons, and a few are taken only when stormy seas whip them close to shore. From the results of archeological excavations in Seri garbage mounds, I was able to infer that one shellfish was the preferred species, and Seri statements, obtained after analysis, corroborated the inference. Flecks of the shell of this mollusc are abundant in breadth, width, and depth, whereas the shell fragments of seasonal species appear in intermittent groups. This positioning applied to other organic residues, and as such provides a useful clue to the constancies and changes in the Seri community over time.

TIME'S ARROW: CONCLUSION

I have considered one important phase of the disorganization path—its beginning in the "inhabited" community. The phenomena identified at Desemboque may not be general, but they are probably not unique. It is noteworthy that the distribution and density of automobiles in an American automobile yard, and the removal of parts from the cars, seem to parallel the trends of smearing, blending, and cycling identified in the hunter-gatherer community. It would be of value to seek and report relevant trends in other communities for the heuristics they can provide.

It is Sir Arthur Eddington who is generally credited with coining the term "time's arrow" with reference to the tendency of the universe to move in the direction of the more probable state of disorder and chaos. Many have found meanings and implications in this general process that extend far beyond its rigorous application in thermodynamics. The meaning of "time's arrow" in the present context, being neither philosophical nor rigorously physical, can be simply stated: in time, every community will become first a "ghost" town, then a cube below ground. The problem of the prehistorian is to reconstruct the community from the cube. Since the connection between the archeological present and the ethnographic past lies along the route of increasing disorder, the advancement of interpretation depends on knowing what happens along that route.

Here we have considered one important phase of the disorganization path—beginning in the "inhabited" community. Such phenomena as cycling and smearing identified at Desemboque may not be general, but they are probably not unique. If trends in other relevant communities are identified, given precise expression, and used, reconstructions may read less like fantasies.

REFERENCES

Ascher, Robert. 1961a. Analogy in archaeological interpretation, *Southwestern Journal of Anthropology* 17:317–25.

—— 1961b. Function and prehistoric art. *Man* 61(84).

—— 1962. Ethnography for archeology: A case from the Seri Indians, *Ethnology* 1:360–69.

Darwin, Horace. 1901. On the movement of stones by worms, *Proceedings of the Royal Society* 68, no. 446.

Kroeber, A. L. 1931. The Seri, *Southwest Museum Papers*, no. 6.

McGee, W. J. 1898. The Seri Indians, *Annual Report of the Bureau of American Ethnology,* no. 17, pt. 1.

Wiener, Norbert. 1954. *The human use of human beings.* New York: Doubleday.

» 12 «

DONALD J. ORTNER • DAVID W. VON ENDT • MARY S. ROBINSON

The Effect of Temperature on Protein Decay in Bone: Its Significance in Nitrogen Dating of Archeological Specimens

An interesting question to consider is how the archeologist, given his short lifetime, can attempt through experiment to reconstruct complex processes of chemical and physical change which proceed only slowly over the course of thousands of years. Ortner and his colleagues discuss two ways to attack the problem. One may take samples recovered from dated archeological contexts, directly compare one to the other, and then correlate the degree of alteration with known age. Such an approach is best suited to changes which are dependent on time alone and which are unaffected by other variables. In the case of nitrogen loss from bone, however, so many other uncontrollable factors come into play that their accumulated effect makes it highly unlikely this approach will give meaningful results.

A second technique—simulation analysis—appears a more workable alternative. Here one starts by experimentally varying the "cause" and determining the "effect" through direct observation. As Ortner et al. demonstrate, once the basic relationship between two variables is established, one may then extrapolate from the short "laboratory" time range to a longer, archeologically relevant one. When multiple factors are responsible for the change— and this is so for bone nitrogen loss—each may be separately examined under controlled laboratory conditions and a quite complex natural process

Reproduced, with minor editorial changes, by permission of the Society for American Archaeology, from *American Antiquity* 37(4), 1972.

may possibly be reconstructed in a stepwise fashion. Although the question he asks is quite a different one, Speth (chapter 1 of this volume) employs what is essentially the same experimental design.

The authors note in passing that human bone seems less resistant to decay than other animal remains. The practical implications are considerable, for if bones from different species are removed at differing rates from the archeological record, a systematic bias of major proportions may result. Although it lies outside the immediate scope of their work, the simulation technique the authors employ might be adapted with little modification to investigate this phenomenon. If cow bone, for example, loses nitrogen less rapidly than its human counterpart at high temperature in a laboratory beaker, then the same relationship most probably holds under actual field conditions as well. Different means, however, may be used to investigate this same question. Turn back to fig. 10.4 and see whether or not their experimental results tend to square with the hypothesis Ortner and his colleagues set forth.

Bone has both structural and metabolic functions in the living individual. In addition to providing a counterforce to muscle activity and gravity, bone is vital in maintaining ionic concentrations of certain elements (for instance, calcium) at constant levels in blood serum. Bone is able to accomplish these functions because it is a complex tissue composed of a protein matrix in close chemical association with its mineral phase. In addition, bone is cellular and has a vascular and nerve supply. Living bone is dynamic—constantly undergoing surface and internal remodeling all during the life of the individual.

After death and burial, changes begin to take place as a result of several factors. Apparently, living cells are needed to maintain the relationship between the protein and mineral phases. At death, this relationship begins to deteriorate. The mineral phase gives sharper X-ray diffraction patterns with time, implying a more systematic relationship between the elements making up the bone crystal lattice. Another factor in the destruction of bone through time is that the protein, which constitutes approximately 20 percent of the total mass in fresh bone, is hydrolyzed to peptides which in turn break down to their constituent amino acids. At each level of degradation, proteinaceous materials become more susceptible to removal by water, with the rate of degradation being influenced by soil and water activity.

In a constant environment, the rate of protein degradation and removal from bone should be constant. Because of this, one should, theoretically, be able to determine the archeological age of a bone sample by determining the amount of protein remaining in the sample. Since protein is the only component in bone which contains nitrogen, this element has been used by many investigators as an index of protein and thus of the archeological age of bone specimens (see Oakley 1950, 1963a, 1963b; Cook and Heizer 1947, 1953; Doberenz and Matter 1965).

All investigators have recognized that the sample application of nitrogen concentration as an index of time is limited because of the numerous variables which affect the decay rate. Cook (1960:229), summarizing Duerst's (1926) study, notes that solute concentration, water, and average temperature affect the rate of protein decay. Soil pH is an additional variable of obvious importance. With the exception of Duerst's research, there has been little or no attempt to control for these variables in the published reports on nitrogen dating. Because of this lack of control, most investigators have limited the use of nitrogen concentration to the relative dating of specimens from the same site.

The use of protein decay in absolute dating remains a tantalizing possibility for several reasons. Nitrogen analysis requires a bone sample in the milligram size range and thus is very economical of valuable archeological specimens. It also requires a much smaller investment for equipment and supplies than radiocarbon dating. The analysis itself can be done by almost anyone having reasonable intelligence and minimal training in chemistry. However, before it is possible to use this method, at least the major variables affecting the decay rate—temperature, water, and pH—must be studied. Such a study represents a substantial investment of time, but without it the potential of nitrogen analysis for dating cannot be evaluated.

During the past three years, the authors have been studying the kinetics of protein decay in compact bone in an attempt to provide a more solid theoretical framework for nitrogen dating of archeological skeletal specimens. In this research, to be published in greater detail elsewhere, we have focused on developing a simple, accurate method for assaying nitrogen. We are also conducting laboratory simulation studies on protein decay with time, as reflected by nitrogen decay. In this paper we report on the effects of temperature on nitrogen loss in bone. In subsequent papers, we shall report on the effects of pH and water volume.

MATERIAL AND METHOD

The bone we have used in this study was from a single fresh bovine tibia obtained from a local butcher. The soft tissue and fat were removed by thoroughly scraping and grinding the inner and outer surfaces, after which the bone was broken into small pieces and ground to less than 50 mesh particle size in a Wiley mill. The bone powder was dried in a desiccator jar using both desiccant and vacuum.

There are two basic methods of determining the relationship between bone protein decay and time. Empirically, one can take bones of known but different archeological ages, determine their nitrogen concentration, and plot the relationship. The problem with this design is that the range of time at any single site is generally inadequate, and one must make the assumption that the immediate environment of the buried bones has been constant since burial. If we use bone samples from several sites, we are faced with the problem of different pH and water concentrations affecting the rate of protein decay in the different localities.

The second method is to establish the ideal relationship between the two variables by simulating the process of protein decay in the laboratory. This method has the advantage of providing control over the variables affecting the decay rate. In our study, we placed 100 mg. samples of the dried bone powder in test tubes containing 5 ml. distilled water. The test tubes were sealed with a flame and placed in a constant temperature bath. In this study, the two dependent variables were the heat of the bath, ranging from 100°C (212°F) to 140°C (284°F), and the length of time the sample was in the bath, ranging up to 5 hours. By determining nitrogen concentration in bone for these varying high temperatures at varying lengths of time in the bath, it is possible to extrapolate back to a time and temperature combination approximating archeological conditions.

A crucial problem in this research is to develop an accurate method for determining percent nitrogen in a bone sample. Bone poses unique problems for analysis because of the high salt concentration formed during the digestion of bone. In our laboratory, we have developed a modified micro-Kjeldahl method which is highly reproducible and relatively uncomplicated.

In essence, there are two phases in micro-Kjeldahl analysis: reduction or digestion, and quantitation. The purpose of reduction is to break down the proteins to the elemental level, freeing the nitrogen from the amino acids and forming ammonium ion (NH_4^+). Reduction is dependent on the length of the reaction and the temperature. The maximum temperature, which needs to be high, is regulated by the addition of a salt (Na_2SO_4). The length of the digestion is regulated to produce the maximum amount of ammonium ion while minimizing loss. The digestion mixture was developed in our laboratory and requires only a single step process. The mixture is a combination of salt (Na_2SO_4), catalyst ($CuSO_4$), and acid (H_2SO_4 + $HClO_4$).

After the nitrogen from the bone protein is in solution in the form of ammonium ions, the next step is to quantify the amount of nitrogen. In our laboratory, we use colorimetric analysis. Nessler's reagent turns amber in a solution containing ammonium ion. The intensity of the color is related to the amount of the ion. By adding more base to the standard Nessler's reagent, it is possible to neutralize the digested protein – acid mixture with the Nessler's reagent and produce a color reaction in one step. The Nesslerized digest is brought up to a standard volume, and the color intensity is read on a Gilford Model 240 spectrophotometer. The light absorption is compared with the absorption of known concentrations of ammonium ion to determine the nitrogen value.

In the actual experiment, test tubes containing the ground bone sample and water were placed in the constant temperature bath set for one of the six temperatures used in the research. At the temperatures of 100°C (212°F) and 110°C (230°F) three samples were removed for nitrogen analysis at one hour intervals up to five hours maximum time. The intervals at higher temperatures were variable and shorter because the reactions take place more rapidly. At 120°C (248°F), samples were removed after 30 minutes, and then at one-hour intervals for the remaining time periods. At 125°C (257°F) the time intervals were 15, 30, 60, 90, and 120 minutes. For 130°C (266°F) they were 10, 15, 30, 40, 45, and 60 minutes, while at 140°C (284°F) the intervals were 10, 15, 20, 30, 40, and 45 minutes. After removal from the bath, the samples were chilled to minimize further protein degradation and filtered to remove the remaining bone particles. Nitrogen analysis of the supernatant was done immediately when possible; otherwise, the samples were frozen until the analysis could be done.

In determining the decay rate for each temperature, each of the three samples removed at a given time interval was divided into two samples for the digestion phase of the analysis. These six samples were further divided in half for the colorimetric analysis, so that each point on the decay curve of a given temperature represents the average of 12 determinations. The decay rates at each temperature were determined using standard regression analysis. By extrapolation from a constant point on each of the temperature curves (63 percent and 95 percent nitrogen loss), the time for the loss of nitrogen was determined for a range of temperatures more appropriate to the archeological environment.

RESULTS

In a kinetic study of this type, the ideal result is one in which the rate of the reaction can be expressed in mathematical terms. If it is assumed that loss of nitrogen is dependent only on the concentration of nitrogen remaining in the bone, then the decay rate can be expressed as

$$\frac{dx}{dt} = k(a - x)$$

(12.1.1)

where dx is the change in nitrogen concentration of the bone, dt is the change in time t, k is a constant defining the slope of the curve, a is the initial concentration of nitrogen, and x is the amount of nitrogen released at time t. The term $a - x$ thus represents the difference between the original nitrogen concentration of bone at time zero, and the amount of nitrogen found in the supernatant at any given time, that is, the amount of nitrogen remaining in bone.

Because nitrogen loss at any point in time is proportional to the amount of remaining nitrogen, the initial loss is greatest, with the subsequent amount of nitrogen lost per mass unit of bone decreasing with time. In order to fit this relationship to a straight line, the above equation needs to be adjusted to compensate for this logarithmic relationship between the two variables. This is done using the integrated form of the above formula

$$1n \frac{\dot{a}}{a} - x = kt$$

(12.1.2)

where $1n$ is the natural logarithm.

The plot of $1n \, \dot{a}/a - x$ with time in hours is given in fig. 12.1. In our research, the initial concentration of nitrogen (a) is a constant. As the amount of nitrogen remaining in bone $(a - x)$ decreases with time, the value of the expression $1n \, \dot{a}/a - x$ increases. If the loss of nitrogen is dependent only on its concentration in bone, our data for any given temperature will form a straight line. Inspection of fig. 12.1 indicates that this is in fact the case. It is clear that the relationship between nitrogen concentration and time is logarithmic as Cook (1960:230) had suggested.

In addition to our interest in the nature of the relationships between time and nitrogen loss, we are, of course, most interested in being able to predict archeological age on the basis of a given nitrogen concentration. The data in fig. 12.1 are rates of nitrogen release at constant temperatures. If we project

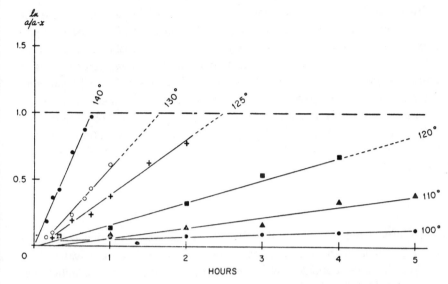

Figure 12.1 The release of nitrogen from bone at 6 temperatures. The vertical coordinate represents the natural logarithm of a ratio between the initial concentration of nitrogen in bone and that which remains at any given time. The horizontal coordinate represents the number of hours each sample was heated. The temperature lines indicate the rate at which nitrogen is lost from bone at a given temperature (in degrees Centigrade). The dotted horizontal line represents those where a/a-x is equal to 2.718 and 1n a/a-x equals 1.

the data for each temperature to the time it would take to reduce the initial concentration of nitrogen by 63 percent ($t_{63\%}$, the dotted horizontal line in fig. 12.1), then $1n\, \dot{a}/a - x$ of equation 12.1.2 equals 1. Using this projection, we can fit the data into the Arrhenius equation

$$k = Ae - \frac{E}{RT} \tag{12.2.1}$$

Here k ie equal to $t_{63\%}$; A, e, and R are constants; E is the activation energy; and T is temperature. On this manner, the integrated form of 2.1.

$$1n\, k = 1n\, A - \frac{E}{RT} \tag{12.2.2}$$

is reduced to a log-linear relationship. We may now use this equation to compare the differences in decay rate (slopes of the lines in fig. 12.1) at various high temperatures, and project the data to predict the rate of nitrogen release at temperatures approximating those found at an archeological site.

By using this formula, we have generated two lines which indicate the relationship between temperature and the time necessary for 63 percent and approximately 95 percent of the nitrogen in bone to be lost (fig. 12.2). Given our experimental conditions of neutral pH and excess water, at the mean annual temperature (M.A.T.) of Washington, D.C. (14.5°C; 58°F), nitrogen should be almost completely gone in 7488 years. In a warmer environment, such as Cairo, with a mean annual temperature of 21.6°C (71°F), the same result would be achieved in 1785 years. An increase in mean annual temperature of a little over 7°C (12.6°F) increased the rate of nitrogen loss by over four times.

DISCUSSION

It is important to remember that the data in this paper were collected under the artificial laboratory conditions of neutral pH and excess water. It is obvious that these conditions represent a rare circumstance at any archeological site. Most soils tend to be on the acidic side of neutrality, although some (such as habitation sites) may be slightly to even strongly alkaline. Soils also are rarely saturated by water during the entire year. However, any chemical method of dating depends on an understanding of the reactions involved in the process under study. We are attempting to provide insight into the process of nitrogen release by bone through a kinetic approach. These and subsequent laboratory experiments will provide a theoretical base upon which the method will rest. Only after this is established can one apply the techniques with confidence, and make accurate corrections for any modifying factors.

In view of the above, caution is urged in applying the findings reported in this paper to specific geographical areas as we have done for illustrative purposes. For example, we have shown on the basis of our time-temperature data that bone nitrogen in Cairo should disappear over four times faster than in Washington, D.C. Empirically, however, we know that samples of Egyptian bone dated between the XX and XXV dynasty (1200–656 b.c.) contain approximately 4.5% nitrogen, while fresh bone contains about 5% nitrogen. On the basis of our kinetic data, we would expect almost no nitrogen to be detected in the Egyptian samples. Clearly, other variables have reduced the impact of temperature on the decay rate of nitrogen. Dry environmental conditions are undoubtedly the major contributing factor of this effect. This, of course, is not surprising. Water is necessary for the reactions associated with protein degradation to take place.

A further complicating factor in nitrogen dating is that decay rates vary

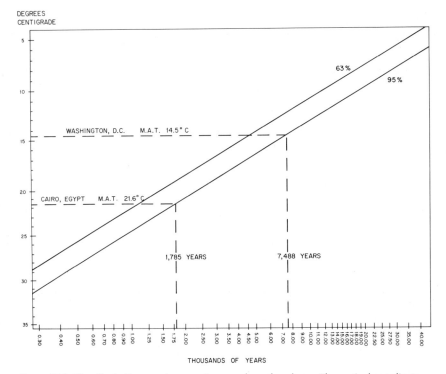

Figure 12.2   The effect of temperature on nitrogen release from bone. The vertical coordinate indicates the temperature in a range found at most archeological sites. The horizontal coordinate indicates time in thousands of years. The 63% and 95% lines represent an extrapolation of the data in fig. 12.1 and show the number of years it takes for bone to lose 63% and 95% of its nitrogen at temperatures from approximately 5° C to 31° C. The dotted lines show how many years it would take all the nitrogen to disappear from bone at the mean annual temperatures of Washington, D.C., and Cairo, Egypt.

between different types of bone (compact and cancellous) from the same individual and in bone from different animals. In this study, we have used cow bone largely because of its ready availability. Preliminary data we have obtained on human bone suggest that protein decay occurs more rapidly in human bone than in cow bone, which is not surprising in view of the importance of the mineral-protein bond. As any archeologist who has excavated both human and nonhuman bone from the same site knows, nonhuman bone appears to be much harder than human bone. With these important reservations in mind, however, there are several significant observations which can be made on the basis of the data we have presented.

It is clear from our simulation studies that mean annual temperature has an important effect on the decay rate of bone protein. Slight differences in temperature can produce substantial differences in estimating the absolute age of an archeological specimen on the basis of nitrogen concentration. There are two implications from this finding. First, in any attempt to determine the absolute date of a bone specimen using nitrogen concentration, one must control the mean annual temperature of the archeological site. Second, some assumption must be made about the average temperature during the entire time period since the burial of the specimen. Butzer's review of the postglacial environment in Europe clearly indicates the danger in assuming that temperatures throughout the effective time range for nitrogen analysis (about 10,000 years) were the same as today (Butzer 1971:526). Likewise, water content, pH, and all other factors contingent upon climate may not have remained constant during this period of time.

In summary, we have conducted kinetic experiments on nitrogen release from bone at high temperatures and projected these data to lower temperatures approximating archeological conditions. In effect, we have developed a "standard curve" against which further experiments, and data collected in the field, can be measured. We have shown that even slight differences in mean annual temperatures can have a significant effect on the rate of nitrogen decay in bone. However, we must emphasize that one cannot correct for temperature alone. Ground water and soil pH must also be considered, since they may either enhance or reduce the effect of temperature. It seems clear that increasing temperature and decreasing pH will accelerate the rate of nitrogen decay. Both of these variables, of course, require the presence of water. We expect to find that, up to the point of water saturation of the soil, increasing amounts of ground water will also accelerate the rate of nitrogen decay.

Currently we are conducting simulation studies on both pH and water volume. When these are complete, the data will be combined with the data on temperature to develop correction factors for a wide range of archeological conditions. With appropriate baseline data for the three most significant variables affecting nitrogen decay, we expect that the ultimate question of the utility of nitrogen analysis in chemical dating can be decided with greater scientific precision.

ACKNOWLEDGMENTS

The authors would like to express their deep appreciation for the advice and assistance of Neil Roth, mathematician; Agnes Bernstein, research assistant; Lisa Rhudy, summer intern; Katharine Hollad, secretary; and George R. Lewis, scientific illustrator, all of the Smithsonian Institution. This research was partially supported by grants from the Smithsonian Research Foundation (SG 3327171) and the National Institutes of Health (HD 03861).

REFERENCES

Butzer, Karl W. 1971. *Environment and archeology*. Chicago: Aldine.

Cook, S. F. 1960. Dating prehistoric bone by chemical analysis. In R. F. Heizer and S. F. Cook, eds., *The application of quantitative methods in archaeology*. *Viking Fund Publications in Anthropology* 28:223–39.

Cook, S. F., and R. F. Heizer. 1947. The quantitative investigation of aboriginal sites: analysis of human bone. *American Journal of Physical Anthropology* N.S. 5:201–19.

—— 1953. Archaeological dating by chemical analysis of bone. *Southwestern Journal of Anthropology* 9:231–38.

Doberenz, A. R., and P. Matter, III. 1965. Nitrogen analysis of fossil bones. *Comparative biochemistry and physiology* 16:253–58.

Duerst, J. U. 1926. Vergleichende untersuchungsmethoden am skellett by saugern. In *Abderhaldens Handbuch der Biologischen Arbeitsmethoden* Abt. VII, Teil 1, Hett 2, pp. 124–530.

Oakley, K. P. 1950. Relative dating of the Piltdown skull. *Advancement of Science* 6:343–44.

—— 1963a. Dating skeletal material. *Science* 140:488.

—— 1963b. Analytical methods of dating bones. In Don R. Brothwell and Eric Higgs, eds., *Science in archeology*. New York: Basic Books, pp. 24–34.

» 13 «

JOHN H. CHILCOTT • JAMES DEETZ

The Construction and Uses of a Laboratory Archeological Site

Imagine the perfect archeological excavation: All personnel are highly trained, sufficient time is available, finance poses no problems, and work proceeds in a most meticulous and painstaking manner. Ascher (chapter 11) argues that even in such ideal circumstances information would, of necessity, be lost. Given this situation, one may ask three questions: For any particular site, how severe is destruction in excavation likely to be? How may it best be minimized? Under what circumstances is it best to avoid excavation completely? As Chilcott and Deetz point out, one cannot assume that material is randomly distributed within a site, and for this reason the efficiency of alternative excavation techniques cannot be directly assessed. In an artificially constructed "laboratory site," where distribution and amount of material is known before excavation, this problem does not arise.

Thus Chilcott and Deetz start with a known pattern. What they test is how variable perception of that pattern may be and what techniques of excavation will produce the least distortion. From their results one may derive a series of conclusions directly applicable to a wide variety of excavation situations. Some are self-evident: Darker objects which more nearly match in color the soil matrix are more likely to slip by unnoticed. Sophistication in archeological interpretation is directly related to the age of student excavators. Yet other conclusions are not so obvious. The authors note, for example, that small objects are significantly more difficult to locate in midden soil than in a natural counterpart. In an instance such as this, one may invoke the law of uniformitarianism to apply results from a laboratory site to a natural counterpart. One

Reproduced, with minor editorial changes, by permission of the Society for American Archaeology from *American Antiquity* 29(3), 1964.

can do more than just point out the special problems which any midden excavation is likely to entail, for within the controlled context of the laboratory site techniques may be devised that keep such loss to a minimum. Chilcott and Deetz provide a specific example of how this may be done.

The recent revival of experimental archeology noted by Sonnenfeld (1962) is primarily concerned with the interpretation of artifactual materials through a process of controlled experimentation with these objects in an effort to understand their proper function more clearly. Since archeology treats objects and their spatial associations in order to reconstruct culture, the objects and their archeological association are both fair game for experimental investigation.

The possibilities offered by this proposition plus a desire to sharpen training methods led us to devise an experimental archeological site which was designed to achieve both ends. The use of artificial sites as instructional aids is not a new idea; Harvard's basement sandbox laboratory served successfully for years, and small-scale, tabletop site replicas have also been employed with considerable effect. In view of the success of such devices, it seems reasonable to assume that a full-scale laboratory site, constructed on a college campus, might serve a similarly useful purpose. This article describes the construction and use of such a site and offers suggestions for others who may want to duplicate the experiment.

The Santa Barbara experimental site grew out of our lunchtime conversations, and rapidly developed into a rather complex first effort that required a year to execute. As the project developed, it could be seen that such a site provided certain advantages which other such constructs lacked, both in the area of field training and in methodological refinement. The immediate advantage over smaller-scale operations, particularly those constructed indoors, was apparent quite early in the development. Since the features were constructed several months prior to their excavation, rodents, water, and limited root growth had an opportunity to affect the condition of the artifacts. The native soil of the site area was used as fill, a rapidly growing and deep-rooted species of erosion-control grass was planted and soon completely obscured the pit outlines, and heavy California winter rains settled the deposits thoroughly. As a result, the excavators were provided with the "feel" of actual field conditions, particularly with respect to moving fill. The simple problem of earth removal in quantity is an urgent one in field training, and the artificial site exactly duplicated this problem. Thus matters of back-dirt disposition, screening areas, and large-scale shoveling were realistically presented and realistically solved.

In addition to these relatively obvious mechanical advantages offered by the experimental site, other advantages were less clearly apparent but of equal importance. It was felt that the laboratory site was actually preferable to natural sites for field training in many instances. Archeological instruction is usually offered either in summer sessions specifically designed for the purpose or in regular academic-course form, with students participating in weekend digging of a rather limited nature. Excavations accomplished in these two types of courses are somewhat different in emphasis and quantity, and thus each type should be discussed separately. The advantages offered by a laboratory site for course training within the framework of the regular academic year are mainly those which result from an increase in efficiency provided by an on-campus site. With the current expansion of the student population in the nation's colleges and the accompanying expansion in anthropological coursework, more facilities are needed to provide beginning students with field experience in archeology. Since much of the student-population expansion occurs in colleges located in urban centers and in community junior colleges, the traditional methods of using actual sites to train students may ultimately prove to be too limited, too costly, or too time-consuming. A laboratory site on the college campus is much less expensive, since it eliminates the cost of transporting students to the field and maintaining them while there. The site's ready availability not only avoids the usual weekend rush to a field site, but also increases the number of contact hours the student may have with field conditions. Such a site also reduces the damage to natural sites wreaked by inexperienced personnel.

Since archeological training on a weekend basis provides a minimum of field experience in any given semester, natural sites quite often provide the student with a correspondingly limited diversity of experience. There is no foolproof method of assuring any particular problem's presentation and solution. A laboratory site, on the other hand, can widen a student's experience in techniques and interpretation by presenting a variety of situations, many of which may not be encountered until he has gained considerable field experience in several different archeological areas. A student can be exposed to such diverse features as burials, housepits, hearths, adobe and stone walls, and rather complex stratigraphy within the brief span of a few days of digging. Since these situations are created under controlled conditions and known before recovery, there is a further advantage in that the techniques used can be evaluated more objectively while in progress. Any damage, dislocation, or misinterpretation can be analyzed with the student, and faulty procedures corrected.

On the other hand, on a natural site, since the situation is unknown beforehand, it is very difficult to diagnose anything other than blatantly incorrect procedures. Clearly, for limited instruction in archeological field methods, a laboratory site is more suitable than a natural site because it is more efficient in terms of time available, because it provides a greater variety of experience in a given amount of time, and because it permits more objective evaluation of a student's progress.

A laboratory site may also be used as an adjunct to a field-school site or as a substitute for it. Field-school sites are usually investigated for a period of six weeks or more during the summer, and are therefore more thoroughly excavated than sites dug during the regular school year. At this level of application of the laboratory site, a common criticism is that such a procedure diverts valuable effort and time from the real sites, which are being removed at an alarming rate by construction, amateurs, and natural forces. While this seems a valid and important criticism at first, a little thought shows that such is not the case. Sites selected for field-school use are frequently chosen for reasons not entirely archeological. Such practical problems as housing, suitability for field instruction with a beginning class (one would not begin a training program at Tikal, for example), accessibility, and proximity to the institution offering the course all bear on field-school site selection. Often the result is that the site selected does not represent the best interests of current research problems in the area.

While the use of a laboratory site does not advance archeological knowledge in an area, the use of certain natural sites provides little improvement of the situation. Furthermore, once a site has been excavated, the data collected must be processed. If this site is not directly involved in current research problems in the area, one is left with a mass of data requiring great amounts of laboratory time to process, while failing to provide a commensurate amount of new knowledge. In the meantime, these collections take up space and consume valuable time.

It is generally estimated that laboratory analysis takes from two to four times the amount of time that excavation of the material involves. The long view indicates that some natural sites should not be excavated if their collections become a burden to the archeologist, as they often do. The use of a laboratory site reduces to nearly none the amount of time required for laboratory analysis because no intrinsically important information is collected. The excavated material from the laboratory site can be reburied by the class at the end of the season to await excavation by other students the following year. If laboratory techniques are to be taught as a part of the field program, any of these can be illustrated by using data recovered from sites which do in fact represent the central research problems of the moment. In this manner an added advantage accrues from the use of students on truly worthwhile problems. An alternative to the exclusive use of a laboratory site for field-school training would be a combination of both types, natural and artificial, shifting emphasis as it seems necessary according to the needs and problems of the moment.

The term "laboratory site" was coined as a descriptive phrase to use in connection with such a site. This term not only avoids the semantic hostility associated with the term "artificial site" but also aptly describes a second application of such a site, the validation of the effectiveness of current archeological techniques. As has been indicated previously, if one is aware of the exact situation prevailing in a feature before its excavation, it is possible to study disruptions of these situations in terms of the variables that cause the disruption. No proper study of the relative effectiveness of different techniques can be accomplished at a natural site. Completely random distribution of artifactual materials is necessary for such a demonstration, and this cannot be shown to be true. Without this type of distribution, technique studies on natural sites require a knowledge of the total site content and the exact locations of all artifacts. Unless the excavator knows what was present at the outset of his work, he cannot possibly make a concise statement of the relative effectiveness of one technique as contrasted with another. Anyone who has done a reasonable amount of excavation knows that adjacent 5-foot-square pits can vary radically in their contents—quantitatively and qualitatively. Through the use of a laboratory site, a variety of excavation techniques with their underlying assumptions can be studied by using identical situations, with absolute control assured. Problems of stratigraphy and seriation are particularly suited to this approach, as is an investigation of the relative efficiency of various excavation techniques.

With the above considerations taken into account, we constructed a laboratory site on the Santa Barbara campus of the University of California during the fall of 1961. An area 50 by 100 feet was cleared of grass, and a pit 7 feet wide and 75 feet long was excavated by machine shovel in this space. This long trench was divided into ten 7-foot-square units, and each of these was built up, layer by layer, into an experimental set of features. Each layer was thoroughly soaked with water and allowed to settle for a week before the next layer was begun. Thus all of the basal layers were put in at the same time, and each successive layer in each 7-foot square followed in unison. Grass was planted on the surface of the filled trench, and charcoal, beer cans, paper, and other refuse were scattered over it. Gophers were active in the area during the "salting" period and during the winter; we had included peanuts in a number of the 7-foot units during their construction to encourage the animals. Prior to excavation, in late April, the grass had sprouted and covered the area with a rank growth, and a 6-inch-deep hardpan had formed at the surface. Fig. 13.1 shows the vertical layout of the site, with the contents of each pit indicated.

Of the ten pits, five were designed as training pits and four were used to investigate relatively simple problems of archeological technique. The training pits were devised to contain three levels of material representing preceramic, ceramic, and historical occupations. At the 1.5-foot level five flowerpots were crushed and scattered in each pit, and at the 2-foot level one flowerpot was broken and scattered in each unit. The training pits were therefore uniform in content and were used to investigate varying perceptions, abilities, and teaching problems in students of different age groups with different degrees of experience.

The experimental pits varied radically in their contents, with each pit designed to investigate a particular field-procedure problem. The four pits in this section were designed to study the effect of the color of small objects and earth composition on recovery of those objects, the effect of gopher activity on stratification in a variety of soil types, the effect of degree of vertical control on stratigraphic interpretation, and the relationship between certain excavation techniques and the recovery of small objects.

Five groups, some with prior field experience, were recruited from local schools and college classes to excavate the training pits during the month of May. Included in the inexperienced groups was a junior high school party of both sexes, a senior high school group of both sexes, and a college group of both sexes. The two experienced groups were a senior high school group of boys whose biology teacher had directed them in competent excavation of a historic Chumash Indian site and a college group of both sexes who had excavated both a Chumash shell midden and portions of the La Purisima Mission complex in Lompoc, California. The inexperienced groups were given a 20-minute orientation in field archeology before beginning work;

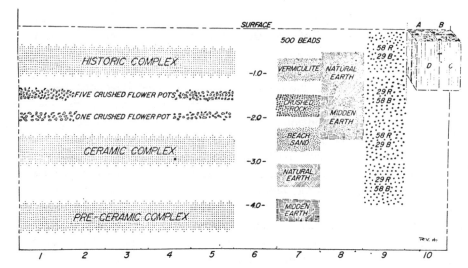

Figure 13.1 Schematic profile of a laboratory site. Pit 6 is sterile. Legends for Pits 1 through 5 refer to single-pit contents.

they were also given some experience on a nearby natural site. Thus, all of these students had the experience of working at both natural and laboratory sites. At the conclusion of each day, the students were interviewed individually concerning their preference for excavation in natural as opposed to artificial sites, and their overall reactions to the work in general.

While the most important aspect of the five excavated training pits was the investigation of their utility as training devices, they also permitted a study of the effect of maturity and experience on recovery. A detailed description of each pit's contents and excavation is impossible here, but the general results are presented and their significance briefly discussed. An inventory of the contents of one of the pits will make the summary statements more meaningful in specific terms.

As noted above, all of the training pits were of the same general type of construction and contained similar materials placed in the same sequence. Pit A2, excavated by inexperienced junior high school students, is typical of these training pits, and was constructed as shown in table 13.1 which shows pit contents and recovered material (fig. 13.2).

Pit A2 was excavated with shovels and trowels, with techniques ranging from gross shoveling to fine trowelwork around features. One of the most obviously striking aspects of the results of this work is the excellent rate of recovery by young inexperienced workers who before excavation had a minimum of understanding of the problems involved. Maturity had little effect on quantitative recovery, since equally excellent recovery records were compiled by the other groups. However, previous experience had a positive effect on quality of recovery. While relatively little breakage was inflicted on the material by the junior high school students, still less was done by the experienced high school and college groups.

On the other hand, maturity is positively correlated with sophistication of interpretation, while differences in experience have little effect on this variable. The older groups produced more imaginative interpretations of what they had exposed, regardless of previous experience. In Pit A2 the students managed to collect 50 percent more human bone from Feature 2 than was originally placed in their pit. This excess bone was apparently taken from adjacent pits also dug by younger inexperienced personnel, since their shortages more than cover the increase and there had been no burials in the area before the construction of the laboratory site. This dislocation is indicative of a rather low degree of careful procedure on the part of the younger workers, which was generally observed; older workers did a more careful job. Thus increased maturity and experience both add to the quality of recovery with less breaking and dislocation.

Since the pit excavated for the laboratory site had been exposed to sun and air for several weeks before construction, a hardpan formed which acted as a reservoir for water during the rainy season. As a result of this artificially formed water table at the base of the site, the lower levels of all pits were waterlogged and fluid when initially exposed. Because of the pressure of time, it was not possible to dry this level before excavation, and a sharp reduction of recovery resulted. However, situations frequently arise in which features must be excavated at once despite the condition of the soil, particularly in connection with salvage operations (Orr 1943). Under such circumstances, one often wonders if it is advisable to proceed with work. As a check on these conditions, the lower levels of three pits were excavated in their wet state, and since their contents were known, a statement of efficiency could be made. The results tabulated for Feature 3 in Pit A2 are typical of the high rate of loss among inexperienced personnel. However, there was a dramatic increase in both recovery and interpretation in the experienced high school group. The authors feel that excavation is warranted in such instances if an experienced, mature crew is employed, since a majority of the material was recovered by the senior high school boys, and interpretations were not severely limited.

The lowest feature in their pit was a hearth surrounded by large milling stones, food remains, and small, chipped-stone artifacts. This precise situation was reconstructed by the workers, although they had not seen the feature in its entirety; the students made the inference from materials dredged from below the surface with their hands. Even all of the smaller projectile points

TABLE 13.1

Excavation of Pit A2 by Inexperienced Junior High School Students

Contents	*Recovered Materials*
Feature 1 (0.5–1.0 feet), historic component	
1. Ox femur	1. recovered, 1.0–1.5
2. Clear glass, 20 pieces	2. recovered, broken (38 pieces), 1.0–1.5
3. Brown bottle	3. recovered, 1.0–1.5
4. Metal bank	4. recovered, 0.0–0.5
5. Pottery (16 pieces)	5. recovered, broken (32 pieces), 0.0–0.5; and (32 pieces), 1.0–1.5
6. Roof tile fragment	6. recovered, 1.0 1.5
7. Brown cup	7. recovered, 1.0–1.5
8. Animal bone (10 pieces)	8. recovered, 1.0–1.5
9. Small glass bottle	9. recovered, 1.0–1.5
10. Ceramic bottle	10. recovered, 1.0–1.5
11. White and blue bowl	11. recovered, broken, 1.0–1.5
12. White glass (2 pieces)	12. recovered, 1.0–1.5 (1 piece chipped)
13. Blue-green bottle (4 pieces)	13. recovered, 0.5–1.0
14. Pottery beer bottle	14. recovered, broken, 4 pieces, 1.0–1.5
15. Human bone: ribs, 2 femora, ulna, vertebrae, radius	15. recovered, ribs broken, femora intact, ulna broken, vertebrae intact, radius sheared in half by shovel
Feature 2 (2.5–3.0 feet), ceramic component	
1. Mortar fragment, large	1. recovered, 2.5–3.0
2. Large rock	2. recovered, 2.5–3.0
3. Large rock	3. recovered, 2.5–3.0
4. Small mortar	4. recovered, 2.5–3.0
5. Pestle	5. recovered, 2.5–3.0
6. Fossil	6. recovered, 2.5–3.0
7. Chert scraper	7. recovered, 2.5–3.0
8. Chert scraper	8. recovered, 2.5–3.0
9. Chert scraper	9. recovered, 2.5–3.0
10. Fossil shell	10. recovered, 2.5–3.0
11. Coyote mandible	11. recovered, broken, 2.5–3.0
12. Coyote cranium	12. recovered, 2.5–3.0
13. Human femur	13. missing
14. Seven potsherds	14. recovered, 2.5–3.0
15. Lidded pot	15. recovered, lid chipped, 2.5–3.0
16. Projectile point	16. missing

(In addition, two pieces of white glass were recovered, source unknown.)

Feature 3 (4.0–4.5 feet), preceramic component

1.	Mortar	1. recovered, 4.0–5.0
2.	Mano	2. missing
3.	Mortar fragment	3. recovered, 4.0–5.0
4.	Pestle	4. missing
5.	Rock fragments	5. recovered, 4.0–5.0
6.	Hearth with shell, bone, and acorn	6. missing
7.	Projectile point	7. missing
8.	Projectile point	8. missing
9.	Projectile point	9. missing
10.	Scraper	10. missing
11.	Projectile point	11. missing
12.	Scrapers (2)	12. missing
13.	Small projectile point	13. missing
14.	Projectile point	14. missing
15.	Projectile point	15. missing
16.	Scraper	16. missing
17.	Projectile point	17. missing
18.	Projectile points (20)	18. missing

a   b

Figure 13.2 Feature 1, Pit A2. [a] at time of construction; [b] after excavation.

and scrapers were recovered. The flowerpots, which were broken and scattered in two levels in the training pits, formed a separate experiment. The effect of a site's richness on the efficiency of recovery can be measured in this manner, if excavation techniques are held constant. All students excavated these levels by shovel-shaving. While one pot was broken and scattered at one level, five pots, broken and scattered a foot higher, created a five-times-richer situation. The results from two pits are shown in table 13.2. With the exception of a rather low recovery by the experienced workers in Pit A5, variations in artifactual richness seem to have had relatively little effect on recovery.

At the conclusion of each day of digging, each student was queried as to his or her preference for excavation between laboratory and natural sites. Most of the students preferred excavating the natural site; however, all but two of the students (junior high school girls) also found the excavation of the laboratory site interesting. Interest in excavation of the laboratory site increased among the experienced and older students. It would seem that the glamor of archeology wears off as students gain more experience and become more mature. Table 13.3 summarizes student preferences for each type of site.

Students who had no previous experience in archeology were also queried as to the changes in their perception of what archeological field work might be like. Most students were surprised by the careful procedures which had to be followed, the smallness of many of the artifacts, the amount of hard work involved, and its dirtiness.

The four pits designed for study of methods and techniques were quite successful in realized results. Only one could be considered a complete failure—a pit designed to measure the direction and degree of dislocation of small objects caused by gopher activity. Design of this pit was simple. A "layer cake" was constructed consisting of .5-foot-thick layers of natural earth, beach sand, midden earth, crushed rock, and vermiculite. Grain was scattered through these layers as an attraction to gophers, whose activity in the area was indicated by numerous burrows and tailings. On the surface of the completed pit, 500 light-blue glass beads ($\frac{1}{16}$ inch in diameter) were scattered. It was hoped that gophers would burrow through the layers and in so doing move the beads downward. Since the layers were of contrasting colors and textures, the nature and extent of the admixture would be obvious. Although there was considerable gopher activity in adjacent pits, the "layer cake" remained undisturbed. This lack of activity seems due in large part to the effect of the vermiculite forming the top layer. Burrows approaching the edge of the vermiculite layer in a lateral direction stopped abruptly upon encountering this material. It served to seal off the underlying layers effectively, so that the entire pit remained undisturbed. The only conclusion which can be made is that some materials serve as a very effective barrier to gopher activity. While this information may be of some value to gardeners, from the archeological standpoint the experiment can be considered a failure.

TABLE 13.2
Recovery of Potsherds (in percent)

Level	Pit A3	Pit A5
5-pot level	72.6	83.2
1-pot level	85.0	52.0

Pit A3 was excavated by an inexperienced high
school group, Pit A5 by an experienced high
school group.

TABLE 13.3
Preferences for Type of Site

Group	Laboratory	Natural	Totals
Secondary	4	18	22
College	4	2	6
Totals	8	20	28

The second experimental pit was designed to measure the effect of both soil and artifact color on recovery of objects. Two layers of earth, one of dark midden fill and the other of tan, silty, native soil, were constructed, and 300 each of red, white, and black beads ($\frac{1}{16}$ inch) were mixed in each level. All fill of this pit was passed through a ¼-inch mesh screen. No beads were recovered from damp native soil. Later, when this earth had dried, beads of all three colors were found simply by troweling. Damp midden fill was more productive of beads when screened. While no black beads were recovered because of their dark color, a few red beads and large quantities of white beads were found adhering to the clumps of midden on the screen. Once these clumps were broken, however, the beads passed unnoticed through the screen. Troweling dry midden earth produced no beads, in marked contrast to the recovery rate from dry native soil. Screening dry midden earth produced beads of all three colors in nearly equal quantities. The failure to find beads by troweling damp midden, and their apparent absence from unscreened dry midden earth, can probably be attributed to the higher oil content of the midden soil, which causes the soil to adhere closely to the smooth surface of the beads when dry. The fact that red, black, and white beads, present in equal quantities, were not recovered in equal proportions indicates a possible source of sampling error when using one technique only. As one might expect, the closer the color of the artifact approaches the color of the soil in which it is found, the more difficult it is to find. On the basis of these controlled results, one might suggest that if the presence of small artifacts such as beads is suspected, a variety of techniques should be used, including sample troweling of dried screen tailings.

The third experimental pit was designed to investigate a simple problem of seriation and stratigraphy through the construction of a clear-cut stratigraphic column characterized by regular variation of two types of objects. Red and blue plastic-covered, cardboard poker chips were mixed with natural earth and deposited in discrete 1-foot levels. A total of four levels was constructed. The relative frequency of red and blue chips was changed in each foot level. Every other level had identical quantities of each color, and the total number of chips was the same in each level. This pit, a 7-foot-square unit, was excavated by experienced college students, using a .25-foot vertical control. Recovered poker-chip frequencies were recorded and compared with the known profile. Table 13.4 shows the expected variation and the observed variation for each level.

Except for a rather low degree of recovery in the first level, observed frequencies repeated expected results, and in view of the technique used—shovel-shaving—the recovery rate was surprisingly high. Since the levels were constructed from the bottom up and excavated from the top down, there is also surprising coincidence between constructed and excavated levels. In two levels, more chips were recovered than were deposited, indicating mixing along the junctions of the levels. The relative inaccuracy in the first layer may result in part from root growth, and partly from the usual problem of penetrating the topmost, sundried, hard topsoil. However, a graphic representation of the quarter-foot level frequencies presents a more confusing picture (fig. 13.3).

While the general trend is still evident, gross examination of this graph may lead one to conclude that nearly identical quantities of red and blue chips were present in the first levels, and certainly that the two types varied in phase. A departure from this pattern occurs at the 2.0–2.5-foot level, but even beyond this depth relative frequencies are far from clear. This pattern has some implications for field archeological problems. The contradictory pattern resulting from finer vertical control is probably due to the method of constructing the deposit. The chips, although mixed with the soil, were not randomly distributed. As a result, there were areas of more intense occurrence within the profile, and this difference in richness creates the pattern observed. This mode of occurrence is not unlike that expected in a midden lacking in clearly visible stratigraphic levels, but nonetheless possessed of discrete living surfaces. The dispersal through the deposit resulting from inadequate mixture in the experiment may have a counterpart in rodent translocation, root disturbance, and similar forces. On the basis of these results, it may be suggested that both discrete and combined frequencies

TABLE 13.4
Recovery of Poker Chips

Level	Expected	Recovered
0.0–1.0	58 red, 29 blue	21 red, 8 blue
1.0–2.0	29 red, 58 blue	31 red, 56 blue
2.0–3.0	58 red, 29 blue	58 red, 31 blue
3.0–4.0	29 red, 58 blue	25 red, 57 blue

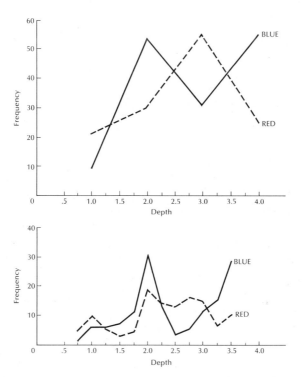

Figure 13.3 Poker-chip frequencies, *a*, plotted by 1-foot levels, Pit 9; *b*, plotted by 3-inch levels, Pit 9.

should be plotted for artifact-frequency variation. In the experimental case, a pattern which is clear-cut in 1-foot increments is totally misleading under finer control.

The fourth experimental pit was designed to determine the influence of excavation technique on the recovery of small objects. The pit was divided into four quadrants, each containing 50 glass beads (⅛ inch diameter). Each quadrant was 1 foot thick. Three of the four quadrants were composed of natural soil, the fourth of screened black midden soil. The three natural-soil quadrants were each excavated by a different technique and the midden-soil quadrant by a technique used on one of the natural-soil sections. Table 13.5 shows the results of this experiment.

Quadrant A was excavated by gross shoveling onto a ⅛-inch mesh screen. Recovery from this quadrant was expectably high, but no higher than the

TABLE 13.5
Excavation Technique and Recovery of Small Objects

Quadrant	Soil Type	Technique	Recovery (%)
A	Natural	Shovel, screen	96
B	Natural	Trowel	96
C	Natural	Shovel, shave	56
D	Midden	Trowel	58

yield of quadrant B, in which identical soil was troweled. Thus, under the circumstances which prevailed, troweling and screening were shown to be equally efficient. Troweling midden soil resulted in a sharp decrease in recovery, and this reduction was probably due to the texture of the soil, the same factor which limited recovery in the second experimental pit, in which troweling damp midden soil produced none of the beads (¹⁄₁₆ inch) present in the fill. If beads were twice as large, some were recovered, but fewer than by certain other techniques. Shovel-shaving of natural soil recovered 56 percent of the beads, the lowest of the recovery rates. However, even this rather gross technique produced over half of the beads in the section.

The four experimental pits described above constitute a basic series of controlled experiments in the investigation of efficiency and accuracy of certain techniques universally employed by archeologists in the field. They are extremely simple, and serve only to indicate the direction which may be taken by more refined and complex experiments and to point out what the authors feel are rather surprising results in a modest effort. Beads and poker chips are in no way meant to represent the full extent of actual archeological assemblages, but experiments in which greater diversity is introduced could and should be devised. Under such closely controlled circumstances, much can be learned regarding the techniques which archeologists accept as a standard part of their field procedures.

As a result of experience gained by this experiment, certain suggestions for devising and constructing an on-campus laboratory site can be made. If the construction is an initial effort, the size of the site should be restricted to an area of not more than 900 square feet, and the depth is best restricted to 2 feet. The site should be excavated an additional 2 feet and filled to a point 2 feet below surface before developing the features to be placed in it. This procedure will permit excess water to seep to the bottom of the pit and keep the features above relatively dry and undisturbed by standing water. The earth used to fill the site should be screened to avoid intrusion of modern objects. It was rather embarrassing to have one of our groups discover a bottle cap associated with a feature representing an early hunting-and-gathering component. Soil of contrasting color can be used to advantage to define the base of certain features and to represent posthole or hearth fill in simulated architectural features. Each feature should be carefully arranged, with each artifact numbered and photographed before covering. This provides the instructor with a complete record of each feature against which he may check excavated results. Covering the features with screened earth must be done with considerable care to avoid displacement or breakage of objects. Filling should be accomplished to approximately 3 inches above the surface to compensate for soil settling. The boundaries of the site should be marked with wooden stakes pounded to ground level, to permit convenient relocation the following season. The Santa Barbara site was constructed during October and excavated in May. This period of time was adequate to permit complete settling and overgrowth by vegetation. Any rapidly growing ground cover can be used to advantage in planting the filled site. A site of this size will require approximately five days for preparation, using three full-time workers, and three days to excavate, using a crew the size of that employed at Santa Barbara.

These instructions are intended for the construction of a laboratory site for the first time and as such are quite modest. With added imagination and effort, many refinements can be made, using knowledge of other archeological features as a source of inspiration. Burials, refuse heaps, pit houses, and similar features can be made with relatively little effort.

A laboratory replica of a Plains earthlodge on the Santa Barbara site has been constructed. Other experimental sites are also in the process of construction or aging, so that a supply of experiments will be assured in coming years. The use of such a device holds promise for both training and methodological refinement.

REFERENCES

Orr, Phil. 1943. Archaeology of Mescalitan Island, and customs of the Canalino. *Santa Barbara Museum of Natural History, Occasional Papers*, No. 5. Santa Barbara.

Sonnenfeld, J. 1962. Interpreting the function of primitive implements. *American Antiquity* 28(1):56–65. Salt Lake City.

» FOUR «

Living Archeology

In American universities, archeology is most often cast as a subdiscipline of anthropology, and this arrangement reflects the widely accepted belief that processes which shape human social and individual actions today were equally important determinants of past behavior. The "general laws"—that holy grail which marks the end of the anthropologist's search—must, by definition, explain past change as well as current diversity. Given this intimate and accepted relationship between past and present, it is not surprising that archeologists draw from the better-documented ethnographic present in their attempt to order and interpret the fragmentary bits and pieces of data preserved from the past. It is difficult to know where else to turn, and just as the ethnographer must, consciously or unconsciously, use knowledge derived from his own cultural experience to understand a nonwestern society, so too—like it or not—the archeologist must use the historic record and the ethnographic present to approach an unknown past. The fact that objects must be named and features described militates toward this end, and few people would quibble with such terms as "post mold," "hearth," or "ceramic jar." Intuitively this is often an eminently reasonable practice.

While the present provides a tempting and possibly unavoidable route to the past, the problems which beset this approach cannot be bypassed lightly. Four of the articles in this section were written after 1968. Of these, three make specific mention of a publication by Freeman which appeared in print that year and which directly and forcefully attacked the "ethnoarcheological approach." Freeman notes, quite sensibly, that *a priori* one may assume that all past ways of life, which cover several million years, are not duplicated in the rather paltry sample of historically known hunting and gathering societies. He argues that primary reference to this limited body of data will not only distort our understanding of the past but will also prevent original discovery. In a similar vein other authors have pointed out that analogy is basic to the application of ethnographic data, and that the archeologist may pick and choose between historically documented alternatives to select an example he finds congenial. Quite rightly, such a "grab bag approach," as it has been termed, lacks even minimal logical rigor. From such criticism one undisputable point emerges: No matter how great the potential interpretive value of the ethnographic present may be, this tool can be applied only with thought and care. Each of the following articles deals, in one way or another, with this basic problem of application.

Two themes run through the articles which follow. First, all authors realize that the ethnographic present offers a controlled situation in which a social "cause" and a material "effect" may be directly observed. Here one need not guess—as the archeologist must—the "cause" on the basis of the excavated "effect," and the relationship between a human or group activity and its material byproduct may be analyzed in a straightforward manner, with relevant variables, in theory at least, susceptible to control. And for this reason, these studies fall within the realm of "Experimental Archeology." Secondly, as some of the authors state, and others imply, ethnographic observations, unless expressly directed toward this end, are rarely of the type relevant to archeological questions. How pots break, animal bones are split, or where garbage eventually comes to rest are rarely prime ethnographic concerns. Thus prehistorians, together with the few social anthropologists directly interested in archeological problems, have themselves undertaken the study of living peoples.

» 14

JOHN E. YELLEN

Cultural Patterning in Faunal Remains: Evidence from the !Kung Bushmen

The 1960s marked a period of change and upheaval in American archeology. "Traditional" approaches which emphasized the establishment and delineation of cultural traditions in time and space were subjected to attack from many sides. These first steps in the long and arduous business of archeological reconstruction became, it was argued, ends in themselves; they overly restricted the archeologist's horizons and substituted the dry bones of descriptive history for the more proper anthropological study of culture and culture process. "Ethnoarcheology," or the emphasis on ethnographic analysis for archeological ends, was explicitly defined and has flourished in the context of these recent changes. The dichotomy between the "new" and "old," however, need exist neither in theory nor practice. As you read this article, consider the uses to which the type of faunal analysis advocated may be put. Yellen argues that the process of butchering is governed, either consciously or unconsciously, by a series of culture-specific rules, and suggests a technique for discerning these regularities in faunal remains. But why attempt such a long and intrinsically dull task in the first place? Yellen casts his answer in terms of "traditional" goals and argues that new approaches can fruitfully be used to attack old problems.

Note also, the crucial, yet essentially negative role ethnoarcheology can serve. Yellen observes, for example, that a number of forces resulting from both human and nonhuman factors determine the particular faunal pattern observed in abandoned Bushman campsites. On this basis he can examine the explanations for different patterns discerned at diverse archeological sites and demonstrate that the assumptions on which these analyses rest are overly simplistic—and therefore open to challenge—because they do not take all the possibly relevant variables into account. In this way, a particular case may refute—or at least cast strong doubt on—general theories or interpretations. To work in the other direction and generalize from a specific instance is a much more difficult procedure.

Note that this article is organized like a site report. Data are presented in a separate section, set apart from interpretation, theoretical considerations, and specific conclusions. The ethnoarcheologist documents societies, many in a state of rapid change, and in the long run the particular data he collects may prove of greater importance to the specific questions he asks of them because the objectives and analytic techniques of archeologists tend to shift in both subtle and not-so-subtle ways over the years.

Archeological interpretation, like religious devotion, requires a "leap of faith." On the one hand pottery designs, stone shapes, faunal remains, assemblage variability, site locations, and other of the observable phenomena which form the basic material of archeological investigation may be described, enumerated, and analyzed. The intuitive or statistically significant patterns toward which empirical analysis of this type leads can often be demonstrated, but the cause of such patterns—the interaction of underlying variables which result in an observable configuration—can only be guessed; and this requires a leap of faith. Deductive approaches, on the other hand, seem, theoretically at least, to offer a solution to this problem. They postulate a set of relationships, and then test how well observable data may comfortably be made to fit within them. But from a practical point of view, relatively few archeological problems have been successfully couched within this framework, and as a rule it is easier to laud the methodological advantages of this approach than to devise models relevant in concrete situations—in part because of the limited and fragmentary nature of archeological data, and in part because of the difficulty of discerning laws which apply to material remains of human culture. These limitations become all the more frustrating since the number of sophisticated techniques for data collection and statistical manipulation are constantly increasing while allied fields such as population biology and animal ethology provide models which are theoretically applicable but practically difficult to apply.

Hypothesis formation (which is the first step in a deductive approach) and interpretation in cultural terms of observed patterns (which represents the last step in an inductive analysis) both require some feel or idea of what may constitute a reasonable explanation. And in either type of study one must ask how "reasonable" the results appear. In such a final assessment, where the subjective element admittedly plays an important role, it may be useful to assess conclusions against two criteria. One may first ask if possibly there are important variables which have not been taken into consideration, and then attempt to discover if there are any other equally or more reasonable models to which conclusions may be compared. In dealing with the unique events of man's prehistory, which by definition have not, and cannot be observed, these criteria can never be conclusively met.

One way to deal with this problem involves viewing man in a wider context and to look for broader, more encompassing regularities in which prehistoric man forms one specific case. For example, man may be viewed as one of many specialized biological organisms—as a unique case within this broader context. Man may be examined as one of a number of predator species, for example, and thus forced to make adaptations common to all of them. On the other hand it is sometimes possible to ignore for a while the overall puzzle and to concentrate on the individual pieces. In this instance these would be the different variables which individually or in various combinations may interact to give an observed pattern. Material drawn from the "ethnographic present" may sometimes be used in this way to provide a tightly controlled test situation or working model which may profitably be investigated by the archeologist. The particular observed configuration is of itself not of central importance, since it almost certainly will vary from case to case, and may in fact be unique. Certainly one instance cannot serve as a basis for generalization across the vast reaches to time, space, and cultural variability. What one can do, using ethnographic material, is to determine in any particular instance the relevant variables which may either cause or distort variation, and evaluate and sharpen manipulative techniques which may serve to elucidate underlying cultural patterning. Such an approach has often been criticized (see Freeman 1968) on the basis that specific observed models *a priori* have a limited applicability; this criticism is a valid one. But if the ethnographic present is perceived not as a factory which stamps out templates against which models of the past can be measured but as a workshop in which analytic tools are forged and fashioned, these objections no longer hold.

In this article I present a body of data that deals with !Kung Bushmen's butchering techniques and analyzes the remains of large antelopes recovered from abandoned Bushmen campsites. My purposes are to present in a straightforward manner a body of data that may be of interest and use to other researchers, and to examine the problem of whether in one specific area—faunal analysis—the ethnographic present may be of use in interpreting the archeological past.

APPROACHES AND PROBLEMS IN FAUNAL ANALYSIS

The questions asked of faunal remains from Paleolithic sites may be broadly grouped in three categories. (I stress the term "Paleolithic," since I wish to avoid the specialized area which deals with the recognition of early domestication and attempts to determine when in specific sequences wild antecedents gave way to their modern counterparts.) In one category of analysis, prime emphasis centers on animals themselves in relation not particularly to man, but to time and to the environment. Species with limited chronological lives serve as time markers, and their presence in an assemblage may help to assign it to a relative slot in the Pleistocene sequence. Elephants, for example, have evolved through a number of species during this time, and the presence of a particular species may provide the crucial chronological clue. In the absence of solid geological means or absolute means of aging, faunal dating of this type is of central importance, and lists of consecutive faunal assemblages (i.e. Coppens 1967) provide a vital research tool. In addition, given the assumption (and it is only an assumption) that prehistoric forms shared adaptations similar to their modern counterparts, numerous attempts have been made to reconstruct past environments and to place them in glacial or interglacial, dry or wet periods.

In a similar way, one may attempt to reconstruct both single periods and to deal with the problems of climatic change. Garrod and Bate (1937), in their analysis of changing percentages of deer and gazelle in the different levels of Mt. Carmel Cave in Israel, provide a pioneering study of this type. In a final, and even more exacting, kind of environmental study, attempts have been made to determine the seasons during which sites were occupied. An examination of faunal remains for seasonal changes in animal anatomy—the development and shedding of antlers for example—as well as for age changes in animal population structure in some cases permit one to infer the season (see, for example Bouchud 1966 and Binford 1971). It must be remembered that animal remains recovered in an archeological context do not present a representative cross-section of the natural population, since they have been killed and brought there by man. However, in approaches of this type the prime emphasis is on the animals themselves rather than on man's use or interaction with them; they are linked more closely to the natural than to the social sciences.

A second group of questions that consider faunal remains deals with actual bones and their possible uses. Years ago, Dart (1957) proposed the still controversial idea that *Australopithecus* fabricated bone tools before the use of stone, and Kitching (1963) has argued that, contrary to accepted belief, Mousterian man made widespread use of bone utensils. Recent discoveries in Kenya's Lake Rudolph area of stone implements over 2 million years old reduce in importance the question of early bone use, but from a methodological point of view an extremely interesting problem still remains: namely, what techniques can be used to determine whether obviously modified fragments of bone are, in effect, tools. Recently Wolberg (1970) and Brain (1967, 1969) have reviewed the South African australopithecine material and arrived at diametrically opposed conclusions. Sadek-Kooros (1972) has used both actual experimentation on fresh bone and statistical analysis of materials recovered in an archeological context to consider the same question.

A third and most interesting group of questions concerns the interrelationship between faunal remains and human activity. If the odd small animal that may have burrowed into an archeological deposit and died there is excluded, it must be assumed that bones recovered in a sealed content were purposely brought there—most often as food. And if only for this fact, they have passed through a cultural filter. It is possible to examine this cultural imprint which bones bear and to infer some aspects of cultural process. On the simplest level, a list of the species represented (and such lists are characteristic of most site reports) indicates the range and relative importance of different prey species. By carrying this type of analysis a step further, one can estimate the number of individuals represented for each species; a number of different techniques exist for doing this (see Chaplin 1971). With this information it is possible to guess at food amount given estimates of the weight of edible as opposed to nonedible portions for different species of animals. Clark (1952) and White (1953a) among others have led the way in this kind of analysis.

In the types of studies outlined immediately above, analysis is concerned exclusively with determining the species and number of individuals present. By examining the treatment, the distribution in space, and the relative number of anatomical parts for different species of animals, it is possible to carry this cultural analysis several steps further, and to discuss such questions as hunting and butchering techniques, sharing and trade, and more general cultural patterning. From a series of excellently preserved and excavated bison kill sites in the Western United States, a number of workers (Frison 1971, Kehoe 1967, Kehoe and Kehoe 1960, Wheat 1967, 1972) have been able to reconstruct in some detail the final stages of the bison drive and the following butchering procedure. Perkins and Daly (Perkins and Daly 1968, Daly 1969) through the analysis of relative frequency of fore- and hindlimb bones from a number of species of animals at Suberde, a Neolithic site in Turkey, feel that they can reconstruct both hunting patterns and following butchering processes. Using a similar technique in his study of sheep remains from Roman sites in England, Chaplin (1969, 1971) has noted a significantly low number of pelvae and femurs, and he suggests that the meat encompassing these choice parts may have been shared or traded away. Employing a different approach, Guilday, Parmalee, and Tanner (1962) have studied cut marks on bone, and from them inferred butchering techniques. The most sophisticated studies in terms of conceptualization, if not actual methodology, were published by White in a series of articles spanning the early 1950s (1952, 1953a,b, 1954, 1955). Working with faunal remains from a number of sites located in the Western United States, White tried not only to interpret observed distributions in terms of hunting and butchering technique, taking such factors as the size of a species into consideration, but also took a larger view and considered assemblages in light of overall patterns. He used observed patterns in such assemblages to determine site similarities, just as one might use pottery or stone-tool types for the same purpose. And he tested his conclusions against these more standard measures.

Perhaps faunal material, by its very nature—it comes in bits and pieces which can, with varying amounts of difficulty, be fit into the predetermined boxes of species and then anatomical portion—favors an inductive approach. Generally three stages are involved: first classification, then manipulation of the numerical results to determine either patterns or glaring irregularities, and finally that interpretive leap of faith, in which an attempt is made to explain observed results most often in cultural terms. Dart, for example, in his study of faunal remains from Makapansgat Cave (1957), noted that for antelope 336 distal ends of the humerus were recovered compared to only 33 proximal ends of the same bone: a ratio of approximately 10:1. Similar irregularities were noted for other longbones as well, and given these nonrandom proportions he postulates that the australopithecine occupants of the cave used bone tools. Bones that would make good tools were brought back to the cave and thus found in large numbers; bones less frequently represented were either discarded outside of the cave or were used as tools away from it. An argument of this type does not simply guess at the cause of observed variation (there is no real way around this) but usually assumes that a single cause for most if not all variation can be isolated. To take one more example: Perkins and Daly (1968) use basically the same approach in their analysis of remains from Suberde and note that for the ox *Bos primigenius* foot bones occur more frequently than do bones from the upper leg. They argue that the upper leg bones were discarded away from camp and that the foot bones were left attached to the skin when the latter was carried home. Again, the assumption is made that a single relevant factor is responsible for observed variation, and Daly, who is aware of this problem, discusses other possible natural sources and states, "In the archaeological context, however, we are not dealing with natural survival, but with the results of man's activity and the differences in survival pattern become of great importance" (1969:149).

With the exception of passing references to butchering practices (e.g. Wilson 1924, Wissler 1910) there is little in the ethnographic literature to serve as an example to buttress or attack assumptions of this type. One worker (Chaplin 1971) has in fact turned to modern English butchery practices to support his arguments. A notable exception is Brain's (1969) controlled study of goat bones collected from modern Namib Desert Hottentot camps, and this work throws considerable doubt on the notion that observed distributions can be explained in terms of single cultural factors. Brain analyzed goat bones from Hottentot refuse heaps and found that the distributions of anatomical parts correspond quite closely to those observed at Makapansgat by Dart. Since the Hottentots do not make tools from goat bones, other explanations must be sought; Brain has suggested that differential preservation, at least in this case, is related to variations in the structural features of bones and the relative times at which longbone epiphyses fuse. My own studies, which are a continuation of Brain's work, indicate that a number of other complicating factors must also be taken into account.

PATTERNING IN FAUNAL REMAINS: THE !KUNG CASE

The speakers of !Kung, or zu/wasi, a Bushman language, inhabit Western Botswana and adjacent portions of South West Africa (Namibia) and Angola; they have been extensively described by Lee (1968), Marshall (1960), and Thomas (1959) among others. While some !Kung groups have been largely absorbed into the surrounding Bantu agricultural and pastoral complex, others have maintained a hunting and gathering way of life, and these latter provide an excellent milieu for controlled faunal studies. My own work with them has proceeded on three distinct analytic levels, and I have attempted to keep each of them separate in the following discussion. The first includes observation and interview: over a period of two and a half years I was able to watch how people treated animal remains from start to finish, and through interview find out why observed procedures were followed. From this it is possible to build up a descriptive framework and to delineate culturally determined patterns with great accuracy and control. Thus the patterns an archeologist might try to infer from the remains he excavated were available to me through direct observation. And these observed "conclusions" could serve as a check in the later stages of my analysis. In effect, I had the answers before the questions had been asked.

The second step in this research involved the collection of faunal samples under tightly regulated circumstances. Therefore several times I provided the !Kung with a large antelope, killed and transferred by me, with the proviso that after they had butchered and consumed it, breaking the bones as they wished, all the fragments should be returned to me. Recovery in these cases was never complete, since one person would always forget, or some fragments would mysteriously disappear; but from such controlled samples it proved possible to arrange the fragments, observe how each bone has been treated, and describe the form the resultant pieces took. And with this kind of sample it is possible to talk directly about cultural patterning.

The third and final step consisted of collecting faunal remains from !Kung campsites which had been abandoned from several weeks to several months before. These camps were treated as archeological sites, and all observed features, as well as the position of all bone fragments, were measured. These fragments, which had been exposed to scavenging and other natural forces, fall into the archeological realm, although quite a recent one. And when an "archeological type analysis" was conducted on this sample, it was then possible to compare these inductively produced results to the "right" or observed answers, to determine the closeness of fit, and to note and attempt to explain the irregularities. In the following sections, each of these steps is considered separately.

!Kung Butchering Practices: Observation and Interview

For large antelope it is useful to distinguish three stages in the butchering and consumption process. The first consists of primary butchering of the freshly dead animal at the kill site, and the incidental cooking and eating by the hunters which takes place there. The second stage, which is sometimes not necessary, includes the further subdivision of the carcass into smaller parcels for distribution to individuals or family groups, while in the final stage these packages are further broken down for the actual cooking and consumption.

My sample in this study includes gemsbok, kudu, and wildebeeste. Adults weigh from 305 to 600 lbs. (114–188 kg) and according to sex and species may provide from 158 to 300 lbs. (49–94 kg) of edible yield (Lee personal communication). The same types of information which have been collected for smaller antelopes (steenbok and duiker), the African porcupine, and springhare will be published elsewhere. In passing, it may be noted that the butchering process, and the resulting configuration of observed faunal remains, is unique for each of these groups and differs very markedly from the patterns observed for the large antelope.

Large animals are hunted with the bow and poisoned arrow. The hunter, either alone or with a companion, tracks and stalks his prey and, if lucky, hits it with a small poisoned arrow. Usually the poison rather than the physical damage caused by the penetration of the arrow causes death, and this may take from several hours to several days to occur. Thus the hunter follows the wounded animal only a short distance before returning to camp since he does not want it to travel far before it dies. Some animals do, in fact, wander aimlessly and die near the place where they were first wounded; others may travel dozens of miles before they die, and the hunters will often abandon the hunt, believing that the effort involved outweighs the possible rewards. On the morning after an animal has been wounded, most or all adult men in a camp will accompany the hunter and follow the tracks with hope of finding the prey either dead or unable to travel further. If unsuccessful on the first day, this procedure will be repeated until the hunters decide to give up the search. When this happens usually depends on the distance the animal has traveled from camp, and the extent to which the animal has weakened.

When an animal is found dead—and this may also include kills scavenged from lions, leopards, or hyenas—there are three possible courses of action. The carcass may merely be butchered and cut into carrying-size pieces for removal to camp; alternatively, further meat preparation is possible and portions of meat may be cut into strips or "biltong," dried on the spot, and then carried back; finally, in some cases the camp itself may be moved to the kill. Which method the hunters use depends on the size of the animal, the distance to camp, the number of carriers available, the availability of water and other resources in the immediate area of the kill, and previously planned group moves. Most often the first course is preferred, but as size and distance increase, or the number of carriers decrease, it becomes more likely that some on-the-spot biltong-making will take place. Only if plans have already been made to shift the camp in the direction of the kill, or if water is available in the immediate area (which happens only during the limited rainy season), will the camp move to the kill site.

The first field butchering serves three purposes. The primary aim is to divide the carcass into smaller, manageable, carrying-size packages. A secondary function is to remove as neatly as possible the few undesirable parts, such as the contents of the digestive system and the horns. Finally special portions of the animal, such as the cannon bones and the liver, are set aside for cooking and consumption at the kill site by the hunters. In this latter regard a consistent pattern is observed: the marrow in the cannon bones and the liver belong to and are usually eaten by the hunters at the kill. Depending on the number of men present, up to 10 ribs, as well as miscellaneous strips of meat which do not contain bones, may also be directly roasted on a fire and eaten. The men say that they eat meat at the kill to give them strength for the long and extremely tiring carrying job that lies ahead of them.

The following summary, which describes the butchering of an adult female wildebeeste weighing approximately 400 lbs. (125 kg), conforms to the standard pattern. The total time involved is approximately two hours, and the tools used include a small metal hatchet as well as three small metal knives, which are constantly resharpened by being stropped against the wildebeeste's horns and hooves. Hatchets, as well as the !Kung adze, which consists of a light metal blade set in a wooden handle, are used primarily to separate the ribs from the vertebral column, to cut the latter into segments, to remove the head, and to split the pelvis. When a hatchet or adze is lacking, however, the same results can be accomplished using either a rock or a whole cannon bone as a hammer in combination with a knife. The wildebeeste butchering proceeded as follows:

1. *By pulling both forelegs, the wildebeeste is dragged about 15 ft. into an area of patchy shade.*
2. *The left side of the animal is skinned and the udder removed in the process.* The animal is placed on its left side and the skin is slit along the ventral midline from the neck to the udder. Cuts are continued along either side of the udder and along the inner portion of both hind legs to the distal end of the cannon bones. Similar cuts are made from the

midline along the inside of each front leg. The skin on the left side is then pulled away from the body and carefully cut away, intact, with a knife. The muscles which twitch the skin are left adhering to the body. Once this process has started, the freed portion of skin is stretched tight and struck near its contact with the body with the butt of the hatchet, and this serves to pull the skin free from the body. By using this technique with selective cutting in places, the skin is completely freed from the left side and from both left legs. The udder is then cut free and placed in a tree.

3. *Removal of cannon bones and hooves.* With a knife, the cannon bones are carefully removed by cutting at the contact between their proximal head and the adjacent articulation. Similarly the hooves are removed by cutting at the cannon's distal ends. The hooves are then tied together and placed in a tree. The heads of all cannons and the adjacent bones are left intact.

4. *Cooking the cannon bones.* A fire is built from small branches located in the immediate area. When it has burned down, all four cannon bones are placed directly in it, allowed to cook for five minutes, and then removed and set aside.

5. *Removing the left forelimb.* Two men removed the left forelimb. While one pulls it away from the body the other, using a knife, severs the attachments which hold the scapula to the rib cage. This is easily accomplished; then the forelimb, which includes the scapula, humerus, and radius-ulna, comes away cleanly with all bones intact. This also is placed in a small tree adjacent to the kill.

6. *Removing the left hindlimb.* As before, one man holds the limb away from the body while the other cuts. An incision is made directly to the head of the femur, and the ligaments which connect it to the acetabulum are severed, thus freeing the hindlimb with the femur and the tibia both intact. This portion is also placed in a tree. All this work is accomplished with a small knife: finesse rather than force is the rule; the hunters know just where the joints are located and can cut directly to them.

7. *Stripping sinew from the left side of the vertebral column.* The muscles which run along each side of the vertebral column are covered with a sheath of sinew which the !Kung carefully remove in a single piece by cutting one end free and then pulling and cutting it gently away from the underlying muscle. This sinew is set aside to dry.

8. *Removing and eating marrow from cannon bones.* The cannon bones, which have now sufficiently cooled, are broken by splitting with an axe. For each bone the pattern is the same, and lengthwise blows are struck on both the proximal and distal heads to gently split the bone lengthwise.

The hot stringy marrow in the shaft cavity, exposed intact and free of bone splinters, is carefully removed with the point of a knife and eaten directly. The bone fragments are then discarded.

9. *Removal of the five most distal left ribs.* These are removed as a single package. A slightly lateral ventral incision is made in the abdominal region so that the intestines are exposed. The ribs are then removed by separating them from the neighboring ribs on one side and the connective tissue on the other with a knife. The rib package is then bent and pulled upward toward the vertebral column, and chopped free adjacent to the dorsal heads with an axe. The dorsal heads of the ribs remain attached to the vertebral column. The rib package is then placed directly in the fire and roasted.

10. *Removal and processing of the digestive system.* An attempt is made to remove the digestive system intact, to prevent the contents from escaping into the chest cavity and contaminating the blood which collects there. A small slit is carefully made in the upper surface of the rumen or first stomach to allow trapped gasses to escape. This decreases the stomach's size, thus increasing its manageability. The slit is then increased in size to allow a hand hold, and as one man pulls it out of the body cavity, another severs the tissues which hold it in place. An attempt is made to remove all four stomachs and the intestines in a single bundle, by cutting at the esophagus and the rectum. This bulky, barely manageable package is then pulled 10–15 ft. away from the body. The rumen is then cut away and slit down the middle. Its half-digested contents are discarded and it is vigorously shaken to remove as much adhering matter as possible. Then it is hung in a tree. The second stomach or reticulum is treated the same way. The third and fourth stomachs, the omasum and abomasum, are carefully cleaned and then turned inside out to form a pouch with an opening at one end only. This is saved for collecting blood from the chest cavity. The intestine is cleaned by cutting small slits at various points along its length and then squeezing out the enclosed matter through them.

11. *Removal of other internal organs.* The heart and lungs are removed as a single package and placed in a tree. The liver is then removed, and the gall bladder carefully cut away and discarded. The liver is then placed directly in the coals to roast. The rectum is then cut away, cleaned, and placed in a tree.

12. *Collecting blood from the chest cavity.* The blood which has collected in this cavity is carefully scooped up in the hands and transferred to the stomach pouch which has previously been prepared. This pouch is then

closed by pressing its open end together, and weaving a thin pointed stick back and forth through the two sides. The pouch must be carried upright.

13. *Removing the head.* The head is removed by chopping it from the vertebral column with an axe. It is then set aside, with the first two vertebrae, still complete, adhering to it.

14. *Removing the remaining ribs not attached to the sternum from the left side.* These ribs are removed in one package, by chopping them from the vertebral column near their dorsal heads with an axe. The dorsal heads themselves remain attached to the vertebral column. These ribs are also placed directly on the fire to cook.

15. *Turning the carcass.* A number of leafy branches are cut and arranged to form a mat on the ground adjacent to and along the length of the wildebeeste's backbone. The animal is then rolled over onto the mat which serves to keep dirt off the meat. The right side of the animal is thus exposed for butchering.

16. – 19. *Removing the skin, forelimb, hindlimb, and sinew from the right side.* These steps proceed in the same order and manner as on the left side.

20. *Removing the right ribs not attached to the sternum.* These ribs are removed in two packages in the same manner as their counterparts on the left side. They are not cooked, however, but placed in a tree.

21. *Removing the muscles which run along either side of the vertebral column.* With a knife, these long slender muscles are carefully removed from each side of the vertebral column. The sinew which adheres to the underside of them is carefully stripped away and saved.

22. *Discarding the bladder.* The bladder is carefully removed intact and thrown away.

23. *Removing the pelvis.* Using both an axe and knife, the vertebral column is cut crosswise just above the sacrum and the pelvis is removed in one piece. The caudal vertebrae are then separated from it and both packages are set aside (*n.b.* In other cases, the pelvis is often split lengthwise with an axe to give two pieces).

24. *Removal of the chest.* The chest includes the sternum and the first few ribs on each side which are attached directly to it. The chest is removed in one piece by cutting each of the ribs near its dorsal head with an axe. The dorsal portions of each rib remain attached to the vertebral column. The chest is then set in a tree.

25. *Removal of the kidneys.* The kidneys are removed and set aside.

26. *Eating.* At this point work stops temporarily, and everyone (including the two anthropologists observing) eats the liver and ribs which had been placed in the fire.

27. *Treatment of the vertebral column.* The uppermost 10 or so most proximal remaining vertebrae are cut in one segment from the vertebral column with a knife. This piece is then split lengthwise, with an axe, to yield two carrying size parcels. Each contains half of each vertebra as well as the dorsal portions of the ribs attached to them. The remainder of the vertebral column is smashed both longitudinally and horizontally with an axe. Enough force is used to shatter most of the vertebrae, but care is taken to maintain the integrity of the whole. The result is a single pliable package which can easily be transported on a carrying pole.

28. *Discarding the horns.* In the final butchering step, the horns are cut from the head with an axe and discarded.

It should be noted that the longbones (with the exception of the cannons), all the smaller bones of the extremities, the scapula, and sometimes the pelvis survive the butchering process intact and are returned to camp this way. The skull remains almost complete, while the ribs and vertebral column (except for the first few vertebrae) are extensively broken. Only the split cannon bones, some ribs from the left side, the horns, and the contents of the digestive system are left to mark the kill site. When butchering is completed, each man cuts a stick of about 3½ feet in length and 2 inches in diameter to use as a carrying device. Bark is removed from the middle portion of the stick, which will rest on the carrier's shoulder, and packages of meat are placed on each end of the stick to give a balanced load, with a maximum weight of 60–70 lbs. (19–22 kg). Some portions, such as the skin or the vertebral column, may be draped directly over the stick; in other pieces, such as the fore- and hindlimbs, slits must be cut, into which the end of the stick is inserted. The loaded carrying stick is then balanced on one shoulder, and a second stick or spear shaft is angled downward behind the other shoulder and under the carrying stick in an attempt to distribute the weight more evenly across both shoulders. Carrying is hard work; men proceed at a slow pace, stopping often to change shoulders and to rest.

There is one variation of the process described above. Sometimes, when the number of carriers is few and the distance from camp great, biltong is cut at the site, which reduces carrying weight and also preserves the meat. Two days and two round trips to the kill site are involved in this process. On the first day the animal is butchered following standard procedure; biltong is made from some parts of the body, and then hung on tree limbs or flimsy, easily constructed drying racks. That first day the men carry as many of the remaining portions back to camp as possible. On the second day they return to the kill site for the biltong as well as whatever else is left and carry this back to camp. Biltong can be made from the fore- and hindlimbs, the muscles which run along the vertebral column, and parts of the pelvis, neck, and chest. An elongated chunk of meat, approximately 1 lb. (.313 kg), is cut away so that the muscle fibers run the length of the bundle. This is then slit lengthwise, almost in half, so that a small bit of uncut meat serves to hold the halves together. Each half is then slit again in a similar way to give a single continuous thin strip. This is then hung in the shade and allowed to dry until it achieves a hard leathery texture. Depending on the season, it may remain edible from several days to several months; the higher the humidity, the sooner putrefaction occurs. It is essential to emphasize that the aim of this procedure is not to separate the meat from the bones and to discard the latter. The nearly clean longbones (and usually meat is removed only from them) contain marrow, which is regarded as a highly desirable food. They are *always* carried back to camp, and there is very little, if any, difference between kill sites where biltong has or has not been made.

The next step in the butchering and consumption process involves distribution; depending on the number of individuals among whom the meat must be shared, further butchering may or may not be necessary. If so, usually only minor cutting is involved; the bones in the fore- and hindlimbs may be neatly separated at points of articulation or further subdivision of the rib packages may occur. The chest may be split lengthwise through the sternum with an axe, or if the pelvic portion has not been split lengthwise this may now be done. No scrap of the animal is discarded during this secondary butchering process, and there are no visible signs to indicate when or where this has occurred. The meat from large animals is always shared, and the !Kung say that some parts should go to specific individuals. The head, for example, goes to the *n!ori kau,* or "owner" of the area. Actually, rules of this type are extremely flexible, and the only hard and fast statement which can be made is that everyone in camp must have something to eat. There is a good reason for this flexibility; the number of adults in a camp may vary from under five to over twenty, and the kinship links which join individuals and families vary not only from camp to camp, but within a single group, depending on its ever-changing composition. Also, outsiders may appear and individuals may give gifts of meat to people from nearby encampments. A description and analysis of one particular distribution may serve to elucidate the general process involved. The following is based on interview notes of Irven DeVore. He has kindly permitted me to use them.

> In early December 1968, the !Kung camp at Dobe, a small waterhole, included nine nuclear family units and one unmarried male (see figure 14.1). During this period, the single male, ≠gau, wounded an adult female kudu with a poisoned arrow while hunting alone. On the following day (day 2) ≠gau, accompanied by his two elder brothers, N!aishe and ≠toma, leave camp, take up the kudu tracks and finding the animal in a severely weakened condition, they shoot it with additional arrows and then dispatch it with a club. During the tracking ≠toma collects a tortoise and ≠gau shoots a hare to increase the meat total. At the kill site, the three brothers butcher the kudu and meat from all four legs, some of the back and some from the pelvic region, is cut into biltong and hung in a tree to dry. The men roast 6 ribs, the 4 cannon bones, the liver, tortoise, and hare at the kill, and eat all but the hare and about half of the liver. Most of the biltong, along with the rumen, is hung in a tree and the remainder of the kudu is distributed on the spot among the three men. Each man basically carries his own share back to Dobe, with a few minor adjustments to even the carrying loads. Upon return to Dobe a second distribution and then a third one take place. On the following day the three brothers, accompanied by /xəshe and dam again set out for the kill. Along the way they see fresh warthog tracks, /xəshe and dam separate to follow and take no part in carrying the remaining meat back to camp. The biltong and the stomach are divided among the brothers and then carried back; two more rounds of distribution occur. By the following day, all the meat has been consumed.

> Through interview it is possible to basically reconstruct the distributions on days 2 and 3, although several of the smaller kudu parts cannot be accounted for (see figure 14.2)

Distribution 1

≠gau receives:
   the remaining ribs
   heart and lungs
   upper portion of the back
   3 sets articulated limb bones (including both scapula)
   the skin
   ⅓ of the remaining liver
   the small intestine
   some biltong

N!aishe receives:
   the head

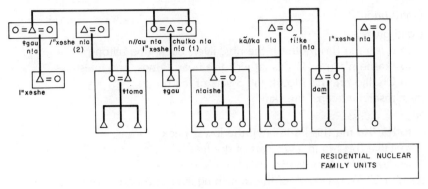

Figure 14.1 Kin ties of Dobe Camp members (late 1967).

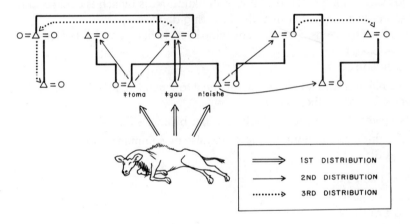

Figure 14.2 Meat distribution on Day 2.

the lower back
upper half of the hare
⅓ of the remaining liver
≠toma receives:
  chest
  neck
  kudu fetus
  ⅓ of the remaining liver
  articulated bones of remaining leg
  lower half of the hare

Distribution 2

≠gau gives:

    to n//au n!a (his mother): the ribs, liver, back, and biltong

    to /x̌əshe n!a (no. 1) (his father): the heart, lungs, and intestines

    to Chu!ko n!a (his MoSi): the 3 sets of leg bones

for himself he keeps: the skin

N!aishe gives:

    to Kā//Ka n!a (his Fa-in-law): the lower back

    to Ti!ke (his Mo-in-law): part of the head

    to dam (his wife's MoBr): ½ of the hare

for himself he keeps: ⅓ of the remaining liver and part of the head.

≠toma gives:

    to /x̌əshe n!a (no. 2) (his Fa-in-law): the chest and neck

    to /x̌əshe n!a (no. 1) (his father): the kudu fetus (which is cooked and

    shared with the adult men the following day)

for himself he keeps: ⅕ of the remaining liver, ½ hare, and 1 set of leg bones.

Distribution 3

N//au n!a and Chu!ko n!a give some meat to ≠gau n!a, their brother, and he gives some to /x̌əshe, his son.

Ti!ke gives some meat to N!aishe n!a her brother's Fa-in-law.

    The three distributions on day 3 may also be summarized as follows (see fig. 14.3):

Distribution 1

≠gau receives:

    part of the stomach

    28 lbs. of biltong

N!aishe receives:

    part of the stomach

    38 lbs. of biltong

≠toma receives:

    part of the stomach

    30 lbs. of biltong

Distribution 2

≠gau gives: biltong and/or stomach to:

  /"x əshe n!a (no. 1) (his father)

  n//au n!a (his mother)

  HaKakoshe, a local Bantu who works for the anthropologist

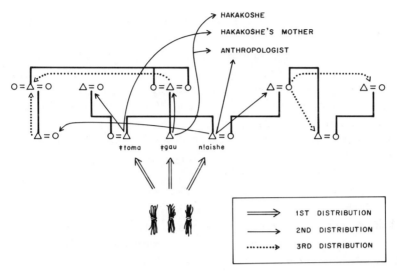

Figure 14.3 Meat distribution on Day 3.

N!aishe gives biltong and/or stomach to:
  Kā//ka n!a (his Fa-in-law)
  /"xəshe (his MoBrSo)
  the anthropologist
  he also keeps some for himself

≠toma gives to:
  /x̌əshe n!a (no. 2) (his Fa-in-law)
  HaKakoshe's mother (who lives about five miles away)
  he also keeps some for himself

Distribution 3

Distribution 3 follows along the same basic lines of its counterpart the previous day.

The pattern observed in these transactions is typical. Meat moves from the hunters and carriers upward through the kinship network to parents and in-laws, and then outward and downward again. When sharing is viewed in a specific instance, such as this one, it can be clearly seen why hard and fast distribution rules cannot apply; each kill must be considered as a specific case; the relationships between families who happen to compose a group at that moment and family size must both be taken into account. These factors have already been considered when the first distribution among the carriers is made. In the above case, on both days the basic pattern is the same. The one unmarried brother gives meat to his parents and his aunt. The other brothers both give primarily to their fathers-in-law, who happen to reside in camp. If all three brothers were married with in-laws present, the secondary distributions would have been quite different. On the third day, an additional factor comes into play. Each of the brothers gives "gifts" of meat to individuals who have no direct claim on a portion. In effect, some meat passes outside of the camp—a typical occurrence that almost always happens when direct contact with either "outsiders" or with other !Kung camps exists.

The above case illustrates two minor points as well: first, the hunter himself does not receive an additional share of the meat, and in fact ≠gau, who wounded the kudu in the first place, was left with no meat for himself at the end of day two. While outward vocal praise of hunting success is avoided, and the hunter will not brag of his success, a certain status is attached to being a good provider and tacit recognition of hunting skill is given. Secondly, only if an individual carries meat back to camp does he have a direct claim on a portion of it. If /x̃əshe and dam had remained with the carrying party on three they would have received such a share; but in setting off after a warthog they forfeited this right.

From the nonbony portions of the animal the sinew is dried and saved either to make twine or as a binding material. The skin from gemsbok and kudu may be stretched, dried, and tanned for women's clothing, or—along with the thicker skins of other large bucks—it may be roasted and eaten, or saved for eating at some future date. Bone itself is used only for three implements, and then only rarely. The olecranon process of the scapula may be cut from the body of that bone, and the shallow depression used as a cup for mixing arrow poison. Fragments of gemsbok tibia may also be employed for making arrow linkshafts, but the heavier and stronger giraffe bone, if available, is preferred for this purpose; during my two and a half year stay at Dobe I never observed large antelope bone actually being worked. Smoking pipes are fashioned from a hollowed section of radius shaft, and goat bone, which has the desired diameter, is the preferred material when available. A grass plug is inserted near one end of the shaft to keep the tobacco away from the smoker's lips. Although large antelope longbone may in a pinch be used for this purpose, the necessity rarely arises and has never been observed by me.

The long, straight horns of the gemsbok are sometimes saved and a tubular segment cut from them near the pointed tip. Detachable leather covers are then fashioned to fit over each end, giving a small carrying case for spare metal arrowheads. As recently as the early 1960s these heads were carved from bone—adults still know how to make them—but the introduction of fence wire, which serves the same purpose more efficiently, has made bone arrowheads obsolete. Finally, small ritual bows and arrows may also be fashioned from small slivers of gemsbok horn.

Meat may be either boiled or roasted, and the former method is preferred because it softens the food more effectively and yields a gravy as well. In roasting, meat is placed either directly in the coals of an open fire or, for the head, in a pit specially dug for this purpose. Clay pots, traded in from areas of Bantu manufacture over 100 miles to the east, have been found in local Late Stone Age sites, and several such pots are used by !Kung in the region today. Informants cannot remember a time when clay vessels were not available, and their original introduction, it may be guessed, greatly altered not only the cooking but the final butchering procedures as well. Within the last ten years three-legged No. 3 iron pots, with a mouth of approximately 12 inches in diameter, have become generally available through trade either with Bantu or anthropologists. Since they can be easily transported, and are nearly impossible to break, these pots have almost completely supplanted their earlier clay counterparts in the Dobe area; each of the families in my study sample owned one. The boiling process is straightforward: chunks of meat and bone are placed in the pot with water, and a small amount of salt is added when available. The meat will then be boiled for over an hour until well done and raw marrow may then be added to enrich the gravy. The meat is then eaten, the bones tossed aside, and the gravy drunk directly from the cooking vessel. In the following description, parts of the carcass are classified on the basis of how each is cooked and eaten.

> 1. The soft, nonbony portions. *These include the viscera (with the exception of the liver which is consumed away from camp), the udder, and the blood. These portions are generally cooked and eaten first, because they rot most quickly. They are cut into chunks and boiled. The stomach and udder are generally boiled with other meat, and the blood is mixed with water and added to meat stew mixtures.*
> 2. The skin. *Pieces of dried skin are placed directly in the coals and roasted.*
> 3. The head. *Edible food from the head includes the brain, tongue, marrow from the mandible body, the nose, ears, meat from the interior of the nasal cavity, the skin, and the external muscles. The meat from the first several vertebrae which are still attached to the head after field butchering is also counted as head meat. The head is roasted whole in a pit specially dug for this purpose. The mandible is then separated cleanly from the cranium with a knife*

and broken at the mandibular symiphisis. The tongue is cut from the former and eaten. The ventral portion of the mandible body may then be chopped away to expose the included marrow. The skin, facial meat, and nose are then cut from the cranium and eaten. The face is separated from the rest of the skull near the intersection of the nasal and frontal bones. Depending on the age of the animal, this may be accomplished either by striking the skull with a stick or chopping crosswise with an axe. Again, depending on the strength of the bone, the facial portion is divided into two segments either by pulling the two halves apart manually, or by splitting it lengthwise along the midline with an axe. The occipital is then removed from the vault by striking it with a stick. The brain may thus be removed and eaten. The first few adhering vertebrae are cut from the base of the skull and the meat adhering to them is eaten directly "off the bone."

4. The hooves. These are the only other portion of large antelope which are always roasted. This is accomplished either in an open fire or in the cooking pit with the head. After cooking, the outer hoof covering is removed in one piece and thrown away. The meat is eaten directly from the bone, and the first two phalanges are sometimes split lengthwise with an axe for removal of the edible marrow. The other smaller extremity bones are discarded unbroken.

5. The vertebral column. The segments of the vertebral column, which have already been extensively cut and chopped in during field butchering, are cut into roughly fist-size segments with a knife. They are placed in a pot and boiled. The !Kung state that the vertebrae are smashed to facilitate carrying and not to expose the insignificant amount of marrow contained within them.

6. The scapula, pelvis, chest and ribs. From all but the last of these categories it is possible to remove the meat and make biltong, and usually a small portion of this meat is thus treated. These parts are cooked by boiling. The packages are rapidly reduced into pot-sized pieces by a combination of cutting and chopping with an axe. No attempt is made to separate the meat from the bone, or to cut the bones at the point of articulation, and size of the pieces is the only relevant consideration. The sternum, ribs, scapula, and pelvis do not contain enough marrow to worry about, say the !Kung.

7. Meat from the long bones and exterior back muscles. Unless eaten immediately after arrival in camp, this meat is cut into biltong if this has not been done at the kill site. The biltong strips are hung to dry and may be eaten in one of three ways. After the first several days they are usually roasted directly on a bed of coals since boiling will not appreciably reduce the toughness. When fresh, however, boiling is the preferred method. Marrow when available is added to the finished stew. One final method consists of roasting fresh biltong and then cutting and pounding it into a fine paste. This is accomplished on a smooth log which is placed on the center of an animal skin. Freshly cooked marrow is added to the finely pounded meat and mixed in thoroughly, giving a rich, greasy, and highly desirable paste which is eaten with no further preparation. I have observed this latter process only once; it took place at the site of the kill.

8. The longbones. With the exception of the cannon bones, which are roasted at the kill site, split lengthwise through both heads, and have the marrow removed, the remaining longbones are broken open at camp. When

*the meat for biltong has been removed from them, the larger bits of meat still
adhering but too small for biltong are cut away and placed in an iron pot. The
bones are then separated at their articulations and the astragalus and
calcaneus only are placed in the pot whole. The longbones are then carefully
broken into fragments and the marrow is removed and set aside. The bone
fragments then are placed in the pot with the other meat and water, and a stew
is made. The marrow is added when cooking has been completed. In breaking
the longbones, an attempt is made to remove the marrow as whole and
uncontaminated as possible, and different bones are treated in varying ways.
!Kung explanation and direct observation confirm that random smashing is not
the rule. Each longbone is treated as follows:*

> *a. HUMERUS. The proximal and distal heads are cut at their respective
> bases from the bone shaft, with an axe. The proximal head is then
> chopped into several pieces, and the distal head, which contains little if
> any marrow, is either left whole or cut the same way. The shaft is then
> carefully split into fragments still using an axe.*
>
> *b. RADIUS. For two large antelope, gemsbok and wildebeeste, the
> radius is first split with an axe through both the proximal and distal heads.
> Once the bone has been cracked in this manner, crosswise blows with an
> axe divide the shaft into smaller fragments. The kudu radius is treated
> differently: the proximal and distal heads are chopped from the shaft
> intact and the shaft is then split with an axe. The !Kung say that the heads
> of the kudu radius do not contain enough marrow to worry about while
> the corresponding segments from the gemsbok and wildebeeste do. This,
> however, is a subjective judgement.*
>
> *c. ULNA. The ulna lacks a distal head. The proximal head is chopped
> from the shaft and then split. The shaft is then chopped into several
> pieces.*
>
> *d. FEMUR. The proximal and distal heads are chopped from the shaft
> near their respective bases and then split into several fragments with an
> axe. The shaft is then carefully split into numerous fragments.*
>
> *e. TIBIA. The proximal head is chopped from the shaft at its base and
> then cut into several fragments. The distal head however is either cut from
> the shaft and then discarded or is split lengthwise, still attached, as the
> shaft is broken. In either case, the shaft is further cut into fragments.*

While some variation is possible, the normal process described above is
usually followed fairly closely. It should be mentioned that meat is not stored,
and drying serves only to lighten a carrying load or prevent immediate
spoilage. For large game, as well as smaller animals and vegetable foods, the
!Kung attitude is the same: when the food is available eat it—when it's gone,
it's gone. Another point to be emphasized is that !Kung treat bones as an
important food source and would not think to discard them uncracked.
Marrow provides the main source of animal fat for the !Kung since the meat
from desert animals is usually very lean. The !Kung themselves discuss this
and recall with fondness animals which they considered especially fat.

Finally, it should be noted that both the final form and the spatial distribution of faunal remains reflect the last steps of the butchering and consumption process. Very few bones are left at the kill site, and in the initial field butchering only the vertebrae, ribs, pelvis, and of course the cannons are badly broken. But after eating is completed, only the small bones from the extremities remain intact. Thus, the way most bones are broken reflects the way they were cooked; and it is this latter variable, rather than any kind of "hunting technique," which is reflected the most clearly in observed patterning in the faunal remains.

!Kung Butchering Practices: Analysis of Controlled Samples

To determine the extent to which the observed patterns already described could be reconstructed from the faunal remains, the broken and discarded bones of an adult kudu and an adult wildebeeste were collected from the !Kung at the Dobe camp. To control the samples as carefully as possible, ensure as complete recovery as practicable, and eliminate the effects of non-random preservation, both animals were shot with a rifle and transported to camp whole in my truck. There primary butchering and distribution were carried out by the !Kung, so that the cannons and ribs usually left at the kill site were thus included in the sample. Each family, in addition to its share of the kill, received a metal bucket with the plea that all fragments of bone be returned to me. It was then possible to analyze this sample and in many instances reconstruct whole bones. This procedure was carried out twice, and in each instance recovery was good, though far from perfect. Fragments of vertebrae, rib, and longbone shaft as well as the smaller bones from the extremities tended to disappear, but I do not believe analysis was seriously affected. This process was purposely repeated, first with a kudu and then with a wildebeeste to permit comparison of results, in order to determine the extent to which patterning was regular. This study was of necessity limited to the bones themselves; it was not possible to analyze sharing patterns, since my own intimate involvement in this entire procedure would likely have seriously biased the results. The basic results are presented in tables 14.1–3.

The first question which may be asked of this data is the extent to which patterning is regular, and determination of similarity or difference may be made on two bases. The first, which rests on statistical comparison, has the advantage of exactness but is susceptible to general difficulty in interpretation; there are also several particular problems derived from the incomplete nature of the sample. One misplaced blow with a stick or an inadvertent footfall, for example, and one large cranial fragment may become ten small ones; such a conversion would alter not only the relative number of cranial fragments but also the ratio of large to small fragments. Much more important than statistical analysis is a comparison of "patterns": both kudu and wildebeeste pelvic remains, for example, are exclusively small, angular fragments, with cut marks visible on most edges. Similarly, although there are significantly more fragments of kudu than wildebeeste crania, for both animals the four major fragments, which make up the majority of the skull, are basically identical. Table 14.4 presents a comparison of the non-longbone portions. Excluding unidentified fragments, 14 statistical comparisons are made and three reveal significant differences. Of these, two, and perhaps the third, can be explained in "noncultural terms"; the reason for relatively more complete and almost complete wildebeeste vertebrae is uncertain and may be of cultural significance. For all but the vertebrae, however, the method of treatment for non-longbone portions is the same for both animals.

For the heads of the longbones in this controlled sample, reconstruction indicates that recovery is complete. While sample size is too small to permit statistical analysis, visual examination reveals several remarkable consistencies. Note, for example, the tibia column in table 14.2. There are four mutually exclusive ways to categorize the proximal head and four corresponding groupings for the distal head. All of the kudu proximal tibia head fragments are categorized as "PF" and the same holds true for the wildebeeste proximal fragments as well. The distal fragments from the kudu tibia fall into two categories, "DC" and "DF and Sh //," showing that one distal

General Notes for Tables 14.1–14.3

For both the kudu and the wildebeeste, shaft fragments from the humerus and the ulna are clearly missing, and it is not possible to correct for this error. With the exception of the first phalange, the small bones of the fore and hind extremities are not included in the sample since most were not returned to me, and in any case they are never broken.

The terms "small" and "large" are relative and reflect both size, in comparison to the complete bone of which they form a part, and the ease with which identification of the fragment is possible. These two criteria generally co-vary together, and "small fragments" would most often be considered as unidentifiable when recovered in an archeological context. Thus, a piece from the blade of a scapula may be 4″ maximum length and still count as a small fragment, while a diagnostic cranial fragment less than 2″ in length may be classed as a large one.

Tables 14.2 and 3

The attribute system employed to categorize longbone fragments is outlined in the key accompanying table 14.2. For all pieces which consist of, or contain, a portion of shaft, a basic distinction is made between parts of shaft which show crosswise cutting (=), and those which have been split lengthwise (//). Split shaft fragments tend toward a long and thin contour, while those cut crosswise are relatively shorter and wider; they may form a complete ring of bone.

TABLE 14.1

Controlled Sample: Kudu – Wildebeeste Non-Longbone Parts

		Wildebeeste	Kudu	Combined Sample	Total
Cranium	Large Fragments	4[a]	8[c]	[12]	
	Small Fragments	4[b]	10[d]	[14]	(26)
Mandible	½ Complete or Almost Complete	2[e]	2[f]	[4]	(4)
Vertebrae	Complete	8[h]	2[i]	[10]	
	Almost Complete	16	6	[22]	
	Large Fragments	13	11	[24]	(154[g])
	Small Fragments	47	51	[98]	
Pelvis	Small Fragments	17	8	[25]	(25[j])
Ribs	Fragments Cut Crosswise	117	53	[170]	(170[k])
Sternum	Small Fragments	2[l]	0	[2]	(2)
Scapula	Small Fragments	23	18	[41]	(41[m])
Unidentified Fragments	Longbone	16	0	[16[n]]	
	Other	72	73	[145[o]]	(161)
Total		341	242	[583]	(583)

a. These include the occipital, almost complete (AC); the right and left halves of the face, and most of the vault including large parts of the parietals, frontal and some of the face. Some fragments show evidence of burning.

b. Two small bits of inner nasal bone, and two fragments from the orbit of the eye.

c. These include the left and the right halves of the face, the occiput (AC), most of the vault including the frontal, parietals and the major portions of both orbits, 2 large fragments of nasal bone, and two halves of the hyoid bone.

d. These include 4 fragments of interior nasal bones, 4 fragments from the base of the skull, and 1 fragment each of orbital and temporal.

e. These two pieces represent an AC mandible split at the epiphisis. The right half lacks two molars, and the left lacks 1 molar and 3 incisors.

f. These two fragments represent an AC mandible split at the epiphysis. The right half is complete whereas all incisors are missing from the left half.

g. The categories for vertebrae classification are self-evident. Small fragments generally consist of either a fragment of body only, or a dorsal or transverse process. Some of the fragments were still attached to one another by connective tissue.

h. These include the first and second vertebrae, 3 caudal vertebrae, and 3 others.

i. These include the first and second vertebrae.

j. The pelvic fragments from both animals vary in size and shape but none exceed 5″ measured on the longest axis. Edges show that most cuts were made with an axe, and very few of them exhibit irregular fracture. None contains more than a small fragment of the acetabulum.

k. The longest rib fragment measured 8″ while the average is approximately 4″. Almost all fragments exhibit sharp cuts at one or both of their ends, and none are split along their length. This pattern holds for both animals.

l. The sternum is represented by two small fragments, both exhibiting cut marks along their edges.

m. The fragments of scapula from both animals closely resemble those of the pelvis in size, shape, and method of treatment.

n. This category includes slivers of longbone shaft only.

o. These include very small, flattish bits possibly from the skull, scapula, pelvis, or sternum.

TABLE 14.2

Controlled Sample: Kudu and Wildebeeste Longbone Fragments

	Humerus	Radius	Ulna	Femur	Tibia	Cannons
Entire Bone C						4k/1w
Half bone split /						
PC		2k/				
PC + Sh–						
PF	6k/6w		1k/1w	5k/4w	4k/6w	
PF + Sh //	1k/	2k/4w				4k/7w
DC			ND		1k/1w	
DC + Sh–			ND			
DF	2k/4w		ND	4k/4w		
DF + Sh //		/4w	ND		2k/2w	4k/7w
ShF=	FMk/1w		FMk/4w	/2w		
ShF //	FMk/7w	5k/4w	FMk/2w	10k/17w	3k/5w	4k/4w
Total	(9k)/(18w)	(9k)/(12w)	(1k)/(7w)	(19k)/(27w)	(10k)/(14w)	(16k)/(19w)

(+ 16 unidentified ShF)

Key:
C Complete   ND No Distal head   – Cut crosswise   // Split lengthwise
F Fragment   D Distal head   = Cut crosswise   k Kudu
P Proximal head   Sh Shaft   both ends   w Wildebeeste
                                                    FM Fragments Missing

TABLE 14.3

Controlled Sample: Kudu and Wildebeeste Combined Longbone Fragments

	Humerus	Radius	Ulna	Femur	Tibia	Cannons
Entire Bone C						
Half bone split /						[5]
PC		[2]				
PC + Sh-						
PF	[12]		[2]	[9]	[10]	
PF + Sh //		[4]				[11]
DC	[1]	[2]	ND			
DC + Sh-			ND		[2]	
DF	[6]		ND	[8]		
DF + Sh //		[4]	ND		[4]	[11]
ShF=	[FM 1]		[FM 4]	[2]		
ShF //	[FM 7]	[9]	[FM 2]	[27]	[8]	[8]
Total	(27)	(21)	(8)	(46)	(24)	(35)

(+ 16 unidentified ShF)   ND = No Distal head

head was cut complete from the shaft and then discarded while the other head was first split and then cut from the shaft. Exactly the same fragment categories, and thus the same set of butchering steps, holds for the distal head of the wildebeeste tibia as well. In four of the six kinds of longbone where kudu–wildebeeste similarities are compared (ulna, femur, tibia, and all cannon bones), no differences are observed, even though the cannons, for example, as a group exhibit quite a different pattern from the tibia. Antelope have four cannon bones and two of each of the remaining longbones. Because each of the kudu tibia was butchered by a different individual, it is possible to get some idea of consistency within a species. And the kudu–wildebeeste comparison often involves the comparable actions of four separate individuals.

For two of the longbones, the humerus and radius, cross-species differences may be observed. The distal head of the kudu radius, as shown in table 14.2, may be either whole or fragmentary while the corresponding distal head from the wildebeeste is, in both instances, split. This pattern was first observed in the faunal sample, and a subsequent interview revealed that !Kung usually don't bother to split the distal head of humerus, because it contains relatively little marrow; for wildebeeste this is not the case. (Remains from two other kudu were studied, and in both instances the distal heads of the humerus were left intact.) The radius reveals significant difference in patterning for both

TABLE 14.4

Comparison of Kudu and Wildebeeste Non-Longbone Remains from Controlled Sample

	Frequency of Each Anatomical Part	Frequency of Sub-types for Each Anatomical Part	Method of Treatment
Cranium	More kudu than wildebeeste cranial fragments (p = .05)	n.s.[a]	The 4 main fragments which constitute 80% of cranium; the same for both animals
Mandible	n.s.	n.s.	Identical
Vertebrae	n.s.	More complete and almost complete vertebrae for wildebeeste; more small fragments for kudu (p = .01)	Slightly different and difficult to assess. For both animals over 50% are small fragments, C1 and C2 are complete, and "Complete" is the smallest category.
Pelvis	n.s.	n.s.	Treatment same for both animals
Ribs	More wildebeeste than kudu rib fragments (p = .01)	n.s.	Treatment same for both animals
Sternum	n.s.	n.s.	Comparison not possible because of small sample size
Scapula	n.s.	n.s.	
Unidentified Fragments	n.s.	more wildebeeste longbone fragments (p = .01)	Treatment same for both animals

[a]n.s. when p = .05

proximal and distal heads and observation has shown that this also is not accidental.

When the relative numbers of shaft fragments split lengthwise are compared to those cut crosswise, bone by bone, the same type of consistency is revealed. (For the humerus and ulna these comparisons are not possible because fragments are missing.) Finally, when the relative number of fragments from each longbone is compared to the total number of longbone fragments for each species, no significant differences are revealed, even though within each species some longbones are represented by significantly more fragments than others.

Three conclusions may be drawn from the wildebeeste – kudu comparison. The first is that "patterning" is a meaningful term: First marked similarities between the kudu and wildebeeste remains exist and they reflect the method by which the bones were originally treated; second, direct observation confirms that variation in butchering technique accounted for the two instances where striking differences were noted—in the radius and the distal head of the humerus; finally, it should be emphasized that comparisons based on counting of anatomical fragments alone can yield results of doubtful value, and the most essential factor to be considered is the method, as far as can be reconstructed, by which these parts have been treated.

In point of fact, when the wildebeeste and kudu are combined to form a single sample (table 14.1 and table 14.3), it is still possible to arrive at a fairly accurate description of the *process* by which each anatomical portion was treated, even if in some cases the ordering of the steps and their cultural significance may only be guessed at. For example, one can say that the occipital and face were removed from the skull, that the face was then split, that the mandible was consistently split into two halves, that the scapula and pelvis were regularly cut into pieces of a certain size, and that ribs were always cut crosswise into fragments of a roughly specified length. It is also possible to see that with the exception of the atlas and axis, vertebrae are usually chopped into small fragments. For all non-longbone fragments, relative numbers mean little in this kind of interpretation. Rib and vertabral fragments (29 percent and 26 percent respectively), as might be guessed, are most common. These are followed by a second group—scapula (7 percent), cranium (4.4 percent), and the pelvis (4.4 percent)—all large bones with considerable surface area. Numerically the mandible and sternum form an insignificant part of the total.

A similar type of analysis applied to the longbones of the combined kudu-wildebeeste sample gives even more interesting results because it is possible to basically reconstruct in order the different steps involved in bone breakage. Different ways of striking a longbone, and the sequence in which these varying blows are applied, yield fragments which are usually distinct and which lend themselves to a simple kind of categorization. This is outlined in table 14.5, which is meant to apply to !Kung material only, since other

TABLE 14.5

Steps in Breaking a Longbone

Step Number:	Resulting Fragment:
1. Proximal head cut off at or near base of shaft	
2. Distal head cut off at or near base of shaft	
3. Proximal head from Step 1 then split	PF
4. Distal head from Step 2 then split	DF
5. Proximal head from Step 1 discarded unsplit	PC or PC + Sh-
6. Distal head from Step 2 discarded unsplit	DC or DC + Sh-
7. Bone split through attached proximal head	PF + Sh //
8. Bone split through attached distal head	DF + Sh //
9. Shaft broken lengthwise and/or crosswise	ShF // and/or ShF=

(n.b. Steps 7 and 8 in sequence may yield half a bone split lengthwise)

alternative steps are also possible. As table 14.6 shows, one can both reconstruct and describe the method of treatment for each of the longbones. Thus, for the humerus the proximal head is cut from the shaft and then split to give several PF; the distal head is then cut from the shaft and either discarded completely to give a PC, or it is split to yield more than one PF. Also, it is possible using this approach to show how different bones may be classed on the basis of their treatment. The humerus, femur, and ulna are all treated in the same fashion. The tibia is sometimes treated as the humerus while in some instances the distal head is butchered differently. The cannon bones are distinct, as is each of the two forms for the radius. It is also possible and worthwhile to consider variation in the two types of shaft fragment in this light,

TABLE 14.6
Process of Breaking Kudu and Wildebeeste Longbones

	Humerus	Radius Kudu	Radius Wildebeeste	Ulna	Femur	Tibia	Cannons
Proximal Head	1 ↓ 3	1 ↓ 5	7	1 ↓ 3	1 ↓ 3	1 ↓ 3	7
	2 2	2		has no	2	2	
Distal Head	↓ or ↓	↓	8	distal head	↓	↓ or 8	8
	4 6	6			4	6	
Shaft	9	9	9	9	9	9	9

but incomplete recovery of these pieces in the controlled sample makes such an analysis difficult. It should be noted however that the ulna is distinct in this regard, for the number of shaft fragments cut crosswise outnumber those split lengthwise, while for all other shaft fragment groups, the split form predominates.

Consideration of the number of fragments and also fragment size gives some interesting results. When the number of fragments from each longbone bone is compared to the total for each of the other five and the significance of the difference is evaluated by X^2, it is noted that the femur is represented by significantly more fragments than any of the other longbones. In the combined kudu – wildebeeste sample, the femur – humerus difference is significant at $p = .05$, while a level of $p = .01$ is observed for the remaining femur – longbone comparisons. The reason for this is uncertain, but in the concluding section of this paper it will be suggested that this phenomenon may apply to—and bias the interpretation of—non-!Kung samples. In another comparison, the lengths of shaft fragments were measured from the four longbones represented by 10 pieces or more and compared to the maximum length of rib fragments as well as pelvis and scapula fragments, measured along their longest axis. (See table 14.7.) These measurements were taken on the remains of a sample of two additional kudu whose remains were recovered in the same manner as the wildebeeste and the original kudu described above. Although significant variance within the sample may be demonstrated, the similarity in maximum length of the different categories is striking, especially when one considers that such disparate forms as the femur and the scapula are both included. The difference in the extreme means—the humerus and the tibia—is only 1.31″. Direct observation reveals the reason for this: maximum fragment length is directly related to pot size; all of the pieces

TABLE 14.7
Lengths of Selected Fragment Classes from Two "Controlled" Kudu

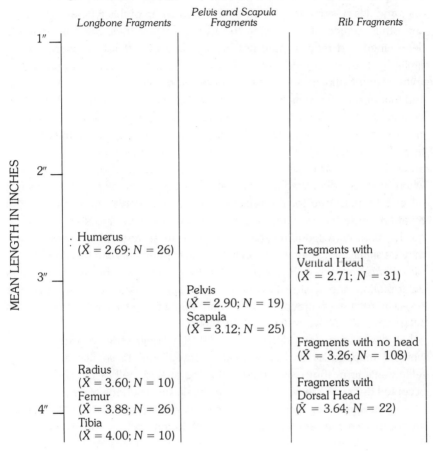

considered above are boiled, and it may be guessed that changes in either cooking utensil or cooking technique would have some effect on fragment size.

!KUNG BUTCHERING PRACTICES: ANALYSIS OF SAMPLES FROM ABANDONED CAMPSITES

In an attempt to determine what kinds of factors affected bones after they had been discarded, and the extent to which these effects were random, a series of large animal bones was collected from abandoned !Kung campsites. These provided, in a sense, a controlled archeological sample, albeit a recent one; and it is possible to treat an abandoned camp of this type as one might any other surface site. The way the !Kung butcher their game is culturally determined and may or may not be repeated by different human groups; similarly, it can be argued that the Northern Kalahari environment presents a unique combination of soil forms, process, temperature, rainfall, and sunshine and that observed results of bone preservation may not be applicable in other situations. In this context it is necessary to distinguish between "absolute" and "relative" patterns of preservation. While it may be assumed the absolute rate of preservation—i.e. the total number of bone fragments which survive in recognizable form—will vary enormously, depending both on the surface where they are deposited and on following geological events, this does not necessarily hold true for the relative pattern of preservation as well. In the Kalahari, preservation is quite poor; longbone heads tend to disappear more quickly than corresponding shaft fragments. In an area where preservation may be significantly better and relatively more fragments can be recovered, it still seems reasonable to hypothesize that shafts will be subject to less deterioration and destruction than heads, since it will be shown that the physical nature of the bone itself and the way it was originally broken determine the relative rate of disintegration.

Large antelope were killed at five out of a larger series of !Kung camps which I mapped as part of a relative study, and these five abandoned settlements form the basis for the following analysis. All of the camps were occupied during the rainy season for relatively short periods of time, and both hunting and gathering activities were carried out at each of them. At most of them other smaller animals were also butchered and consumed, but since there is significant variation in the treatment of animals according to their size, only large antelope are considered herein. The camps are located in areas of loosely compacted Kalahari sand, with only slight plant cover. The top inch or two of sand is extremely dry and forms an even covering for the more compact underlying layer of the same material. Bones move easily downward through this top several inches. Rain and dew are limited to about four months of the year and, as might be expected, drainage is excellent. During the summer months the surface temperature of the sand rises to over 120°F (49°C).

I visited each campsite after it had been abandoned and took several of the inhabitants with me. For each camp day-by-day activity schedules were reconstructed, with emphasis on activities related to hunting and butchering. It was possible in this way to determine not only the total number of kills, but also the hunting and butchering steps from start to finish for each one. At each site a grid was constructed and all surface features and individual objects were mapped to the nearest inch. All faunal material was numbered and returned to my camp for further analysis, and selected portions of each site were excavated to determine whether a significant amount of material had been pushed down below the surface of the sand. Further excavations were carried out in several cases. The !Kung then helped me to identify the bone fragments I had collected. Independent cross-checking with different informants showed the accuracy to be very high; on this basis it was possible to identify by species and anatomical position over 99.5 percent of the bones recovered. The five camps under consideration are all located in a region where gemsbok constitutes the prime large antelope prey. As it happens, gemsbok was the only large animal killed at them, and neither kudu nor wildebeeste was successfully hunted. I obtained no controlled samples of gemsbok remains, since I observed that gemsbok and wildebeeste are treated identically. From table 14.8 it can be seen that the total sample of six animals consists primarily of immature males (which !Kung say are the easiest to hunt); that four of the five camps contained one animal only; and that two gemsbok were killed at the remaining camp. The interval between camp abandonment by the !Kung and mapping and collection of bones by me varied from two weeks to eight months.

It may be noted in passing that Polly Weissner has demonstrated that the spatial distribution of faunal remains reveals something of the nature of the sharing and distribution process. Figure 14.4 shows the distribution of gemsbok remains at Camp number 10; gemsbok, like all large animals, are shared among all members of a camp, and this is clearly reflected in the dispersal of gemsbok bones near all of the huts. For comparison, figure 14.5 presents the distribution of porcupine remains from Camp 11. These two camps were occupied sequentially, and their membership was identical. A porcupine belongs to the man who kills it and generally porcupine meat is not shared—a fact reflected in the concentration of porcupine remains in front of a single hut.

One conclusion immediately apparent is that the rate of preservation and recovery from the abandoned camp series is extremely low. The control kudu–wildebeeste sample yielded an average of 387 bone fragments per animal while the average is only 41.5 per individual from the abandoned

TABLE 14.8

Gemsbok Sample from Abandoned Campsites

Camp	Number of Individuals	Age	Sex	Length of Time Camp Occupied	Interval: Camp Abandonment-Bone Collection	Butchering Notes
Camp 2 ≠tum ≠toa 2	1	adult	male	9 days	32 weeks	some ribs, the head, and all cannons left at kill site
Camp 6 Hwanasi	1	immature ca. 1 year old	male	3 days	2 weeks	some ribs, 2 tibia. all cannon bones, and one horn left at kill site
Camp 8 /twi dum (Upper)	1	?	?	30 days	4 weeks	?
Camp 10 //gakwe ≠dua 1	2	both immature	both male	12 days	2 weeks	for both animals, cannon bones and some ribs left at kill site
Camp 13 n/on/oni ≠toa 2	1	immature ca. 7 months old	male	5 days	5 weeks	carried whole to camp

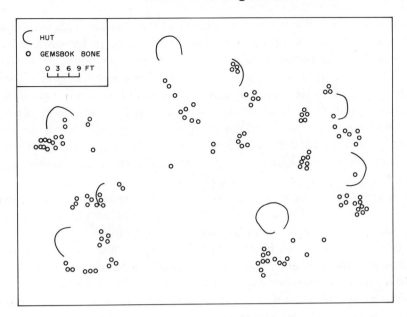

Figure 14.4 Camp 10. Gemsbok remains.

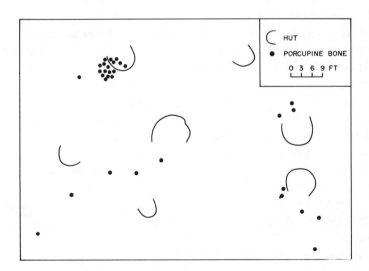

Figure 14.5 Camp 11. Porcupine remains.

camp series. Secondly, there are marked differences between preservation at different sites within the abandoned series itself. Camp 13 for example has significantly fewer gemsbok fragments than all the other camps ($p = .01$), while at the same level of significance Camp 8 has fewer fragments than either Camps 2 or 10. Camps 2, 6, and 10 seem to form a single grouping, and testing reveals no significant differences among them. The length of time between mapping and abandonment does not explain this disparity: the interval for Camp 13, with the worst recovery rate, is 5 weeks while for Camp 2, where the rate was relatively good, eight months elapsed before mapping. Another likely hypothesis, that fewer parts of the gemsbok were brought back to camp at some of the sites, is also incorrect since interview confirms that this had not occurred. In fact, at Camp 13 the gemsbok was carried whole back to the site. And at none of the camps were dogs present.

There are three main factors which may explain the disappearance of bones. The first rapid and natural selective structural decomposition of bone, which will be discussed in detail below would, it must be supposed, operate at approximately the same rate at all five sites, and cannot be used to explain variation between sites. Scavenging by carnivores, which abound in the northern Kalahari, provides a second destructive factor. Tracks indicate that all of the abandoned sites were visited by hyenas, and some by jackals as well as other smaller animals. While some bones, especially small uncracked bones from the extremities, certainly are removed in this way, my own guess is that carnivores cause less disruption than might be expected since little is left when the !Kung have finished with the bones. The massive jaws of the hyena, for example, are adapted to cracking the marrow-rich longbones, but the !Kung always do this themselves—and boil and pick the bones clean. Noncarnivorous animals provide the final destructive factor, for porcupine as well as most of the larger antelope are known to eat the bones themselves. I am not certain why antelope do this, but cattle feed in much of the Kalahari is supplemented with bone meal and it may be guessed that when antelope eat dry bones exposed on the surface they are trying to compensate for the same dietary deficiency. Antelope and porcupine enter abandoned camps more or less by chance and do not purposely search them out as scavengers do. The effects of their accidental discoveries are evident in the bone totals presented in table 14.9.

By combining the gemsbok remains into a single group and then comparing this group with the combined kudu–wildebeeste controlled sample, it is possible to determine the extent to which destruction of different anatomical parts has proceeded in a random fashion.

TABLE 14.9
Gemsbok Bones From Abandoned Campsites

		Camp 2 ≠tum ≠toa 2	Camp 6 Hwanasi	Camp 8 /tui dum (Upper)	Camp 10 //gakwe ≠dua	Camp 13 n/on/oni ≠toa	Combined Sample	Total
Cranium	Large Fragments		2[a]				[2]	(13)
	Small Fragments		5[b]		5[c]	1	[11]	
Mandible	Ramus		1[d]				[1]	(1)
Vertebrae	Complete		1[f]	4[h]			[5]	(85)
	Almost Complete			2[i]			[2]	
	Large Fragments	1[e]	2[g]	3			[6]	
	Small Fragments		1	1	4		[6]	
	Transverse Process	3					[3]	
	Dorsal Process	13	7	4	39		[63]	
Pelvis	Small Fragments		2	7	14		[23]	(23[j])

TABLE 14.9
Gemsbok Bones From Abandoned Campsites

		Camp 2 #tum ≠toa 2	Camp 6 Huanasi	Camp 8 /tui dum (Upper)	Camp 10 //gakwe ≠dua	Camp 13 n/on/oni ≠toa	Combined Sample	Total
Ribs	Almost Complete				4		[4]	(64)
	Dorsal Head + ShF			2	3		[5]	
	Ventral Head + ShF			4	6		[10]	
	ShF=	11	5	5	18		[39]	
	ShF//	5	1				[6]	
Sternum	Small Fragments			1	1		[2]	(2)[k]
Scapula	Small Fragments	1			17		[18]	(18)[l]
Humerus	ShF//	2	4		6	1	[13]	(15)
	ShF=		1		1		[2]	
Radius	ShF//		3		3		[6]	(6)
Ulna	ShF//				2		[2]	(4)
	ShF=		1			1	[2]	
Femur	ShF//	16	9		8		[33]	(34)
	ShF=		1				[1]	
Tibia	ShF//	7			1		[8]	(9)
	PF			1[m]			[1]	
Cannons	DF			2[n]			[2]	(2)
First Phalange	Split Lengthwise				2[o]		[2]	(2)

Third Phalange	Complete	1^p					[1]	(1)
Sesamoids	Complete		2				[2]	(2)
Hooves	Front	1^q					[1]	(5)
							[4]	
	Rear	2^r	2^s					
Unidentified Longbone		1	1				[2]	(2)
Fragments								
Total		59	51	37	138	3		(288)

a. Left and right halves of face from frontal bone forwards, including all molars (two pieces).
b. One fragment of occiput; 4 fragments of nasal bone.
c. Four fragments of occiput; 1 hyoid bone.
d. One almost complete left ramus.
e. Both transverse and dorsal processes are present.
f. Atlas.
g. Both dorsal and transverse processes are present; most of body is missing.
h. All are caudal vertebrae.
i. Both are caudal vertebrae.
j. All fragments are small; most show hack-marks on edges; a few show signs of smashing.
k. All fragments are small.
l. All fragments small; most show signs of hacking.
m. PF plus Sh//
n. DF plus Sh// right rear, and DF plus Sh//, left rear.
o. Each contains one half of the proximal and distal heads connected by half of the split shaft.
p. From right hindlimb.
q. From right forelimb.
r. From right and left hindlimbs.
s. From right and left hindlimbs.

The results of this analysis are presented next; the interpretation follows.

X^2 testing of the frequencies of individual parts for the non-longbone portion of the two samples reveals a difference significant at $p = .01$ (see table 14.10). When the "Unidentified fragment" category is removed from both samples, however, the differences in relative proportions become nonsignificant.

Several regularities noted in the controlled kudu–wildebeeste sample are repeated in their abandoned camp counterpart: rib and vertebra fragments again occur in the greatest numbers; these are followed by the large flattish bones—the cranium, scapula, and pelvis—all represented by approximately the same number of fragments, all significantly less frequent than the first group. Two highly significant differences (14 percent and 26 percent respectively) may be noted between the number of vertebra fragments (relatively more were from the abandoned camps), and the number of unidentified non-longbone fragments (none were found at abandoned camps). A discrepancy which cannot be statistically tested, however, involves the extremely small number of complete bones recovered from abandoned camps. In all, only 1 atlas, 4 caudal vertebrae, 1 third phalange, and 2 sesamoids were found in this context. Admittedly, a number of these bones are small and may actually have been overlooked in collection, but this case cannot be made for the calcaneum and astragalus, and especially for the mandible halves, which are both large and extremely tough.

When the kinds of fragments which represent each anatomical portion are compared between the two samples in the same way, it can be seen that the pelvis, scapula, and sternum types are identical. This, of course, would be expected, since they were represented solely by small fragments in the controlled samples. Four interesting differences between the controlled and the abandoned camp samples may be noted however. The first difference is that in the abandoned camp sample the ratio of small cranial fragments to their larger counterparts is significantly increased. Secondly, the relative numbers of complete vertebrae remain fairly constant, but the proportions of almost complete vertebrae and large fragments decrease markedly in the abandoned camp series while the proportion of small fragments increases significantly. The difference in relative frequency of small fragments between the two samples is significant at $p = .01$ (see table 14.11). A third, extremely significant, difference ($p = .01$) may also be noted in the form of the unidentified fragments; in the controlled series 145, or 90 percent, of such pieces are non-longbone in nature whereas not one fragment of this type was

TABLE 14.10

Comparison of Non-Longbone Fragments: Controlled Series and Abandoned Camps

	Kudu – Wildebeeste Controlled Series		Series from Abandoned Camps	
	Number	Percent	Number	Percent
Cranium	26	5	13	6
Mandible	4	*	1	1
Vertebrae	154	27	85	41
Pelvis	25	4	23	11
Ribs	170	30	64	31
Sternum	2	*	2	1
Scapula	41	7	18	9
Unidentified Fragments	145	26	0	0

*less than 1%

recovered at an abandoned camp. Finally, it appears that there is more variation in rib form in the abandoned camp series. While most ribs are cut crosswise, four examples are almost complete and an additional six are split lengthwise. In the controlled comparisons, all rib fragments show crosswise cutting at either one or both ends.

TABLE 14.11

Comparison of Vertebrae Classes: Controlled Series and Abandoned Camps

	Kudu – Wildebeeste Controlled Series		Series from Abandoned Camps	
	Number	Percent	Number	Percent
Complete	10	6	5	6
Almost Complete	22	15	2	2
Large Fragment	24	16	6	7
Small Fragment	98	63	72	85

The relative numbers of longbone fragments in the controlled group (24 percent) and the abandoned camp series (26 percent) are not significantly different. When the two samples are compared by X^2 on the basis of relative frequency of fragments from each longbone the difference is significant at $p = .01$. It may be seen from table 14.12 however that one major source of variance lies in the numbers of cannon bone fragments; when these are removed from the sample, X^2 testing now indicates no significant difference (see table 14.13). Also, with the cannon bones removed, the ordering of bones on the basis of relative number of fragments is identical. Within the abandoned camp series itself X^2 was again used to test for significant differences

TABLE 14.12
Comparison of Longbone Fragments (in Order of Decreasing Frequency):
Controlled Series and Abandoned Camps

	Kudu–Wildebeeste Controlled Series			Series from Abandoned Camps	
	Number	Percent		Number	Percent
Femur	46	29	Femur	34	49
Cannons	35	21	Humerus	15	21
Humerus	27	17	Tibia	9	13
Tibia	24	15	Radius	6	9
Radius	21	13	Ulna	4	5
Ulna	8	5	Cannons	2	3

in the number of fragments from each longbone, and the results are very much like those observed when this identical procedure was carried out for the controlled sample. The femur is represented by significantly more fragments than any of the other longbones. The difference between the femur and humerus is significant at $p = .01$, yet this latter bone occurred significantly more often than the radius, ulna, and the cannons.

TABLE 14.13
Comparison of Longbone Fragments, excluding Cannons (in order of Decreasing Frequency): Controlled Series and Abandoned Camps

	Kudu–Wildebeeste Controlled Series			Series from Abandoned Camps	
	Number	Percent		Number	Percent
Femur	46	37	Femur	34	50
Humerus	27	21	Humerus	15	22
Tibia	24	19	Tibia	9	13
Radius	21	17	Radius	6	9
Ulna	8	6	Ulna	4	6

The most striking difference between the two series lies in the relative numbers of longbone shaft and head fragments: in the controlled series 93 out of 161 fragments (58 percent) include some longbone head, while from the abandoned camps the comparable figure is 2 out of 71, or 3 percent. When the relative numbers of heads are compared to their respective total samples (longbone plus non-longbone) it can be stated with an extremely high level of confidence ($p = .005$) that fragments of longbone head are underrepresented in the abandoned camp series. Interestingly enough, on the same basis of comparison, fragments of longbone shaft are more common than would be expected by chance ($p = .005$).

Finally, within the longbone samples it is possible for each longbone and for each sample to compare the numbers of shaft fragments split lengthwise to those cut crosswise, and these data are presented in table 14.14.

Although these totals are too small for statistical manipulation, visual comparison indicates that for each of the longbones the relative numbers of each type of shaft fragment are the same in each of the two samples. It may be concluded that this ratio is not affected by natural "postdepositional" factors.

TABLE 14.14

Comparison of Distribution of Longbone Shaft Fragments:
Controlled Series and Abandoned Camps

	Kudu–Wildebeeste Controlled Series		Series from Abandoned Camps	
	ShF //	ShF =	ShF //	ShF =
Humerus	7	1	13	2
Radius	9		6	
Ulna	2	4	2	2
Femur	27	2	33	1
Tibia	8		8	1
Cannon	8			

What kind of order, if any, can be made of the welter of facts which have been presented above? Several definite statements can be made: the overall preservation of remains varies significantly from site to site; it is not correlated with the length of time between abandonment and bone collection and it is suggested that bone eating by noncarnivorous animals is responsible for this disparity. This can not be proven however. Secondly, analysis of these faunal remains by anatomical part and type of fragment conclusively shows that relative preservation is not random: some parts such as shaft fragments are extraordinarily well preserved while others such as the corresponding head fragments disappear very quickly. Statistical analysis shows that the likelihood of such distributions occurring by chance is minuscule. The interesting question to ask is whether factors can be isolated which account for this nonrandom patterning, and the answer is definitely yes. The observed variability (defined in relation to the controlled kudu–wildebeeste sample) can be explained on the basis of five factors:

1. *Primary Butchering Practices.* The sole effect of kill site butchering and consuming is reflected in the difference in number of cannon bone fragments between the controlled and the abandoned camp series. In the former

sample, I purposely included the cannon bones in order to describe how they were split, while observation shows that hunters break and discard these bones at the kill site. This observed difference is therefore "artificial" and results from problems involved in my own research design.

2. *Variation in Cooking Practices.* Observation shows that a cut of meat may be cooked in more than one way. Ribs are usually chopped crosswise into pot-sized pieces and then boiled; but at the kill site hunters roast rib packages directly on the fire, pick the meat from them, and then discard the bones in the same state as when they were originally cut from the animal. That several almost complete rib fragments were found in the abandoned camp series whereas they were totally absent in the controlled counterpart is most likely explained by the roasting of several ribs at the abandoned camps.

3. *Simple smashing of fragments.* Pieces of bone, after they have been discarded on the ground, are vulnerable to simple mechanical breakage. Either people or animals may tread on them, or heavier pieces which have been slightly broken during butchering may fall apart of their own weight. Not surprisingly, a relative increase in the number of small cranial fragments over large ones, and a similar rise in the number of small vertebra fragments was observed, although in this latter case another factor is also at work.

4. *Disintegration of exposed spongy bone tissue.* A number of authors (i.e. Cornwall 1956; Chaplin 1971) have discussed the different kinds of tissue which make up a bone and have also differentiated between the spongy, relatively soft material which, covered by a thin layer of compact tissue, forms the longbone heads and the harder very compact structure which makes up the shafts. Brain (1969), in fact, has related the differential preservation of goat bones to just such structural properties and has used the specific gravity of a bone section as a rough measure of its compactness or strength. My own information bears out Brain's contention that the stronger portions of a bone are more likely to be preserved, but one specific and extremely important qualification must be made: *for portions with spongy tissue, likelihood of destruction is significantly increased only if the bone has been broken and the inner tissue is directly exposed.* Unfortunately it is not possible to support this contention with the "large animal data," but comparative analysis of steenbok and duiker (small antelope), African porcupine, and even smaller springhare provide overwhelming confirmation of this fact. When springhare and porcupine are butchered, the longbones are usually broken once across the middle of the shaft, and the longbone heads remain intact. Collections

from abandoned camps show that in comparison with other anatomical parts, and also with controlled collections, the longbone heads are relatively well preserved and constitute a major class of recovered fragment. This, of course, is in direct contrast to the large antelopes. Even more convincing are the small-antelope data, because some longbone heads are cracked during butchering and others are left intact. And the rate of recovery of intact heads from abandoned sites is far greater than for their broken counterparts.

Considering this one variable alone it is now possible to explain major anomalies observed between the controlled and the abandoned camp series. The heads of all gemsbok longbones are split and thus remarkably few of the fragments are preserved. For the shafts (composed of compact tissue) recovery is excellent—so high in fact that the total number of fragments from the abandoned camps is equal to that from the controlled series. And it may be concluded that not only are shaft fragments being differentially preserved but also that fragments with a portion of both head and shaft are being converted to shaft fragments only. If one looks at the totals for unidentified fragments, the same phenomenon may be observed: the relative numbers of unidentified shaft fragments are about the same in both series, while for unidentified non-shaft fragments (mostly bits of cranium, vertebrae, pelvis, and scapula) destruction in the abandoned camp series is complete. These latter bits are composed for the most part of spongy tissue covered with a thin compact covering, and thus their rapid disappearance is not surprising. The vertebrae provide another example of this phenomenon: in the abandoned camp series the relative number of vertebrae increases significantly in relation to other anatomical portions, and within the vertebra class itself a similar significant increase in the relative number of small fragments may be noted. What happens is that the exposed spongy tissue of the vertebra body is destroyed, leaving intact the more solid transverse and especially dorsal processes which are classed as "small fragments." In this context it is significant to note that the relative numbers of complete vertebrae remain unchanged, and it is the almost complete vertebrae and the large fragments (in both of these classes the spongy tissue is directly exposed) which decrease significantly in frequency.

5. *Selective carnivore activity.* No direct evidence exists to support this assumption, and the following argument, admittedly a bit hypothetical, is devised to explain the fact that almost none of the complete bones known to be left at abandoned campsites are recovered. These bones include the calcaneum and astragalus, the remaining small bones from the extremities,

and the mandible halves. While the smaller of these bone types may have escaped my notice, this case cannot be made for the mandible, calcaneum, or astragalus. These bones are usually not cracked in butchering, and the mandible consists of extremely compact tissue, so the likelihood of the differential destruction through weathering is not great. This leaves the possibility of carnivores that are interested not in the bones themselves but in either meat or marrow. When the !Kung are through with an animal very little of either are left, since meat is picked clean from all the bones and marrow has been extracted from the main bones which contain it. Carnivores do visit abandoned camps regularly, and all that is really left for them is marrow in those bones which the !Kung ignore. And these are precisely those complete bones missing from the abandoned sites. Interestingly enough, with the exception of the mandible, these are the same bones which are so badly underrepresented in the controlled kudu – wildebeeste sample, which was collected at the Dobe base camp; and Dobe abounds with lean and hungry Bushman dogs. Speculation, but interesting, and I think possible nonetheless.

Anthropologists have at times created a hypothetical archeologist, placed him in a known ethnographic situation, and on the basis of material remains guessed the kinds of conclusions he might draw. Although difficult, it is possible to construct such a hypothetical situation in an even-handed manner, and with the gemsbok remains from the abandoned camps it actually may prove instructive to do so. One point to be emphasized at the outset is that the degree of specificity of bone identification as presented in table 14.9 (only 2 of 288 pieces, or .007 percent, are classified as "unidentified fragments") would never be replicated in a true archeological analysis. The accuracy achieved for the abandoned camp series was possible for two reasons: first the situation was a controlled one, and there was no question about the species represented; gemsbok was the only large animal present. Because of the generally small fragment size, it would have been impossible in most instances to distinguish between gemsbok and kudu or wildebeeste if either of the latter had also been represented. Secondly, almost all of the identification was done by !Kung (its high accuracy was independently checked through multiple identifications using different informants), and the !Kung are uncanny in the accuracy with which they can determine anatomical position. Compare these levels of identification with those of archeologists who specialize in this field: Reed (1963:205) notes that: "At large excavations where . . . quantities of broken bone rapidly accumulate preliminary field sorting is necessary, since 90 of the bulk may be unidentifiable chips."

To choose one specific example, Perkins and Daly (1968:97) started their analysis with a sample of 300,000 individual pieces of bone. Preliminary sorting reduced the total to 25,000 and the final sample they analyzed consisted of about 14,000 pieces, or 4.6 percent of the original number.

The first question which may be asked is: given the table 14.9 totals, how many individuals would the hypothesized archeologist conclude were represented in the combined sample? The answer (based on the number of right or left rear hooves) would be two: an error of 67 percent. Given the small size of the longbone-shaft fragments, not even a much more exacting reconstruction approach (such as Chaplin 1971 suggests) would increase this total. Note what would happen as the sample increased. If Camp 2 were considered alone, it would be concluded that one individual was present. Suppose Camp 6 bones, in this hypothetical situation, were combined with the Camp 2 sample and the determination of minimum number of animals was again made. Again, one would be forced to conclude that one animal only was present, and the total error would be 50 percent. If Camp 8 were next added to the series, again one could not determine that more than one individual was present, and the error would increase to 67 percent. This process can be continued step by step until all the camps are included in the sample, and in figure 14.6 one can see how the amount of error in the calculation of minimum number increases in relation to sample size. Its magnitude need not be emphasized. For comparison, an identical calculation based on a series of 32 porcupines also collected from abandoned sites is included, and it is immediately evident that the error is both smaller and systematically different. The reason is that in smaller animals bones are not so extensively broken, and either complete bones or longbone fragments which contain complete heads are more likely to survive in recognizable form. Up to a certain point, the smaller the animal the better the relative preservation.

What correct conclusions, then, could this hypothetical archeologist make? He might guess that most if not all of the non-longbone portions of the animals were returned to camp. From examining the size and shape of the fragments from the pelvis and scapula, and by noting the chopping marks along their edges, he could deduce the manner in which they were broken, although the reason for this might escape him. He might also speculate that on the basis of the two complete face halves the face was removed from the skull in the butchering process and then split in half. And from the types, relative numbers, and sizes of rib fragments he might conclude that entire ribs were brought back to camp and then cut crosswise into a number of

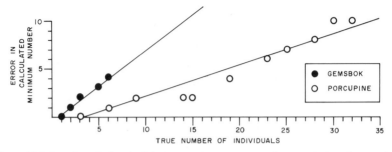

Figure 14.6 Error in calculated minimum number vs. true number gemsbok and porcupine.

fragments. He might, through inspired intuition, guess that the cannon bones were usually left at the kill site. Finally, a comparison of the relatively well preserved shaft fragments might permit him a few speculations on methods of treatment for the different longbones. However, given the amount of information that can be gained through direct observation and the analysis of controlled samples, the above conclusions would be slim indeed. But this, most archeologists themselves would agree, is a cross they must bear.

Without making a dolt of the fellow, where would the archeologist most likely go wrong? Given only one mandible fragment, he might conclude that the mandibles had been removed and left at the kill site, presumably after the tongue had been removed. Another disparity that might very likely catch his eye are the significantly large number of humerus and especially femur fragments, in comparison with the lower two sets of longbones. And this could lead to another not improbable conclusion: that the lower longbones, which have relatively little meat, were usually left at the kill site and only the uppermost ones were carried back to camp, along with the hooves (which are relatively well represented in the sample). In fact, among Alaskan Eskimo a very similar pattern is actually observed today (Dennis Stanford: personal communication). I refrain from continuing to more speculative realms—bone tools from longbone heads and cranial saucers (see Kitching 1963).

CONCLUSION

In the preceding section I have attempted to illustrate how the form, frequency, and spatial distribution of faunal material which might be recovered from an abandoned !Kung campsite is based not on chance, but assumes a pattern determined by both cultural and natural factors. Strictly archeological materials can, from a logical point of view, be subjected to the same kinds of influences although the ways they vary, interact, and combine may differ drastically, and other unknown factors may also make their presence felt. It is useful to distinguish between "cultural" and "natural" variables, since the the archeologist seeks the cultural variables whereas the natural variables work to obscure them. Based on the !Kung data, with several additions which have been noted by other workers, a list of cultural variables which may leave their mark on the patterning of faunal remains may be presented as follows:

1. *An evaluation of "worthless parts" left at the kill site.* For the !Kung this includes only the horns; evidence from Alaskan Eskimo (Stanford: personal communication) and from Paleo-Indian bison kills shows how subjective this evaluation can be. Also, it may change within a single group depending on the amount of meat and other resources that may be available.

2. *Consumption of parts of the kill away from camp.* The !Kung, for example, generally consume the cannons and some ribs at the kill and often many of these bones never reach camp. This is a culturally prescribed !Kung rule which has no cross-cultural type of logic behind it, and might be expected to vary from tribe to tribe.

3. *The method of primary butchering for return of meat to camp.* In the process of treating the kill and dividing it into manageable, carrying-size pieces the bones may be affected in a number of ways. !Kung, for example, snap the ribs near the dorsal head, and smash the vertebrae in more than one direction to make a pliable package.

4. *Means of preparing meat for cooking and consumption.* For the !Kung, the major cultural patterning takes place at this stage. There are rules that determine which bones are to be broken and how this is to be accomplished. The most important factors considered are the amount of marrow (if any) the bone contains, whether a portion is to be cooked by boiling or roasting, and the size of the pot. Wissler (1910) and Leechman (1951) have described the technique used by some groups of North American Indians to smash bones into small fragments for boiling and the preparation of bone grease; from a practical point of view this destroys bones completely. Again, it might be expected that variation will depend largely on the amount of fat available from the soft parts of the animal, and the amount of meat generally available, to any particular group. Even within a single area this may change radically from season to season.

5. *Use of Bone Tools.* The !Kung make relatively little use of bone as a raw

material for tools, and this factor has no noticeable effect on bone patterning. Extensive use of bone is known for other groups however and the Eskimo provide an excellent case in point. It is interesting to speculate on the effect more extensive use of bone tools would have on the patterning of faunal remains, and it would seem to me that three factors must be considered: (1) the extent to which bone is used for this purpose; (2) the parts of the animal skeleton employed for this end (if longbone shafts and either whole ribs or rib fragments provided the main blanks for tool making, the effect on overall faunal patterning may well be negligible, since these parts generally are classed as unidentifiable or unimportant fragments in faunal analysis; if the heads of longbones or an entire bone, such as the scapula, were consistently used, the effect would then be quite different); (3) the social and spatial contexts in which tool making occurs (this determines where the unwanted bone fragments will fall, and among other things their consequent likelihood of archeological recovery). For the !Kung, tool making takes place around the cooking hearths, and the resultant byproducts are intermingled with discarded food remains.

6. *Distribution of meat outside of camp.* From the example presented earlier, it can be seen that not all meat is consumed within and by members of the camp, and that some sharing beyond the physical and social boundaries of the group occurs even when a "surplus" is not present. These portions are, of course, effectively removed from the sample. Chaplin (1969) suggests that such a process was operable in influencing patterning of sheep remains in Roman Britain sites.

In a similar way it is possible to examine some of the "natural" factors which may lead to differential preservation and recovery of faunal remains. These include:

1. *The size of the bone.* Very small bones, such as the hyoid, sesamoids, and some of the other extremity bones, which are likely to be preserved intact, can easily be missed in the excavation process.

2. *Natural fragility.* Through simple crushing of a mechanical nature some portions are likely to be destroyed. These include, for example, the inner portions of the face such as the ethmoid bones.

3. *Type of tissue from which the bone is formed.* Parts composed primarily of spongy tissue are subject to relatively rapid disintegration in comparison to those formed solely from compacted cells.

4. *Extent of structural damage to bones through cooking.* Chaplin points out that roasting as well as prolonged boiling can remove much of the organic

matrix from a bone, leaving it brittle and easily destroyed. It is, he notes, "the tabular bones and tabular processes that are the most susceptible" (1971:14).

5. *Selective and Nonselective destruction by carnivores and other animals.* Porcupine, other rodents, and in some cases larger animals eat bones for the elements they contain, and the destructive effect of these actions, while probably random, may nonetheless be considerable. Action of dogs and other carnivores may also have a major effect, and it is likely nonrandom in nature. In part this will depend on the amounts of meat and marrow contained in the discarded parts.

An additional factor which must be considered is the length of time which a bone remains exposed on the living floor. Although the !Kung data are not adequate to prove it, small bones as a rule tend to be pushed downward through the top inch or two of loose dry sand, and in the long run they are better preserved. Brief examination of abandoned !Kung campsites of over several years in age reveal that little bone was preserved on the surface. But excavation at these sites indicates that at least a number of the buried bones have survived intact.

While it is convenient to separate cultural from natural factors, as done in the outline above, this process is in part a dangerous one; these two elements interact, and not always in expected ways. The likelihood of preservation and the effect of natural process are in part determined by the cultural treatment an individual bone receives. Consider, for example, the vertebral fragments recovered in the abandoned campsite series (see table 14.8). Why the small numbers of "almost complete" vertebrae, "large fragments," and "small fragments"? This results from both cultural and natural factors: the vertebrae were cracked during primary butchering and the exposed spongy tissue disintegrated rapidly thereafter. Why the extremely high number of dorsal processes (63 out of 85 pieces, or 74 percent)? Because the dorsal process is formed from compact tissue in contrast to the vertebrate body and thus is more likely to remain intact after the body disappears. Then why the low number of transverse processes (3 out of 85 pieces, or 4 percent), especially since each vertebra has two of them and only one dorsal process? For a cultural reason: when the rib heads are cut from the vertebrae, the transverse processes are usually smashed. Similar kinds of arguments can be made for the longbone heads or any part which contains spongy tissue, for preservation is based not only on the nature of the bone itself, but also on the extent to which this inner portion is exposed during the culturally determined butchering process. As a general rule, the less a portion of a bone is broken, and the more compact tissue it contains, the greater the likelihood of its preservation in an archeological context.

In light of the information presented above, let us finally return to a point raised in the introduction and examine in terms of inherent assumptions or "leaps of faith" some conclusions which have been made from observed patternings in faunal remains. The first great leap usually concerns preservation of faunal material within the archeological context and it is usually taken as an article of faith that destruction, if it occurs, is random. To quote White (1952:337), for example:

> Although the numerical count of the elements is subject to the accidents of preservation and the size of the excavation, the distribution of the various elements from an excavation which meets the archaeological requirements is probably a reasonably accurate reflection of the parts brought into camp, since one element has as good a chance of being preserved as another.

Daly (1969:149) sums it up even more succinctly when she states that "In the archaeological context, however, we are not dealing with natural survival, but with the results of man's activity. . . ." Given this extremely dubious first assumption, it is possible to count different bones or portions thereof, note discrepancies, and then proceed in more than one direction.

One jump can lead to tool use. Observed discrepancies must have some cause, and anatomical parts are overrepresented because they were used as tools at the site; or to turn the argument around, parts that are unexpectedly rare are tools that were employed away from camp. Stein (1963:218), for example, assumes:

> As far as the longbones are concerned, it is reasonable to suppose that these would be brought to villages in roughly equal numbers because the limbs supply a large part of the meat. Those absent from the collection were most likely used for the manufacture of artifacts.

Dart also makes this same assumption in analysis of faunal remains from the Makapansgat australopithecine caves, and is led astray on this basis. In this context it is interesting to compare the preponderance of distal over proximal humerus heads from this site to observations on !Kung kudu butchering. In the three cases (six humeri) observed, the proximal head was split in all instances while five out of six distal heads were left intact.

Alternatively, one may leap in a different direction and assume that significant discrepancies in anatomical proportions reflect hunting techniques and primary butchering practices alone. Thus Perkins and Daly (1968) choose to interpret the relative scarcity of open upper leg bones in comparison with those from the extremities to mean that the former were left at the kill site while the latter, still attached to the skin as convenient handles, were brought back to camp. Their argument is a bit more complex than this since they note that a quite different pattern is observed for sheep and goats, but !Kung information indicates that cross-species comparisons of this type are at best hazardous and at worst completely misleading.

Chaplin, who has done quite sophisticated work along these lines, has tentatively suggested that trade in one instance may be the factor which accounts for nonrandom distribution. His study takes clear note of problems involved in interpretation and is worth a careful second look, since it illustrates how difficult it can be to arrive at a single cultural cause on the basis of observed frequency variation. Chaplin (1969) in a study of sheep remains from a Saxon site at Whitehall, London, determined the minimum numbers of various bones which were present (see table 14.15). His technique for doing this is relatively complex, since in reconstructing minimum longbone numbers, the heads counted and the fragments of shaft are both taken into consideration (1971). In examining his totals, Chaplin noted a significantly low number of femurs (compared to the other longbones), and a low number of pelves as well. He concluded, and possibly correctly, that this discrepancy could be explained in cultural terms and hypothesized the removal of the rear haunch perhaps for sale or trade.

If one assumes, and I think it is a fair assumption to make, that the more pieces into which a bone tends to be broken the greater the likelihood of underestimating its minimum number, then some disturbing parallels between the English sheep and the Kalahari kudu and wildebeeste samples may be noted. As table 14.15 indicates, the kudu and wildebeeste bones that are broken into the most fragments during butchering are precisely the ones that are least common in the sheep sample. In fact, Chaplin's ordering of sheep longbones from smallest minimum number to largest is basically the same as a kudu – wildebeest ordering from most fragments per longbone to least. In the sheep sample, which is based on minimum number, X^2 testing indicates that the femur alone shows significant differences from the other longbones; when the same test is used on the number of fragments from the kudu and wildebeeste sample, the femur alone is the "odd man out." When the non-longbone portions which Chaplin calculates (mandible, scapula, pelvis) are compared in the same fashion the results are slightly equivocal. In the sheep sample the greatest anomaly lies in the extremely high minimum

TABLE 14.15.

Comparison of English Sheep and Kudu – Wildebeeste Remains

Chaplin's English Sheep Sample[a] Minimum Number of Parts (Listed in Order of Increasing Number)			Kudu – Wildebeeste Controlled Sample Total Number of Fragments (Listed in Order of Decreasing Number)	
		Non-Longbone		
Pelvis	14		Scapula	41
Scapula	28		Pelvis	25
Mandible	43		Mandible	4
		Longbone		
Femur	7		Femur	46
Humerus	29		Humerus	27
Tibia	37		Tibia	24
Metacarpal (Cannon)	38		Radius	21
Radius	43			
Metatarsal (Cannon)	43		Cannons	17.5[b]

[a]From Chaplin (1969:233)

[b]Since front and rear cannons both included, the total has been divided by two for comparability to Chaplin's sample.

number of mandibles, and this is reflected similarly in the low number of mandibular fragments in the kudu – wildebeeste series. In the sheep sample, however, there are significantly more scapulae than pelves while in the other group a significant difference is also observed but in the wrong direction. Thus, there would be little definite factual basis on which to choose between two possible ways to explain the anomalies observed in the English sheep sample: perhaps trade or sale of the rear haunch explains these discrepancies, as Chaplin suggests. But on the other hand, differential bone breakage and the resulting difficulties in computation can just about fill the bill as well.

If we turn in a slightly different direction, it is possible to examine a different kind of argument and set of assumptions which is based not on relative frequency of anatomical portions but on the shapes of bone fragments themselves. Kitching (1963), in a largely subjective analysis of faunal remains from Paleolithic levels in Pin Hole Cave, Derbyshire, notes that certain anatomical portions exhibit similar final forms. On this basis he concludes that these fragments of bone are tools, purposely shaped to perform specific functions. Sadek-Kooros (1972) employs statistical analysis for much the same ends and attempts to isolate formal fragment categories. She states (1972:370): "Bone broken through natural agencies or through random human breaking does not accidentally result in formal categories; such categories reflect purposeful fracturing of bone with the object of producing specific shapes."

She then suggests that the resulting formal categories are, in fact, bone tools. In both Kitchings' and Sadek-Kooros' studies the assumption, which I consider unwarranted, is that breaking of bones in the butchering process is random and that "patterning," or "formal categories," of remains must be associated with something else. The !Kung data reveal unambiguously that such patterns do exist and in this instance are based on the desire to extract marrow from longbones as efficiently, and with as few bone inclusions, as possible. The bone fragments are then cooked along with the bits of remaining meat, picked clean, discarded, and never used as tools.

Thus, in all the studies considered above, patterning is related to a single variable based usually on either primary butchering or tool use. It is instructive that, in the !Kung case, these factors have extremely little effect on the final form of faunal remains, and that far more important are the last stages of butchering for cooking and direct consumption and then selective destruction by natural processes after the bones and bone fragments have been discarded. With the exceptions of Brain's (1969) study of Hottentot goat bones, and Olsen's (1967) examination of fish remains from archeological sites on the South Coast of Varanger Fjord, Norway, almost no attention has been given to these two factors, and because of this, I have grave reservations concerning the validity of most of the "cultural" explanations of observed faunal patterning, with which I am familiar. From this, I would exclude only those which deal with Paleo-Indian bison kill sites, where remains are in a clear cultural context, preservation is excellent, samples are large, and fairly direct ethnographic parallels are available.

Fault finding, while at times necessary, is not a pleasant task. The data on large animal butchering in this paper provide, in one way, an acid test since preservation of such material is extremely poor and few archeologists, if they recovered such material in an archeological context, would spend much time analyzing it. For smaller animals, in the !Kung case at least, preservation is decidedly better and the data are correspondingly richer. In many archeological contexts—numbers of cave sites come immediately to mind—conditions of preservation are excellent; and while the problem of differential preservation must always be considered first and most carefully, it will likely prove possible to make fairly detailed cultural inferences.

The conclusion of this research that I find most encouraging is that !Kung, and I very strongly suspect *all*, groups leave a distinct cultural imprint on the faunal materials which are the final and incidental byproducts of meat consumption (excluding bone tools from consideration). The final form of these remains results from a series of ordered rules on how a carcass is to be treated, and while some cultural decisions are tightly tied to the nature of the animal skeleton itself (scapula bodies, for example, cannot be split for marrow) others clearly embody a subjective element. Faunal remains, then, as do house and settlement patterns, or tool forms, constitute the visible end product of a series of cultural rules and can, with care, be examined in the same light. The very complexity which poses such interpretive problems also provides excellent opportunities, and it is possible to pass beyond such elementary questions as "what is left at a kill site?" or "what parts of the skeleton might be used for tools?"

These observations have several implications in terms of research strategies which may best be employed. First, controlled studies—especially those which can help to define the effects of natural agencies on discarded bone— are essential. Secondly studies of the detailed type, which deal with differing butchering techniques and how they are reflected in bone remains (i.e. Guilday et al. 1962), can also be of great value. Finally, in faunal studies which attempt cultural reconstruction of this type, it will be necessary to shift the basic unit of analysis from entire bones, or even the heads of bones themselves, to smaller units and to devise smaller categories, or attribute systems which will permit one to ask the question of how—by what steps—was the bone broken. In retrospective examination of my own controlled studies, and of other analyses presented in the literature, I am struck by the fact that interpretation based on the counting of anatomical parts provides the least trustworthy information, while a more detailed analysis of the kind proposed here seems to yield not only more, but also more accurate, results. And although I disagree with her interpretations, I believe that Sadek-Kooros (1972) has taken a great methodological step forward in this direction. Admittedly detailed work of this kind is time-consuming and devoid of almost all intrinsic interest, but I can see no way around this.

Finally, I would like to indicate briefly how faunal analysis of this kind fits into the broader archeological framework. One obvious way to consider it is in terms of "system analysis," and although butchering actually does form a "system" as that term has come to be used in the archeological literature, its potential significance extends well beyond this fact. By using analysis of faunal remains as a tool, it is also possible to approach "traditional" archeological questions concerned with cultural relationships through time and space. Just as stone-tool forms and ceramic forms, both of which reflect cultural rules and patterns, are used to define and compare archeologically known cultures, comparison in the patterning of faunal remains may be used in the same way. Frenchmen not only call their cuts of meat by different names than do Americans, but in fact they butcher their animals in a different way. Although this study has not been done, I am fairly confident that if large and representative samples of bone scraps were collected from French and American households these differences would be readily apparent. Defining archeological cultures on this basis would, from a practical point of view, be a thankless and probably hopeless task. But there are a number of cases where the evidence from faunal analysis might throw a welcome additional light on already existing problems. In two areas with which I am familiar, the Upper Paleolithic of France and the stone age in Eastern and Southern Africa, there are a number of instances in which it would be interesting to know if conclusions drawn on the basis of lithic analysis would be supported by possible faunal analysis. T. E. White (1953b), who was the original pioneer in this field, did undertake an analysis of this type; the results were encouraging.

ACKNOWLEDGMENTS

This paper is based on data collected between 1968 and 1970. I thank the National Institutes of Mental Health (MH 13611), the Wenner-Gren Foundation of Anthropological Research (Grant Number 2476), and the Department of Anthropology, Smithsonian Institution, whose financial support has made this work possible. My intellectual debt to Irven DeVore, Richard Lee, Hallam L. Movius Jr., Desmond Clark, Richard Gould, Bob Brain, Brian Fagan, and Revel Mason is deep, and I am happy to acknowledge the contributions, both direct and indirect, which they have made. My wife, Alison S. Brooks, William W. Fitzhugh, and Robert J. Bigart were kind enough to read this paper and their suggestions have improved it considerably. I also wish to thank Niel Roth for his mathematical assistance, G. Robert Lewis for drafting the figures, and Rosemary M. DeRosa who typed the final version. My final and deepest thanks go to my !Kung friends both for their faunal identifications and for their strong and continued moral support. As tradition requires, I alone am responsible for all and sundry errors.

REFERENCES

Binford, L. R. 1971. Interassemblage variability—the Mousterian and the "functional" argument. Research Seminar on Archaeology and Related Subjects, Sheffield, Dec. 14–16, 1971.

Bouchud, J. 1966. *Essai sur le renne et la climatologie du Paléolithique moyen et supérieur.* Imprimerie Magne, Périgueux.

Brain, C. K. 1967. New light on old bones. Paper presented at the Annual Congress of the Museum Association, Bulawayo.

—— 1969. The contribution of Namib Desert Hottentots to an understanding of australopithecine bone accumulations. *Scientific Papers of the Namib Desert Research Station,* No. 39, pp. 13–22.

Chaplin, R. E. 1969. The use of nonmorphological criteria in the study of animal domestication from bones found on archaeological sites. In P. J. Ucko and G. W. Dimbleby eds. *The domestication and exploitation of plants and animals,* pp. 231–45. Chicago: Aldine.

—— 1971. *The study of animal bones from archaeological sites.* London and New York: Seminar Press.

Clark, J. G. D. 1952. *Prehistoric Europe: The economic basis.* London: Methuen and Co.

Coppens, Y. 1967. Les faunes de vertébres quaternaires du Tchad. In W. W. Bishop and J. D. Clark eds. *Background to evolution in Africa,* pp. 89–98. Chicago: University of Chicago Press.

Cornwall, I. W. 1956. *Bones for the archaeologist.* London: Phoenix House.

Daly, P. 1969. Approaches to faunal analysis in archaeology. *American Antiquity* 34(2):146–53.

Dart, R. A. 1957. The Osteodontokeratic culture of *Australopithecus prometheus. Transvaal Museum Memoir* No. 10.

Freeman, L. G. Jr. 1968. A theoretical framework for interpreting archaeological materials. In R. B. Lee and I. DeVore, eds. *Man the hunter,* pp. 262–67. Chicago: Aldine.

Frison, G. C. 1971. The buffalo pound in northwestern plains prehistory: Site 48CA302, Wyoming. *American Antiquity* 36(1):77–91.

Garrod, D. A. E. and D. M. A. Bate. 1937. *The stone age of Mount Carmel.* 2 Vols. Oxford: Oxford University Press.

Guilday, J. E., P. W. Parmalee and D. P. Tanner. 1962. Aboriginal butchering techniques at the Eschelman Site (36 La 12), Lancaster County, Pennsylvania. *Pennsylvania Archaeologist* 32(2):59–83.

Kehoe, T. F. 1967. The boarding school bison drive site. *Plains Anthropologist,* Memoir 4, Lincoln.

Kehoe, T. F. and A. B. Kehoe. 1960. Observations on the butchering technique at a prehistoric bison kill in Montana. *American Antiquity* 25(3):420–23.

Kitching, J. W. 1963. *Bone, tooth and horn tools of Paleolithic man.* Manchester: Manchester University Press.

Lee, R. B. 1965. *Subsistence ecology of !Kung Bushmen.* Doctoral dissertation, University, of California, Berkeley.

———1968. What hunters do for a living, or, how to make out on scarce resources. In R. B. Lee and I. DeVore eds. *Man the hunter,* pp. 30–48. Chicago: Aldine.

Leechman, D. 1951. Bone grease. *American Antiquity* 16(4):355–56.

Marshall, L. 1960. !Kung Bushman bands. *Africa* 30:325–55.

Olsen, H. 1967. Varanger-Funnene IV Osteologisk Materiale Innledning—Fish—Fugl. *Tromso Museums Skrifter* 7(4) Tromso, Oslo, Bergen.

Perkins, D. Jr. and P. Daly. 1968. A hunters' village in Neolithic Turkey. *Scientific American* 219(5):96–106.

Reed, C. A. 1963. Osteo-archaeology. In D. Brothwell and E. Higgs, eds. *Science in Archaeology,* pp. 204–16. New York: Basic Books.

Sadek-Kooros, H. 1972. Primitive bone fracturing: A method of research. *American Antiquity* 37(3):369–82.

Stein, W. T. 1963. Mammal remains from archaeological sites in the Point of Pines region, Arizona. *American Antiquity* 29(2):213–20.

Thomas, E. M. 1959. *The harmless people.* New York: Knopf.

Wheat, J. B. 1967. A Paleo-Indian bison kill. *Scientific American* 216(1):44–52.

—— 1972. The Olsen-Chubbuck Site: A Paleo-Indian bison kill. *Memoirs of the Society for American Archaeology,* No. 26; *American Antiquity* 37(1), pt. 2.

White, T. E. 1952. Observations on the butchering technique of some aboriginal peoples, no. 1. *American Antiquity* 17(4):337–38.

—— 1953a. A method of calculating the dietary percentage of various food animals utilized by aboriginal peoples. *American Antiquity* 18(4):396–98.

—— 1953b. Observations on the butchering technique of some aboriginal peoples, no. 2. *American Antiquity* 19(2):160–64.

—— 1954. Observations on the butchering technique of some aboriginal peoples, nos. 3–6. *American Antiquity* 19(3):254–64.

—— 1955. Observations on the butchering technique of some aboriginal peoples, nos. 7–9. *American Antiquity* 21(2): 170–78.

Wilson, G. L. 1924. The horse and dog in Hidatsa culture. *Anthropological Papers of the American Museum of Natural History* 15, pt. 2.

Wissler, C. 1910. Material culture of the Blackfoot Indians. *Anthropological Papers of the American Museum of Natural History* 5, pt. 1.

Wolberg, D. L. 1970. The hypothesized osteodontokeratic culture of the Australopithecinae: A look at the evidence and the opinions. *Current Anthropology* 11(1):23–37.

» 15 «

MICHAEL C. ROBBINS • RICHARD B. POLLNAC

A Multivariate Analysis of the Relationship of Artifactual to Cultural Modernity in Rural Buganda

Ethnographic data provide the basis for analogy, and when archeologists turn to living peoples their goal, most often, is to find information which may be used in this way. One observes, for example, that pointed bone objects— harpoons—are used today to spear fish and marine mammals. When similar objects are recovered in an archeological context, one argues by analogy that the term "harpoon" fits them, and a particular function is therefore ascribed. If one searches the ethnographic literature and can discover no other purpose to which such objects were put, the analogy becomes all the more likely; if alternate functions are noted, the probability the analogy is a valid one decreases accordingly. Likewise, the strength of analogical reasoning increases if the archeological site in question is located near a seacoast, river, or lake, and if fish or aquatic mammal bones are found in association with the barbed bone points. Finally the more complex the objects under comparison, the greater the likelihood that a suggested analogy holds true. If one found, for example, an object in all major respects identical to a modern sextant in an unexpected early site, one would be on pretty safe ground in assuming that it served the same purpose as its modern counterpart. On the other hand, a small rounded stone, holed at one end, may have weighted down a fishing line, but may equally well have functioned as a spindle whorl, loom weight, or bolas stone.

The analogy which Robbins and Pollnac examine involves the correspon-

dence, not between object and function, but between object and idea. To what extent, they want to know, is that complex association of beliefs an individual, both consciously and unconsciously, carries around in his head reflected in the objects he owns and uses? The ethnographic present, as they point out, provides a tightly controlled situation in which relationships of this kind may be assessed. One can see what an individual has, then ask him what he believes, and finally determine how closely the one body of data reflects the other. If the fit, as one would hope, is tight, it may then be feasible for the archeologist to employ analogy and to work backward from objects to ideas.

It is appropriate that the authors focus their attention on the question of change—change in ideology and change in material culture—for change of necessity requires time, and is thus particularly amenable to archeological investigation. The conclusions reached are far from encouraging and the article serves to sound a note of caution. But it also illustrates quite neatly how study of the present is relevant to an understanding of the past.

Of fundamental concern to anthropologists working with "material culture" is the problem of discerning the nonmaterial social and cultural significance of material artifacts and remains. Most anthropologists are not simply interested in the "things" themselves, but primarily in the amount and kind of information they can provide about the culture, society, and behavior of their makers and users. Moreover, if we agree with Goodenough that "all we can see of a culture is its products and artifacts, the things people make, do, and say" (1966:265), then it follows that everyone interested in learning about the culture of a population first-hand must eventually do so through the study of some form of its artifacts. If we exempt, for the moment, those who *do* archeology, it appears that recently most anthropologists have neglected, rather seriously, the first of these three main information sources (i.e. what people make and use). This seems especially unfortunate because the possession, use, and arrangement of material artifacts provide relatively permanent, objective data which can be both reliably and validly measured and documented (see Pelto 1970:235–37).

One of the great advantages in studying living populations is the opportunity to collect and intercorrelate data not only on what people "make" and "use" but also on what they "say" and "do." One is thus not only better able to reveal both the functional interrelationships of a community's material artifacts to its observable events, settings, and social relationships and differentiation, but also their cultural significance—to examine the relationship of material artifacts to the ideational order of the individual members of a local population: their beliefs, attitudes, aspirations, values, ideas, preferences, principles of action, percepts, concepts, etc. In addition, these data, collected on living populations, can be of considerable value to prehistorians who must use the information contained in material artifacts and their arrangements to understand the nature of the culture, society, and behavior of prehistoric populations; for in large part, they depend on analogies of artifact-behavior-culture interrelationships of ethnographically known populations in making their interpretations. Furthermore, most prehistorians use the nature of material artifacts and their spatial distributions as evidence for social, behavioral, and cultural change through time.

Goodenough (1964, 1966, 1970) and others who subscribe to a cognitive theory of culture have observed that because we learn about culture by studying its artifacts, we quite frequently and easily confuse artifacts with culture; the artifacts themselves are often confused with the cultural standards, values, and concepts that guided their production. Moreover, the conceptual distinction between the phenomenal order of events, surroundings, behavior, and artifacts on the one hand, and the ideational order of beliefs, values, ideas, and principles of action of the members of a community on the other, becomes crucial for understanding the nature of change; for it is possible that change in one order will not correspond to change in the other. As Goodenough (1966) succinctly notes:

> Observers commonly make the mistake of assuming that observed changes in material, behavioral, or social artifacts and their arrangements in a community necessarily reflect a change in its members' culture: in their values, principles of action, and standards for getting things done (p. 268).

Several anthropologists have recognized, and profitably employed, this distinction in their studies of the relationship of behavioral to cultural change. In fact, one anthropologist has gone so far as to call the "effective, theoretical separation between cultural codes—cognitively based normative systems—and their enactment in behavior" one of the major breakthroughs in cultural anthropology (Keesing 1969).

SCOPE OF THE PRESENT STUDY

We propose to examine the extent to which changes in certain aspects of the material style of life of a rural population in the Buganda region of Uganda can be used to explain (or predict) changes in certain aspects of the culture of its members. More specifically, we shall attempt to provide information on two basic questions:

(1) Over all, are differences in the possession and use of certain modern material artifacts related to differences in the expression of certain attitudes, aspirations, beliefs, and values? That is, do individuals who possess modern material artifacts also express what we would define as modern beliefs, attitudes, and values?

(2) Which material possessions offer the best prediction of the expression of what cultural items?

In our view, these questions warrant careful consideration if one recognizes both the multifunctional role of material artifacts and the variety of potential factors involved in their manufacture, adoption, maintenance, and use. On the surface it might appear that the possession and use of certain modern material items would constitute more accurate predictors of cultural modernity than others. For example, the use of wristwatches, Western clothing, and radios could perhaps be more easily construed as symbols and badges of modern cultural identities than, say, kerosene lanterns, bicycles, or metal roofs. But one cannot be sure. The opposite conclusion is possible or the use of either or both might merely reflect some other factor. That is, both of these kinds of items might be adopted and used simply because of their perceived utility as tools and functional equipment (or perhaps as indicators of socioeconomic distinctions) and not be related, at least in any significant way, to a change in the culture of their users. The essential point is that, in any given instance, whether artifactual change is in fact related to cultural change becomes questionable and must be answered by empirical research.

POPULATION AND PROCEDURES

Our fieldwork was conducted in Buganda, a former Interlacustrine Bantu kingdom in Uganda. The Baganda are a well-known East-African agricultural population, and several excellent accounts of their sociocultural system are available. Although the Baganda retain a strong sense of their separate cultural identity, they have eagerly accepted Western education, religion, and technology, and for the most part seem committed to modernization (Richards 1969). Throughout our research, we were impressed by the considerable range of intrasocietal variation in modernization. For example, some individuals, educated in the West, owning automobiles and television sets, may live within walking distance of others who live in traditional thatched homes and wear traditional clothing. This marked range of variation provides an opportunity to explore several economic, social, and psychocultural concomitants of the relative extent of modernization and the factors responsible. Additional information on our previous investigations, the area, and population with whom we worked, can be found in several other places.

The quantitative data which form the basis for examining the relationships of artifactual to cultural change are derived from responses to a social survey interview schedule. This schedule was administered in 1967 in Luganda, to 109 household heads (57 females and 52 males), randomly sampled from a rural parish (Mulaka) near the town of Masaka. The households contained 519 individuals, approximately one-fourth of the parish population. The interview schedules were designed to collect basic demographic, socioeconomic, and cultural information which could provide both a description of the population and data for assessing the modernization process occurring in this area. Included in the schedule were several items concerning the ownership of both traditional and modern, personal and household, material possessions. The schedule also contained several questions which were constructed to provide data on both traditional and modern beliefs, aspirations, attitudes, and values. Both sets of items are described below. It should be noted, however, that the present study is based on a secondary analysis of these materials. They were not collected primarily for the purposes of this paper. The disadvantage of this, of course, is the potential danger that we committed errors of omission and commission in the selection and use of both the material and cultural items. Had we gone into the field with the present objectives in mind, we would have collected more information of both kinds, including much more qualitative, or contextual, data from key informants, participant-observation, and unstructured interviewing. On the other hand, we feel we can quite confidently claim that we did not knowingly prejudice, or bias, our chances of objectively investigating these relationships because the data were not collected with the present purposes in mind. Nevertheless, the qualifications noted above place our study much more firmly in the exploratory than in the definitive category.

MODERN MATERIAL CULTURE

In table 15.1 we have listed the material items used and their percent distribution. A considerable amount of additional information on their availa-

TABLE 15.1
Percent Distribution of Material Items

Item[a]	Percent	Item	Percent
(12) clock	27	(23) concrete walls	
(13) watch	29	main buildings	23
(14) radio	39	(24) metal or tile roof	
(15) bicycle	48	on other buildings	40
(16) drum	17	(25) photographs on walls	68
(17) motorcycle	06	(26) magazines	47
(18) automobile	07	(27) wears kanzu at home or	
(19) camera	06	while visiting relatives	
(20) iron	69	and friends	78
(21) stove	47	(28) floor tile or concrete	
(22) metal or tile roof on		in main house	22
main building	72		

[a]Variable identity numbers will be used for variable identification in subsequent tables.

bility, use, and meaning to the members of this population, as well as the social, economic, and cultural consequences of their adoption, can be found in extended discussion published elsewhere (Robbins and Kilbride, n.d.).

The modernity of most of these items is quite obvious. Two traditional material items were also included. These refer to the possession of a Kiganda drum and a report by the respondent as to whether he (or her husband, in the case of a female) wears a *Kanzu* (a traditional ankle-length white gown worn by men) at home or while visiting relatives and friends (Robbins and Pollnac 1969b:278). Material item responses were scored as either absent (1) or present (2). For the last two items (*Kanzu* and drum), we felt that negative responses could be interpreted as indicators of modernity.

CULTURAL MODERNITY

The items used to assess "cultural modernity" were selected on the basis of several considerations, and require more discussion. Initially, they were selected because of both their face validity and the theoretical expectation that they would be valid predictors of attitudinal modernity. Furthermore, several similar items have been used in other studies conducted among the Baganda by other investigators (e.g. Doob 1960; Ainsworth and Ainsworth 1962); in other closely related Interlacustrine Bantu populations (e.g. the Banyankole, see Segall, n.d.); and in other African and nonwestern societies (e.g. Graves 1967; Smith and Inkeles 1966; Rodgers 1969; etc.). These studies have shown that most of these items are reliable and valid predictors of other, more obvious, indicators of modernity (e.g. education, occupation, exposure to mass media, etc.). Finally, our preliminary field research and several subsequent analyses of these materials had suggested that for the most part they had an acceptable degree of reliability, and interrelationship with other, more ostensible, indicators of modernization in our research community (cf. Robbins and Pollnac 1969; Robbins, et al. 1969).

The cultural items and their percent distribution are listed in table 15.2.

Each item is briefly described below as is the rationale for its inclusion.

1. If *your daughter (or if you had a daughter who) had a chance to go to the University, would you let her go?":*

A response of "yes" was coded **2**, modern, a response of "no" was coded **1**. This was based on the assumption that people's aspirations for a modern education for their children (especially their daughters) would indicate the possession of modern values (Peshkin and Cohen 1967).

2. *"Do you think it is proper for the husband and wife to eat at the same table?":*

Again, a response of "yes" was coded as **2** and a "no" was coded **1**. This question was constructed to determine if the respondent was accepting the modern emphasis toward the equality of sexual status (cf. Peshkin and Cohen 1967; LeVine 1970).

3. *"Should more than one person drink out of the same straw?":*

"Yes" was coded as **1**, and "no" was **2**. Traditionally, many Baganda drank from the same gourd and straw as a symbol of social solidarity. Public health propaganda, however, has tried to discourage these practices for hygienic reasons. This item might determine if the person has been exposed to or has accepted this information.

4. *"Do you prefer drinking from a gourd or a glass?":*

The response "gourd" was coded **1**, "glass" **2**. The choice of a traditional Kiganda gourd for drinking rather than a glass is often used to symbolize that one is a "pure" Muganda *(Muganda wawu)*. Moreover, one who refuses a gourd, or chooses a glass, is usually trying to indicate to others that he is both modern and refined.

5. *"Do African women look more beautiful in Kiganda or European clothing?":*

A response "Kiganda" was coded **1**, and "European" **2**.

6. *"Are there any diseases a Kiganda doctor can cure better than a European doctor?":*

TABLE 15.2
Percent Distribution of Cultural Modernity
Items

Variable[a]	Response[a]		
	1	2	3
1	06	94	
2	31	69	
3	10	90	
4	44	56	
5	92	08	
6	42	58	
7	59	06	35
8	94	06	
9	43	02	55
10	19	70	11
11	57	28	15

[a]See text for variable name, description, and response code. These variable identification numbers will be used for variable identification in subsequent tables.

If the respondent named any diseases, he was coded **1**; if he stated there were no diseases, he was coded **2**. This is admittedly a dubious item. We felt, however, that those who either did not believe there were any diseases that a Kiganda doctor could cure better, or who would not mention one, were reflecting either considerable exposure to modernity or a desire to present a modern impression of themselves to us during the interview.

7. *"Do you believe that the second child should not arrive before the first child is weaned?":*

"Yes" was coded **1**, a response of "maybe," "possibly," "didn't know for sure," "couldn't say," etc. was coded as **2**, and a definite "no" was coded **3**. This question was designed to measure whether or not people were adhering to, or expressing, traditional attitudes toward the customary postpartum sex taboo.

8. *"Should poor, helpless clan members be supported?":*

"Yes" was coded **1**, "no" was coded **2**. This question intended to measure whether people felt that, irrespective of a person's contribution, an ascribed membership in a kin-group nevertheless entitles him to support. A response of "no," it was felt, would indicate emphasis on the relatively more modern form of economic individualism (Mboya 1969).

9. *"Do you believe that deceased ancestors can do people harm?":*

Again, a response of "yes" was coded **1**, a response of "not sure," "possibly," etc. was coded **2**, and a definite "no" was coded **3**. This question was aimed at determining whether people felt that traditional sources of social control in the form of deceased ancestral kin were important. We decided on an ordinal measure because of the corresponding belief that if a person denies the power of deceased ancestors, there is an even greater certainty that he will in fact be harmed. Therefore, those who feared to respond negatively or were unsure of how to respond seemed to be clearly intermediate.

10. *Gratification Pattern*

The nature of gratification patterns was determined by responses to an open-ended question concerning consumption aspirations: "If someone gave you 1000 shillings (C.A. $143), what would you do with it?" The response was coded **3** *deferred goal gratification* if the response indicated that the money would be used for future rewards, e.g. investment of the money in farms, bank savings, school fees, goods for trading, etc.; **1** *immediate goal gratification* if the individuals indicated they would buy a radio, cigarettes, food, etc.; and **2** *mixed* if the response indicated a combination of the two patterns. In table 15.3 we present, in rank order, the frequency distribution of the range of responses on consumption aspirations.

Several recent studies (e.g. Doob 1960; Graves 1967; Rodgers 1967) have been concerned with patterns of goal gratification among individuals in societies undergoing modernization and have noted that the tendency to voluntarily postpone more immediate desires in order to obtain more substantial future rewards is a characteristic of people beginning to modernize. A more complete description of the nature of gratification patterns in this community and their relationship to other measures of modernization has been presented elsewhere (cf. Robbins and Pollnac 1969b).

11. *Self-Identity*

The nature of a person's self-image as a modern person was based on his response to the question "Do you consider yourself to be mainly a traditional Muganda **(1)**, a modern European-type person **(3)**, or a 'mixture' **(2)**?" This item was included because its more subjective nature allowed respondents to map *themselves* onto a modernity continuum, and because one's self-image is a cognitive and motivational system of strong emotional concern. Several anthropologists have investigated and disclosed the crucial relationship of both self-identity and reference group change to rapid sociocultural change (e.g. Berreman 1964; Chance 1965; Goodenough 1966, chs. 8 and 9; Parker 1964; Wallace 1968; etc.).

TABLE 15.3
Frequency and Percent of Consumption Aspiration Responses

Response	Fq.	%	Response	Fq.	%
farming[a]	45	41	bicycle	3	03
trading[a]	27	25	cloth	2	02
school fees[a]	18	17	shoes	1	01
house	13	12	radio	1	01
bank[a]	7	06	cigarettes	1	01
food	6	06	paraffin	1	01
clothes	4	04	wife	1	01
house furnishings	3	03	musical instrument	1	01
sewing machine	3	03	busuuti (women's dress)	1	01

[a] Coded as deferred, all others coded as immediate.

THE RELATIONSHIP OF ARTIFACTUAL TO CULTURAL MODERNITY

The first step in the analysis was to determine whether there is any overall significant relationship between the possession of material artifacts and the expression of modern cultural attitudes. Canonical correlation was used to examine this relationship. With canonical correlation one can determine the strength of association between two *sets* of variables and test the significance of this association. Canonical correlation also provides information that indicates the manner in which the two sets of variables can be combined to maximize their correlation. This information is provided in the form of loadings which indicate the degree to which the individual variables contribute to the canonical variates. This technique was selected for two reasons: first, preliminary factor analyses indicated that we could not assume that either the material or the cultural sets of variables could be reduced to a unidimensional scale; and second, canonical analysis is scale free and thus would not be affected by the mixture of nominal and ordinal scales present in our data. The results of the canonical analysis are presented in table 15.4.

As can be seen, this analysis indicates that the overall relationship between the possession of material items and traditional–modern attitudes is not statistically significant at the .05 level. The reason for this lack of statistical significance with a relatively high canonical correlation coefficient (.64) is that as the number of variables in each set is increased, the probability is also increased that some weighted combination of variables will be highly correlated by chance. See Bartlett (1941) for the rationale of this statistical test.

The contribution that each variable of the two sets makes to the maximum canonical correlation is also presented in table 15.4. The loadings indicate that the attitudes concerning a husband and wife eating at the same table, the

TABLE 15.4

Relation of Modern Artifactual to
Modern Cultural Items: The
Maximum Canonical Vector

Cultural Items		Material Items	
(4)	0.548	(27)	0.519
(5)	0.469	(14)	0.424
(7)	0.411	(21)	0.371
(2)	0.303	(19)	0.361
(1)	0.251	(26)	0.290
(11)	0.200	(28)	0.270
(9)	0.056	(24)	0.104
(8)	0.004	(20)	0.034
(10)	−0.007	(25)	0.020
(6)	−0.056	(23)	−0.123
(3)	−0.103	(15)	−0.128
		(16)	−0.142
		(12)	−0.177
		(13)	−0.219
		(18)	−0.222
		(22)	−0.250
		(17)	−0.374

Canonical Correlation $= 0.64$; $x^2 = 207.9$;
$D_f = 187$; P œ 05; $n = 109$

arrival of a second child before the first is weaned, drinking from a gourd versus a glass, and Kiganda versus European style clothing for women from the cultural item set, and the radio, camera, stove, and wearing of a *Kanzu* from the material item set, are the variables that contribute the most to the canonical vector, which explains most of the variance in the two sets. It should be remembered, however, that this association was not statistically significant at the .05 level.

Since the canonical analysis failed to indicate any overall significant relationship between the material and cultural variables, the next step was to determine whether any of the dimensions derived by means of the factor analyses mentioned above were significantly related. See table 15.5.

Factor scores were calculated for each household on each factor, and these scores were then intercorrelated.[9] The factor score correlation matrix is presented in table 15.6. The correlations between the cultural and material factors are extremely low, and although one correlation reaches statistical significance, it accounts for only 9 percent of the variance in the factor scores of the two factors. Considering that material item factor II and cultural factor II

TABLE 15.5
Orthogonally Rotated Factors (Varimax)[a]

Material Item Factor Analysis					Cultural Item Factor Analysis			
Variable	I	II	III	h^{2b}	Variable	I	II	h^{2b}
12	.253	−.289	.447	.347	1	.676	.069	.462
13	.081	−.536	.184	.328	2	.360	−.320	.232
14	.248	−.610	.221	.482	3	−.095	−.291	.094
15	.055	−.350	.263	.195	4	.140	−.629	.415
16	.004	.022	.249	.063	5	.010	−.203	.041
17	.054	−.408	−.157	.194	6	−.008	.123	.015
18	.402	−.301	.065	.256	7	−.054	.319	.105
19	.125	−.284	.063	.100	8	−.426	−.015	.182
20	.154	−.572	.202	.392	9	.127	−.060	.020
21	.302	−.678	.164	.578	10	.375	.064	.145
22	.232	−.185	.508	.346	11	−.035	−.415	.173
23	.788	−.143	.148	.663	Percent			
24	.405	−.226	.511	.476	Total	8.7	8.4	
25	−.016	−.253	.586	.408	Variance			
26	.124	−.024	.555	.324				
27	.219	−.180	.003	.080				
28	.787	−.149	.241	.700				
Percent								
Total	11.5	13.0	10.4					
Variance								

[a]Initial communality estimates were squared multiple correlations. Final communalities are the result of a maximum of 15 iterations.
[b]h^2 were calculated from the patterns presented. Criterion for number of factors rotated: eigenvalue of 0.7000.

only explain respectively 13 and 8.4 percent of the variance of their respective data sets, the relationship does not have much predictive power.

Stepwise multiple regression was next applied to determine how much we could increase the amount of variance explained by increasing the number of factors used as predictor variables. The criterion variables were the two cultural factors taken singly, and the predictor variables, the material item factors, added in a stepwise fashion in terms of the amount of variance explained. The results of this analysis are also presented in table 15.6. The multiple correlation between the material item factors and cultural factor I never reaches statistical significance at the .05 level, whereas the multiple correlations between the material item factors and cultural factor II are significant at the .01 level at each step. Although statistically significant, this multiple correlation accounts for only 11 percent of the variance, and, considering the amount of the variance in the data set explained by the

TABLE 15.6
Intercorrelations And Multiple Correlations of Material Item And Cultural
Item Factors

	(1)	(2)	(3)	(4)
(1) Cultural Factor I	——			
(2) Cultural Factor II	−.046	——		
(3) Material Factor I	.086	−.173	——	
(4) Material Factor II	−.120	.300	−.096	——
(5) Material Factor III	.137	.021	.120	−.140

R 1.45 = .170 P .05   R 2.34 = .333 P .01
R 1.345 = .181 P .05   R 2.345 = .335 P .01

n = 109

factors involved, the relation, once again, is not very meaningful in terms of predictive power.

The final step in the analysis was to determine the relationships between the possession of specific material items and the expression of specific cultural attitudes. The results of this analysis are presented in table 15.7. They reveal essentially the same pattern of cultural and material item intercorrelation as the canonical, factor, and multiple correlation analyses presented and discussed above. In addition, however, it can be seen that the ownership of an automobile and/or motorcycle is also related to a few cultural items (#6 and #8). These relationships, however, could quite easily be spurious because of the small number of motor vehicle owners (table 15.1).

In general, the results of this analysis support the others to the effect that there is little or no relationship between the ownership of modern material items and the expression of modern cultural attitudes. In fact, the few significant relationships that are present in table 15.7 are close to the number that would be expected by chance.

DISCUSSION AND CONCLUSION

Considering the two original objectives, the results suggest that in terms of the procedures we used, (1) there is little or no overall relationship between the ownership and use of certain modern material and the expression of certain modern cultural attitudes in this community, and (2) because little or no relationship was discovered between the material items on the one hand and the cultural items on the other, and the relationships that were found could rather easily be attributed to chance, the question regarding the best predictor of cultural items from material items becomes inconsequential.

TABLE 15.7
Intercorrelation (Phi) of Material and Cultural Items

Material Items					Cultural Items						
	1	2	3	4	5	6	7	8	9	10	11
12	.096	.112	.023	.024	.007	.080	.061	.070	.065	.080	.171
13	.018	.150	.110	.077	.020	.154	.078	.164	.171	.027	.190
14	.063	.189[a]	.103	.236[a]	.046	.134	.079	.140	.096	.168	.216
15	.029	.165	.076	.077	.020	.111	.066	.102	.109	.202	.053
16	.048	.031	.127	.015	.022	.150	.070	.045	.080	.082	.230
17	.030	.037	.014	.007	.008	.406[a]	.189	.402[a]	.028	.090	.141
18	.009	.081	.036	.067	.029	.351[a]	.140	.347[a]	.075	.119	.057
19	.030	.123	.014	.088	.271[a]	.047	.091	.063	.136	.044	.124
20	.049	.306[a]	.002	.175	.018	.123	.202	.105	.186	.146	.249[a]
21	.101	.298[a]	.089	.188[a]	.008	.120	.097	.120	.130	.123	.131
22	.071	.154	.093	.047	.052	.165	.086	.156	.132	.216	.137
23	.012	.212[a]	.002	.189[a]	.014	.168	.040	.143	.209	.139	.196
24	.006	.105	.128	.093	.028	.129	.110	.150	.117	.070	.118
25	.005	.279[a]	.070	.006	.024	.146	.151	.160	.166	.160	.188
26	.025	.113	.022	.055	.014	.095	.148	.091	.108	.058	.102
27	.114	.180	.079	.364[a]	.132	.104	.132	.082	.126	.063	.208
28	.004	.176	.012	.063	.004	.195[a]	.091	.150	.192	.050	.182

[a]Significant P < .05; n = 105

One possible explanation for these rather unexpected results can perhaps be found in the nature of the differential acquisition of material items within certain subgroups of the population. In this rural region of Buganda, differences in occupation, cash income, land ownership, and formal education have all contributed to a rather marked socioeconomic stratification of the population which bears a strong relationship to age. Of interest here is the fact that there are, among the younger population, individuals with a modern outlook on life acquired from a good deal of formal education and exposure to other modernizing influences (e.g. mass media exposure). Representative of this group would be primary school teachers, clerks, small businessmen, medical assistants, etc. Although less affluent than the older rural elite, they nevertheless possess the desire and economic means to obtain a modern material style of life. Among this segment of the population one can quite ostensibly observe a positive relationship between cultural and material modernity.

In contrast, most older members of the population are peasant farmers who adhere rather strongly to traditional Kiganda culture. They often have little or no education and speak only Luganda. On the whole, they have been comparatively less exposed to modernizing influences than the younger group. With the exception of a few older, wealthy, land-owning families, they tend to lack the economic means of obtaining an elaborate material style of life or participating as intensively in modern sociocultural activities. Moreover, their relatively small cash reserves are often put aside to provide for their children's and younger relative's education. Nevertheless, through them, they have accumulated a rather impressive array of modern material items, particularly those which provide for a more comfortable and efficient lifestyle (e.g. metal roofs, lanterns, bicycles, etc.). It is therefore among this subgroup that one observes the greatest disparity between cultural and material modernity. Given these considerations, we would suspect that the overall relationship between cultural and material modernity for the population as a whole has been obfuscated by the nature of these subgroup differences.

In an effort to explore this possibility, we divided the total sample into two subgroups based on age—those under 40 ($N = 44$) and 40 and older ($N = 65$).[10] Using canonical correlation, the overall relationship between the material and cultural factors (table 15.5 above) was examined within each subgroup. The results of these secondary analyses indicate, as expected, that among the younger group there is a positive and significant relationship ($R_c = .55$, $X^2 = 15.33$, $d.f. = 6$, $p \leqslant .02$) between cultural and material modernity;

whereas among the older group the relationship was not statistically significant ($R_c = 40$, $X^2 = 11.93$, $d.f. = 6$, $p = .05$). These findings suggest that in the present case intrapopulation variation probably contributed to our inability to discover a relationship between material and cultural modernity for the population as a whole.

Perhaps the most significant lesson to be learned from this study is the potential, and in this instance the very real, hazards of making superficial inferences about one domain from the other. While our results are far from definitive and, of course, do not necessarily apply elsewhere, they do seem especially pertinent to research which attempts to use information concerning "material culture" to infer the nature of the nonmaterial culture of both past and present populations. Many archeological investigators, for example, have called for caution with regard to making inferences from material to nonmaterial culture. Eoin McWhite (1956) presents a table of inferences arranged in a series of seven levels corresponding to the degree of abstraction involved. Level seven, the highest, is the psychological level which consists of "complex inferences from material culture to the behavioral and ideological culture of a social group or of an individual person" (p. 5). He warns that on the higher levels of his scale, the inferences become increasingly hypothetical, and that at the highest level, "intuition (in the popular sense of the word) replaces the more logical processes" (p. 6). Willey and Phillips (1958:50) warned that "under special conditions even a primitive population may exhibit revolutionary changes in material culture without losing its identity as a society." Chang (1968:35) agrees with this position and notes that "isolated and idiosyncratic shifts in stylistic tastes and fashions may occur on a grand scale irrespective of the social order which continues." In short, these theorists seem to agree that the degree of reliability in such inferences is in an inverse proportion to the degree of abstraction from the artifacts involved. Recently, L. R. Binford (1968), after citing a number of authors who have subscribed to the preceding position, has attempted to develop an argument against this more cautious approach. We believe that the evidence presented here embarrasses Binford's position (although we do not deny the existence of a relationship between material and nonmaterial culture). David L. Clarke (1968) has argued that the complex relationships involved have "tended to lead to either a desperate oversimplification of the relationship or a denial of its existence" (p. 359). He feels that the solution to this problem lies in the field of social anthropology. The means by which social anthropology can help solve this problem have been exemplified by several authors (Anderson 1969; Ascher

1962; Goggin and Sturtevant 1964; Heider 1967; Robbins 1966a). We feel that our present ethnographic example also supports the cautious position described above. Only with more ethnographic research which quantitatively assesses the empirical relationship between material and nonmaterial culture can we approach a solution to this problem. The solutions are beyond the stage of armchair speculation.

In conclusion, we would also like to suggest that our study supports the value of conceptually distinguishing the phenomenal order of a community's artifacts, events, and surroundings from the ideational order, or culture, of its members. This would appear to be especially important with respect to change. In this instance, there is clearly a lack of correspondence in the direction of change in the two orders for the population as a whole. We do not want to imply, however, that there could never be a strong relationship between them. Hypothetically, long-term sociocultural stability and isolation could potentially result in a more invariant relationship between the two orders. Rather, what we want to stress is the necessity of examining the specific nature of possible relationships, in an empirical manner, before making generalizations about one from the other.

ACKNOWLEDGMENTS

We would like to take this opportunity to acknowledge and express our gratitude for the generous support and assistance of several persons and institutions. In particular we would like to thank the Makerere Institute of Social Research, Makerere University College, Kampala, Uganda, for their help during our tenure there as Research Associates in 1967 and 1969. Our fieldwork in 1967 was supported by a grant from the Agricultural Development Council, Inc. and a National Science Foundation institutional grant administered by Pennsylvania State University. Our fieldwork in 1969 and the data analysis for both periods have been supported by the Wenner-Gren Foundation for Anthropological Research, a grant from the Graduate School Research Support Fund at the University of Missouri, and by a Biomedical Sciences Support Grant, Fr–07053, from the General Research Support Branch, Division of Research Resources, Bureau of Health Professions, Education, and Manpower Training, National Institutes of Health. We would also like to thank Robert Benfer, John Bregenzer, Richard Diehl, James Gavan, Ward Goodenough, Philip Kilbride, Marvin Loflin, John Page, Pertti Pelto, and Ralph Rowlett for reading and commenting on various drafts of this paper.

REFERENCES

Ainsworth, M. and L. Ainsworth. 1962. Acculturation in East Africa IV. Summary and discussion. *Journal of Social Psychology* 57: 417–32.

Anderson, K. 1969. Ethnographic analogy and archaeological interpretation. *Science* 163: 133–38.

Ascher, R. 1962. Ethnography for archaeology: a case from the Seri-Indians. *Ethnology* 1: 360–69.

Bartlett, M. 1941. The statistical significance of canonical correlations. *Biometrika* 32: 29–38.

Berreman, G. 1964. Aleut reference group alienation, mobility and acculturation. *American Anthropologist* 66: 231–50.

Binford, L. 1968. Archeological perspectives. In S. and L. Binford, eds., *New Perspectives in Archeology.* Chicago: Aldine.

Chance, N. 1965. Acculturation, self-identification, and personality adjustment. *American Anthropologist* 67: 372–93.

Chang, K. 1968. *Settlement archeology.* Palo Alto: National Press Books.

Clarke, D. 1968. *Analytical archeology.* London. Methuen and Co. Ltd.

Cooley, W. and P. Lohnes. 1962. *Multivariate procedures for the behavioral sciences.* New York: Wiley and Sons.

Doob, L. 1960. *Becoming more civilized.* New Haven: Yale University Press.

Fallers, L. 1961. Ideology and culture in Uganda nationalism. *American Anthropologist* 63: 677–86.

Fallers, M. 1960. The eastern lacustrine Bantu (Ganda, Soga). London: International African Institute.

Goggin, J. and W. Sturtevant. 1964. The Clausa: a stratified non-agricultural society (with notes on sibling marriage). In W. Goodenough, ed., *Explorations in cultural anthropology.* New York: McGraw-Hill.

Goodenough, W. 1964. Introduction to *Explorations in cultural anthropology.* New York: McGraw-Hill.

Goodenough, W. 1966. *Cooperation in change: An anthropological approach to community development.* New York: Wiley and Sons.

Goodenough, W. 1970. *Description and comparison in cultural anthropology.* Chicago: Aldine.

Graves, T. 1967. Psychological acculturation in a tri-ethnic community. *Southwestern Journal of Anthropology* 23: 337–50.

Heider, Karl G. 1967. Archeological assumptions and ethnographic facts: A cautionary tale from New Guinea. *Southwestern Journal of Anthropology* 23: 52–64.

Holloway, R. 1969. Culture: a human domain. *Current Anthropology* 10: 395–412.

Hotelling, H. 1936. Relations between two sets of variates. *Biometrika* 28: 321–77.

Inkeles, A. 1966. The modernization of man. In M. Weiner, ed., *Modernization: the dynamics of growth.* New York: Basic Books Inc.

Inkeles, A. 1969. Making men modern: on the causes and consequences of individual change in six developing countries. *The American Journal of Sociology* 75: 208–25.

Kay, P. 1964. A guttman scale of Tahitian consumer behavior. *Southwestern Journal of Anthropology* 20: 160–67.

Keesing, R. 1969. On quibblings over squabblings of siblings: new perspectives on kin terms and role behavior. *Southwestern Journal of Anthropology* 25: 207–27.

Kilbride, P. and M. Robbins. 1969. Pictorial depth perception and acculturation among the Baganda. *American Anthropologist* 71: 293–301.

Kilbride, P. 1970. Individual modernization and pictorial perception among the Baganda of Uganda. Ph.D. Thesis, The University of Missouri.

Koons, P. 1962. Canonical analysis. In H. Borko, ed., *Computer application in the behavioral sciences.* Englewood Cliffs: Prentice-Hall.

Laumann, F. and J. House. 1970. Living room styles and social attributes: the patterning of material artifacts in a modern urban community. *Sociology and Social Research* 54: 321–42.

Lebar, F. 1964. A household survey of economic goods on Romonum Island, Truk. *In* W. Goodenough, ed., *Explorations in cultural anthropology.* New York: McGraw-Hill.

LeVine, R. 1970. Personality and change. In J. Paden and E. Soja, eds. *The african experience.* Evanston: Northwestern University Press.

Lewis, O. 1969. The possessions of the poor. *Scientific American* 221: 115–124.

Maxwell, R. 1966. Onstage and offstage sex: exploring an hypothesis. *Cornell Journal of Social Relations* 1: 75–84.

McWhite, E. 1956. On the interpretation of archeological evidence in historical and sociological terms. *American Anthropologist* 58: 3–25.

Mboya, T. 1969. The impact of modern institutions on the East African. In P. Gulliver, ed., *Tradition and transition in East Africa.* Berkeley and Los Angeles: University of California Press.

Parker, S. 1964. Ethnic identity and acculturation in two Eskimo villages. *American Anthropologist* 66: 325–40.

Pelto, P. 1970. *Anthropological research: The structure of inquiry.* New York: Harper and Row.

Peshkin, A. and R. Cohen. 1967. The value of modernization. *The Journal of Developing Areas* 2: 7–22.

Richards, A. 1969. *The multicultural states of East Africa.* Montreal: McGill-Queens University Press.

Richardson, M. and L. Thomas. 1970. Behavioral cycles and land use in Puntarenas, Costa Rica. Paper presented at the Southern Anthropological Society Meeting, Athens, Georgia.

Robbins, M. 1966a. House types and settlement patterns: an application of ethnology to archeological interpretation. *The Minnesota Archaeologist* 28: 3–35.

Robbins, M. 1966b. Material culture and cognition. *American Anthropologist* 68: 745–48.

Robbins, M. and R. Pollnac. 1969a. Drinking patterns and acculturation in rural Buganda. *American Anthropologist* 71: 276–85.

Robbins, M. and R. Pollnac. 1969b. Gratification patterns and acculturation in rural Buganda. Paper presented at the meetings of the Southwestern Anthropological Society, New Orleans.

Robbins, M., A. Williams, P. Kilbride and R. Pollnac. 1969. Factor analysis and case selection in complex societies: a Buganda example. *Human Organization* 28: 227–34.

Robbins, M. and P. Kilbride. n.d. The role of microtechnology in a parish in rural Buganda. In H. Bernard and P. Pelto, eds., *Technological innovation and cultural change*. New York: Macmillan (in press).

Rodgers, W. 1967. Changing gratification orientations: Some findings from the Out Island Bahamas. *Human Organization* 16:200–05.

Rodgers, W. and R. Gardner. 1969. Linked changes in values and behavior in the Out Island Bahamas. *American Anthropologist* 71: 21–35.

Rodgers, E. 1969. *Modernization among peasants: The impact of communication.* New York: Holt, Rinehart and Winston, Inc.

Rummel, R. 1970. *Applied factor analysis.* Evanston: Northwestern University Press.

Schensul, S., A. Paredes and P. Pelto. 1968. The twilight zone of poverty: A new perspective on an economically depressed area. *Human Organization* 27:30–40.

Segall, M., D. Campbell, and M. Herskovits. 1966. *The influence of culture on visual perception.* Indianapolis: Bobbs-Merrill Co., Inc.

Segall, M. n.d. Personal communication.

Smith, D. and A. Inkeles. 1966. The OM scale: A comparative socio-psychological measure of individual modernity. *Sociometry* 4: 353–77.

Southwold, M. 1965. The Ganda of Uganda. In J. Gibbs, ed., *Peoples of Africa.* New York: Holt, Rinehart and Winston, Inc.

Wallace, A. 1968. Anthropological contributions to the theory of personality. In E. Norbeck, D. Price-Williams and W. McCord, eds., *The study of personality: An interdisciplinary appraisal.* New York: Holt, Rinehart and Winston, Inc.

Willey, G. F. and P. Phillips. 1958. *Method and theory in American archeology.* Chicago: University of Chicago Press.

16

GEORGE M. FOSTER

Life Expectancy of Utilitarian Pottery in Tzintzuntzan, Michoacán, Mexico

Paradoxically, what may seem one of the easiest questions for the archeologist to answer proves in fact to be extremely difficult. Even when a site is completely excavated, its boundaries clearly defined, and the preservation of materials excellent, it is exceedingly difficult to determine how long it was occupied, and how many families or individuals lived there. One way to attack this question lies in the search for relationships among time, group size, and the absolute amount of material which litters an abandoned site. All three of these variables are susceptible to quantification, and the last may be determined directly through excavation. Foster uses the controlled context of the ethnographic present to examine one aspect of this problem: the rate at which one class of material, pottery, is created, passes through a society, and is discarded to form part of the archeological record. As Foster realizes, his work provides the first of many steps necessary to move toward this general goal.

The basic problem which confronts Foster is this: How can one move from the specific, in this case a single Mexican community, and derive results applicable in a wide range of archeological occurrences from both the Old and New Worlds? As a first step, he must determine whether within the single village itself any regularity can be discerned. For this reason he compares the rates at which pots are broken in different households. A pattern does emerge, and on this basis Foster may proceed to the second step of his analysis which is to isolate those general factors regulating the frequency of breakage. To be of widespread use, these factors must first account for most

Reproduced, with minor editorial changes, by permission of the Society for American Archaeology from *American Antiquity* 25 (4), 1960.

of the broken pots, and secondly be universal enough in nature so that they apply in a wide range of circumstances. Foster describes five such causes which range from the basic strength of the pot to the expense in time and effort involved in obtaining it. One may then ask the extent to which each of these factors is relevant in any particular archeological situation. As Foster notes, some of them—such as the cause of breakage, or basic pot strength— can be determined through analysis of the sherd itself or of the context in which it is unearthed. This approach provides, in fact, a valuable first step in the desired direction. What next? As Foster and most of the other authors in this section agree, the next step requires the expansion, testing, and refining of such models on the basis of a cross-cultural ethnographic sample to determine which factors have been omitted and which may represent limited cultural idiosyncrasies.

How long does a pot last, on the average, in primitive and peasant communities? Six months? A year? Ten years? How many pots does the average housewife in such communities have in her kitchen? Ten? Twenty five? A hundred? The archeologist is unable to answer these questions for the villages he excavates, for there is no known way to tell how long a sherd served as a part of a functioning vessel before accident overtook it, or how many siblings the vessel had as of a given date. Yet if it were possible to assign an average life to the pottery remnants of a particular archeological site, and if it were possible to estimate the average number of pots in a kitchen, the total sherd count at any period would permit calculation both of population size and duration of occupancy.

Pottery and its uses in contemporary primitive and peasant communities give data which are applicable to this problem. It is not unreasonable to assume that the factors determining pottery use and pottery life today also functioned in similar communities in earlier periods, so that if these factors are recognized and their effect known, archeological interpretation will be facilitated. The data and ideas presented here are a first step in this direction. They stem from research in Tzintzuntzan, Michoacán, Mexico, during the summer of 1959. Tzintzuntzan is a peasant community of about 1700 inhabitants on the shores of Lake Pátzcuaro, 250 miles west of Mexico City. The villagers' most important occupation is manufacturing pottery on a home workshop basis, for local consumption and export over a wide trade area.

The mode of manufacture of Tzintzuntzan pottery has been described in detail (Foster 1948:79–101). Briefly, a "red" and a "white" earth are pulverized and mixed dry in approximately equal quantities, moistened to form the paste, and shaped in or over molds. No temper is added. Neither the wheel nor the simpler methods of coiling or shaping from a single lump of clay are used. Vessels are fired in the primitive circular Mediterranean kiln, introduced by the Spaniards shortly after the Conquest. Most vessels subsequently receive a lead glaze—also a Spanish introduction—and are refired at a temperature of about 900°C. This technique produces a relatively sturdy and durable ware, as compared to unglazed pottery fired without a kiln.

As in most of rural Mexico (and in many city homes as well), the iron age has had little influence in the kitchen: pottery vessels serve to carry and store water, to cook, and as eating and drinking receptacles. With increasing frequency a visitor finds a few glasses and porcelain plates in kitchens, but the bulk of the kitchen economy is based on locally made pottery which comes in a bewildering variety of named forms and sizes (Foster 1948:85).

In this article I report on observations in four kitchens, which reveal something about the range of forms and uses of pottery vessels, the numbers found at a given time, life expectancies of various types, and the factors that cause breakage. Then I summarize the evidence and suggest its applicability to archeological work. Two of the housewives—Otila Zavala and Carmen Peña—are potters who work with their husbands. The other housewives — Micaela Gonzáles (in whose home I lived) and Concepción Tzintzún—buy or receive as gifts all of their ware.

Otila Zavala. Otila cooks on a large, square waist-high *chimenea* with three places for small fires so that several dishes may cook at the same time. Her kitchen has an earth floor. She estimates that eight medium-size, well-blackened cooking pots in daily use range in age from four months to one year. A large casserole, not in daily use, is about five years old, and two smaller casseroles are six months old. About 20 assorted pieces—plates, bowls, pitchers—rest on wooden shelves along one wall; these range from one to five years in age. It is difficult to know exactly, says Otila, since when one breaks it may be replaced from current production, almost without thought. Above the shelves 33 cups *(boleros)* hang on the adobe wall. Most of these are about ten years old, made and hung shortly after she and her husband moved into this house 12 years earlier. They are used mostly for fiestas and large gatherings. Two big unglazed *tinaja* water jars rest on a raised adobe bench against one wall; these are accurately dated at 12 years, since they were set up when the family moved into this house. Otila estimates that a cooking vessel in daily use has a life expectancy of approximately one year. There are about 75 pottery vessels of all kinds in this kitchen. With the exception of a couple of gifts, all were made by Otila and her husband.

Micaela Gonzáles. Micaela and her grown daughters also cook on a raised *chimenea,* and on an oil stove. The small but efficient kitchen has a tile floor. The work of ten different local potters is represented in this kitchen, the accretion of gifts and purchases, the latter made particularly at the time of major fiestas when guests may be expected. A year ago Micaela bought a number of new cooking vessels, and these were the ones principally used at the time of observation. Thus, the milk-boiling pot, the bean pot, the pot for making *nixtamal,* and a frequently used small casserole are all a year old. A second casserole is eight months old. The unglazed water *tinaja,* protected in a wooden frame beneath a filter, is two years old, and should last indefinitely. She recalls a *tinaja,* in another house, which rested on a raised adobe bench against a wall, which lasted, we calculated, more than 22 years; a wandering pig finally bumped into it. The oldest *cántaro* (for carrying water) was acquired four years ago. A large casserole, used only for fiestas, is eight years old. Micaela independently gave the same estimate as Otila for the life expectancy of a cooking vessel in daily use: one year. This kitchen has about 60 pottery vessels of all kinds (this figure does not include numerous flower-pots, found in all Tzintzuntzan homes).

Carmen Peña. Carmen cooks on a low *chimenea* raised less than a foot off the earth floor, and hence pottery is more exposed to wandering animals and children than in the other homes described. Of the cooking vessels in daily use one casserole is two years old, a second six months, and a third three months. Five well-blackened cooking pots were acquired during the Fiesta of Nuestro Señor del Rescate in February—the time of year when most new pottery is acquired—and hence are six months old. A variety of small cooking pots range from brand new to 2½ years old. The *tinaja* is six months old, as is the comal (griddle for tortillas). An enormous *olla de a 2 reales,* used for making the hominy-like *pozole* of fiestas, and with a capacity of 45 liters, is the oldest vessel recorded any place. It was acquired by her husband's grandfather, when he was *carguero (mayordomo* in the more common Latin American terminology) between 40 and 50 years ago. Her kitchen has a total of perhaps 50 pottery objects.

Concepción Tzintzún. This kitchen, with fine *chimenea,* a hood for smoke, tile floor and plastered walls, and large glass windows, is the most modern of the four described. Although data are incomplete, two casseroles in daily use are about 18 months and three years old respectively. Two small cups for drinking chocolate are a year old, and two dinner plates of ornamental *loza negra* and *loza blanca* are about six months old. The *tinaja* under the water filter is about five years old. Other pottery pieces not in daily use are estimated at from one month to six or seven years old. Concha estimates the average life of pottery, types not specified, at four to five years, a figure which seems to me to be disproportionately high. However, it may be noted (see below) that few children and animals have access to this kitchen.

If the data here presented are examined in the light of our knowledge of the productive process and the quality of Tzintzuntzan ware, at least four types of factors—and perhaps five—may be noted that affect the life expectancy of pottery vessels. These factors, while induced from the Tzintzuntzan picture, certainly are true for most if not all pottery-using groups.

1. *Basic strength.* Pottery life varies directly with the hardness of the ware. Tzintzuntzan informants agree that, although there are differences in the quality of pottery finish, the basic strength of the product of all potters is essentially the same. That is, all are apparently equally workmanlike in selecting and mixing clays, in molding, and in firing ware. The strength of Tzintzuntzan ware, therefore, reflects the presence of a primitive kiln permitting 900°C (1652°F) temperatures and the strong lead glaze. The unglazed, burnished *tinaja* ware used primarily for water jars is fired but once, and is less strong. The life expectancy of pottery will be less in villages where lack of the kiln and lack of glaze mean a more fragile ware, other factors being equal.

2. *Pottery uses.* The various uses of pottery are important in determining life expectancy. *Comales* and bean pots are used daily, and, in spite of their glaze, appear to have the shortest life of all. Casseroles, and plates and cups, also in daily use, last but little longer. *Tinaja* jars have a much longer life expectancy; their protected position more than compensates for their greater intrinsic weakness. The very large fiesta pots and casseroles have a long life expectancy, both because they are used only a few times a year, and because they are enormously thick and strong. We are probably safe in saying that cooling and eating vessels in daily use last the shortest time (an average of a year), *tinaja* water storage jars an intermediate time, and festive cooking ware the longest time. This general sequence probably is true in most pottery-using villages, regardless of the quality of the ware.

3. *Mode of use.* By this term I refer particularly to whether cooking is done on or near the ground, on the traditional three-stone hearth or a low *chimenea,* or on a raised stove of some type. Objects that customarily are used at waist height appear to last longer than those customarily used on or

near the ground. Thus, for a housewife who cooks in the traditional fashion on three stones on the ground, a group of pots will not last as long as those used by a second housewife with raised stove. This is true also of water storage jars. If they are enclosed within a frame or raised on an adobe bench they last longer than if they are simply propped in a corner. To the extent that archeological excavations reveal the mode of use of pottery we can hypothesize that—other factors being constant—life expectancy will be similar to, superior to, or inferior to that of Tzintzuntzan, depending on how favorable circumstances are.

4. *Causes of breakage.* The most common threats to pottery longevity appear to be the housewife's carelessness, the fumblings and blunderings of children, and the presence of domestic animals in the kitchen, probably in the order given. Since the first two causes must be more or less constant in most societies, the presence or absence of animals, in conjunction with other factors, is the variable to be noted. In Tzintzuntzan a surprising amount of breakage results from cats, chickens, dogs, and pigs bumping pots or knocking them over. Since only a cat usually climbs, the raised stove offers a great safety factor over an otherwise identical situation, with ground level cooking. From the standpoint of archeological interpretation, we can assume that in those cultures with numerous domestic animals (the Old World) life expectancy—assuming other factors always remain constant—will be less than in cultures with few or no domestic animals (the New World).

5. *Pottery costs.* The foregoing four factors influencing pottery life expectancy are directly observable. The fifth, pottery costs, is logical, but can be proved only on the basis of comparative study. Pottery is inexpensive in Tzintzuntzan. Even for those who are not potters, it does not represent a significant item in the yearly budget. I have never heard dismay expressed when a common pot was broken, and there appears never to be a problem about replacement. The fact that pottery is so easily obtained may lead to carelessness in its use. Perhaps in villages where it is more costly greater care is taken of it, so that technically inferior vessels last longer than would be the case in Tzintzuntzan.

For the guidance of the archeologist who might wish to use the data given here for comparison with a site, I would suggest that the average life expectancy of one year for vessels in daily use is longer, and the average number of pottery objects in a kitchen—50 to 75—is probably higher than will be the case in most prehistoric sites. Tzintzuntzan ware, because of the kiln and glaze, is stronger than most preconquest American pottery and preglaze Old

World pottery. Again, the factors that favor long life—particularly the raised stove—are not often found in early sites. Finally, the speed and facility with which pottery is made in Tzintzuntzan is superior to any other situation known to me, except for advanced wheel-using potters, so comparatively pottery is cheap and plentiful, and can be had in quantity by nearly everybody. Although it is only a guess, I suggest that preglaze, pre-kiln cooking vessels in daily use might better be calculated as having an average life of six months rather than one year.

The data and ideas offered are suggestive of a number of problems. Significant archeological interpretation, however, will require much more comparative material. It would be particularly desirable to have information from contemporary communities where unglazed, open-fired, tempered-paste pottery made by the coiling and other primitive techniques is utilized.

ACKNOWLEDGMENT

My colleague, Robert F. Heizer, stimulated me to make the observations here recorded. Some of the kinds of problems he had in mind are discussed in Baumhoff and Heizer 1959.

REFERENCES

Baumhoff, M. A. and R. F. Heizer. 1959. Some unexploited possibilities in ceramic analysis. *Southwestern Journal of Anthropology* (3): 308–16.

Foster, G. M. 1948. Empire's children: The people of Tzintzuntzan. *Smithsonian Institution, Institute of Social Anthropology, Publication,* no. 6.

17

R. A. GOULD

Some Current Problems in Ethnoarcheology

A common refrain runs through each of the articles in this section: To what extent is the individual society a "typical" or a "unique" case? For if generalizations or specific techniques derived from study of a single group are not applicable, across the board, to the entire range of relevant extant peoples, they cannot serve as a safe framework for the interpretation of past cultures, objects, and events. Recourse to a wide range of ethnographic data—a cross-cultural approach—provides a necessary and desirable stepping stone from the single present-day society to the broad and varied past. Gould has conducted ethnoarcheological research among both Tolowa (California Indians) and Aborigines from the Western Desert of Australia, and the advantages which accrue when sample size is doubled are readily apparent in his presentation.

The sword cuts two ways. On the one hand, useful regularities can emerge and one can speculate, for example, on what constitutes "minimal archeological visibility." Thus Gould may compare a series of Tolowa and Aborigine campsites which range from large to small, long-term to short-term, and suggest where a cutoff point may lie. On one side smaller sites are highly likely to escape future archeological notice; on the other the chances of discovery are great. But cross-cultural comparison indicates that for other aspects of culture no such simple regularities or patterns may be observed. The basic principles used by Tolowa and by Aborigines to classify stone implements are not the same and neither corresponds to the commonly accepted archeological criterion intended to accomplish the identical task. Thus, it seems likely any general classificatory scheme proposed by the

Reprinted, with minor editorial changes, from Monograph 4, Archaeological Survey, Institute of Archaeology, UCLA. Used by permission of the Institute.

prehistorian must be imposed from the outside and cannot reflect the criteria of the tool maker.

Gould also draws the extremely important distinction between continuous and discontinuous models. In the former instance—and this includes his site of Puntutjarpa—a direct genetic link extends from the present back into the past. Provided no major climatic changes have occurred, application of ethnographic data is a relatively straightforward affair. But in the majority of archeological instances a discontinuity separates the past and present; then, Gould argues, the best source for analogy is societies whose environmental settings are most similar.

I shall examine the proposition that there is what can be called an "archeological point of view" which can be brought to bear upon ethnographic evidence in ways that offer valid cultural explanation of excavated data. In applying this point of view to technographic evidence, the archeologist is faced with certain problems. This article is a brief review of some of them; it proceeds on the basic assumption that most if not all of these problems can be solved. The archeologist, as always, is in the position of trying to make the most of limited and intractable data. To be sure, attempts to relate ethnographic and archeological evidence must always be made with caution, but they must be made.

At the outset I wish to distinguish between ethnoarcheology in the general sense and what I have elsewhere referred to as "living archeology" (Gould 1968b). As I would define it here, living archeology is the actual effort made by an archeologist or ethnographer to do fieldwork in living human societies, with special reference to the "archeological" patterning of the behavior in those societies. Ethnoarcheology, as I see it, refers to a much broader general framework for comparing ethnographic and archeological patterning. In this latter case, the archeologist may rely entirely upon published and archival sources or upon experimental results (use and manufacture of pottery, stone tools, etc.) for his comparisons without having to do the actual fieldwork himself. Thus ethnoarcheology may include studies of "living archeology" along with other approaches as well.

THE RISE OF ETHNOARCHEOLOGY

Without attempting a detailed historical treatment, it seems fair to say that American anthropology has pioneered in relating archeological evidence to ethnographic behavior ever since the American Indian was unequivocally accepted as having produced the archeological antiquities of North America. The presence of living Indian societies in areas where stratigraphic excavations were being carried out helped to create an awareness of the continuities between the living people of the historic present and the dead people of the prehistoric past. The first efforts at integrating archeology and ethnography in North America took the form of using archeological evidence to test Indian oral traditions (Fewkes 1893; Hodge 1897; Kroeber 1916), with only partial success. However, interest in integrative studies in archeology and ethnography continued to appear in American anthropology, with a tendency to become broader both in terms of the problems and the regions being studied (Swanton 1928; Parsons 1940; Steward 1942). During the last 25 years, it has become commonplace for American archeologists to use ethnographic evidence to help them reconstruct prehistoric remains and behavior patterns, as is shown particularly by the work of De Laguna in sub-Arctic Alaska, Jennings in the Great Basin, Heizer in California, Larsen, Rainey, and Giddings in Arctic Alaska, Wedel in the Great Plains, and others. In the light of all this interest, it has seemed natural that some scholars, particularly those trained in the American tradition of holistic anthropology, should want to find and study living societies in terms of archeological problems.

This approach has recently come to be called ethnoarcheology, and for the first time a self-conscious, theoretical body of literature has begun to appear on the subject. It should be remembered, however, that American archeologists were making regular use of ethnographic analogies in archeology long before this approach received any kind of formal recognition. On the whole, most of this recent literature has tended to be cautionary in nature, stressing the limitations and ambiguities of this approach.

In approaching the subject of ethnoarcheology, I shall be echoing comments made by Colin Turnbull during discussions at the "Man the Hunter" conference in 1966:

> I have noticed a great difference in the tone of the presentations by archeologists and those of social anthropologists. The archeologists have shown a great awareness of the limitations of their data and the interpretations of it, while the rest of us have all spoken as though we knew what we were talking about. (Turnbull 1968:288)

I would go further, in fact, and suggest that while archeologists have generally been cautious and critical in accepting archeological evidence, they have not always applied this same critical awareness to the evidence offered by cultural anthropologists. The principal misuse of ethnographic evidence in making archeological interpretations occurs when archeologists fail to apply the same rigorous standards of empirical observation which they have developed in their own field to the evidence afforded by ethnography. When this happens, the archeologist finds himself using weak and ambiguous analogies which make assumptions out of the very things he should be trying to find out. Many archeologists today are testing ethnoarcheological approaches in the field, and it is no accident that this is happening particularly in places like North America, Australia, and New Guinea, where there still are or recently have been living traditional cultures in areas where stratigraphic archeology is being undertaken. Can a positive approach be found which, while recognizing the many problems that exist, will make most of these opportunities while they are still present? I shall attempt to provide a framework for such an approach, drawing particularly on evidence gathered in California and Australia to illustrate aspects of it.

THE PROBLEM OF "ARCHEOLOGICAL VISIBILITY"

The problem of "archeological visibility" has three aspects. First, there is the question of preservation of organic materials generally and the fact that what remains in the ground after these materials have deteriorated may not represent a useful sample of the past behavior of the society being studied. This point has been raised by Heider in relation to his studies among the Dugum Dani, a horticultural society of the West New Guinea highlands (Heider 1967) and by Lee in his study of a Kalahari Bushman campsite (Lee 1966). These two studies stress the incompleteness of the potential archeo-logical record in relation to overall behavior in these two ethnographic cases. Also, a cautionary view has been applied to what might be termed the second aspect of this problem, namely the transitory nature of many ethnographic sites (particularly the camps of hunter-gatherers) and the danger that they will not remain visible archeologically due to natural factors like erosion or to cultural factors like disturbances caused when the sites are reoccupied. Deetz has suggested that threshold values of archeological visibility be established on the basis of size, mobility, and intensity of occupation in particular societies, and he goes on to state:

> If in our studies of known hunters in the ethnographic present we were to consider how they relate to this threshold value, we might be able to come up with some statement of minimal "archaeological visibility" which could then be used with advantage in our archaeological interpretation. The Californians are certainly very visible, as are the Upper Paleolithic inhabitants of much of

Europe. Less visible, except at their kill sites, are the pedestrian hunters of the Plains prior to the coming of the Europeans with their horses, or the Shoshonean peoples of the Great Basin. Presumably these groups are well above the threshold, and the Bushmen are below. (Deetz 1968:285)

This view has also been applied to the open-air camps of ethnographic Australian Aborigines by Peterson (1971:242). These ideas have merit and reveal clearly the limitations and obstacles that exist in making archeological reconstructions. In a sense, however, these difficulties have always been recognized, at least implicitly, whenever archeologists have had to consider the ravages of decay and erosion on the prehistoric remains they are studying. These difficulties have arisen, too, in making inferences about the totality of human behavior when most of the evidence available relates to the prehistoric technology and economy or other limited spheres of human activity. Archeologists everywhere must make the most of inadequate samples of human behavior in the form of bits and pieces that survive in the ground.

Finally, there is the third aspect of this problem, namely the risk of skewed and misleading samples of behavior. Thomson, in his studies of the Wik Munkan Aborigines of the Cape York Peninsula of Australia, recognized that:

an onlooker, seeing these people at different seasons of the year, would find them engaged in occupations so diverse, and with weapons and utensils differing so much in character, that if he were unaware of the seasonal influence on food supply, and consequently upon occupation, he would be led to conclude that they were different groups. (Thomson 1939:209)

With cautionary cases like this in mind, archeologists more and more have turned to seasonal models to explain differences in artifact assemblages in different sites within a particular region (Binford 1968:287). Such models are one way the archeologist has of overcoming the limitations posed by such evidence which, if seen in another way, might lead to a complete misinterpretation of the ancient behavior patterns in the region.

In the two principal areas where I have done most of my fieldwork—northwestern California and the Western Desert of Australia—archeological visibility is a highly variable matter. The indigenous cultures of these two areas, though qualifying as "pristine" hunter-gatherers (they show little if any influences from agricultural societies outside their areas [Deetz 1968:283]), represent extremes in the spectrum of hunter-gatherer adaptations. The Tolowa Indians of northwestern California lived in large, almost year-round settlements in a region of high rainfall and dependable seasonal resources, while the Ngatatjara-speaking Aborigines and their neighbors in the Western Desert of Australia adhered to no seasonal pattern in their frequent movement over long distances in small groups in search of water and food. It comes as no surprise that the large Tolowa settlements along the coast should be well-preserved and clearly visible to the archeologist, whereas task-specific seasonal sites like smelting camps along the coast or acorn-collecting camps in the interior are hard to find. Smelting camps, in particular, were occupied only for a short time in late summer, and these sites were located in sand dunes near the shore, where wind erosion is severe. Stratigraphic and cultural associations of Tolowa smelting camps are virtually nonexistent. Interior acorn-collecting camps, though harder to find than other kinds of sites owing to heavy vegetation cover, offer some possibility of stratigraphic associations and will require further research. In the case of the desert Aborigines, most open-air sites, whether habitational camps or task-specific sites like hunting blinds or roasting sites for game, are exposed to wind and surface water erosion and tend not to be preserved stratigraphically. However, exceptions to this rule do occur, in such cases as open-air camps which are partially shielded from heavy winds by nearby rock formations or sites inside rockshelters (no longer inhabited by Aborigines on a regular basis but definitely inhabited in the past). Thus, in these two cases, we can see both examples of and exceptions to the cautionary principles of archeological visibility mentioned in the literature.

THE PROBLEM OF ROCKSHELTER SITES

Archeologists in many parts of the world depend heavily on sequences derived from excavations in caves and rockshelters, yet it is rockshelter sites which present some of the most acute difficulties in the area of cultural sampling. Jelinek, for example, in reviewing the evidence from Tabūn Cave in Israel, has noted that rockshelters tend to be atypical places for human habitation, and the processes of soil and artifact distribution within them tend to differ from those occurring in open sites (Jelinek 1972:15–16). Peterson takes a more negative view of this problem, noting on the basis of his studies of cave sites in Arnhem Land, Australia, that:

> If a single occupation were to survive in a place such as a cave where it might be preserved for many years, the rates of deposition are so slow that a second use of the cave even several hundred years later would result in the mixing of artifacts. (Peterson 1971:242)

While the observations no doubt hold true for many of the rockshelter sites in Arnhem Land and elsewhere in the world, it would be misleading to assume that this must be the case in rockshelters everywhere and at all times. For the ethnoarcheologist, this problem can be viewed as a challenge to find out how and in what ways the evidence from rockshelter sites is skewed and, further, to determine the natural and cultural processes which account for this skewing of the evidence.

Ethnoarcheologists are hampered at the outset, of course, by the fact that few living societies actually live in caves or use them for any appreciable amount of time. Recent publicity surrounding the discovery of the Tasaday, a hunter-gatherer society in the tropical forests of Mindanao, is a case in point, since so much of this publicity has been focused on the fact that these people reside in caves. Another tantalizing ethnographic example, which in this case can no longer be studied firsthand, is that of the Veddas of Ceylon, many of whom were living as hunter-gatherers and were residing in caves into the early 1900s (Allchin 1966:126–27). There are several archeologists who currently think there is a possibility of finding some hunter-gatherer groups in parts of southeast Asia and the Philippines that use caves for at least part of the year and could be studied with the problems of cave use in mind (P. Bion Griffin and Karl Hutterer, personal communication).

Some rockshelters occur in the Western Desert of Australia, although these are used infrequently by the Aborigines. Present-day uses include visits for sacred purposes and shelter from extreme daytime heat or torrential rains while on foraging trips. Aborigines show no reluctance to enter caves, but they do not actually live in them, mainly because at this time none of these caves has a reliable source of water nearby. The Australian desert Aborigines today depend primarily for their subsistence on seven staple plant food species along with a number of supplemental varieties of plants and small game (Gould 1969:258–65, 1970:63–65). Only on occasions when there has been heavy local rainfall for at least two seasons, leading to an abundance of large game (mainly kangaroos, euros, and emus) in the affected area, do large groups come together. The largest groups of this kind range from about 100 to 150 individuals, and they tend to fragment as soon as the hunting starts to decline (Gould 1967:56). Such maximal groupings based upon hunting of large game are exceptional and occur at unpredictable intervals, since rainfall is highly unpredictable throughout the Western Desert region. About three miles from the Warburton Ranges Mission, in the heart of the Western Desert, there is a rockshelter site called Puntutjarpa which was observed by the early missionaries there (from 1934 on) to have been used as a hunting-trap, a function which has been confirmed through interviews with living Ngatatjara Aborigines from this area. Kangaroos and wallabies were driven by means of fire over the edge of the 26-foot-high escarpment in which the rockshelter lies, and they were sometimes roasted and butchered in or near the rockshelter. The rockshelter itself is ideally situated as a hunting camp, since it is elevated high enough to command an excellent view of the acacia-covered plain to the north as far as the Warburton Ranges—an area which in early contact times was exceptionally rich in game when compared to the surrounding desert country. Today the area for several miles around the Mission is denuded of vegetation and poor in game, but this is the result of pressure by abnormal concentrations of populations (300–400 individuals) living year round at the Mission.

So, stated in its simplest terms, the problem in the Western Desert is to consider how remains contained in caves like Puntutjarpa can be related to the economic and seasonal patterns of a society which does not currently use caves as habitations. An interim report on this site has been published (Gould 1971), but some more of the evidence bearing upon this question can be discussed here, since it suggests how Puntutjarpa fit in as one aspect of the overall human adaptation to post-Pleistocene desert conditions in this region.

Stratigraphy and radiocarbon dates at Puntutjarpa indicate that this cave was used and regularly revisited as a habitation site from at least 10,000 years ago until about the time the Warburton Ranges Mission was founded. Large amounts of butchered animal bones, mainly of various species of modern desert macropods (kangaroo, euro, wallaby), were found at every level in the Puntutjarpa excavations. Detailed faunal identifications indicate that only modern species of the same varieties known from the Western Desert in historic times (excluding, of course, all introduced species like rabbits and feral cats) occur there, even as far back as 10,000 years ago (M. Archer, personal communication; Tedford in Gould 1968a:184–85). Carbonized plant remains, recovered by means of flotation, and a small number of stone seed-grinders and grinding slabs have been found, the latter occurring in contexts from 7000 years ago to the present. The carbonized seed remains still await identification, but on present evidence it appears that Puntutjarpa Rockshelter served mainly as a hunting base at which butchering and consumption of game were important cultural activities. This view is reinforced by the discovery of an elongated hearth identical to modern Aborigine earth ovens for kangaroos. This earth oven occurred at a depth between four to six inches below the modern surface and was radiocarbon-dated to within the last 185 years.

Within the excavated portions of the interior of the rockshelter, three clearly defined and well-preserved living surfaces (camps) were uncovered. The earliest ones appeared as two oval-shaped, rock-free areas at the back of the cave, each containing hearths, fragments of butchered animal bones, and stone tools and débitage. Their good archeological visibility resulted from the fact that they had been constructed by removing stones from a layer of rockfall, thus leaving a clear outline of each camp. Radiocarbon dates and stratification indicate that these two camps were reused on successive visits over a fairly long period between 10,000 and 7000 years ago. The other well-preserved living surface occurred directly beneath another layer of rockfall which fell at a later date than the lower rockfall and is preserved stratigraphically in the upper levels of the site fill throughout the interior of the cave. This living surface appears to represent a single season (or at the most a couple of seasons) of occupation until its use was terminated by the rockfall. It contains features like hearths, grinding slabs, chipped stone tools and débitage, and faunal remains. Radiocarbon dating of the hearth material on this living surface indicates that it was inhabited 435 ± 90 years ago. In terms of shape, area, internal features, and artifact contents, all three of these archeological living surfaces closely resemble ethnographic Aborigine camps. In only one important respect do they differ, and that is in the high concentrations of faunal material found in and around them. Most of the 41 ethnographic camps which were mapped and studied in detail in the course of this field study showed far lower concentrations of faunal material, mainly because of the preponderantly vegetarian diet of the people living at these camps.

The data from Puntutjarpa Rockshelter is thus skewed away from the prevailing ethnographic pattern with respect to the occurrence of faunal remains. The fact that the rockshelter forms a semi-enclosed and confined space also enhances this skewing by restricting any scattering of these remains which might normally occur on an open campsite. However, even taking this natural factor into account, the site fill at every level shows extremely high concentrations of butchered and charred animal bones, making it clear that this site was more important as a hunting camp than would be the case for most ethnographic Aborigine camps—with one exception. As mentioned earlier, there are occasions when, under conditions of increased local rainfall (particularly in areas characterized by acacia vegetation), game animals will appear in large numbers and hunting becomes a profitable activity, leading to temporary concentrations of population. Present evidence suggests that, throughout its history, Puntutjarpa Rockshelter was just such a site, which people used to good advantage as a base for hunting large macropods under climatic and ecological conditions much like those of today.

There remains the problem of water at Puntutjarpa. Today the nearest sources of water are Hughs Creek, about 1500 feet away, which contains water only after heavy rains, and a dependable native well about two miles away. However, excavations in the West Cave at Puntutjarpa, about 20 feet west of the main rockshelter and habitation area, revealed the existence of a large pit which has been interpreted as a natural freshwater seepage which was dug out periodically by the Aborigine inhabitants of the site and used as a water hole until abandoned about 3800 years ago. The site continued in use right up to the present, but it probably served less often as a habitation and more as a focus for brief visits, which has been the pattern of use for this site in historic times.

Thus a comparison between excavated data from Puntutjarpa Rockshelter and data on observed ethnographic camp behavior and subsistence among the Western Desert Aborigines provides a cultural explanation for the skewed faunal remains within the rockshelter. Moreover, the Puntutjarpa excavations themselves demonstrate that under certain conditions (in this case of rockfall layers within the cave), the archeological visibility of habitational remains will be better than might have been supposed from the cautionary statements cited earlier. Although it is only a single case, and others will be needed before positive statements can be made, the ethnoarcheological approach used at Puntutjarpa Rockshelter seems to point to a useful way for the archeologist to understand the processes behind the patterning of cave remains.

THE PROBLEM OF NATIVE VS. "ARCHEOLOGICAL" CLASSIFICATIONS OF ARTIFACTS

In any discussion of taxonomic approaches to the classification of artifacts, the recurrent question is asked, "Did the maker of the artifact see it as the archaeologist does?" (Deetz 1971:42). Archeologists have debated this point, with some, like Ford (1954), deciding that archeological types are determined solely by the archeologist for purposes of analysis and others, like Spaulding (1953), assuming that native categories can be inferred through the application of various statistical techniques to the artifact assemblage. With these discussions in mind, and also with an awareness of the "ethno-science" approach to culture being tried by ethnographers like Frake (1962), it seemed worthwhile to investigate the nature of ethnographic classification of stone tools in Tolowa Indian and Western Desert Aborigine culture as a first step toward comparing native taxonomies with classifications offered by archeologists looking at the same material.

In the Tolowa study, five informants were independently shown a collection of 478 chipped stone projectile points (38 were surface-collected from sites within known historic Tolowa territory, and 97 came from an excavated archeological site at Point St. George). These projectile points were exceptionally well made by any standards and showed stylistic elaboration over and above strictly functional considerations. Indeed, their symmetry and regularity of pressure-flaking place them among the finest examples of stone chipping in North America. The informants questioned in these interviews did not manufacture stone tools themselves, but they all conversed regularly in their native Athabaskan language and recalled their older traditions in detail. They all remembered having seen such tools in use, and most had close relatives who had made and used such implements.

Each Indian informant was asked separately to sort the chipped stone points into whatever groupings he thought were significant. The results of these interviews were remarkably consistent and revealed the essential characteristics of the native classification. The largest hollow-base points were identified as harpoon-tips (taliậ). These were set into a groove at the end of a carved bone harpoon-toggle used, they said, mainly for hunting sea lions. As independent confirmation of this statement, it should be noted that many of these large, hollow-base points had been found embedded among the butchered sea lion bones at the Point St. George site, sometimes with broken harpoon-toggles nearby.

Small hollow-base points and tanged points were classed together as arrowheads (ậhậšteytx). These Tolowa informants classified their stone projectile points by function, with size, not shape, as the main criterion. Thus the category based on size and function cross-cuts any which might be based on shape.

The Western Desert Aborigines do not make stone projectile points, nor do they attempt in any way to enhance the appearance of their stone tools by means of retouch and other techniques. Also, unlike the Tolowa, they still were making and using the full range of their stone implements, although tools of metal and glass were coming into common use at the time of this study. But, like the Tolowa, their basic classification of stone tools is based on criteria of function rather than form.

The Western Desert Aborigines classify their flaked stone tools into two categories: purpunpa (tools for scraping hard wood) and tjimari (knives for cutting sinew, fibrous materials, skin, etc.). Purpunpa can range in size from large, hand-held unifacial scraper-choppers (sometimes termed "handaxes") to small discoidal scrapers (adzes) hafted onto ends of spearthrowers or clubs. All show some unifacial retouch along the working edge, which is characteristically steep (an ethnographic sample studied in the Western Desert had a mean edge angle of 67°). Tjimari, on the other hand, consist of steep-edged flakes (most are untrimmed, but a few show some retouch along the working edge) with a mean working edge angle on the order of 39.5°. These are always hand-held in use, although sometimes a small blob of spinifex (Triodia sp.) resin is added as a kind of handle. They are more uniform in size than are purpunpa. In terms of form, these two classes of tool can be distinguished by the cross-section of the working edge rather than in terms of overall shape or size. The Aborigines select and classify flakes according to the angle of the working edge, but this selection is always made relative to the intended function of the tool. That is, if a man needs a tool for scraping hard wood, he selects a flake with a steep working edge, which he then trims and refers to as purpunpa. For the Australian desert Aborigines the important thing about a stone tool is the shape of the working edge—all other considerations of size, overall shape, retouch, and other attributes are of little or no importance. This situation resembles that described by White in his analysis of prehistoric chipped stone tools from the New Guinea highlands, where he suggests, "that retouched and used edges be studied in their own right" by archeologists (1969:22).

In terms of the question asked earlier, it should be clear at least in these two cases that classifications based on shape and size, two of the most widely applied criteria used by archeologists in establishing stone tool types, cannot be expected to give the archeologist an accurate picture of the native classification. Thus it may be unrealistic for archeologists to hope that ethnoarcheological studies will provide unambiguous evidence for relating native and archeological classifications of tool types, at least in the realm of stone tools.

THE PROBLEM OF MODELS IN ETHNOARCHEOLOGY

As stated earlier, the ethnoarcheologist is concerned primarily with establishing ethnographic models, that is, describing patterns of ethnographic behavior which can be usefully compared with patterns of artifacts, faunal and floral remains, and features in archeological sites. The models referred to in this case are general models of the way whole societies adapt to their biotic and geographical surroundings rather than specific models pertaining to archeological details like house construction, artifact typology, and the patterning of butchered animal remains. Such comparisons, if applied in a controlled manner, can give satisfying results, where the "fit" between the ethnographic and prehistoric patterns is close, and where no other model, whether derived logically or on the basis of other ethnographic models, will fit more closely. In looking at work done so far along these lines, there appear to be two basic kinds of ethnographic models which archeologists can use in developing interpretations of their site data: *discontinuous* and *continuous* models.

Discontinuous models can be applied in areas where the ethnographic or historic people no longer lead traditional lives and where the ethnographic literature is incomplete. Here the ethnoarcheologist must derive his interpretive model from ethnographic studies made in an area in which the basic ecology, resources, and technology are similar to those of the area in which he is carrying out his excavations, but where the two areas may be widely separated in time and space. Ascher refers to this as the "new analogy" by which he means, in its simplest terms, the archeologist must "seek analogies in cultures which manipulate similar environments in similar ways" (Ascher 1961:319).

As suggested earlier, this general approach is not new to archeology, though it has sometimes been misused to the point of presenting improbable analogies. Ascher (1961:319–22), Clark (1953:355), Heider (1967:62), and Freeman (1968:263–64) all rightly argue for caution in applying such analogies. However, recent work by White and Peterson in Arnhem Land, Australia, shows that such long-distance analogy can apply convincingly to archeological evidence. In this case the model of transhumant exploitation of different ecosystems at different seasons by the same people, as described by Thomson (1939) for the Wik Munkan Aborigines of Cape York, was applied to the patterning of post-Pleistocene archeological remains from a series of excavated sites in Arnhem Land (an area which lies about 600 air-miles from Cape York). Other, alternative models were considered, too, but the most economical explanation for the archeological patterning at these sites was found to be a transhumant seasonal exploitation of estuary lowland and highland plateau ecosystems by the people rather than the separate occupation of these areas by distinct subcultures (White and Peterson 1969). Although there is no historical or geographic continuity between the Wik Munkan Aborigines and the sites reported by White and Peterson, their arguments for interpreting their excavated data in a seasonal framework are logically convincing.

Continuous models depend upon situations in which the living, ethnographic societies on which the model is based can be shown to be historically continuous with the prehistoric cultures being excavated in the same region. Situations like this are less common than the long-distance analogies discussed above, but they offer an inherently higher degree of probability in interpretation and should be sought out by ethnoarcheologists whenever possible. The more strongly one can demonstrate both continuity and conservatism between the prehistoric and ethnographic culture patterns in a particular area, the greater the probability that the model derived in the present is applicable to the past in that region. The Puntutjarpa Rockshelter site in the Western Desert of Australia, mentioned earlier, offers a case in point. The sequence of human occupation at Puntutjarpa began around 10,000 years ago and has continued uninterrupted to the present day. On present evidence, it appears that the post-Pleistocene human occupation of this part of the Western Desert has been characterized by a remarkably stable and nonseasonal adaptation to an undependable and impoverished physical environment along lines closely similar to that of the present day Western Desert Aborigines. This conservatism is suggested by long-term continuities in the lithic assemblage excavated at Puntutjarpa but is shown even better by continuities in camp structure (as revealed by the ancient campsites found at the site which are virtually identical to ethnographic Aborigine camps), and by continuities in the faunal assemblage. There were changes in certain aspects of the lithic technology, such as the appearance of backed blades and fluctuations in the relative popularity of different kinds of lithic raw materials, but these do not appear to reflect important adaptive changes and were clearly outweighed by the long-term continuities mentioned above.

The ethnoarcheologist may shift from a continuous to a discontinuous model should either of the following two situations occur:

1. There may be further archeological manifestations which fit the continuous model but which lack present day or historic ethnographic examples. In such a case, one can take the continuous model and apply it as a discontinuous model in another region, provided the new area can be shown to have had the same basic ecology in the past as the area in which the model was

developed. For example, the adaptive model developed at Puntutjarpa, which includes both past and present hunter-gatherer adaptations in that region, may also fit other parts of arid Australia. However, most Australian desert Aborigines were not studied from an "archeological" point of view, and the data available in published ethnographies on these other parts of the desert are rarely detailed enough for one to develop models for each area where excavation is planned. Instead, the archeologist will have to apply the Western Desert model to the excavated sequences in these areas, testing each one to find out to what extent the archeological patterning in each of these areas corresponds to the ethnographic model derived from the Western Desert.

2. The archeologist may excavate sequences in which there is an interruption or a cultural break, suggesting an important adaptive change. In such cases, different kinds of models will need to be applied to different phases of the sequence. The excavations at the Point St. George site in northwestern California offer an ethnoarcheologist the opportunity to apply both a continuous and a discontinuous model to the same sequence.

In these excavations, two natural units containing cultural material were distinguished. The upper one consisted of shell midden deposits with stone projectile points, bone needles, stone net-sinkers, and a wide variety of distinctive artifacts making up an assemblage closely resembling that of the ethnographic Tolowa Indians. Although no radiocarbon dates have been obtained for this occupation, this proto-historic midden layer is thought, on stratigraphic grounds, to date sometime between 1000 years ago and the first direct contact with whites in this area in 1828. The cultural materials contained in this occupation layer were labeled Point St. George II. Underlying this midden deposit in one part of the site, there was a layer of smooth, dark brown sand, varying from two to four feet in thickness and containing chipped stone projectile points and other artifacts differing considerably in style from those occurring in the midden levels. This earlier occupation was designated as Point St. George I, and it has been radiocarbon-dated to around 300 b.c. (the earliest evidence of human habitation so far discovered along the northwestern California–southern Oregon coast).

The Point St. George II occupation is clearly the historic antecedent of ethnographic Tolowa culture in this area and can thus be treated within the framework of a continuous model. Ethnographic and ethno-historical research into Tolowa culture has already assisted in many aspects of interpretation of Point St. George II archeological patterning (Gould 1966). However, in view of the stratigraphic change as well as what appear to be important stylistic and cultural differences between Point St. George I and II, it would be inappropriate to apply such a model to Point St. George I culture. As yet, Point St. George I is poorly understood, and further excavations will be needed before enough will be known about the archeological patterning of this phase to justify comparison with any kind of ethnographic model. But when such an attempt is made, it will have to be in terms of a discontinuous model derived from some group other than the historic Tolowa Indians. At this stage of research, it can be seen that the Point St. George archeological sequence can best be interpreted through the application of both a continuous and a discontinuous model, and, no doubt, many other archeological sequences in different parts of the world will lend themselves to this same sort of dual—or multiple-model—ethnoarcheological approach.

In discussing the way the archeologists should view ethnographic behavior, Heider has commented:

> Studies of house-building and pottery-making are all very well, but for the archaeologist the emphasis should be on function and disposal rather than on manufacture: how are houses and pots used, and what happens to them afterwards? (Heider 1967:62)

This statement points the way toward what I have referred to elsewhere as "living archeology" (Gould 1968b), that is, the observed patterns by which material remains like stone tools and débitage, camp structures, hearths, butchered animal bones, and potsherds are arranged by the native inhabitants of sites as they go about their lives. By recording these patterns in a systematic and empirical manner, the ethnoarcheologist is able to build a model which is of use to the archeologist who must try to infer the behavior of ancient people from the patterned material remains in the sites he excavates. This approach has been demonstrated effectively by Stanislawski (1969a, 1969b) in his studies of ethnographic Hopi pottery making and use. Of special interest is the way Stanislawski describes how Hopi potsherds are disposed of or reused in patterned ways which would affect their distribution within the pueblo and thus give clues to the archeologist on how to interpret the potsherds he finds in his prehistoric pueblo excavations. Another example along similar lines recently came to my attention during a graduate seminar at the University of Hawaii. Bonito fishing hooks made of shell on San Cristobal in the Solomon Islands are distinctive in terms of form, yet are found infrequently in coastal sites known to have been associated with bonito fishing. When one studies the actual behavior of bonito fishermen on San Cristobal, it is clear that most fishhooks are lost at sea, either because they are broken and discarded or because the line breaks and they are carried away by the fish (M. Kaschko, personal communication). For the archeologist working in this area, the relative absence of bonito fishing hooks in coastal sites does not necessarily indicate a relative absence of bonito fishing as an activity.

These examples, as well as the case I have described from the Western Desert of Australia, suggest that the archeologist as ethnographer works most effectively when his approach is site-oriented. Each site is a particular case of patterned behavior, whether the site is ethnographic or prehistoric, and any ethnoarcheological model, if it is to be useful to the archeologist, must be based on observations that describe the human behavior and/or natural phenomena that account for the patterning of material remains at particular sites. Later, after one has described each case, it should be possible to relate the array of different ethnographic sites into a systemic model which can then be used for comparison with prehistoric site remains. Ideally, the archeologist will eventually uncover an array of contemporaneous sites of different kinds, but, owing to factors of poor preservation and archeological visibility, the chances are that he will recover only a few site types which represent only a fragment of the whole cultural system. His job will then be to fit that fragment of prehistoric behavior into a wider model which offers a reasonable approximation of the whole cultural system. This site-oriented view offers a way of reconciling the somewhat idealistic aims of systemic archeology with the realities of poor archeological preservation. As Heider correctly points out, simple and unempirical ethnographic models are likely to be ambiguous and misleading (1967:63). So, too, are approaches "framed in terms of areas rather than sites" (Peterson 1971:246), since they lack the specific archeological detail of cultural patterning needed by the archeologist as the first step in relating his data to an ethnographic model. I would restate this by saying, "Sites first, and then areas."

ACKNOWLEDGMENTS

I would like to acknowledge, with thanks, the advice and criticism offered by David Tuggle on this manuscript and also for the ideas suggested by P. Bion Griffin, Carmel White-Steiger, and Leslie G. Freeman in discussions.

Thanks go, too, to the Social Science Research Institute of the University of Hawaii for its assistance in preparing the manuscript for publication. Responsibility for the views expressed in this paper is, of course, mine.

REFERENCES

Allchin, B. 1966. *The stone-tipped arrow,* New York: Barnes and Noble.

Ascher, R. 1961. Analogy in archaeological interpretation. *Southwestern Journal of Anthropology* 17:317–25.

Binford, L. R. 1968. Discussion on archaeological visibility of food-gatherers. In R. B. Lee and I. DeVore, eds., *Man the hunter,* pp. 285–87. Chicago: Aldine.

Clark, J. G. D. 1953. Archaeological theories and interpretations: Old World, in *Anthropology Today,* Kroeber (ed.), pp. 348–60. Chicago: University of Chicago Press.

Deetz, J. 1968. Discussion on hunters in archaeological perspective, In R. B. Lee and I. DeVore, eds., *Man the hunter,* pp. 281–85. Chicago: Aldine.

—— 1971. *Man's imprint from the past.* Boston: Little, Brown.

Fewkes, J. W. 1893. A-wa-to-bi: an archaeological verification of a Tusayan legend. *American Anthropologist* 6:363–75.

Ford, J. A. 1954. The type concept revisited. *American Anthropologist* 56:42–53.

Frake, C. O. 1962. Cultural ecology and ethnography. *American Anthropologist* 64:53–59.

Freeman, L. G. 1968. A theoretical framework for interpreting archaeological materials. In R. B. Lee and I. DeVore, eds., *Man the hunter,* pp. 262–67. Chicago: Aldine.

Gould, R. A. 1966. Archaeology of the Point St. George and Tolowa prehistory. *University of California Publications in Anthropology* 4:1–41.

—— 1967 Notes on hunting, butchering, and sharing of game among the Ngatatjara and their neighbors in the Western Australian Desert. *Kroeber Anthropological Society Papers* 36:41–66.

—— 1968a Preliminary report on excavations at Puntutjarpa Rockshelter, near the Warburton Ranges, Western Australia. *Archaeology and Physical Anthropology in Oceania* 3:161–85.

—— 1968b Living archaeology: the Ngatatjara of Western Australia. *Southwestern Journal of Anthropology* 24:101–22.

—— 1969 Subsistence behavior among the Western Desert Aborigines of Australia. *Oceania* 39:253–74.

—— 1970 Journey to Pulykara. *Natural History* 79:56–67.

—— 1971 The archaeologist as ethnographer: a case from the Western Desert of Australia. *World Archaeology* 3:143–77.

Heider, K. G. 1967. Archaeological assumptions and ethnographic facts: a cautionary tale from New Guinea. *Southwestern Journal of Anthropology* 23:52–64.

Hodge, F. W. 1897. The verification of a tradition. *American Anthropologist* 10:299–302.

Jelinek, A. J. 1972. A consideration of the evidence for seasonal patterns in the paleolithic cultures of the Near East. Paper read at the Conference on Seasonality and Prehistory, School of American Research, Santa Fe.

Kroeber, A. L. 1916. Zuni potsherds. *Anthropological Papers of the American Museum of Natural History* 18:1–37.

Lee, R. B. 1966. Kalahari-1: a site report. In *The Study of Early Man*. Anthropology Curriculum Study Project.

Parsons, E. C. 1940. Relations between ethnology and archaeology in the southwest. *American Antiquity* 5:214–20.

Peterson, N. 1971. Open sites and the ethnographic approach to the archaeology of hunters-gatherers, in *Aboriginal Man and Environment in Australia,* Mulvaney and Golson (eds.), pp. 239–48, Canberra.

Spaulding, A. C. 1953. Statistical techniques for the discovery of artifact types. *American Antiquity* 18:303–13.

Stanislawski, M. B. 1969a. What good is a broken pot? An experiment in Hopi-Tewa ethnoarchaeology. *Southwestern Lore* 35:11–18.

—— 1969b. The ethno-archaeology of Hopi pottery making. *Plateau* 42:27–33.

Steward, J. H. 1942. The direct historical approach to archaeology. *American Antiquity* 7:337–43.

Swanton, J. R. 1928. The interpretation of aboriginal mounds by means of Creek Indian customs. *Annual Report of the Smithsonian Institution for 1927,* pp. 495–506.

Thomson, D. F. 1939. The seasonal factor in human culture. *Proceedings of the Prehistoric Society* n. s. 5:209–21.

Turnbull, C. 1968. Discussion on the use of ethnography in reconstructing the past. In R. B. Lee and I. DeVore, eds., *Man the hunter,* 288–89. Chicago: Aldine.

White, C. and N. Peterson., 1969. Ethnographic interpretations of the prehistory of Western Arnhem Land. *Southwestern Journal of Anthropology* 25:45–67.

White, J. P. 1969. Typologies for some prehistoric flaked stone artifacts of the Australian New Guinea highlands. *Archaeology and Physical Anthropology in Oceania* 4:18–46.

» 18 «

MICHAEL B. STANISLAWSKI

Ethnoarcheology of Hopi and Hopi-Tewa Pottery Making: Styles of Learning

Compare the articles in this section. Each uses the controlled context of the ethnographic present, yet in each case the questions asked, and the final goal, are different. Yellen examines faunal remains to seek "patterns" of potential value in cross cultural comparison of assemblages. Robbins and Pollnac are interested primarily in ideology and try to determine if ideological differences between individuals are reflected in their material belongings. Foster wants to know if group size and length of occupation at a particular site can be determined through quantitative analysis of debris, and Gould searches for ways to reconstruct subsistence activities. Stanislawski, however, considers quite a different question. Is it possible, he asks, to reconstruct social structure from observed regularities in archeological remains?

He raises several interesting points. First, he notes that a particular ethnographic regularity on which more than one archeologist has depended—that female Hopi-Tewa learn the pottery-making procedure from their mothers—had, in fact, never been specifically confirmed in the field although it was, and still is, possible to study this question. In the course of a single summer's work, Stanislawski and his wife neatly lay this assumption to rest. In retrospect one may ask why it took so many years before someone decided to undertake the relatively straightforward fieldwork necessary to validate or refute this point.

Secondly, Stanislawski illustrates, by example, the value of participant observation. He argues that this approach, where feasible, is superior to study of museum specimens, ethnographic documents, and interviews with informants about "old objects" which are no longer used. What archeologists dig from the ground—with the exception of written documents—are the end products of actual, rather than ideal behavior. How people act, how they say they should act, and how, in fact, they remember acting in the past rarely coincide exactly. Thus, even if Hopi-Tewa informants would tell the ethnographer that mothers teach their daughters how to make pots, this idealized statement is not a sufficient basis for archeological interpretation. What one wants to know is just how often people conform to this stated norm. Suppose only 50 percent of mothers and daughters follow this rule? Will this be sufficient to result in a pattern which may be described by some future-day archeologist? To what extent, in any particular situation, is compliance necessary before observed data fit the predicted pattern? Ethnoarcheological studies can, and should, be devised with such aims in mind.

> It cannot be that axioms established by argumentation
> can suffice for the discovery of new works, for the
> subtlety of Nature exceedeth many times over the subtlety
> of argument.—Francis Bacon.

I discuss two major things in this paper: the relationship of ethnoarcheology and "scientific" archeology within the general field of archeology in the 1970s; and, by way of example, the present techniques and social meaning of pottery making among the Hopi and Hopi-Tewa of northeastern Arizona. The data presented in the second half of the paper are based on direct ethnographic field observations and interviews during the summers of 1968–73. The study was designed to fall within the field of ethnoarcheology, which I define as "the direct observation or participant observation study of the form, manufacture, distribution, meaning, and use of artifacts and their institutional setting and social unit correlates among living (generally nonindustrial) peoples." This kind of study can contribute to the development of more probable and more testable hypotheses and theoretical models in archeology. For example, it can enable us to better explore the nature and limitations of archeological analogy and inference; to consider alternative methods for the development of the explanatory models used by modern archeologists in their attempts to reconstruct the processes of social evolution; and to collect and preserve ethnographic information on material culture products and their social contexts in the American Southwest, so that, in the future, generations of anthropologists might have a better baseline from which to analyze social change.

In addition, the data presented concerning the origin and transmission of a new style of Hopi and Hopi-Tewa whiteware pottery can serve as a test case concerning the transmission, learning, and change of pottery-making techniques in the Western Pueblo Southwest. (Additional specific data are now in press: Stanislawski 1975; Stanislawski and Stanislawski 1975; Stanislawski et al. 1975; or have been published: Stanislawski 1973 and 1974a.)

Finally, the material is also used in discussing a matrilocal-matrilineal model of transmitting the learning of pottery-making styles and their social unit correlates. William Longacre, James Hill, and others suggest and utilize this model to reconstruct and explain social organization in the prehistoric Southwestern Pueblo area. Much of the theoretical discussion is devoted to this problem.

THEORETICAL BASE

Systems Archeology

The proponents of "systems" archeology wish to study cultural evolution in terms of systems of interaction and adaptation. These interrelated systems may be cultural or ecological. The cultural systems, involving at least sociological, technological, and ideological artifact indicators, seem to be considered in functional terms, similar to Malinowski's definition of an Institution of Culture (Malinowski 1943). Thus the goals or functions of such institutions should, in part, be directly related to the nature of the artifacts involved: and these, in turn, should reflect the nature of the systems of adaptation involved. This is important, for as archeologists we can only study man's artifacts—i.e., any object made, modified, or used by man, which is then the preserved physical end result of man's activities. Thus it is only from the formal, contextual, and temporal study of these artifacts that we can hope to reconstruct possible models of prehistoric man's activities, systems of interactions, and cultural evolution. In the words of Binford (1962:217), artifacts "represent the structure of the total cultural system," and there is no real dichotomy between material and nonmaterial culture (Binford 1968a:21).

As Flannery has recently stated the problem (1967:120), then, our first-stage goal is "to discover the role of the trait or implement by determining what it is functionally associated with"—in short, to discover the nonrandom clustering of elements in a site. All possible correlations between artifact components, artifacts and other artifacts, and artifacts and their social and environmental contexts must be studied in order to reconstruct processes of cultural interaction. When we understand these processes we may "reconstruct the events which form the context in which the archaeological record was produced" (Binford 1968a:12); or as Longacre (1968:91) has recently put it, "the patterning of material remains in an archaeological site is the result of the patterned behavior of the members of an extinct society . . . this patterning is potentially informative as to the way the society was organized . . . the patterned relationships among classes of artifacts should document the context in which they were made, used, and lost or abandoned. . . . the structure of this covariation, once delimited, should reflect the organizational and behavioral aspects of the society that produced it."

However, Binford argues that in each different class of artifacts is a variety of independently varying attributes, each of which may be related to a different set of ultimate determinants. Each determinant might inform us about a different aspect of the total cultural system of the past (Binford 1968a:22). Thus, "there is no reason to expect that our units of observation are, in their form and distribution, referable to the operation of a single variable in the past" (Binford 1968a:24). It will not be easy to judge which are the important variables. We must try to understand all possible correlations of artifacts, all the variability in the archeological record, in order to formulate laws of cultural dynamics. For this purpose, it is of course assumed that the artifacts the excavator has found are in the position their makers and users left them in; that they were lost or abandoned at about the same time during one, or a few, similar events; and that there has been no disturbance, no mixing, and no reuse of materials by members of a different, or more recent, group. However, these conditions are not always to be expected. Recent work of my own on the Hopi Mesas (Stanislawski 1969a) suggests that Hopi and Hopi-Tewa potters frequently collect, stockpile in their homes, and reuse potsherds of their own make, of other potters' manufacture, and from prehistoric ruins nearby. Thus any stratigraphic unit counts made by future archeologists working on prehistoric or modern Hopi Mesas sites might be seriously misleading. There is also evidence of similar *prehistoric* reuse and reassort-ment of potsherds in northeastern Arizona. A. J. Lindsay (1968) has noted the use of potsherds as chinking in the mortar of prehistoric Pueblo house walls, in a manner reminiscent of their Hopi and Hopi-Tewa use today.

ETHNOARCHEOLOGY: THE DEVELOPMENT AND USE OF ANALOGY MODELS

Even if we assume that the necessary data may be accurately preserved for us, how do we work out a few reasonable models which will allow us to penetrate the maze of alternate explanations? According to Flannery (1967) and Binford (1968a, 1968b), we maintain the following approach: first, we collect ethnographic information emphasizing material culture (hopefully from members of a group whose cultural history and assemblage of artifacts show direct historical continuity with those of the archeological site); second, we make one or several analogies between the general classes of artifacts of a site, and those similar ones made by members of the nearby living group; third, based on the distribution pattern of the artifacts of this living group, a prediction is made as to the pattern of the archeological debris left by the prehistoric group; a prediction is made as to the pattern of the archeological debris left by the prehistoric group; fourth, we test this model against the actual remains found; fifth, if there is a match, we may attempt to "explain" the cultural meaning of the distribution of prehistoric artifacts by reference to the meaning of the modern distribution; or, if there is *no* match, or an imperfect match, there may then result a new class of data, the difference between observed and expected, and the attempt to explain this may lead to new inference models for testing. Thus archeology may go beyond what we may observe of present living groups, for there has inevitably been change from past to present. We can and must learn more than an ethnographic analogy alone can contribute, for there are problems that the ethnographer cannot clarify for us, such as covariation of traits not now found among living peoples, or cultural change processes over long periods of time.

Binford's major point is that we cannot *prove* our statements by reference to ethnographic analogy alone, for archeological "facts do not speak for themselves" (Binford 1968a:13). We must test all such analogy models, as any scientific hypothesis must be tested for verification. In this process we may be able to produce comparable measures of verification in statistical terms (e.g., Hill 1968:139). Binford does note that studies of direct historical continuities are important, and that we are thus indebted to ethnographers for providing us with much information concerning form, function, and structure of existing cultural systems which can serve as models for our hypothesis building and the testing of these hypotheses. He particularly mentions modern "action archeology" studies (1968b:268–73).

This need for ethnographic information for archeological model building and testing has led some other archeologists to suggest that entire horizontal stratigraphic settlement levels should be cleared at one time, and that the archeologists involved should have ethnographic experience with living peoples similar to those who might have inhabited the archeological site settlement. For example, Richard Lee (1968:345–46) and Morton Fried

(1968:351) suggest that we offer graduate programs in "interpretive archeology," wherein the student would do ethnography, living with a nonwestern group for three to six months in order to collect information useful for archeological analysis in his area. In particular, Lee notes the need for anthropologists to "study the actual fit between the observed post-marital residence pattern and the distribution of stylistic techniques and technology" (1968:346). Moreover, archeologists will have to do this work. DeVore (1968:349) points out that social anthropologists have simply not provided us with much adequate material for archeological testing; but he and Karl Heider (1967:62) warn that a variety of ethnographic models for testing must be provided, not just one "paternal" hypothesis model. Possibly the emphasis to be followed might be that suggested by Heider, i.e., an emphasis on function (use) and disposal rather than manufacture. He would apply a double test: ask one student to translate a living culture to archeological remains, and then ask another group to translate this set of remains back to living culture. This, he says, should reveal the difficulties of archeological reconstruction of systems or events. It should be recognized that there are several ways to collect the ethnographic information which can be used for general or direct historical analogies and the inferences from them.

First, we may study preserved museum collections, or collect data published in the literature by ethnographers, archeologists, and historians referring to the use and disposal of material culture products of members of a society perhaps now extinct or acculturated to our way of life. In many cases, though, such studies do not analyze comparable sociocultural units or problems, and even if they do, the data presented may not meet modern demands of classification or precision.

Second, we can ask individual members of a living nonwestern society assumed to represent the descendants of the people who inhabited the archeological site under study to view the prehistoric artifacts, or see them at the site in context; and we can then question these informants as to the manufacture, distribution, use, and disposal of these items in their native cultural contexts. However, using individual informants, as Anderson points out in his excellent discussion on Hopi-Kayenta Anasazi analogy and interpretation (1969), results in a short discussion of the object out of its original context by men or women who may not themselves work with such specific materials, and may themselves not have frequently seen them before. Such isolated informants who willingly come from their villages may be the more acculturated members of the population, and less aware of the traditional patterns. Anderson notes that contradictory evidence may be presented by such informants, or may be perceived by the anthropologist in terms of the contrast between the informant's statements and archeological context of the object (Anderson 1969:136–37). Thus, taken out of context, all informants' responses are subject to doubt. The informant may have a strong desire to please the anthropologist by giving an answer whether he knows it or not. Finally, many artifacts are multipurpose tools, and thus no one informant's data may be adequate.

Third, we can live with members of a nonwestern society and observe as a participant the social use, meaning, distribution, and disposal, and infer function. This type of approach to analogy and inference seems to me to be much the most reliable. We can observe the full range and original contexts of the materials, collect information on the ideal and the real, and observe the individual variations which may occur, and which may be the basis of innovation. There is less chance of the anthropologist or an acculturated informant subtly altering the meaning of the material by unconscious reference to the standards of his own society.

Thus ethnoarcheology techniques will put us on safer paths of comparison than any other single form of analogy building, and may suggest the best models for testing. Moreover, if, as Binford has said, each artifact may be the result of the operation of a multitude of past variables, if many artifacts are multipurpose tools, and if, as Ascher (1961:322) and Heider (1967:62) say, there is nearly always more than one ethnographic analogy model which may apply, then data on a *number* of equal and alternate models will need to be collected, used as multiple working hypotheses, and tested for best fit. If archeological facts do not speak for themselves, neither does one logical ethnographic model speak for any, or all, similar archeological situations. Observation studies, revealing the range and complexity of ongoing material culture systems, appear to be an essential part of any systems archeology study.

CERAMIC ANALYSIS AND THE RECONSTRUCTION OF PREHISTORIC SOCIAL SYSTEMS

One of the major interests of systems archeologists who have worked in the prehistoric Pueblo Southwest is that of the reconstruction of prehistoric social units and processes (e.g., descent, coresidence, corporate or noncorporate units, extent of social integration). This is done by the analysis of the spatial distribution, context, and covariation of specific stone and ceramic types and elements (e.g., Hill 1967, 1968; Leone 1968; Longacre 1964, 1966, 1968; Martin 1964). Many of the studies noted above have been done in the analysis of material from sites in the area of eastern Arizona which have been identified both ethnographically and archeologically (post 1000–1150 a.d.) as Western Pueblo (Eggan 1950, 1966; Reed 1950),and are presumably ancestral to the modern Hopi and Zuni societies. For several reasons, Southwestern archeologists have frequently chosen to analyze pottery. In the first place, we still can study pottery making among living groups (Guthe 1925; Bunzel 1929; H. S. Colton 1953; Stanislawski 1969a, 1969b) who are directly related to prehistoric groups—for example, those of the Hopi Mesa region (Eggan 1966; Woolf and Dukepoo 1969). Second, pottery has been made in the Southwest for more than 2000 years, and has been one of the major containers for storage, cooking, etc. Once fired it is relatively permanent, but it is highly breakable and frequently needs to be replaced, providing the archeologist with a quantity of artifact data spanning thousands of years. Thirdly, because of the need for many pots, and their frequent breakage, pottery has had to be continuously hand-produced, generation after generation. Kubler (1967:71) notes "sustained repetition of any sort is impossible without the drift occasioned by tiny unwanted variations." Each pot made must vary from the last one, even the last one produced by the same potter. Watson Smith (1962) lucidly discusses this problem of ceramic variation as it applies to the analysis of the prehistoric Hopi pottery of the village of Awatovi. Southwestern pottery making gave free rein to the maker in terms of change, for the variations in forms made from the plastic clay, the variations in color, slip, design layouts, panels, and motifs is nearly endless—not to mention the variations in manufacture, temper, firing, molding-smoothing-polishing, paint types, etc. Finally, Southwestern pottery may be quite precisely dated (often to the generation) by a combination of stratigraphic correlation, radiocarbon dates, and most importantly, by the absolute dates achieved by use of the dendrochronology method (Breternitz 1966).

Thus the analysis of ceramic artifacts should give us a very sensitive indication of style change through time; and if we measure the covariation of ceramic artifacts, burials, and architectural units, "this patterning is potentially informative as to the way the society was organized" (Longacre 1968:91).

William Longacre (1964, 1966, 1968) has been particularly noted for his application of systems-archeology techniques to Southwest archeology and social-unit reconstruction, and thus a brief discussion of his published work may serve as a convenient starting point. In his work specifically on the archeological patterns of the Carter Ranch site in east-central Arizona, Longacre proceeded as follows:

First, a detailed design-element analysis was made from a sample of over 6000 potsherds, resulting in classification of 175 design attributes which he then plotted in distribution throughout the site. In addition, several major pottery types were recognized and their distribution plotted.

Second, it was found that the design elements tended to cluster in association with room, burial, kiva, and other site features in a nonrandom way, so that three major room-kiva-burial clusters were postulated. In addition, five major clusters of pottery types were recognized to be in direct correlation with architectural units.

Third, it was found that certain design elements, and the five major pottery type clusters, were seemingly associated with certain blocks of rooms within these three major room clusters.

The assumptions made in explanation of these nonrandom associations of types and design elements at the Carter Ranch Site were based upon Longacre's reading of the ethnographic literature concerning living Western Pueblo groups, and the perceived analogies between the artifacts and their cultural meaning for the groups (as described in the literature) and his artifact classes from the Carter Ranch Site. Longacre felt that in the past as in the present the females would probably be the potters, that descent would probably be matrilineal, and that the lineage would be organized in corporate clan groups.

From the data suggesting the nonrandom clusters of ceramic elements in the prehistoric site, and utilizing the ethnographic models drawn from descriptions of Western Pueblo society, Longacre suggested that matrilineal descent and matrilocal residence may have been practiced in the past, and that design elements and techniques were probably inherited in the female line, with the daughter following the mother's ceramic techniques (perhaps often unconsciously). Thus the same pottery types and design elements would be made by members of the same lineage, and would be associated with the lineage homes in the same room block along with the lineage kivas, burials, and other features. He also suggested the corporate nature of such prehistoric matrilineal-matrilocal units, the multiple function and differential use of rooms in the room blocks, and the sexual division of labor found in modern Western Pueblo groups.

Recently Longacre has somewhat retreated from this position and has noted in conferences and in at least one footnote in the literature (1968:100) that it is very difficult, if not impossible, to infer descent rules from archeological data. Deetz (1968) and Hill (1966) have also made this point. However, many scholars are still utilizing some of the original contentions (e.g., Binford 1968b:270; Hill 1966:17, 21, 23); other scholars have extended the possible correlation of ceramic type and design and lineage unit (particularly within the context of matrilineal and matrilocal society) to the eastern United States (e.g., Whallon 1968); and Longacre himself, in a paragraph immediately following his recent cautionary footnote on the subject, apparently continues to make such inferences, at least at the level of "likely" possibility (Longacre 1968:100).

Overall, it is important to note that the premise of this interesting and logical-sounding ceramic teaching model hypothesis explaining ceramic clusters in prehistoric Pueblos had never been tested by direct-observation ethnographic field techniques. In short, the validity of the *antecedents* of the hypothesis was unproven, leading to the possibility that a circular argument was involved, resulting in what philosophers of science call "the fallacy of affirming the consequent"—i.e., the danger of assuming that a correct hypothesis prediction thus also validates all of the *conditions* stated in the hypothesis (e.g., Salmon 1973; Morgan 1973).

Longacre, in primary support of his hypothesis, cites statements of Ruth Bunzel (1929) that each Southwestern Pueblo village or group had its own ceramic ware by 1925, that typical village forms are guided by a definite (if unconscious) sense of ideal form, and that women said that they had learned to make pottery from their mothers. However, in addition to these quoted statements, Bunzel *also* noted: "It is therefore of particular significance, not that all women mention their mothers' teachings, which is natural, but that practically all recognize other sources of inspiration as well" (1929:54). She says that Hopi women in the 1920s frequently acquired ideas from the study of prehistoric potsherds and borrowed designs within the village and between villages, and that ceramic manufacturing was performed in potting groups composed of relatives and friends. Each woman used a slightly different set of designs, she said, although any woman could use any particular designs of the Pueblo if she wished (1929:57, 63–68). Bunzel does *not* say that any particular style of pottery or set of designs is associated with individuals or particular social groups; she stresses the individuality of the pottery, and the alternate learning models that may apply.

Thus these premises (antecedents) of the model suggested by Longacre, Hill, and others were not yet supported by evidence from the field; our fieldwork was designed, in part, to consider this model and its antecedent conditions as one example of the possible value and contributions of ethnoarcheology.

THE HOPI AND HOPI-TEWA CERAMICS PROJECT

The Modern Hopi and Hopi-Tewa

In the summers of 1968–70 my wife and I lived in traditional Hopi houses in the village of Polacca, below First Mesa in northeastern Arizona; in the summers of 1971–73 we worked out of the Museum of Northern Arizona, Flagstaff. We had the opportunity to observe and interview more than 40 Hopi and Hopi-Tewa potters from five villages and two farm settlements. We used open-ended, nondirective interview techniques for the most part and were never able to take notes, pictures, or drawings in front of any of the women or men. We interviewed and observed each potter at least twice, and more than a dozen potters have been interviewed intensively over the five seasons of work.

We also studied traders' collections at several nearby posts, and in Winslow, Flagstaff, and other nearby towns. We photographed and studied the Hopi ceramic collections of the Museum of Northern Arizona, and studied the collections in the Arizona State Museum, Tucson, and the Lowie Museum in Berkeley, California; we photographed and studied all the pottery submitted and sold at the 1968–70 Hopi Craftsman exhibits at the Museum, and records on all of the Hopi shows back to 1930. We thus have a large amount of information about specific pottery made by specific individuals from each of the First Mesa villages, and several Second and Third Mesa villages as well.

Genealogies have been structured by the use of interview data, the 1938 Hopi Tribal Census, and B.I.A. Keams Canyon Agency records. A major difficulty in all such studies is that the Hopi and Hopi-Tewa dislike using their own names, or those of relatives or friends, and are particularly unhappy about using the name of any person now dead (e.g., Woolf and Dukepoo 1969:31). Moreover, their names may change several times during their lifetimes, following renaming at important ceremonies, and they may have several names simultaneously, used under varying circumstances (e.g., Dozier 1954; Stanislawski et al. 1975).

The modern Hopi-Tewa are the descendants of a group of Rio Grande Tewa-speaking people invited by the Hopi of Walpi to settle on First Mesa in about 1700 A.D. Their job was to guard the trail to the Mesa top, and for the last 275 years their village, Hano or Tewa village, has been established at the head of the entrance road on the Mesa top as the northernmost of the three villages of First Mesa (e.g., Dozier 1954, 1966; Stanislawski 1974c). Over the years, Hano or Tewa village developed to the south by the addition of new parallel rows of houses and squares to the original three-sided or square room block, and by 1929 had become contiguous with "Middle" village, the Walpi colony of Sichomovi. The Tewa village borders are marked by three or four small shrines and are well known by all.

Dozier (1954:286–89) states that in the 1950s there were about 400 Tewa tracing clan membership to Hano clans; a current figure would be about 615 to 625. These lived in Hano, Polacca, on ranches on the flat near and to the south of Keams Canyon, on Antelope Mesa, near Awatovi, in other Hopi villages, or in white communities. Nearly all Tewa have two houses, however, including one in Hano to which they return for ceremonies. Dozier's data indicate that of slightly more than 400 Tewa clan members, 340 live near or in Hano; perhaps about 450 do so now. About half of these were women, and half of these, in turn, were married women above the age of eighteen. Adult married women living near the Mesas are almost always the potters, and thus there would have been a maximum *potential* Tewa pottery-making population of about 85 to 90 adult females in 1954, and 112 to 115 in the 1970s. Dozier (1954:359) indicates that 27 females may have been potters, about one out of three. Our preliminary data suggest a *minimum* of 50 to 60 currently producing Hopi-Tewa potters; and thus a *minimum* of one out of two local adult women are potters by the 1970s. (In 1890, by comparison, the data of Donaldson [1893:45] indicate that probably *all* adult females were pottery makers.) The total Hopi population is about 6000 of whom 75 females are known potters on First and Third Mesa villages.

But are the conditions of modern Hopi-Tewa pottery making representative of the Hopi, too, and are they similar to those of the earlier prehistoric people of the area? I suggest that they may be, in part. Dozier (1954, 1966) and Eggan (1966) say that the Hopi-Tewa kinship system is very different from that of the Tewa of the Rio Grande, and is nearly identical to the matrilineal, matrilocal corporate clan system of the Hopi, with whom they have intermarried in the last 250 years. The major revival of Hopi Mesa area pottery making in 1890–1895 was initiated by the Tewa woman, Nampeyo, of Hano; but she was said to have been an expert Hopi-trained potter (taught by her Hopi Snake clan mother-in-law from Walpi village) when she rediscovered the Sikyatki revival style; and this school of design rapidly spread throughout *all* of the First Mesa villages (Hopi or Hopi-Tewa) where it is still predominant (e.g., Nequatewa 1951; Colton and Colton 1951). Official U.S. census data of the 1890 period (Donaldson 1893:45) indicate that pottery was then still being made by nearly all adult Hopi and Tewa women, in all seven existing villages. It was not, then, a dying craft, although artistic and technological skills may not impress us as being the match of those in either the earlier or more recent periods. Finally, the early "revival" potters seem to have copied pots and potsherds from Sikyatki and other nearby prehistoric ruins, and this copying of old designs and vessel forms helped to maintain the traditional style.

In short, both the Hopi and Hopi-Tewa ceramic industries are in large part, at least, similar; they still seem to follow traditional forms and designs, and utilize traditional artifacts and technology in their manufacture (e.g,, Bunzel 1929; M. F. Colton 1951; Danson 1965; Douglas 1932, Stephen 1936). Changes have been more in the introduction of some new forms (cookie jar, cylindrical vase, wedding vase, etc.), a few new manufacturing techniques (use of dung fuel, stove drying of pottery, tooled decoration of redware, etc.), and some differences in distribution, use, and meaning of pottery outside Hopi homes.

Hopi-Tewa Pottery Wares

The modern Hopi-Tewa potter makes two "use" classes: undecorated cooking, ceremonial, and storage wares in brown and polished red and yellow, and decorated serving and ornamental wares. Few women still make the undecorated brown storage jars, bean cooking pots, or pitched canteens, but many still make the polished red and yellow bowls and jars. Tooled and polished redware has become popular lately, and large yellow piki bowls are still widely made and are used on all three of the Mesas during weddings and ceremonies.

The great majority of pottery produced by the Hopi-Tewa is painted. (Several women commented that only women with poor eyesight would make plainware!) The fired base, or slip color, may be "natural" yellow, red, or white; the color difference is due, in part, to different clay or slip, and firing techniques used. Color styles are recognized by the Hopi-Tewa as being different in appearance and technology, and women who specialize in yellow or redware, for example, often say that whiteware is too difficult for them to make. The paint applied for decoration may be black, red, or white and may be applied in bichrome or polychrome designs. However, one more rarely sees black-on-white, pure white, or pure black. A minimum of ten color or paint background classes are produced, as well as several more rare incised, pitched, or tooled varieties.

The data presented here specifically focus on the Hopi and Hopi-Tewa whiteware, and its makers. This is a pottery style which is still comparatively rare and of relatively recent origin (ca. 1925); and it is one the naked eye can easily distinguish from other Hopi pottery styles. There is evidence that makers of this style are recognized by other Hopi and Tewa as being in possession of unique technological skills; and whiteware makers, in turn, often feel that other types of pottery (red slipped, and "natural" yellow) are difficult for them to produce. In short, the styles are recognized as being different in appearance and technology by the Hopi and Tewa, as well as by the anthropologist.

At least 41 potters produced whiteware in the 1970s period, 19 Hopi of seven clans and 22 Hopi-Tewa of five clans. There are at least nine adult women who make quantities of pottery slipped white on both surfaces; five are Hopi and four are Tewa. They are closely related by marriage or descent and include members of at least two Hopi and two Tewa clans. Six of the nine rarely make any other style; three make yellow and red; one makes pitched black Navajo style wares! There are also at least twelve women (five Tewa and seven Hopi) who make occasional pieces of pure white. Included are related women of at least seven Hopi and Tewa clans. Finally, a minimum of twelve women (including some of the ones mentioned above) occasionally make pottery which is black-on-red on the outside and black, red, and white on the inside. Included are six Tewa of three clans, six Hopi of at least four clans. Two related women also make occasional pottery pieces which are yellow outside and white inside (for complete data lists, see Stanislawski and Stanislawski 1975, Stanislawski et al. 1975).

The *technology* of Hopi-Tewa whiteware is traditional, and generally follows the descriptions of Hopi pottery making given by Mary Colton (1951), Harold Colton (1953), and F. H. Douglas (1932). Thus I shall mainly mention here those features of technology particularly important in the making of whiteware alone.

Clays

The clays for red and yellow pottery are dug from deposits under the First Mesa villages, near Sikyatki and Awatovi ruins, and at Keams Canyon. These deposits (for red in particular) are now deeply tunneled and dangerous to work; women have been killed in them by rockfalls. Therefore, much of the redware made today is actually yellowware slipped red. The base clay used for whiteware is usually the grey clay dug near Keams or Awatovi; the whiteware makers claim that this clay takes the white slip best, and is easier to smooth and polish than the others. The clay used for the white slip is a kaolin, iron-free clay, which may come from deposits twelve miles southeast of Walpi, or ten miles south of Mishongnovi (Stephen 1936:1190; Hough 1915:77; Colton 1953:9). It is said to be the same clay used to whiten wedding robes. Every scrap of clay broken or scraped off a pot during manufacture is saved and reused, and women stockpile in the winters, and prospect for new sources constantly. The whiteware makers crush and soak the grey clay pieces, usually add crushed potsherd or sand temper, and then knead the mass by hand, and strain it through window screens or other similar devices. It is then poured out on the ground in a one- or two-inch layer on top of half of a bedspread or tablecloth, the other half of which is folded over the top. It will be left for two or three hours to dry, or until stiff enough to hold a fingerprint, and then it is rolled off the sheet into a ball for use or storage for a day or two. The temper process is not often mentioned for Hopi pottery, but whiteware makers said that it was essential, for otherwise the clay would be too hard to smooth, scrape, polish, and slip. Whiteware makers frequently use an old method of refining the white kaolin clay slip material. They soak the material, put it into a burlap or muslin bag, and hang it from a stepladder or hook to drip into a bucket below. Such straining may be done twice for the best slip results.

Tools and Materials

Traditional Hopi ceramic tools and methods are used. Often the woman sits on the ground, back to wall, legs straight out in front, and works on a lapboard which she may swivel to turn the pot. Some of her own cracked pots or modern glass jars will be nearby, holding shredded yucca brushes; in addition, there will be small, smooth, size-graded, and water-worn chert pebbles for polishing (these are often collected in prehistoric sites), sandstone or sandpaper for smoothing, and ovoid gourd pieces, small flat wood sticks, or (rarely) potsherds for scraping. She will invariably use a dark-color, fine-grain, rectangular indurated-sandstone paint mortar with one or two pecked basins for mixing (these are made from a stone found near Awatovi), and several pails of water. Her paints are traditional, too. She will use a yellow limonite, which fires red; a kaolin white; and a mixture of ground hematite and tansy mustard to fire black. The red and white slip clays have been described, and one of the few recent major innovations is a pink slip mixed from part grey and part yellow native clays.

Manufacturing

The Hopi-Tewa still hand coil and mold each piece of pottery, pinching off one coil at a time, and they make each part of the pot (handle, spout, rim) separately, pinching them and smoothing them together at the end. The pot will be thinned by scraping with a curved ovoid gourd piece or, more rarely, pottery pieces. Gourd is said to be best because it is flexible, does not scratch, and does not stick to the clay. However, flat wood pieces, including popsicle sticks, are used to scrape exterior flat areas, or to add bits of clay to gouged areas. Molding is usually done in daylight when shape can be better judged, the women believe. Each woman does her own molding, for bad work will allow air bubbles which will cause cracks during drying and firing. Thus women may get together in groups to mold, but each does her own work.

Next the pots will be dried for one to four days on a windowsill, in the oven, or under the wood stove. If the vessel cracks at this stage, it will be cut down, or the bowl center will be used as a plaque, or the piece may be broken up and ground down and the clay reused. Nothing is thrown away. Pieces which dry well to a leatherlike surface are smoothed at great length with sandstone hunks or sandpaper. This is the dirtiest and most time-consuming job, and other women may come by and help out. During the following slipping and polishing work, a group of women may again work together in applying the white slip clay with a rag and then polishing the surface with the small water-worn pebbles. Whiteware is often slipped twice, for potters say that the first slip just covers the smoothing scratches, and the second slip is needed to give the bone-white appearance desired. It is important to get a dense but even slip so that it will not burn yellow in firing. Some potters also claim that whiteware must be polished when still damp from the slip, or it will not get a smooth luster (redware and yellowware potters often polish the pottery with a warm moist rag for luster).

Painting and Firing

Most whiteware makers paint black-and-red polychrome designs in Sik-yatki revival style. However, the designs are often more open, with more empty space around them than is common for some other wares. Vessel forms are similar to those used by other Hopi and Tewa potters, although wedding vases are emphasized, and two of the important whiteware makers are also known for their round tiles and plaques, and candlesticks and turtle and swan effigies respectively. The painting is done freehand using a little finger as a "compass" for circular lines. No sketching is done on the pot, and the design is drawn from memory. Shredded yucca brushes are still used in painting, and chert pebbles may be used to spread the paint in solid design areas. Women will often paint for each other, particularly close neighbors, in-laws, or clan relatives; and communal painting groups are common.

Firing is an individual job and is a crucial stage in the production of whiteware. All the Hopi and Tewa fire in the open near the Mesa edge or near their houses on the flat. Nearly all begin firing at 4:00–5:00 a.m. when the air is still. Four types of fuel are used: juniper wood collected on Black Mesa, which may be used to start the fire; sheep-dung cakes collected from the Hopi ranch or bought from Navajo traders at $30.00 a wagonload (in 1974); corncobs dried and stacked near the houses; and coal dug from seams near the Mesas or purchased from a small Hopi mine near Keams Canyon. Most commonly, juniper kindling is used to start sheep-dung cakes smoldering, and after a bed of embers is produced more sheep-dung cakes are put on, intermixed with two or three rows of coal. Then stones and large potsherds are placed down under the four or five pieces of pottery to be fired, more sherds are placed around the pots to cover them, and a beehive of sheep dung is packed around the pots and set aflame, The pile may then be covered with a tin washbasin and protected from the wind by another propped-up basin.

Some whiteware potters will only use coal to fire, and all whiteware makers favored using as much coal as possible, particularly in the winter when it takes much other fuel to get sufficient firing heat. Coal is superior to dung, because each load of dung burns differently and must be tested before use. Even then, however, the dung may be a bit damp or too dry and may thus smoke too much or burn with a sudden flare, and fire-cloud or yellow the whiteware pottery; it settles as it burns, too. Coal, on the other hand, holds its shape as it burns and does not settle and allow the pottery to touch the fuel. In addition, it burns hot and with a steady heat for a long time. Whiteware potters say that they need a fuel like coal because whiteware must be fired for a long period at relatively high, but steady, heat with the fuel packed tightly around it (perhaps to produce a reducing atmosphere?). The pottery should then be cooled very slowly until quite cold. If allowed to touch the fuel, if there are heat flares, or if it is removed from the fire when hot, it will yellow or oxidize. A clear whiteware surface thus depends on care in preparation and application of the special slip, on the choice of fuel and firing temperature, on packing of fuel, and on cooling. Hopi and Tewa who do not make whiteware usually claim they could if they wanted, but note that it is too hard, and that their pots always turn yellow or break. Another suggestion of the difficulty of making pure whiteware is that some women can fire the interior of bowls white, but not the outside, which they slip and fire red. The outside surface, of course, is the area hardest to protect from oxygen, burning fuel flares, settling of fuel, etc.

THE LEARNING AND SOCIAL CORRELATION OF CERAMIC STYLES

Learning

For nearly fifty years, writers such as Ruth Bunzel (1929), Virgil Hubert (1951), and Edward Danson (1965) have been commenting on the stability of Hopi ceramic forms and designs. They note that experimentation is possible in the arrangement of units, forms, and motifs, but that traditional technology and school of design have continued with little change since the fifteenth century. It is particularly noted that while technology is taught, design is not. Design is an individual thing, and each potter makes her own designs, using elements and motifs which are shared communitywide but which may be selected and emphasized in different frequency and used in different arrangements and layouts. Parents and relatives do influence their kin, of course, but in the communal painting groups, composed of neighbors and in-laws as well as clan kin, and in the continuation of the old patterns of copying prehistoric potsherd designs, these writers might lead us to expect a traditional village or Mesa-wide style pattern rather than a lineage or clan style. Data collected in 1968–73 seem to suggest the validity of this latter idea.

In general, Hopi-Tewa potters said the same thing: "All women from First Mesa can make pottery, all teach their daughters, but any can make any style if they are good enough." Another lady said, "I could make all white if I wanted. No one would be mad. They would tell me how. We should not be jealous of one another." And one lady said (with no coaching from the anthropologist!) "we do not just teach in clans here—anyone can make any style." As Bunzel noted in 1929, they do seem to dislike it when other women copy their designs without permission. A Hopi-Tewa whiteware potter noted, "a lady down there is always trying to come by and copy my designs." Yet while they do not like people stealing their designs, they will freely paint for others in communal painting groups, and will teach in-laws, neighbors, or friends who request aid. Moreover, they continue to collect potsherds from such nearby prehistoric sites as Sikyatki, Old Walpi, and Awatovi, and most admitted stockpiling such sherds in their homes and using them for designs. Bunzel previously noted that the Hopi did this more than any other Western Pueblo group (1929:55–57), Some of the modern Tewa also have copies of Fewkes's early B.A.E. reports on Hopi ceramics, and other books on prehistoric Hopi-area pottery. For all, however, the important point was whether the designs were Hopi or not; several ladies told us that they had refused jobs to make white man's designs or Ute Indian designs.

Modern whiteware was originated, or revived, by a Kachina clan Tewa lady and a Bear clan Tewa lady who lived side by side in Polacca. They were in-laws, and often worked on pottery (it is also claimed that Nampeyo, of the Tewa Corn clan, and a Spider clan Tewa lady were making whiteware at about this time, too). The new whiteware differs from the simpler and older Polacca polychrome whiteware style in having Sikyatki revival vessel forms and Sikyatki designs applied on a dense, clear, uncrackled, bone white surface. It probably does not date earlier than 1920; although from the data and pictures shown us by informants, we cannot yet trace the styles back beyond 1927, at which time the Bear clan lady exhibited a large cylindrical whiteware vase in a fair in San Diego. Presumably she was known as an expert potter before this time, but how long before this she had been making whiteware, we do not know. The red exterior–white interior style may only have developed in the late 1950s, according to Danson (1965:7–8) and it may be significant that this was the same period at which the daughter of one of its best skilled makers married into the family of the Kachina clan lady, who was one of the early developers of the style. Thus in the beginning, or revival, of this whiteware style, women of several different Tewa clans were working together.

As noted in table 18.1, there are at least six common teaching models, and eight other more rare ones. Our data indicate that the Kachina clan woman (known as Frog Lady from the signature mark on the bottom of her pottery), trained her daughter, now known as Frog Lady. The daughter now lives on Antelope Mesa, south of Keams Canyon. The first Frog Lady also trained her daughter-in-law, a Tewa of the Stick or Fir clan (now known as Soft Feather from her pottery signature mark). She lives in Polacca. These two women of the second whiteware generation are currently the best-known and respected producers of the style, but note that they live in different villages, and are in-

TABLE 18.1
Learning Models of Whiteware Potters
Hopi Mesas, Arizona

Group I: In-Clan Models: (27 cases)

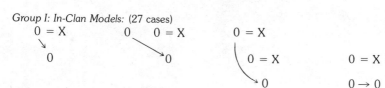

a. Mother (14)   b. Mother's sister   c. Mother's mother   d. Sister
                          (5)   (1)   (5)

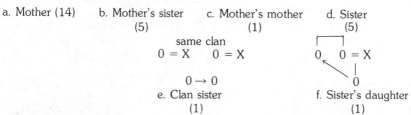

same clan

e. Clan sister   f. Sister's daughter
      (1)   (1)

Group II: Non-Clan Models: (17 cases)

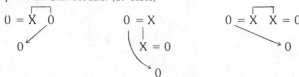

a. Father's sister   b. Father's mother   c. Father's brother's wife
      (0)   (1)   (1)

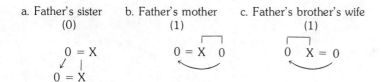

d. Husband's mother   e. Husband's sister   f. Brother's wife
      (3)   (2)   (1)

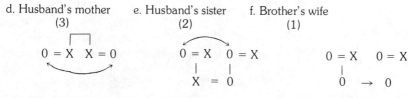

g. Husband's brother's wife   h. Son's or daughter's   i. Non-kin
      (2)   mother-in-law (2)   (5)

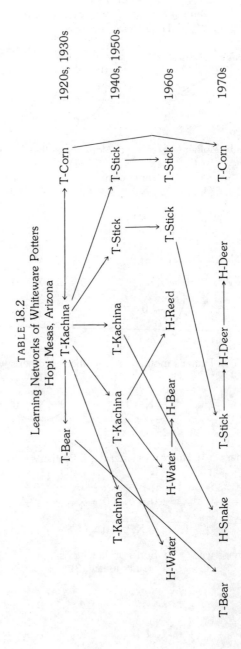

TABLE 18.2
Learning Networks of Whiteware Potters
Hopi Mesas, Arizona

laws of different clans. The first Frog Lady also taught at least two or three of her sisters in the Kachina clan, who, in turn, taught at least three of their daughters, who still make occasional pieces of whiteware. (Teaching thus certainly does go on within the clan or lineage, too.) See tables 18.1–18.3 for a schematic view of this model; or Stanislawski and Stanislawski 1975.

The second-generation Kachina clan Frog Lady has also been training other potters. She trained her sister-in-law (her husband's sister) and her sister-in-law's mother, Hopi from First Mesa of different clan. They both live on Antelope Mesa, near Frog Lady. The Hopi sister-in-law may also have helped to train *her* mother, and definitely trained *her* sister-in-law (her husband's brother's wife), a Bear clan Hopi lady from the Second Mesa village of Mishongnovi. These women also now live near Frog Lady. Finally,

TABLE 18.3

Spread of Identification Marks on Hopi and Hopi-Tewa Pottery

T. Kachina (9)	H. Sand (1)	T. Corn (2)	H. Water (1)		1930s
H. Coyote (1)	H. Deer (1)	T. Stick (2)	T. Corn (1)		1940s, 1950s
H. Bear (1)	T. Sand (1)	T. Tobacco (1)	T. Corn (2)	H. Corn (1)	1960s
T. Bear (1)	T. Kachina (1)	T. Corn (5)	H. Water (2)		1970s

Frog Lady is training at least two of her daughters, and one daughter-in-law, a Hopi girl from Walpi who lives in Walpi near her Hopi mother, a well-known potter who does *not* make whiteware.

Thus, as we trace the expansion of whiteware teaching along one major network alone, note that both Hopi and Tewa are involved; they come from at least three villages and two mesas. Women from a minimum of seven Tewa and five Hopi clans are involved, and they now live on Antelope Mesa, in Polacca, and in Walpi. But to further complicate the affair, the first and second Frog Ladies are said to have painted all of their in-laws' pottery for them at one time or another; and the Hopi sister-in-law of the second Frog Lady also sometimes paints for *her* mother, daughters, and Second Mesa Hopi sister-in-law. Thus, both teaching and communal painting are involved.

If we continue to follow the line of instruction, we can note that Soft

Feather has also been training her in-laws who live next door in Polacca, and her cousin in her own Fir or Stick clan, a Tewa woman who lives above, in Hano, on the entrance road. This Hano woman makes excellent red-exterior – white-interior pottery, and occasional pieces of black-on-white.

The Tewa Bear clan woman who was a co-originator of the style with first Frog Lady is now in her 80s, still producing pottery and still living in her original house in Polacca, which she now shares with her daughter and granddaughter's families. She taught her sister, a Hano Bear clan woman, to make whiteware.

Among the approximately 40 women we are currently aware of who make any quantity of whiteware, two are particularly important producers in terms of quantity and quality of work. One is a noted Tewa potter of the Spider clan or lineage now living in Hano. She says that she learned to make pottery from her mother and the first Frog Lady. Frog Lady's husband and this woman's father were brothers, however, and the girls frequently played together; thus again we may have an example of in-law teaching involving members of two different Tewa clans. The other prominent whiteware maker is a Hopi of Walpi (now living in Polacca), and is related by a daughter's marriage to one of the original whiteware maker's families. She seems to have learned to make whiteware only *after* this marriage, and again we may have evidence of in-law training. About 60 percent of the cases of teaching we have touched on are in-clan models (27 cases) and at least 40 percent cross clan cases (17 cases).

Teaching Methods

Bunzel noted in 1929 that little formal teaching goes on, and that which does is technological training. Most women said that they learned from "watching" relatives or friends; only a few noted that they had asked their older relatives or in-laws to teach them how to make pottery. Apparently women begin to learn when they are between 5 and 15 years old if their relatives are potters; if not, they will learn in their mid-30s or 40s from friends or relatives. Women often give up pottery making from the age of 20 to 35 or so, for they frequently cannot work on pottery when they have small children. In such cases, active potters, such as grandmothers or aunts, may do much of the teaching of the young children. This, again, should reinforce the conservative traditions of manufacture. Unfortunately, however, sixty years ago a generation of women was discouraged from making pottery because of lack of outside interest; now again the young women are not so much interested in making pottery, for they see more financial advantages in other work.

To give some specific teaching examples, Frog Lady said that her mother first let her observe the pottery-making process, then allowed her to paint the frog symbol on the pot bottom, and finally allowed her to mold and paint the whole pot. We also noted that her own daughters would sometimes make miniature pots like her big ones, or would sometimes help her scrape or polish pots. She would sometimes rub out her daughters' poor painting, redo it for them, and give it back as an example.

In general, an informal apprenticeship seems to be the rule, and it involves aunt and niece or granddaughter and grandmother as often as mother and daughter when it remains within the lineage or clan. However, it just as frequently involves in-laws from different clans and lineages. Pride in work-manship in technological terms is stressed, and instruction in design style is minimal. The result is an unconscious continuation of the old styles, and their common use and possession by members of the entire village, or First Mesa community. Freeman (1968:266) may well be correct in his guess that the temporary special-purpose work group composed of a variety of kin and nonkin, who join together to do a common job (such as pottery making), is often the most important source of archeological remains. Thus, we should *not* assume that nonrandom localization of ceramic remains of particular styles necessarily implies the presence of any specific type of corporate, or kin, group. Residence, friendship, or at least some type of physical propin-quity, seem to be the keys in learning and production of ceramic crafts.

CONCLUSIONS

The Southwestern "Systems" archeologists have argued that by the study of the covariation of artifacts and nonartifactual evidence we can reconstruct the past variables (events, activities, etc.) which results in the artifacts' pres-ence at the site. The problem is to choose among the many possible prehistoric determinants, and this I suggest is best approached by observing living descendant peoples and comparing the observed patterns of their technology with that predicted or expected at the sites nearby, thus giving models to test for best fit. In particular, Southwestern "Systems" archeolo-gists have set up several models attempting to explain the covariation of pottery types and design elements in prehistoric Western Pueblo sites. They have suggested that modern ethnographic data allow the inference that clustering of ceramic design styles and types in prehistoric sites in northeast-ern Arizona implies that in the past the females were the potters, and that they inherited ideas of pottery technology, design elements, and styles from their mothers as part of a matrilineal, matrilocal, corporate lineage or clan group. It would appear that archeologists raised a logical, ethnographic model to certainty before direct observation studies had verified its antecedents. As Hill notes (1966:22), there are a minimum of seven different social-organization clusters involving descent and residence which might result in nonrandom localized distribution of artifacts. Clearly neither descent nor locality may be certainly reconstructed by the simple statement of nonrandom distribution of artifacts, as Deetz (1968:41–48), Aberle (1968:353–59), Freeman (1968:262–67), and others have noted. These same authors, and Edward Dozier (1968:352–53), have noted that the corporate structure of the group may be a very important point. Localized, nonrandom distribution of ceramic designs, however (often assumed to indicate kin-based, private corporate control), may not prove this point; for localized corporate groups need not be kinship groups (as Aberle notes, Southwestern kiva groups are not), and localized, temporary, and noncorporate work groups may be of even more importance, as we have seen. Thus, nonrandom localized distribution of ceramic styles need not indicate matrilineal descent, matrilocality, or corporate descent groups. (See also Stanislawski 1975 for settlement pattern data and locality correlates).

In emphasizing material concerning whiteware potters we have shown that this technological style requires unique slipping and firing techniques, but that in general these are only variations of the traditional Hopi and Tewa pottery-making techniques traced back at least 500 years. There has never been a break in the tradition, and for each decade since the 1870s, pottery has been produced on at least two mesas (Stanislawski 1974a–c). Tools, fuels, and materials are still traditional and locally collected and made. The same may be said for the majority of Sikyatki designs and vessel forms used. (While the forms have, however, remained stable, their use and distribution have changed, for now most pottery is being sold commercially.) The Hopi-Tewa are willing to teach any nearby neighbor, in-law, or lineage or clan relative who asks them, and they commonly work together in noncorporate, localized work groups in the scraping, smoothing, and painting of pottery. The traditional designs are learned by watching others work, or by copying potsherds from prehistoric Hopi ruins. The ideal is that any potter can make any style, and thus the women of First Mesa may well share in the manufacture of one clearly distinguishable style, and the nearly common possession of one general set of design elements.

This is not to say that individual women do not sometimes "invent" their own new design elements (although usually in traditional Sikyatki style!), or that they do not sometimes continue to make or emphasize a popular selling style of selected designs originated by their mothers (as the Nampeyo daughters have done). However, one daughter may continue her mother's designs, while another daughter will select new painting styles. It is generally a matter of individual emphasis, and selection of known elements such as rim forms or marks, which distinguish a woman' style, as well as her ability at line work and painting, and her ability at molding and firing. Of approximately 15 unique design elements we have specifically studied, two or three are shared by clan members, two or three by clan and nonclan members, and the rest seem to be currently used by only one woman.

Our study, of course, is not strictly comparable to those of Longacre (1964; 1966; 1968), Deetz (1965; and 1968), and others who have mainly classified, defined, and quantified data on potsherd ceramic design elements and types. We have emphasized technological processes and learning situations, and the study of major wares, types, or styles of whole pots. Quantification of individual potsherd design elements in an entire village community, correlated with specific genealogical controls, would be necessary for a precisely equivalent study. While such quantification may, however, be necessary for the archeologist who needs to find some reliable method of proving the actual association of specific groups of objects with specific building units—i.e., the actual clusters which exist—it does not seem necessary in the work of the ethnographer who can directly observe the association of people, whole pottery, and houses, and who can also elicit and cross-check information concerning ceramics, genealogies, and housing from the living people involved. In short, the major problem is not that of the association of ceramic elements and kinship units, but rather that of eliciting the meaning or explanation of this physical association. We can show that the matrilineal–matrilocal teaching and inheritance model, given as the major explanation for the association of pottery types and building units in some prehistoric Southwestern Pueblo site reports, does not always hold today, nor is it the only important teaching model in use. Today, among the Hopi and Hopi-Tewa whiteware makers at least, people who live near or next to one another may or may not produce the same wares; they may teach both relatives and nonrelatives; and they may copy old designs from sherds rather than learning designs from their mother or their clan mates. Related people who live in several different villages may make the same style, while non-clan–related people living near each other may learn to make the same style. Neither locality, lineage, nor clan rules necessarily seem to control the production of major ceramic styles or wares.

We are thus not denying the existence of the matrilineal–matrilocal corporate kin teaching model, but rather emphasizing that ethnoarcheology field work in Western Pueblo Societies indicates variability in teaching models, several of which might result in a similar production and distribution of ceramic artifacts. Thus we stress the great variability present, and the additional model for equal testing which may be necessary for archeological reconstruction, rather than the "validation" as but one of the logical possibilities. Ethnoarcheology field work allows one to see multiple solutions to the same problem, all of which may need to be tested for best fit.

Binford (1968b), Heider (1967), and Ascher (1961) have said there may be several ultimate determinants (thus, several ethnographic models), which might equally well explain an existing archeological situation. One of modern archeology's most pressing needs is emphasis on direct-observation studies of human technology, concentrating this on an observed range of real and ideal forms, uses, meanings, and functions, which will help us as archeologists to explain the variation we see in the distribution of artifacts in archeological sites. Archeologists will probably have to do this work themselves; we must now begin, before our theories are those only of the imagination, rather than those immensely more complex systems of currently still existent, nonwestern peoples.

POSTSCRIPT: 1975

This manuscript is essentially as written in 1970. Some changes in dates and data have, however, been made to ensure that it correlates with more recent papers of mine quoted. We have all, of course, somewhat changed our theoretical stance in the last five years (Bill Longacre is now doing ethnoarcheology in the Philippines; Binford in Alaska), but the general problems remain the same.

ACKNOWLEDGMENTS

From the beginning of this project we were encouraged and stimulated by the advice and friendship of Dr. Edward P. Dozier of the University of Arizona, who freely gave to us of his time, and who gave us vital introductions to many of his Hopi-Tewa friends on First Mesa. In the Hopi Mesa area, we owe most to the many Tewa and Hopi women who were so kind to us during the summer and who suffered so many foolish questions pleasantly. In deference to Hopi custom, we rarely mention their names, but their help was greatly appreciated. We should also like to offer our thanks to D. Boone

Lacewell, principal of the Polacca Day School, who made facilities of the school available to us; Mr. Beck of the B.I.A. office in Keams Canyon; Byron Hunter, in charge of the Polacca Trading Post, who aided us throughout with his expert knowledge of Hopi crafts.

Our work was made much more pleasant by the excellent cooperation of the Museum of Northern Arizona, whose Director, Edward B. Danson, Assistant Director, William D. Lipe, and Curator of Anthropology, Alexander J. Lindsay, Jr., provided us with living quarters, research space, clerical help, and other advantages. Barton Wright, Curator of the Museum, and his wife, Margaret Wright, and Ann Hitchcock, Registrar of Anthropological Collections, made available to us several unique opportunities to study Museum Show pottery collections and records. Our work could not have been done without this help. We should also like to thank Katharine Bartlett, Librarian of the Museum, who gave us much help in locating sources of material, and made available to us much of her unique knowledge of Hopi culture; Marc Gaede and Anne Pollack, who did photography for us; Mary Swank, Museum ethnologist, and Calvin Jennings, archeologist, both of whom offered us help, facilities, and advice during the project.

We also wish to thank the participants in the May 1969 SAA Symposium, "The Archaeological Implications of the Ethnographic Analysis of Ceramics," in which a shorter version of this paper was presented (David Biernoff, Dean Arnold, Frederick Matson, Donald Lathrap, Margaret Hardin Friedrich); the discussants in that Symposium (Irving Rouse, Raymond Thompson); and the co-organizer of that Symposium, Donald Lathrap, for their comments, criticisms, and suggestions concerning the paper. Members of the Symposium audience also gave us many stimulating comments at this time (and later by letter) which will help us do better work in the future.

My wife, Barbara, was an equal participant on the project and was a partner on all of the field work that went into it. To her I owe a major debt of thanks for her support and encouragement throughout.

REFERENCES

Aberle, D. F. 1968. Comments. In *New perspectives,* pp. 353–59.*
Anderson, K. M. 1969. Ethnographic analogy and archaeological interpretation. *Science* 1963 (3863).

New perspectives will be used in this list to refer to S. R. Binford and L. R. Binford, eds., 1968. *New perspectives in archaeology.* Chicago: Aldine Publications.

Ascher, R. 1961. Analogy in archaeological interpretation. *Southwestern Journal of Anthropology* 17:317–25.

Binford, L. R. 1962. Archaeology as anthropology. *American Antiquity* 28(2):217–25.

—— 1968a. Archaeological perspectives. In *New perspectives,* pp. 5–32.

—— 1968b. Methodological considerations of the archeological use of ethnographic data. In R. B. Lee and I. DeVore, eds., *Man the hunter,* pp. 268–73. Chicago: Aldine Publications.

Breternitz, D. A. 1966. *An appraisal of tree-ring dated pottery in the Southwest.* Tucson: University of Arizona Press.

Bunzel, Ruth. 1929. *The Pueblo potter, a study of creative imagination in primitive art.* New York: Columbia University Press.

Colton, H. S. 1953. Potsherds. *Museum of Northern Arizona Bulletin 25.*

Colton, M. F. 1951. Arts and crafts of the Hopi Indians. In Hopi Indian arts and crafts, pp. 1–30. *Museum of Northern Arizona Reprint Series 3,*

Colton, M. F. and H. S. Colton. 1951. An Appreciation of the art of Nampeyo and her influence on Hopi pottery. In Hopi Indian arts and crafts, pp. 91–93. *Museum of Northern Arizona Reprint Series 3.*

Danson, E. B. 1965. New dimensions in Hopi ceramic crafts. In *New dimensions in Indian art.* Scottsdale (Ariz.): National Indian Arts Council.

Deetz, J. 1965. The dynamics of stylistic change in Arizona ceramics. *Illinois Studies in Anthropology* 4. Urbana: University of Illinois Press.

——1968. The inference of residence and descent rules from archaeological data. In *New Perspectives,* pp. 41–48.

DeVore, Irven. 1968. Comments. In *New perspectives,* pp. 346–49.

Donaldson, Thomas. 1893. Moqui Pueblo Indians of Arizona and Pueblo Indians of New Mexico. *Extra Census Bulletin: Eleventh Census of the United States.* Washington, D.C.

Douglas, F. H. 1932. Hopi Indian pottery. *Denver Art Museum Leaflet 47.*

Dozier, E. P. 1954. The Hopi-Tewa of Arizona. *University of California Publications in American Archaeology and Ethnology* 44(3).

—— 1966. Hano, a Tewa Indian community in Arizona. In G. and L. Spindler, eds., *Case Studies in Cultural Anthropology.* New York: Holt, Rinehart and Winston.

—— 1968. Comments. In *New perspectives,* pp. 352–53.

Eggan, F. 1950. *Social organization of the Western Pueblos.* Chicago: University of Chicago Press.

—— 1966. *The American Indian: Perspectives for the study of social change.* Chicago: Aldine Publications.

Flannery, K. V. 1967. Review of, An introduction to American archaeology, vol. 1, North and Middle America, by F. R. Willey. In *Scientific American* 217(2):119–22.

Freeman, L. G., Jr. 1968. A theoretical framework for interpreting archaeological materials. In R. B. Lee and I. DeVore, eds., *Man the hunter,* pp. 262-67. Chicago: Aldine Publications.

Fried, M. G. 1968. Comments. In *New perspectives,* pp. 350-52.

Guthe, C. E. 1925. *Pueblo pottery making.* New Haven: Yale University Press.

Heider, K. G. 1967. Archaeological assumptions and ethnographical facts: A cautionary tale from New Guinea. *Southwestern Journal of Anthropology* 23(1).

Hill, J. N. 1966. A prehistoric community in eastern Arizona. *Southwestern Journal of Anthropology* 22(1):9-30.

—— 1967. Structure, Function and Change at Broken K Pueblo. In P. S. Martin et al. eds., Chapters in the prehistory of eastern Arizona, III, pp. 158-67. *Fieldiana: Anthropology* 57. Chicago.

—— 1968. Broken K. Pueblo: Patterns of Form and Function. In *New perspectives,* pp. 103-42.

Hough, W. 1915. *Th Hopi Indians.* Cedar Rapids, Iowa: The Torch Press.

Hubert, V. 1951. An introduction to Hopi pottery design. In Hopi Indian arts and crafts, pp. 80-87. *Museum of Northern Arizona Reprint Series* 3. Flagstaff.

Kubler, G. 1967. *The shape of time: remarks on the history of things.* New Haven: Yale University Press.

Lee, R. B. 1968. Comments. In *New perspectives,* pp. 343-46.

Leone, M. P. 1968. Neolithic economic autonomy and social distance. *Science* 162:150-1152.

Lindsay, A. J., Jr. 1968. Personal comment.

Longacre, W. A. 1964. Archeology as anthropology: A case study. *Science* 144 (3625):1454-55.

—— 1966. Changing patterns of social integration: A prehistoric example from the American Southwest. *American Anthropologist* 68(1):94-103.

—— 1968. Some aspects of prehistoric society in east-central Arizona. In: *New perspectives,* pp. 89-102.

Malinowski, B. 1943. *A scientific theory of culture.* Chapel Hill: University of North Carolina Press.

Martin, P. S. 1964. Summary. In P. S. Martin et al., eds. Chapters in the prehistory of eastern Arizona, II, pp. 216-26. *Fieldiana: Anthropology* 55. Chicago.

Morgan, C. G. 1973. Archaeology and explanation. *World archaeology* 4:259-76.

Nequatewa, E. 1951. Nampeyo, famous Hopi potter. In Hopi Indian arts and crafts, pp. 88-90. *Museum of Northern Arizona Reprint Series* 3. Flagstaff.

Reed, E. K. 1950. East-central Arizona archaeology in relation to the Western Pueblos. *Southwestern Journal of Anthropology* 6(2):120-38.

Salmon, W. C. 1973. Confirmation. *Scientific American* (May) 75-83.

Smith, W. 1962. Schools, pots, and potters. *American Anthropologist* 64(6):1165-78.

Stanislawski, M. B. 1969a. What good is a broken pot? *Southwestern Lore* 35(1):11–18.

—— 1969b. The Ethno-archaeology of Hopi pottery making. *Plateau* 42(1).

—— 1973. Review of, archaeology as anthropology, by W. A. Longacre. *American Antiquity* 38:117–22.

—— 1974a. The relationships of ethno-archaeology, traditional, and systems archaeology. *Monograph IV, Archaeological Survey,* pp. 15–26. Institute of Archaeology, U.C.L.A.

—— 1974b. History of Hopi-Tewa pottery making: etics and emics. Presented at the Society for Historic Archeology. January 1974, Berkeley.

—— 1974c. Hano, the Hopi-Tewa of Arizona. *Handbook of North American Indians.* Smithsonian Institution. (In Press).

—— 1975. Ethnoarchaeology and settlement archaeology. Paper presented at the Society for American Archaeology, 38th Annual Meeting, May 4, 1973. (In Press: *Ethnohistory,* 1975).

Stanislawski, M. B. and B. B. Stanislawski. 1975. Hopi and Hopi-Tewa ceramic networks. Paper presented at the Annual Meeting of the American Anthropological Association, November 1974. (In Press in I. Hodder, ed. *Spatial organization of culture.* England: Duckworth Press.)

Stanislawski, M. B., B. B. Stanislawski and A. Hitchcock. 1975. Identification marks on Hopi and Hopi-Tewa pottery. *Plateau.* Flagstaff, Ariz.: In press.

Stephen, A. M. 1936. Hopi journal of Alexander M. Stephen, ed. E. C. Parsons. *Columbia University Contributions to Anthropology* 23. New York.

Whallon, R., Jr. 1968. Investigations of late prehistoric social organization in New York State. In *New perspectives,* pp. 223–44.

Woolf, C. M. and F. C. Dukepoo. 1969. Hopi Indians, inbreeding and albinism. *Science* 164(3875):30–37.